A·N·N·U·A·L E·D·I·

Global Issues 02/03

Eighteenth Edition

EDITOR

Robert M. Jackson

California State University, Chico

Robert M. Jackson is a professor of political science and dean of the School of Graduate, International, and Sponsored Programs at California State University, Chico. In addition to teaching, he has published articles on the international political economy, international relations simulations, and political behavior. His special research interest is in the way northern California is becoming increasingly linked to the Pacific Basin. His travels include China, Japan, Hong Kong, Taiwan, Singapore, Malaysia, Portugal, Spain, Morocco, Costa Rica, El Salvador, Honduras, Guatemala, Mexico, Germany, Belgium, the Netherlands, Russia, and Czechoslovakia.

McGraw-Hill/Dushkin

530 Old Whitfield Street, Guilford, Connecticut 06437

Visit us on the Internet

http://www.dushkin.com

Credits

1. **Global Issues in the Twenty-First Century: An Overview**
   Unit photo—© 2002 by PhotoDisc, Inc.
2. **Population and Food Production**
   Unit photo—United Nations photo by Paul Heath Hoeffel.
3. **The Global Environment and Natural Resources Utilization**
   Unit photo—United Nations photo by JL.
4. **Political Economy**
   Unit photo—© 2002 by PhotoDisc, Inc.
5. **Conflict**
   Unit photo—United Nations photo.
6. **Cooperation**
   Unit photo—United Nations photo by Yutaka Nagata.
7. **Values and Visions**
   Unit photo—United Nations photo.

Copyright

Cataloging in Publication Data
Main entry under title: Annual Editions: Global Issues. 2002/2003.
1. Civilization, Modern—20th century—Periodicals. 2. Social prediction—Periodicals.
3. Social problems—20th century—Periodicals. I. Jackson, Robert, *comp.* II. Title: Global issues.
ISBN 0–07–250683–0 909.82'05 85–658006 ISSN 1093–278X

Eighteenth Edition

Cover image © 2002 PhotoDisc, Inc.
Printed in the United States of America 1234567890BAHBAH5432 Printed on Recycled Paper

Editors/Advisory Board

Members of the Advisory Board are instrumental in the final selection of articles for each edition of ANNUAL EDITIONS. Their review of articles for content, level, currentness, and appropriateness provides critical direction to the editor and staff. We think that you will find their careful consideration well reflected in this volume.

Staff

To the Reader

In publishing ANNUAL EDITIONS we recognize the enormous role played by the magazines, newspapers, and journals of the public press in providing current, first-rate educational information in a broad spectrum of interest areas. Many of these articles are appropriate for students, researchers, and professionals seeking accurate, current material to help bridge the gap between principles and theories and the real world. These articles, however, become more useful for study when those of lasting value are carefully collected, organized, indexed, and reproduced in a low-cost format, which provides easy and permanent access when the material is needed. That is the role played by ANNUAL EDITIONS.

The beginning of the new millennium was celebrated with considerable fanfare. While there is indeed much for which to congratulate ourselves, it is equally true that the issues confronting humanity are uniquely complex and diverse. The events of September 11, 2001, were a stark reminder of the intense emotions and methods of destruction available to those determined to challenge the status quo. While the mass media may focus on the latest crisis for a few days or weeks, the broad forces that are shaping the world are seldom given the in-depth analysis that they warrant. Scholarly research about these historic change factors can be found in a wide variety of publications, but these are not readily accessible. In addition, students just beginning to study global issues can be discouraged by the terminology and abstract concepts that characterize much of the scholarly literature. In selecting and organizing the materials for this book, we have been mindful of the needs of beginning students and have, thus, selected articles that invite the student into the subject matter.

Each unit begins with an introductory article providing a broad overview of the area to be explored. The remaining articles examine in more detail some of the issues presented. The unit then concludes with an article (or two) that not only identifies a problem but suggests positive steps that are being taken to improve the situation. The world faces many serious issues, the magnitude of which would discourage even the most stouthearted individual. Though identifying problems is easier than solving them, it is encouraging to know that many of the issues are being successfully addressed.

Perhaps the most striking feature of the study of contemporary global issues is the absence of any single, widely held theory that explains what is taking place. Therefore, we have made a conscious effort to present a wide variety of ideologies and theories. The most important consideration has been to present global issues from an international perspective, rather than from a purely American or Western point of view. By encompassing materials originally published in many different countries and written by authors of various nationalities, the anthology represents the great diversity of opinions that people hold on important global issues. Two writers examining the same phenomenon may reach very different conclusions. It is not a question of who is right and who is wrong. What is important to understand is that people from different vantage points have differing perceptions of issues.

Another major consideration when organizing these materials was to explore the complex interrelationship of factors that produce social problems such as poverty. Too often, discussions of this problem (and others like it) are reduced to arguments about the fallacies of not following the correct economic policy or not having the correct form of government. As a result, many people overlook the interplay of historic, cultural, environmental, economic, and political factors that form complex webs that bring about many different problems. Every effort has been made to select materials that illustrate this complex interaction of factors, stimulating the beginning student to consider realistic rather than overly simplistic approaches to the pressing problems that threaten the existence of civilization.

In addition to an annotated *table of contents* and a *topic guide,* included in this edition of *Annual Editions: Global Issues* are *World Wide Web* sites that can be used to further explore topics addressed in the articles.

Finally, we selected the materials in this book for both their intellectual insights and their readability. Timely and well-written materials should stimulate good classroom lectures and discussions. We hope that students and teachers will enjoy using this book. Readers can have input into the next edition by completing and returning the postage-paid *article rating form* in the back of the book.

I would like to acknowledge the help and support of Ian Nielsen. I am grateful for his encouragement and helpful suggestions in the selection of materials for *Annual Editions: Global Issues 02/03.* It is my continuing goal to encourage the readers of this book to have a greater appreciation of the world in which we live. I hope each of you will be motivated to further explore the complex issues faced by the world as we enter the twenty-first century.

Robert M. Jackson
Editor

Contents

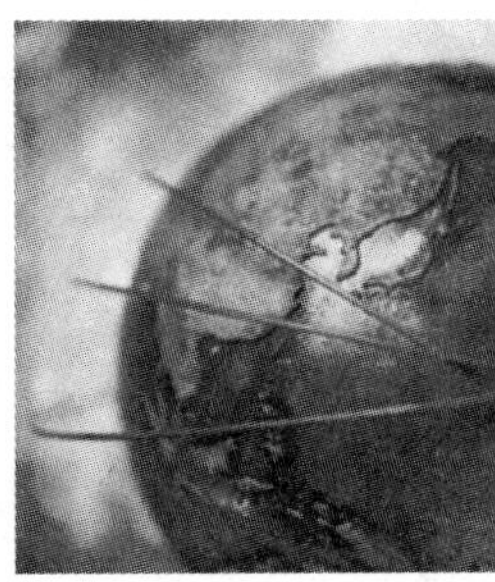

UNIT 1
Global Issues in the Twenty-First Century: An Overview

Four articles in this section present distinct views on the present and future state of life on Earth.

UNIT 2
Population and Food Production

Three selections in this section discuss the contributing factors in the world's population growth and the challenge of providing food for this added strain on the world's capacity.

The concepts in bold italics are developed in the article. For further expansion, please refer to the Topic Guide and the Index.

UNIT 3
The Global Environment and Natural Resources Utilization

Four articles in this section discuss natural resources and their effects on the world's environment.

The concepts in bold italics are developed in the article. For further expansion, please refer to the Topic Guide and the Index.

UNIT 4
Political Economy

Eight articles present various views on economic and social development in the non-industrial and industrial nations.

The concepts in bold italics are developed in the article. For further expansion, please refer to the Topic Guide and the Index.

UNIT 5
Conflict

Six articles in this section discuss the basis for world conflict and the current state of order and disorder in the international community.

The concepts in bold italics are developed in the article. For further expansion, please refer to the Topic Guide and the Index.

UNIT 6
Cooperation

Five selections in this section examine patterns of international cooperation and the social structures that support this cooperation.

UNIT 7
Values and Visions

Six articles discuss human rights, ethics, values, and new ideas.

The concepts in bold italics are developed in the article. For further expansion, please refer to the Topic Guide and the Index.

The concepts in bold italics are developed in the article. For further expansion, please refer to the Topic Guide and the Index.

Topic Guide

This topic guide suggests how the selections in this book relate to the subjects covered in your course. You may want to use the topics listed on these pages to search the Web more easily.

On the following pages a number of Web sites have been gathered specifically for this book. They are arranged to reflect the units of this *Annual Edition.* You can link to these sites by going to the DUSHKIN ONLINE support site at *http://www.dushkin.com/online/.*

ALL THE ARTICLES THAT RELATE TO EACH TOPIC ARE LISTED BELOW THE BOLD-FACED TERM.

World Wide Web Sites

The following World Wide Web sites have been carefully researched and selected to support the articles found in this reader. The easiest way to access these selected sites is to go to our DUSHKIN ONLINE support site at *http://www.dushkin.com/online/*.

AE: Global Issues 02/03

The following sites were available at the time of publication. Visit our Web site—we update DUSHKIN ONLINE regularly to reflect any changes.

General Sources

U.S. Information Agency (USIA)

http://www.usinfo.state.gov

USIA's home page provides definitions, related documentation, and discussions of topics of concern to students of global issues. The site addresses today's Hot Topics as well as ongoing issues that form the foundation of the field.

World Wide Web Virtual Library: International Affairs Resources

http://www.etown.edu/vl/

Surf this site and its extensive links to learn about specific countries and regions, to research various think tanks and international organizations, and to study such vital topics as international law, development, the international economy, human rights, and peacekeeping.

UNIT 1: Global Issues in the Twenty-First Century: An Overview

The Henry L. Stimson Center

http://www.stimson.org

The Stimson Center, a nonpartisan organization, focuses on issues where policy, technology, and politics intersect. Use this site to find varying assessments of U.S. foreign policy in the post–cold war world and to research other topics.

The Heritage Foundation

http://www.heritage.org

This page offers discussion about and links to many sites having to do with foreign policy and foreign affairs, including news and commentary, policy review, events, and a resource bank.

IISDnet

http://iisd1.iisd.ca

The International Institute for Sustainable Development presents information through links to business, sustainable development, and developing ideas. "Linkages" is its multimedia resource for policymakers.

The North-South Institute

http://www.nsi-ins.ca/ensi/index.html

Searching this site of the North-South Institute, which works to strengthen international development cooperation and enhance gender and social equity, will help you find information and debates on a variety of global issues.

UNIT 2: Population and Food Production

The Hunger Project

http://www.thp.org

Browse through this nonprofit organization's site, whose goal is the sustainable end to global hunger through leadership at all levels of society. The Hunger Project contends that the persistence of hunger is at the heart of the major security issues threatening our planet.

Penn Library: Resources by Subject

http://www.library.upenn.edu/resources/websitest.html

This vast site is rich in links to information about subjects of interest to students of global issues. Its extensive population and demography resources address such concerns as migration, family planning, and health and nutrition in various world regions.

World Health Organization

http://www.who.int

This home page of the World Health Organization will provide you with links to a wealth of statistical and analytical information about health and the environment in the developing world.

WWW Virtual Library: Demography & Population Studies

http://demography.anu.edu.au/VirtualLibrary/

A definitive guide to demography and population studies can be found at this site. It contains a multitude of important links to information about global poverty and hunger.

UNIT 3: The Global Environment and Natural Resources Utilization

Friends of the Earth

http://www.foe.co.uk/index.html

This nonprofit organization pursues a number of campaigns to protect Earth and its living creatures. This site has links to many important environmental sites, covering such broad topics as ozone depletion, soil erosion, and biodiversity.

National Geographic Society

http://www.nationalgeographic.com

This site provides links to material related to the atmosphere, the oceans, and other environmental topics.

National Oceanic and Atmospheric Administration (NOAA)

http://www.noaa.gov

Through this home page of NOAA, part of the U.S. Department of Commerce, you can find information about coastal issues, fisheries, climate, and more. The site provides many links to research materials and to other Web resources.

Public Utilities Commission of Ohio (PUCO)

http://www.puc.state.oh.us/consumer/gcc/index.html

PUCO's site serves as a clearinghouse of information about global climate change. Its links explain the science and chronology of global climate change.

SocioSite: Sociological Subject Areas

http://www.pscw.uva.nl/sociosite/TOPICS/

This huge site provides many references of interest to those interested in global issues, such as links to information on ecology and the impact of consumerism.

United Nations Environment Programme (UNEP)

http://www.unep.ch

Consult this home page of UNEP for links to critical topics of concern to students of global issues, including desertification, migratory species, and the impact of trade on the environment.

UNIT 4: Political Economy

Belfer Center for Science and International Affairs (BCSIA)
http://ksgwww.harvard.edu/csia/
BCSIA is the hub of Harvard University's John F. Kennedy School of Government's research, teaching, and training in international affairs related to security, environment, and technology.

Communications for a Sustainable Future
http://csf.colorado.edu
Information on topics in international environmental sustainability is available on this Gopher site. It pays particular attention to the political economics of protecting the environment.

U.S. Agency for International Development
http://www.info.usaid.gov
Broad and overlapping issues such as democracy, population and health, economic growth, and development are covered on this Web site. It provides specific information about different regions and countries.

Virtual Seminar in Global Political Economy/Global Cities & Social Movements
http://csf.colorado.edu/gpe/gpe95b/resources.html
This site of Internet resources is rich in links to subjects of interest in regional environmental studies, covering topics such as sustainable cities, megacities, and urban planning. Links to many international nongovernmental organizations are included.

World Bank
http://www.worldbank.org
News, press releases, summaries of new projects, speeches, publications, and coverage of numerous topics regarding development, countries, and regions are provided at this World Bank site. It also contains links to other important global financial organizations.

UNIT 5: Conflict

DefenseLINK
http://www.defenselink.mil
Learn about security news and research-related publications at this U.S. Department of Defense site. Links to related sites of interest are provided. The information systems BosniaLINK and GulfLINK can also be found here. Use the search function to investigate such issues as land mines.

Federation of American Scientists (FAS)
http://www.fas.org
FAS, a nonprofit policy organization, maintains this site to provide coverage of and links to such topics as global security, peace, and governance in the post–cold war world. It notes a variety of resources of value to students of global issues.

ISN International Relations and Security Network
http://www.isn.ethz.ch
This site, maintained by the Center for Security Studies and Conflict Research, is a clearinghouse for information on international relations and security policy. Topics are listed by category (Traditional Dimensions of Security, New Dimensions of Security, and Related Fields) and by major world region.

The NATO Integrated Data Service (NIDS)
http://www.nato.int/structur/nids/nids.htm
NIDS was created to bring information on security-related matters to within easy reach of the widest possible audience. Check out this Web site to review North Atlantic Treaty Organization documentation of all kinds, to read *NATO Review,* and to explore key issues in the field of European security and transatlantic cooperation.

UNIT 6: Cooperation

American Foreign Service Association
http://www.afsa.org/related.html
The AFSA offers this page of related sites as part of its Web presence. Useful sites include DiploNet, Public Diplomacy, and InterAction. Aso click on Diplomacy and Diplomats and other sites on the sidebar.

Carnegie Endowment for International Peace
http://www.ceip.org
An important goal of this organization is to stimulate discussion and learning among both experts and the public at large on a wide range of international issues. The site provides links to *Foreign Policy,* to the Moscow Center, to descriptions of various programs, and much more.

Commission on Global Governance
http://www.cgg.ch
This site provides access to *The Report of the Commission on Global Governance,* produced by an international group of leaders who want to find ways in which the global community can better manage its affairs.

OECD/FDI Statistics
http://www.oecd.org/statistics/
Explore world trade and investment trends and statistics on this site from the Organization for Economic Cooperation and Development. It provides links to many related topics and addresses the issues on a country-by-country basis.

U.S. Institute of Peace
http://www.usip.org
USIP, which was created by the U.S. Congress to promote peaceful resolution of international conflicts, seeks to educate people and to disseminate information on how to achieve peace. Click on Highlights, Publications, Events, Research Areas, and Library and Links.

UNIT 7: Values and Visions

Human Rights Web
http://www.hrweb.org
The history of the human rights movement, text on seminal figures, landmark legal and political documents, and ideas on how individuals can get involved in helping to protect human rights around the world can be found in this valuable site.

InterAction
http://www.interaction.org
InterAction encourages grassroots action and engages government policymakers on advocacy issues. The organization's Advocacy Committee provides this site to inform people on its initiatives to expand international humanitarian relief, refugee, and development-assistance programs.

We highly recommend that you review our Web site for expanded information and our other product lines. We are continually updating and adding links to our Web site in order to offer you the most usable and useful information that will support and expand the value of your Annual Editions. You can reach us at: *http://www.dushkin.com/annualeditions/*.

World Map

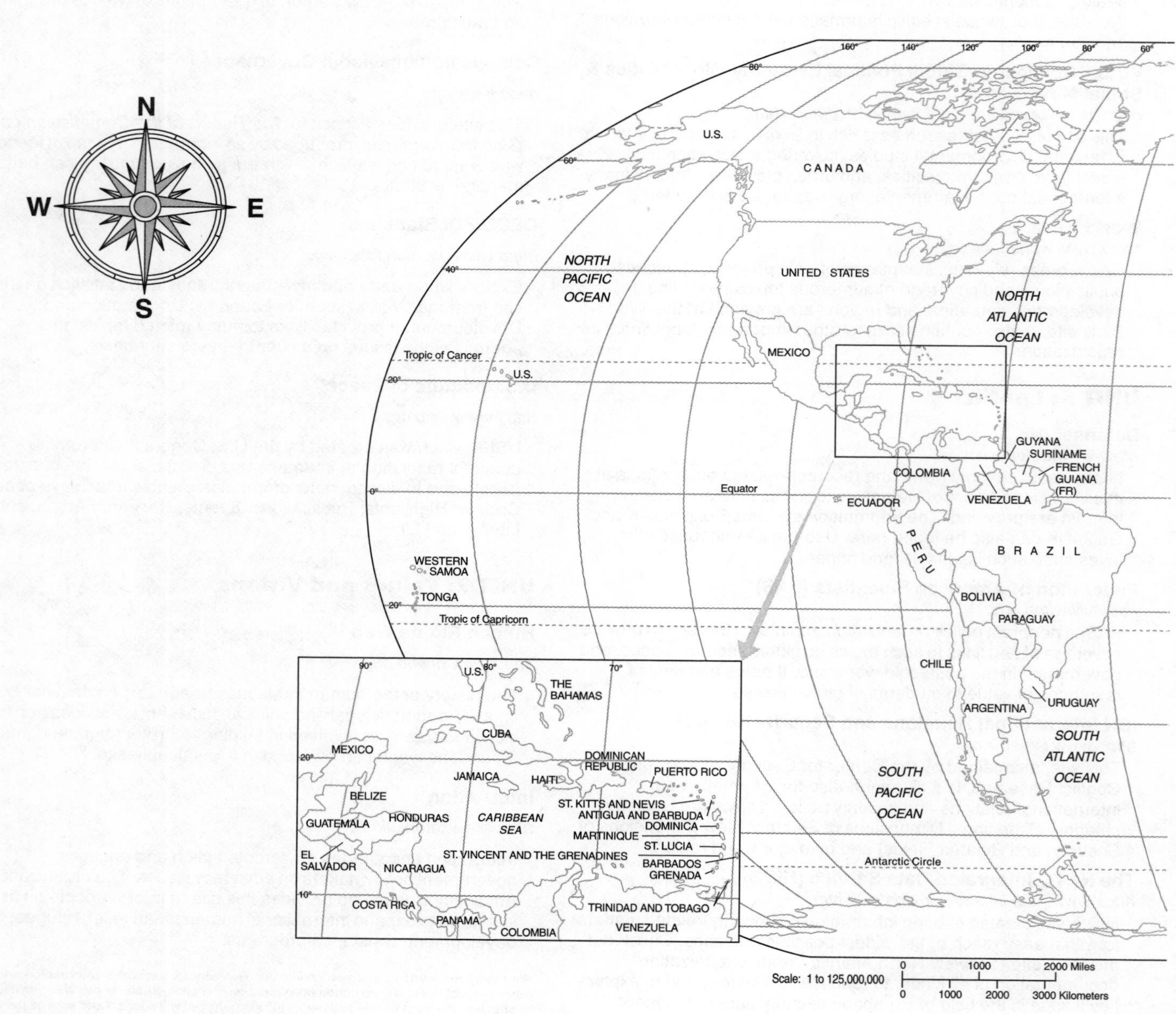

N
W
E
S
U.S.
CANADA
NORTH PACIFIC OCEAN
UNITED STATES
NORTH ATLANTIC OCEAN
MEXICO
Tropic of Cancer
U.S.
GUYANA
SURINAME
FRENCH GUIANA (FR)
COLOMBIA
Equator
ECUADOR
VENEZUELA
PERU
BRAZIL
WESTERN SAMOA
TONGA
BOLIVIA
Tropic of Capricorn
PARAGUAY
CHILE
ARGENTINA
URUGUAY
SOUTH ATLANTIC OCEAN
SOUTH PACIFIC OCEAN
Antarctic Circle
U.S.
THE BAHAMAS
CUBA
MEXICO
DOMINICAN REPUBLIC
JAMAICA
HAITI
PUERTO RICO
BELIZE
ST. KITTS AND NEVIS
ANTIGUA AND BARBUDA
GUATEMALA
HONDURAS
CARIBBEAN SEA
DOMINICA
MARTINIQUE
ST. LUCIA
EL SALVADOR
NICARAGUA
ST. VINCENT AND THE GRENADINES
BARBADOS
GRENADA
COSTA RICA
TRINIDAD AND TOBAGO
PANAMA
COLOMBIA
VENEZUELA
Scale: 1 to 125,000,000
0 1000 2000 Miles
0 1000 2000 3000 Kilometers

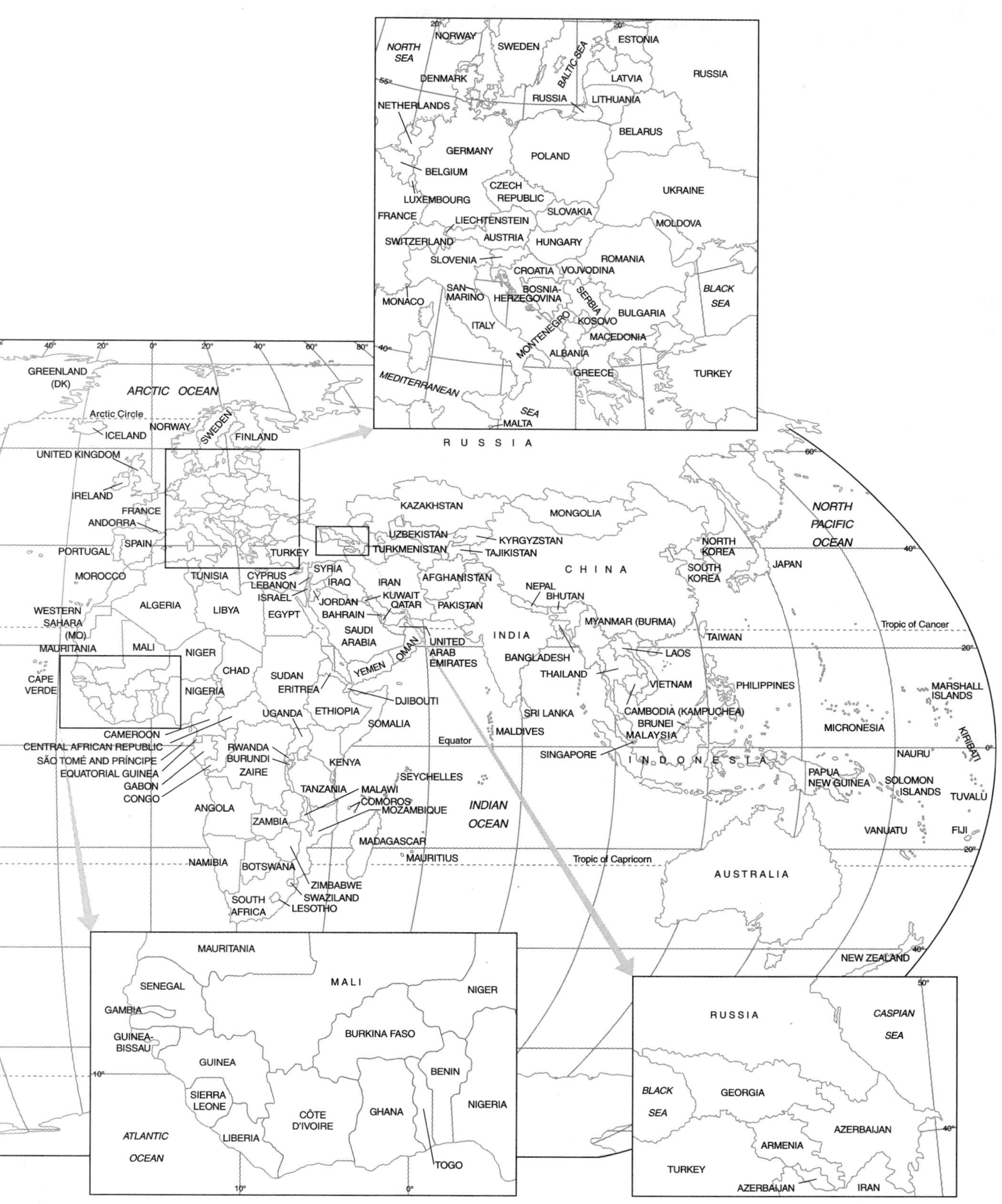
NORTH SEA
NORWAY
SWEDEN
BALTIC SEA
ESTONIA
RUSSIA
LATVIA
DENMARK
LITHUANIA
NETHERLANDS
BELARUS
GERMANY
POLAND
BELGIUM
CZECH REPUBLIC
UKRAINE
LUXEMBOURG
SLOVAKIA
FRANCE
LIECHTENSTEIN
MOLDOVA
SWITZERLAND
AUSTRIA
HUNGARY
SLOVENIA
ROMANIA
CROATIA
VOJVODINA
SAN MARINO
BOSNIA-HERZEGOVINA
SERBIA
BLACK SEA
MONACO
KOSOVO
BULGARIA
ITALY
MONTENEGRO
MACEDONIA
ALBANIA
GREECE
TURKEY
MEDITERRANEAN SEA
MALTA
GREENLAND (DK)
ARCTIC OCEAN
Arctic Circle
ICELAND
FINLAND
UNITED KINGDOM
IRELAND
ANDORRA
PORTUGAL
SPAIN
MOROCCO
TUNISIA
CYPRUS
LEBANON
ISRAEL
SYRIA
IRAQ
JORDAN
IRAN
KUWAIT
QATAR
BAHRAIN
SAUDI ARABIA
OMAN
YEMEN
UNITED ARAB EMIRATES
WESTERN SAHARA (MO)
ALGERIA
LIBYA
EGYPT
MAURITANIA
MALI
NIGER
CHAD
SUDAN
ERITREA
DJIBOUTI
ETHIOPIA
SOMALIA
CAPE VERDE
NIGERIA
CAMEROON
CENTRAL AFRICAN REPUBLIC
SÃO TOMÉ AND PRÍNCIPE
EQUATORIAL GUINEA
GABON
CONGO
UGANDA
RWANDA
BURUNDI
ZAIRE
KENYA
TANZANIA
MALAWI
COMOROS
MOZAMBIQUE
SEYCHELLES
ANGOLA
ZAMBIA
MADAGASCAR
MAURITIUS
NAMIBIA
BOTSWANA
ZIMBABWE
SWAZILAND
SOUTH AFRICA
LESOTHO
KAZAKHSTAN
UZBEKISTAN
TURKMENISTAN
KYRGYZSTAN
TAJIKISTAN
AFGHANISTAN
PAKISTAN
MONGOLIA
C H I N A
NEPAL
BHUTAN
INDIA
BANGLADESH
MYANMAR (BURMA)
LAOS
THAILAND
VIETNAM
CAMBODIA (KAMPUCHEA)
BRUNEI
MALAYSIA
SINGAPORE
SRI LANKA
MALDIVES
I N D O N E S I A
NORTH KOREA
SOUTH KOREA
JAPAN
TAIWAN
PHILIPPINES
NORTH PACIFIC OCEAN
Tropic of Cancer
Equator
Tropic of Capricorn
INDIAN OCEAN
MARSHALL ISLANDS
MICRONESIA
KIRIBATI
NAURU
PAPUA NEW GUINEA
SOLOMON ISLANDS
TUVALU
VANUATU
FIJI
AUSTRALIA
NEW ZEALAND
R U S S I A
SENEGAL
GAMBIA
GUINEA-BISSAU
GUINEA
SIERRA LEONE
LIBERIA
CÔTE D'IVOIRE
GHANA
TOGO
BENIN
BURKINA FASO
ATLANTIC OCEAN
CASPIAN SEA
GEORGIA
AZERBAIJAN
ARMENIA

UNIT 1

Global Issues in the Twenty-First Century: An Overview

Unit Selections

1. **A Special Moment in History**, Bill McKibben
2. **The Many Faces of the Future**, Samuel P. Huntington
3. **The Clash of Ignorance**, Edward W. Said
4. **Mr. Order Meets Mr. Chaos**, Robert Wright and Robert Kaplan

Key Points to Consider

- Do the analyses of any of the authors in this section employ the assumptions implicit in the allegory of the balloon? If so, how? If not, how are the assumptions of the authors different?
- All the authors point to interactions among different factors. What are some of the relationships that they cite? How do the authors differ in terms of the relationships they emphasize?
- What assets that did not exist 100 years ago do people have now to solve problems?
- What events during the twentieth century had the greatest impact on shaping the realities of contemporary international affairs?
- What do you consider to be the five most pressing global problems of today? How do your answers compare to those of your family, friends, and classmates?

Links: www.dushkin.com/online/
These sites are annotated in the World Wide Web pages.

The Henry L. Stimson Center
http://www.stimson.org

The Heritage Foundation
http://www.heritage.org

IISDnet
http://iisd1.iisd.ca

The North-South Institute
http://www.nsi-ins.ca/ensi/index.html

Imagine a clear, round, inflated balloon. Now imagine that a person begins to brush yellow paint onto this miniature globe; symbolically, the color yellow represents *people.* In many ways the study of global issues is ultimately the study of people. Today, there are more people occupying Earth than ever before. In addition, the world is in the midst of a period of unprecedented population growth. Not only are there many countries where the majority of people are under age 16, but because of improved health care, there are also more older people alive than ever before. The effect of a growing global population, however, goes beyond sheer numbers, for this trend has unprecedented negative impacts on natural resources and social services. An examination of population trends, in short, is an appropriate topic to begin the study of global issues.

Imagine that our fictional artist dips the brush into a container of blue paint to represent the world of *nature.* The natural world plays an important role in setting the international agenda. Shortages of raw materials, drought and crop failures, and pollution of waterways are just a few examples of how natural resources can have global implications.

Adding blue paint to the balloon also reveals one of the most important concepts found in this book of readings. Although the balloon originally was covered by yellow and blue paint (people and nature as separate conceptual entities), the two combined produce an entirely different color: green. Talking about nature as a separate entity or about people as though they were somehow removed from the forces of the natural world is a serious intellectual error. The people-nature relationship is one of the keys to understanding many of today's most important global issues.

The third color added to the balloon is red. It represents the *meta* component (i.e., those qualities that make human beings different from animals). These include new ideas and inventions, culture and values, religion and spirituality, and art and literature. The addition of the red paint immediately changes the color green to brown, again emphasizing the relationship among all three factors.

The fourth and final color added is white. This color represents *social structures.* Factors such as whether a society is urban or rural, industrial or agrarian, planned or decentralized, and consumer-oriented or dedicated to the needs of the state fall into this category. The relationship between this component and the others is extremely important. The impact of political decisions on the environment, for example, is one of the most unusual features of the contemporary world. Historically, the forces of nature determined which species survived or perished. Today, survival depends on political decisions—or indecision. Will the whales or bald eagles survive? The answer to this question will often depend on governmental activities, not evolutionary forces.

Understanding this relationship between social structure and nature (known as "ecopolitics") is important to the study of global issues. If the painter continues to ply the paintbrush over the miniature globe, a marbling effect will become evident. In some areas, the shading will vary because one element is greater than another. The miniature system appears dynamic. Nothing is static; relationships are continually changing. This leads to a number of theoretical insights: (1) there is no such thing as separate elements, only connections or relationships; (2) changes in one area (such as the weather) will result in changes in all other areas; and (3) complex relationships make it difficult to predict events accurately, so observers are often surprised by unexpected processes and outcomes.

This book is organized along the basic lines of the balloon allegory. The first unit explores a variety of perspectives on the forces that are shaping the world of the twenty-first century. Unit 2 focuses on population and food production. Unit 3 examines the environment and related issues. The next three units look at different aspects of the world's social structures. They explore issues of economics, national security, conflict, and international cooperation. In the final unit, a number of "meta" factors are discussed.

The reader should be aware that, just as it was impossible to keep the individual colors from blending into new colors on the balloon, it is also impossible to separate global issues into discrete chapters in a book. Any discussion of agriculture, for example, must take into account the impact of a growing population on soil and water resources, as well as new scientific breakthroughs in food production. Therefore, the organization of this book focuses attention on issue areas; it does not mean to imply that these factors are somehow separate.

With the collapse of the Soviet empire and the end of the cold war, the outlines of a new global agenda have begun to emerge. Rather than being based on the ideology and interests of the two superpowers, new political, economic, environmental, and security issues are interacting in an unprecedented fashion. Rapid population growth, environmental decline, uneven economic growth, and global terrorist networks are all parts of a complex situation for which there is no historic parallel. As we begin the twenty-first century, signs abound that we are entering a new era. In the words of Abraham Lincoln, "As our case is new, so we must think anew." Compounding this situation, however, is a whole series of old problems such as ethnic and religious rivalries.

The authors in this first unit provide a variety of perspectives on the trends that they believe are the most important to understanding the historic changes at work at the global level. This discussion is then pursued in greater detail in the following units.

It is important for the reader to note that although the authors look at the same world, they often come to different conclusions. This raises an important issue of values and beliefs, for it can be argued that there really is no objective reality, only differing perspectives. In short, the study of global issues will challenge each thoughtful reader to examine her or his own values and beliefs.

Article 1

A Special Moment in History

Bill McKibben

We may live in the strangest, most thoroughly different moment since human beings took up farming, 10,000 years ago, and time more or less commenced. Since then time has flowed in one direction—toward *more*, which we have taken to be progress. At first the momentum was gradual, almost imperceptible, checked by wars and the Dark Ages and plagues and taboos; but in recent centuries it has accelerated, the curve of every graph steepening like the Himalayas rising from the Asian steppe....

But now—now may be the special time. So special that in the Western world we might each of us consider, among many other things, having only one child—that is, reproducing at a rate as low as that at which human beings have ever voluntarily reproduced. Is this really necessary? Are we finally running up against some limits?

To try to answer this question, we need to ask another: *How many of us will there be in the near future?* Here is a piece of news that may alter the way we see the planet—an indication that we live at a special moment. At least at first blush the news is hopeful. *New demographic evidence shows that it is at least possible that a child born today will live long enough to see the peak of human population.*

Around the world people are choosing to have fewer and fewer children—not just in China, where the government forces it on them, but in almost every nation outside the poorest parts of Africa.... If this keeps up, the population of the world will not quite double again; United Nations analysts offer as their mid-range projection that it will top out at 10 to 11 billion, up from just under six billion at the moment....

The good news is that we won't grow forever. The bad news is that there are six billion of us already, a number the world strains to support. One more near-doubling—four or five billion more people—will nearly double that strain. Will these be the five billion straws that break the camel's back?...

LOOKING AT LIMITS

The case that the next doubling, the one we're now experiencing, might be the difficult one can begin as readily with the Stanford biologist Peter Vitousek as with anyone else. In 1986 Vitousek decided to calculate how much of the earth's "primary productivity" went to support human beings. He added together the grain we ate, the corn we fed our cows, and the forests we cut for timber and paper; he added the losses in food as we overgrazed grassland and turned it into desert. And when he was finished adding, the number he came up with was 38.8 percent. We use 38.8 percent of everything the world's plants don't need to keep themselves alive; directly or indirectly, we consume 38.8 percent of what it is possible to eat. "That's a relatively large number," Vitousek says. "It should give pause to people who think we are far from any limits." Though he never drops the measured tone of an academic, Vitousek speaks with considerable emphasis: "There's a sense among some economists that we're *so* far from any biophysical limits. I think that's not supported by the evidence."

For another antidote to the good cheer of someone like Julian Simon, sit down with the Cornell biologist David Pimentel. He believes that we're in big trouble. Odd facts stud his conversation—for example, a nice head of iceberg lettuce is 95 percent water and contains just fifty calories of energy, but it takes 400 calories of energy to grow that head of lettuce in California's Central Valley, and another 1,800 to ship it east. ("There's practically no nutrition in the damn stuff anyway," Pimentel says. "Cabbage is a lot better, and we can grow it in upstate New York.") Pimentel has devoted the past three decades to tracking the planet's capacity, and he believes that we're already too crowded—that the earth can support only two billion people over the long run at a middle-class standard of living, and that trying to support more is doing damage. He has spent considerable time studying soil erosion, for instance. Every raindrop that hits exposed ground is like a small explosion, launching soil particles into the air. On a slope, more than half of the soil contained in those splashes is carried downhill. If crop residue—cornstalks, say—is left in the field after harvest, it helps to shield the soil: the raindrop doesn't hit hard. But in the developing world, where firewood is scarce, peasants burn those cornstalks for cooking fuel. About 60 percent of crop residues in China and 90 percent in Bangladesh are removed and burned, Pimentel says. When planting season comes, dry soils simply blow away. "Our measuring stations pick up African soils in the wind when they start to plough."

The very things that made the Green Revolution so stunning—that made the last doubling possible—now cause trouble. Irrigation ditches, for instance, water 27 percent of all arable land and help to produce a third of all crops. But when flooded soils are baked by the sun, the water evaporates and the minerals in the irrigation water are deposited on the land. A hectare (2.47 acres) can accumulate two to five tons of salt annually, and eventually plants won't grow there. Maybe 10 percent of all irrigated land is affected.

... [F]ood production grew even faster than population after the Second World War. Year after year the yield of wheat and corn and rice rocketed up about three percent annually. It's a favorite statistic of the eternal optimists. In Julian Simon's book *The Ultimate Resource* (1981) charts show just how fast the growth was, and how it continually cut the cost of food. Simon wrote, "The obvious implication of this historical trend toward cheaper food—a trend that probably extends back to the beginning of agriculture—is that real prices for food will continue to drop.... It is a fact that portends more drops in price and even less scarcity in the future."

A few years after Simon's book was published, however, the data curve began to change. That rocketing growth in grain production ceased; now the gains were coming in tiny increments, too small to keep pace with population growth. The world reaped its largest harvest of grain per capita in 1984; since then the amount of corn and wheat and rice per person has fallen by six percent. Grain stockpiles have shrunk to less than two months' supply.

No one knows quite why. The collapse of the Soviet Union contributed to the trend—cooperative farms suddenly found the fertilizer supply shut off and spare parts for the tractor hard to come by. But there were other causes, too, all around the world—the salinization of irrigated fields, the erosion of topsoil, and all the other things that environmentalists had been warning about for years. It's possible that we'll still turn production around and start it rocketing again. Charles C. Mann, writing in *Science*, quotes experts who believe that in the future a "gigantic, multi-year, multi-billion-dollar scientific effort, a kind of agricultural 'person-on the-moon project,'" might do the trick. The next great hope of the optimists is genetic engineering, and scientists have indeed managed to induce resistance to pests and disease in some plants. To get more yield, though, a cornstalk must be made to put out another ear, and conventional breeding may have exhausted the possibilities. There's a sense that we're running into walls.

... What we are running out of is what the scientists call "sinks"—places to put the by-products of our large appetites. Not garbage dumps (we could go on using Pampers till the end of time and still have empty space left to toss them away) but the atmospheric equivalent of garbage dumps.

It wasn't hard to figure out that there were limits on how much coal smoke we could pour into the air of a single city. It took a while longer to figure out that building ever higher smokestacks merely lofted the haze farther afield, raining down acid on whatever mountain range lay to the east. Even that, however, we are slowly fixing, with scrubbers and different mixtures of fuel. We can't so easily repair the new kinds of pollution. These do not come from something going wrong—some engine without a catalytic converter, some waste-water pipe without a filter, some smokestack without a scrubber. New kinds of pollution come instead from things going as they're supposed to go—but at such a high volume that they overwhelm the planet. They come from normal human life—but there are so many of us living those normal lives that something abnormal is happening. And that something is different from the old forms of pollution that it confuses the issue even to use the word.

Consider nitrogen, for instance. But before plants can absorb it, it must become "fixed"—bonded with carbon, hydrogen, or oxygen. Nature does this trick with certain kinds of algae and soil bacteria, and with lightning. Before human beings began to alter the nitrogen cycle, these mechanisms provided 90–150 million metric tons of nitrogen a year. Now human activity adds 130–150 million more tons. Nitrogen isn't pollution—it's essential. And we are using more of it all the time. Half the industrial nitrogen fertilizer used in human history has been applied since 1984. As a result, coastal waters and estuaries bloom with toxic algae while oxygen concentrations dwindle, killing fish; as a result, nitrous oxide traps solar heat. And once the gas is in the air, it stays there for a century or more.

Or consider methane, which comes out of the back of a cow or the top of a termite mound or the bottom of a rice paddy. As a result of our determination to raise more cattle, cut down more tropical forest (thereby causing termite populations to explode), and grow more rice, methane concentrations in the atmosphere are more than twice as high as they have been for most of the past 160,000 years. And methane traps heat—very efficiently.

Or consider carbon dioxide. In fact, concentrate on carbon dioxide. If we had to pick one problem to obsess about over the next fifty years, we'd do well to make it CO_2—which is not pollution either. Carbon *mon*oxide is pollution: it kills you if you breathe enough of it. But carbon *di*oxide, carbon with two oxygen atoms, can't do a blessed thing to you. If you're reading this indoors, you're breathing more CO_2 than you'll ever get outside. For generations, in fact, engineers said that an engine burned clean if it produced only water vapor and carbon dioxide.

Here's the catch: that engine produces a *lot* of CO_2. A gallon of gas weighs about eight pounds. When it's burned in a car, about five and a half pounds of carbon, in the form of carbon dioxide, come spewing out the back. It doesn't matter if the car is a 1958 Chevy or a 1998 Saab. And no filter can reduce that flow—it's an inevitable by-product of fossil-fuel combustion, which is why CO_2 has been piling up in the atmosphere ever since the Industrial Revolution. Before we started burning oil and coal and gas, the atmosphere contained about 280 parts CO_2 per million. Now the figure is about 360. Unless we do everything we can think of to eliminate fossil fuels from our diet, the air will test out at more than 500 parts per million fifty or sixty years from now, whether it's sampled in the South Bronx or at the South Pole.

This matters because, as we all know by now, the molecular structure of this clean, natural, common element that we are adding to every cubic foot of the atmosphere surrounding us traps heat that would otherwise radiate back out to space. Far more than even methane and nitrous oxide, CO_2 causes global warming—the greenhouse effect—and climate change. Far more than any other single factor, it is turning the earth we were born on into a new planet.

... For ten years, with heavy funding from governments around the world, scientists launched satellites, monitored weather balloons, studied clouds. Their work culminated in a long-awaited report from the UN's Intergovernmental Panel on Climate Change, released in the fall of 1995. The panel's 2,000 scientists, from every corner of the globe, summed up their findings in this dry but historic bit of understatement: "The balance of evidence suggests that there is a discernible human influence on global climate." That is to say, we are heating up the planet—substantially. If we don't reduce emissions of carbon dioxide and other gases, the panel warned, temperatures will probably rise 3.6° Fahrenheit by 2100, and perhaps as much as 6.3°.

You may think you've already heard a lot about global warming. But most of our sense of the problem is behind the curve. Here's the current news: the changes are already well under way. When politicians and businessmen talk about "future risks," their rhetoric is outdated. This is not a problem for the distant future, or even for the near future. The planet has already heated up by a degree or more. We are perhaps a quarter of the way into the greenhouse era, and the effects are already being felt. From a new heaven, filled with nitrogen, methane, and carbon, a new earth is being born. If some alien astronomer is watching us, she's doubtless puzzled. This is the most obvious effect of our numbers and our appetites, and the key to understanding why the size of our population suddenly poses such a risk.

STORMY AND WARM

What does this new world feel like? For one thing, it's stormier than the old one. Data analyzed last year by Thomas Karl, of the National Oceanic and Atmospheric Administration, showed that total winter precipitation in the United States has increased by 10 percent since 1900 and that "extreme precipitation events"—rainstorms that dumped more than two inches of water in twenty-four hours and blizzards—had increased by 20 percent. That's because warmer air holds more water vapor than the colder atmosphere of the old earth; more water evaporates from the ocean, meaning more clouds, more rain, more snow. Engineers designing storm sewers, bridges, and culverts used to plan for what they called the "hundred-year storm." That is, they built to withstand the worst flooding or wind that history led them to expect in the course of a century. Since that history no longer applies, Karl says, "there isn't really a hundred-year event anymore... we seem to be getting these storms of the century every couple of years." When Grand Forks, North Dakota, disappeared beneath the Red River in the spring of last year, some meteorologists referred to it as "a 500-year flood"—meaning, essentially, that all bets are off. Meaning that these aren't acts of God. "If you look out your window, part of what you see in terms of weather is produced by ourselves," Karl says. "If you look out the window fifty years from now, we're going to be responsible for more of it."

Twenty percent more bad storms, 10 percent more winter precipitation—these are enormous numbers. It's like opening the newspaper to read that the average American is smarter by 30 IQ points. And the same data showed increases in drought, too. With more water in the atmosphere, there's less in the soil, according to Kevin Trenberth, of the National Center for Atmospheric Research. Those parts of the continent that are normally dry—the eastern sides of mountains, the plains and deserts—are even drier, as the higher average temperatures evaporate more of what rain does fall. "You get wilting plants and eventually drought faster than you would otherwise," Trenberth says. And when the rain does come, it's often so intense that much of it runs off before it can soak into the soil.

So—wetter and drier. *Different*....

The effects of... warming can be found in the largest phenomena. The oceans that cover most of the planet's surface are clearly rising, both because of melting glaciers and because water expands as it warms. As a result, low-lying Pacific islands already report surges of water washing across the atolls. "It's nice weather and all of a sudden water is pouring into your living room," one Marshall Islands resident told a newspaper reporter. "It's very clear that something is happening in the Pacific, and these islands are feeling it." Global warming will be like a much more powerful version of El Niño that covers the entire globe and lasts forever, or at least until the next big asteroid strikes.

If you want to scare yourself with guesses about what might happen in the near future, there's no shortage of possibilities. Scientists have already observed large-scale shifts in the duration of the El Niño ocean warming, for instance. The Arctic tundra has warmed so much that in some places it now gives off more carbon dioxide than it absorbs—a switch that could trigger a potent feedback loop, making warming ever worse. And researchers studying glacial cores from the Greenland Ice Sheet recently concluded that local climate shifts have occurred with incredible rapidity in the past—18° in one three-year stretch. Other scientists worry that such a shift might be enough to flood the oceans with fresh water and reroute or shut off currents like the Gulf Stream and the North Atlantic, which keep Europe far warmer than it would otherwise be. (See "The Great Climate Flip-flop," by William H. Calvin, January *Atlantic*.) In the words of Wallace Broecker, of Columbia University, a pioneer in the field, "Climate is an angry beast, and we are poking it with sticks."

But we don't need worst-case scenarios: best-case scenarios make the point. The population of the earth is going to nearly double one more time. That will bring it to a level that even the reliable old earth we were born on would be hard-pressed to support. Just at the moment when we need everything to be working as smoothly as possible, we find ourselves inhabiting a new planet, whose carrying capacity we cannot conceivably estimate. We have no idea how much wheat this planet can grow. We don't know what its politics will be like: not if there are going to be heat waves like the one that killed more than 700 Chicagoans in 1995; not if rising sea levels and other effects of climate change create tens of millions of environmental refugees; not if a 1.5° jump in India's temperature could reduce the country's wheat crop by 10 percent or divert its monsoons....

We have gotten very large and very powerful, and for the foreseeable future we're stuck with the results. The glaciers won't grow back again anytime soon; the oceans won't drop. We've already done deep and systemic damage. To use a human analogy, we've already said the angry and unforgivable words that will haunt our marriage till its end. And yet we can't simply walk out the door. There's no place to go. We have to salvage what we can of our relationship with the earth, to keep things from getting any worse than they have to be.

If we can bring our various emissions quickly and sharply under control, we *can* limit the damage, reduce dramatically the chance of horrible surprises, preserve more of the biology we were born into. But do not underestimate the task. The UN's Intergovernmental Panel on Climate Change projects that an immediate 60 percent reduction in fossil-fuel use is necessary just to stabilize climate at the current level of disruption. Nature may still meet us halfway, but halfway is a long way from where we are now. What's more, we can't delay. If we wait a few decades to get started, we may as well not even begin. It's not like poverty, a concern that's always there for civilizations to address. This is a timed test, like the SAT: two or three decades, and we lay our pencils down. It's *the* test for our generations, and population is a part of the answer....

The numbers are so daunting that they're almost unimaginable. Say, just for argument's sake, that we decided to cut world fossil-fuel use by 60 percent—the amount that the UN panel says would stabilize world climate. And then say that we shared the remaining fossil fuel equally. Each human being would get to produce 1.69 metric tons of carbon dioxide annually—which would allow you to drive an average American car nine miles a day. By the time the population increased to 8.5 billion, in about 2025, you'd be down to six miles a day. If you carpooled, you'd have about three pounds of CO_2 left in your daily ration—enough to run a highly efficient refrigerator. Forget your computer, your TV, your stereo, your stove, your dishwasher, your water heater, your microwave, your water pump, your clock. Forget your light bulbs, compact fluorescent or not.

I'm not trying to say that conservation, efficiency, and new technology won't help. They will—but the help will be slow and expensive. The tremendous momentum of growth will work against it. Say that someone invented a new furnace tomorrow that used half as much oil as old furnaces. How many years would it be before a substantial number of American homes had the new device? And what if it cost more? And if oil stays cheaper per gallon than bottled water? Changing basic fuels—to hydrogen, say—would be even more expensive. It's not like running out of white wine and switching to red. Yes, we'll get new technologies. One day last fall *The New York Times* ran a special section on energy, featuring many up-and-coming improvements: solar shingles, basement fuel cells. But the same day, on the front page, William K. Stevens reported that international negotiators had all but given up on preventing a doubling of the atmospheric concentration of CO_2. The momentum of growth was so great, the negotiators said, that making the changes required to slow global warming significantly would be like "trying to turn a supertanker in a sea of syrup."

There are no silver bullets to take care of a problem like this. Electric cars won't by themselves save us, though they would help. We simply won't live efficiently enough soon enough to solve the problem. Vegetarianism won't cure our ills, though it would help. We simply won't live simply enough soon enough to solve the problem.

Reducing the birth rate won't end all our troubles either. That, too, is no silver bullet. But it would help.

There's no more practical decision than how many children to have. (And no more mystical decision, either.)

The bottom-line argument goes like this: The next fifty years are a special time. They will decide how strong and healthy the planet will be for centuries to come. Between now and 2050 we'll see the zenith, or very nearly, of human population. With luck we'll never see any greater production of carbon dioxide or toxic chemicals. We'll never see more species extinction or soil erosion. Greenpeace recently announced a campaign to phase out fossil fuels entirely by mid-century, which sounds utterly quixotic but could—if everything went just right—happen.

So it's the task of those of us alive right now to deal with this special phase, to squeeze us through these next fifty years. That's not fair—any more than it was fair that earlier generations had to deal with the Second World War or the Civil War or the Revolution or the Depression or slavery. It's just reality. We need in these fifty years to be working simultaneously on all parts of the equation—on our ways of life, on our technologies, and on our population.

As Gregg Easterbrook pointed out in his book *A Moment on the Earth* (1995), if the planet does manage to reduce its fertility, "the period in which human numbers threaten the biosphere on a general scale will turn out to have been much, much more brief" than periods of natural threats like the Ice Ages. True enough. But the period in question happens to be our time. That's what makes this moment special, and what makes this moment hard.

Bill McKibben is the author of several books about the environment, including *The End of Nature* (1989) and *Hope, Human and Wild* (1995). His article in this issue will appear in somewhat different form in his book *Maybe One: A Personal and Environmental Argument for Single-Child Families*, published in 1998 by Simon & Schuster.

Excerpted from *The Atlantic Monthly*, May 1998, pp. 55-76. © 1998 by Bill McKibben. Reprinted by permission.

THE MANY FACES OF *the Future*

Why we'll never have a universal civilization

By Samuel P. Huntington

Conventional Wisdom tells us that we are witnessing the emergence of what V.S. Naipaul called a "universal civilization," the cultural coming together of humanity and the increasing acceptance of common values, beliefs, and institutions by people throughout the world. Critics of this trend point to the global domination of Western-style capitalism and culture (*Baywatch*, many note with alarm, is the most popular television show in the world), and the gradual erosion of distinct cultures—especially in the developing world. But there's more to universal civilization than GATT and David Hasselhoff's pecs.

If what we mean by universal culture are the assumptions, values, and doctrines currently held by the many elites who travel in international circles, that's not a viable "one world" scenario. Consider the "Davos culture." Each year about a thousand business executives, government officials, intellectuals, and journalists from scores of countries meet at the World Economic Forum in Davos, Switzerland. Almost all of them hold degrees in the physical sciences, social sciences, business, or law; are reasonably fluent in English; are employed by governments, corporations, and academic institutions with extensive international connections; and travel frequently outside of their own countries. They also generally share beliefs in individualism, market economies, and political democracy, which are also common among people in Western civilization. This core group of people controls virtually all international institutions, many of the world's governments, and the bulk of the world's economic and military organizations. As a result, the Davos culture is tremendously important, but it is far from a universal civilization. Outside the West, these values are shared by perhaps 1 percent of the world's population.

The argument that the spread of Western consumption patterns and popular culture around the world is creating a universal civilization is also not especially profound. Innovations have been transmitted from one civilization to another throughout history. But they are usually techniques lacking in significant cultural consequences or fads that come and go without altering the underlying culture of the recipient civilization. The essence of Western civilization is the Magna Carta, not the Magna Mac. The fact that non-Westerners may bite into the latter does not necessarily mean they are more likely to accept the former. During the '70s and '80s Americans bought millions of Japanese cars and electronic gadgets without being "Japanized," and, in fact, became considerably more antagonistic toward Japan. Only naive arrogance can lead Westerners to assume that non-Westerners will become "Westernized" by acquiring Western goods.

A slightly more sophisticated version of the universal popular culture argument focuses on the media rather than consumer goods in general. Eighty-eight of the world's hundred most popular films in 1993 were produced in the United States, and four organizations based in the United States and Europe—the Associated Press, CNN, Reuters, and the French Press Agency—dominate the dissemination of news worldwide. This situation simply reflects the universality of human interest in love, sex, violence, mystery, heroism, and wealth, and the ability of profit-motivated companies, primarily American, to exploit those interests to their own advantage. Little or no evidence exists, however, to support the assumption that the emergence of pervasive global communications is producing significant convergence in attitudes and beliefs around the world. Indeed, this Western hegemony encourages populist politicians in non-Western societies to denounce Western cultural imperialism and to rally their constituents to preserve their indigenous cultures. The extent to which global communications are dominated by the West is, thus, a major source of the resentment non-Western peoples have toward the West. In addition, rapid economic development in non-Western societies is leading to the emergence of local and regional media industries catering to the distinctive tastes of those societies.

The central elements of any civilization are language and religion. If a universal civilization is emerging, there should be signs of a universal language and a universal religion developing. Nothing of the sort is occurring. Despite claims from Western business leaders that the world's language is English, no evidence exists to support this proposition, and the most reliable evidence that does exist shows just the opposite. English speakers dropped from 9.8 percent of the world's population in 1958 to 7.6 percent in 1992. Still, one can argue that English has become the world's lingua franca, or in linguistic terms, the principal language of wider communication. Diplomats, business executives, tourists, and the service professionals catering to them need some means of efficient communication, and right now that is largely in English. But this is a form of *intercultural* communication; it presupposes the existence of separate cultures. Adopting a lingua franca is a way of coping with linguistic and cultural differences, not a way of eliminating them. It is a tool for communication, not a source of identity and community.

The linguistic scholar Joshua Fishman has observed that a language is more likely to be accepted as a lingua franca if it is not identified with a particular ethnic group, religion, or ideology. In the past, English carried many of those associations. But more recently, Fishman says, it has been "de-ethnicized (or minimally ethnicized)," much like what happened to Akkadian, Aramaic, Greek, and Latin before it. As he puts it, "It is part of the relative good fortune of English as an additional language that neither its British nor its American fountainheads have been widely or deeply viewed in an ethnic or ideological context for the past quarter century or so." Resorting to English for intercultural communication helps maintain—and, indeed, reinforce—separate cultural identities. Precisely because people want to preserve their own culture, they use English to communicate with people of other cultures.

A universal religion is only slightly more likely to emerge than a universal language. The late 20th century has seen a resurgence of religions around the world, including the rise of fundamentalist movements. This trend has reinforced the differences among religions, and has not necessarily resulted in significant shifts in the distribution of religions worldwide.

Of course, there have been increases during the past century in the percentage of people practicing the two major proselytizing religions, Islam and Christianity. Western Christians accounted for 26.9 percent of the world's population in 1900 and peaked at about 30 percent in 1980, while the Muslim population increased from 12.4 percent in 1900 to as much as 18 percent in 1980. The percentage of Christians in the world will probably decline to about 25 percent by 2025. Meanwhile, because of extremely high rates of population growth, the proportion of Muslims in the world will continue to increase dramatically and represent about 30 percent of the world's population by 2025. Neither, however, qualifies as a universal religion.

The argument that some sort of universal civilization is emerging rests on one or more of three assumptions: that the collapse of Soviet communism meant the end of history and the universal victory of liberal democracy; that increased interaction among peoples through trade, investment, tourism, media, and electronic communications is creating a common world culture; and that a universal civilization is the logical result of the process of global modernization that has been going on since the 18th century.

The first assumption is rooted in the Cold War perspective that the only alternative to communism is liberal democracy, and the demise of the first inevitably produces the second. But there are many alternatives to liberal democracy—including authoritarianism, nationalism, corporatism, and market communism (as in China)—that are alive and well in today's world. And, more significantly, there are all the religious alternatives that lie outside the world of secular ideologies. In the modern world, religion is a central, perhaps *the* central, force that motivates and mobilizes people. It is sheer hubris to think that because Soviet communism has collapsed, the West has conquered the world for all time and that non-Western peoples are going to rush to embrace Western liberalism as the only alternative. The Cold War division of humanity is over. The more fundamental divisions of ethnicity, religions, and civilizations remain and will spawn new conflicts.

The new global economy is a reality. Improvements in transportation and communications technology have indeed made it easier and cheaper to move money, goods, knowledge, ideas, and images around the world. But what will be the impact of this increased economic interaction? In social psychology, distinctiveness theory holds that people define themselves by what makes them different from others in a particular context: People define their identity by what they are not. As advanced communications, trade, and travel multiply the interactions among civilizations, people will increasingly accord greater relevance to identity based on their own civilization.

Those who argue that a universal civilization is an inevitable product of modernization assume that all modern societies must become Westernized. As the first civilization to modernize, the West leads in the acquisition of the culture of modernity. And as other societies acquire similar patterns of education, work, wealth, and class structure—the argument runs—this modern Western culture will become the universal culture of the world. That significant differences exist between modern and traditional cultures is beyond dispute. It doesn't necessarily follow, however, that societies with modern cultures resemble each other more than do societies with traditional cultures. As historian Fernand Braudel writes, "Ming China... was assuredly closer to the France of the Valois than the China of Mao Tse-tung is to the France of the Fifth Republic."

Yet modern societies could resemble each other more than do traditional societies for two reasons. First, the increased interaction among modern societies may not generate a common culture, but it does facilitate the transfer of techniques, inventions, and practices from one society to another with a speed and to a degree that were impossible in the traditional world. Second, traditional society was based on agriculture; modern society is based on industry. Patterns of agriculture and the social structure that goes with them are much more dependent on the natural environment than are patterns of industry. Differences in industrial organization are likely to derive from differences in culture and social structure rather than geography, and the former conceivably can converge while the latter cannot.

Modern societies thus have much in common. But do they necessarily merge into homogeneity? The argument that they do rests on the assumption that modern society must approximate a single type, the Western type. This is a totally false assumption. Western civilization emerged in the 8th and 9th centuries. It did not begin to modernize until the 17th and 18th centuries. The West was the West long before it was modern. The central characteristics of the West—the classical legacy, the mix of catholicism and protestantism, and the separation of spiritual and temporal authority—distinguish it from other civilizations and antedate the modernization of the West.

In the post–Cold War world, the most important distinctions among people are not ideological, political, or economic. They are cultural. People and nations are attempting to answer a basic human question: Who are we? And they are answering that question in the traditional way, by reference to the things that mean the most to them: ancestry, religion, language, history, values, customs, and institutions. People identify with cultural groups: tribes, ethnic groups, religious communities, nations, and, at the broadest level, civilizations. They use politics not just to advance their interests but also to define their identity. We know who we are only when we know who we are not, and often only when we know who we are against.

Nation-states remain the principal actors in world affairs. Their behavior is shaped, as in the past, by the pursuit of power and wealth, but it is also shaped by cultural preferences and differences. The most important groupings are no longer the three blocs of the Cold War but rather the world's major civilizations (*See* map):

S Sinic

All scholars recognize the existence of either a single distinct Chinese civilization dating back at least to 1500 B.C., or of two civilizations—one succeeding the other—in the early centuries of the Christian epoch.

J Japanese

Some scholars combine Japanese and Chinese culture, but most recognize Japan as a distinct civilization, the offspring of Chinese civilization, that emerged between A.D. 100 and 400.

H Hindu

A civilization—or successive civilizations—has existed on the Indian subcontinent since at least 1500 B.C. In one form or another, Hinduism has been central to the culture of India since the second millennium B.C.

I Islamic

Originating on the Arabian peninsula in the 7th century A.D., Islam spread rapidly across North Africa and the Iberian Peninsula and also eastward into central Asia, the Indian subcontinent, and Southeast Asia. Many distinct cultures—including Arab, Turkic, Persian, and Malay—exist within Islam.

W Western

The emergence of Western civilization—what used to be called Western Christendom—is usually dated at about 700 A.D. It has two main components, in Europe and North America.

LA Latin American

Latin America, often considered part of the West, has a distinct identity. It has had a corporatist, authoritarian culture, which Europe had to a much lesser degree and North America did not have at all. Europe and North America both felt the effects of the Reformation and have combined Catholic and Protestant cultures, while Latin America has been primarily Catholic. Latin American civilization also incorporates indigenous cultures, which were wiped out in North America.

O Orthodox

This civilization, which combines the Orthodox tradition of Christianity with the Slav cultures of Eastern Europe and Russia, has resurfaced since the demise of the Soviet Union.

A African

There may be some argument about whether there is a distinct African civilization. North Africa and the east coast belong to Islamic civilization. (Historically, Ethiopia constituted a civilization of its own.) Elsewhere, imperial-

The Real World

The civilizations shaping the new global order

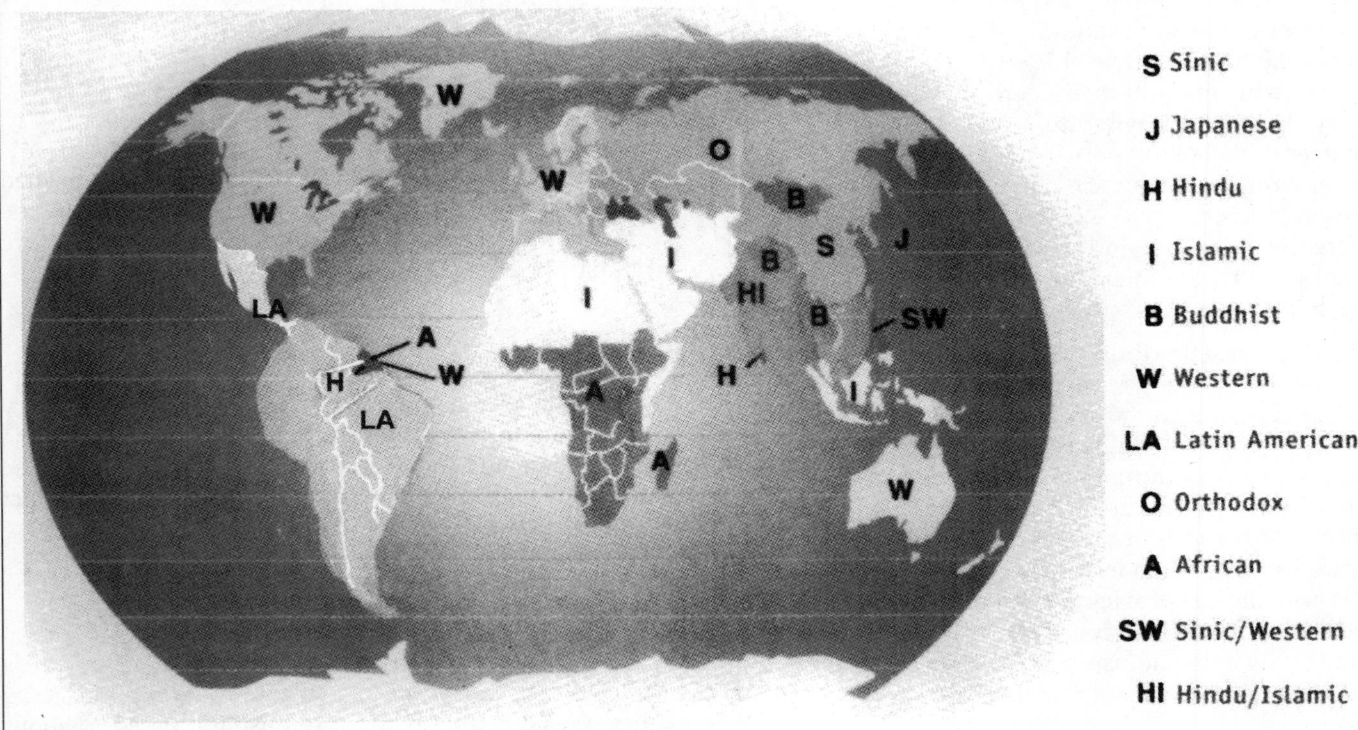

ism brought elements of Western civilization. Tribal identities are pervasive throughout Africa, but Africans are also increasingly developing a sense of African identity. Sub-Saharan Africa conceivably could cohere into a distinct civilization, with South Africa as its core.

B Buddhist

Beginning in the first century A.D., Buddhism was exported from India to China, Korea, Vietnam, and Japan, where it was assimilated by the indigenous cultures and/or suppressed. What can legitimately be described as a Buddhist civilization, however, does exist in Sri Lanka, Burma, Thailand, Laos, Cambodia; and Tibet, Mongolia, and Bhutan. Overall, however, the virtual extinction of Buddhism in India and its incorporation into existing cultures in other major countries means that it has not been the basis of a major civilization.

(Modern India represents a mix of Hindu and Islamic civilizations, while the Philippines is a unique Sinic-Western hybrid by virtue of its history of Spanish, then American rule.)

As Asian and Muslim civilizations begin to assert the universal relevance of *their* cultures, Westerners will see the connection between universalism and imperialism and appreciate the virtues of a pluralistic world. In order to preserve Western civilization, the West needs greater unity of purpose. It should incorporate into the European Union and NATO the western states of central Europe; encourage the Westernization of Latin America; slow the drift of Japan away from the West and toward accommodation with China; and accept Russia as the core state of Orthodoxy and a power with legitimate interests.

The main responsibility of Western leaders is to recognize that intervention in the affairs of other civilizations is the single most dangerous source of instability in the world. The West should attempt not to reshape other civilizations in its own image, but to preserve and renew the unique qualities of its own civilization.

Samuel P. Huntington is Albert J. Weatherhead III University Professor at Harvard University.

From *Utne Reader,* May/June 1997, pp. 75–77, 102–103. Adapted from *The Clash of Civilizations and Remaking of World Order* by Samuel P. Huntington.

THE CLASH OF IGNORANCE

EDWARD W. SAID

Samuel Huntington's article "The Clash of Civilizations?" appeared in the Summer 1993 issue of *Foreign Affairs,* where it immediately attracted a surprising amount of attention and reaction. Because the article was intended to supply Americans with an original thesis about "a new phase" in world politics after the end of the cold war, Huntington's terms of argument seemed compellingly large, bold, even visionary. He very clearly had his eye on rivals in the policy-making ranks, theorists such as Francis Fukuyama and his "end of history" ideas, as well as the legions who had celebrated the onset of globalism, tribalism and the dissipation of the state. But they, he allowed, had understood only some aspects of this new period. He was about to announce the "crucial, indeed a central, aspect" of what "global politics is likely to be in the coming years." Unhesitatingly he pressed on:

"It is my hypothesis that the fundamental source of conflict in this new world will not be primarily ideological or primarily economic. The great divisions among humankind and the dominating source of conflict will be cultural. Nation states will remain the most powerful actors in world affairs, but the principal conflicts of global politics will occur between nations and groups of different civilizations. The clash of civilizations will dominate global politics. The fault lines between civilizations will be the battle lines of the future."

Most of the argument in the pages that followed relied on a vague notion of something Huntington called "civilization identity" and "the interactions among seven or eight [*sic*] major civilizations," of which the conflict between two of them, Islam and the West, gets the lion's share of his attention. In this belligerent kind of thought, he relies heavily on a 1990 article by the veteran Orientalist Bernard Lewis, whose ideological colors are manifest in its title, "The Roots of Muslim Rage." In both articles, the personification of enormous entities called "the West" and "Islam" is recklessly affirmed, as if hugely complicated matters like identity and culture existed in a cartoonlike world where Popeye and Bluto bash each other mercilessly, with one always more virtuous pugilist getting the upper hand over his adversary. Certainly neither Huntington nor Lewis has much time to spare for the internal dynamics and plurality of every civilization, or for the fact that the major contest in most modern cultures concerns the definition or interpretation of each culture, or for the unattractive possibility that a great deal of demagogy and downright ignorance is involved in presuming to speak for a whole religion or civilization. No, the West is the West, and Islam Islam.

The challenge for Western policy-makers, says Huntington, is to make sure that the West gets stronger and fends off all the others, Islam in particular. More troubling is Huntington's assumption that his perspective, which is to survey the entire world from a perch outside all ordinary attachments and hidden loyalties, is the correct one, as if everyone else were scurrying around looking for the answers that he has already found. In fact, Huntington is an ideologist, someone who wants to make "civilizations" and "identities" into what they are not: shut-down, sealed-off entities that have been purged of the myriad currents and counter-currents that animate human history, and that over centuries have made it possible for that history not only to contain wars of religion and imperial conquest but also to be one of exchange, cross-fertilization and sharing. This far less visible history is ignored in the rush to highlight the ludicrously compressed and constricted warfare that "the clash of civilizations" argues is the reality. When he published his book by the same title in 1996, Huntington tried to give his argument a little more subtlety and many, many more footnotes; all he did, however, was confuse himself and demonstrate what a clumsy writer and inelegant thinker he was.

The basic paradigm of West versus the rest (the cold war opposition reformulated) remained untouched, and this is what has persisted, often insidiously and implicitly, in discussion since the terrible events of September 11. The carefully planned and horrendous, pathologically motivated suicide attack and mass slaughter by a small group of deranged militants has been turned into proof of Huntington's thesis. Instead of seeing it for what it is—the capture of big ideas (I use the word loosely) by a tiny band of crazed fanatics for criminal purposes—international luminaries from former Pakistani Prime Minister Benazir Bhutto to Italian Prime Minister Silvio Berlusconi have pontificated about Islam's troubles, and in the latter's case have used Huntington's ideas to rant on about the West's superiority, how "we" have Mozart and Michelangelo and they don't. (Berlusconi has since made a half-hearted apology for his insult to "Islam.")

Labels like Islam and the West mislead and confuse the mind, which is trying to make sense of a disorderly reality.

But why not instead see parallels, admittedly less spectacular in their destructiveness, for Osama bin Laden and his followers in cults like the Branch Davidians or the disciples of the Rev. Jim Jones at Guyana or the Japanese Aum Shinrikyo? Even the normally sober British weekly *The Economist,* in its issue of September 22–28, can't resist reaching for the vast generalization, praising Huntington extravagantly for his "cruel and sweeping, but nonetheless acute" observations about Islam. "Today," the journal says with unseemly solemnity, Huntington writes that "the world's billion or so Muslims are 'convinced of the superiority of their culture, and obsessed with the inferiority of their power.'" Did he canvas 100 Indonesians, 200 Moroccans, 500 Egyptians and fifty Bosnians? Even if he did, what sort of sample is that?

Uncountable are the editorials in every American and European newspaper and magazine of note adding to this vocabulary of gigantism and apocalypse, each use of which is plainly designed not to edify but to inflame the reader's indignant passion as a member of the "West," and what we need to do. Churchillian rhetoric is used inappropriately by self-appointed combatants in the West's, and especially America's, war against its haters, despoilers, destroyers, with scant attention to complex histories that defy such reductiveness and have seeped from one territory into another, in the process overriding the boundaries that are supposed to separate us all into divided armed camps.

This is the problem with unedifying labels like Islam and the West: They mislead and confuse the mind, which is trying to make sense of a disorderly reality that won't be pigeonholed or strapped down as easily as all that. I remember interrupting a man who, after a lecture I had given at a West Bank university in 1994, rose from the audience and started to attack my ideas as "Western," as opposed to the strict Islamic ones he espoused. "Why are you wearing a suit and tie?" was the first retort that came to mind. "They're Western too." He sat down with an embarrassed smile on his face, but I recalled the incident when information on the September 11 terrorists started to come in: how they had mastered all the technical details required to inflict their homicidal evil on the World Trade Center, the Pentagon and the aircraft they had commandeered. Where does one draw the line between "Western" technology and, as Berlusconi declared, "Islam's" inability to be a part of "modernity"?

One cannot easily do so, of course. How finally inadequate are the labels, generalizations and cultural assertions. At some level, for instance, primitive passions and sophisticated know-how converge in ways that give the lie to a fortified boundary not only between "West" and "Islam" but also between past and present, us and them, to say nothing of the very concepts of identity and nationality about which there is unending disagreement and debate. A unilateral decision made to draw lines in the sand, to undertake crusades, to oppose their evil with our good, to extirpate terrorism and, in Paul Wolfowitz's nihilistic vocabulary, to end nations entirely, doesn't make the supposed entities any easier to see; rather, it speaks to how much simpler it is to make bellicose statements for the purpose of mobilizing collective passions than to reflect, examine, sort out what it is we are dealing with in reality, the interconnectedness of innumerable lives, "ours" as well as "theirs."

In a remarkable series of three articles published between January and March 1999 in *Dawn*, Pakistan's most respected weekly, the late Eqbal Ahmad, writing for a Muslim audience, analyzed what he called the roots of the religious right, coming down very harshly on the mutilations of Islam by absolutists and fanatical tyrants whose obsession with regulating personal behavior promotes "an Islamic order reduced to a penal code, stripped of its humanism, aesthetics, intellectual quests, and spiritual devotion." And this "entails an absolute assertion of one, generally de-contextualized, aspect of religion and a total disregard of another. The phenomenon distorts religion, debases tradition, and twists the political process wherever it unfolds." As a timely instance of this debasement, Ahmad proceeds first to present the rich, complex, pluralist meaning of the word *jihad* and then goes on to show that in the word's current confinement to indiscriminate war against presumed enemies, it is impossible "to recognize the Islamic—religion, society, culture, history or politics—as lived and experienced by Muslims through the ages." The modern Islamists, Ahmad concludes, are "concerned with power, not with the soul; with the mobilization of people for political purposes rather than with sharing and alleviating their sufferings and aspirations. Theirs is a very limited and time-bound political agenda." What has made matters worse is that similar distortions and zealotry occur in the "Jewish" and "Christian" universes of discourse.

The 'Clash of Civilizations' thesis is better for reinforcing self-pride than for a critical understanding of the interdependence of our time.

It was Conrad, more powerfully than any of his readers at the end of the nineteenth century could have imagined, who understood that the distinctions between civilized London and "the heart of darkness" quickly collapsed in extreme situations, and that the heights of European civilization could instantaneously fall into the most barbarous practices without preparation or transition. And it was Conrad also, in *The Secret Agent* (1907), who described terrorism's affinity for abstractions like "pure science" (and by extension for "Islam" or "the West"), as well as the terrorist's ultimate moral degradation.

For there are closer ties between apparently warring civilizations than most of us would like to believe; both Freud and Nietzsche showed how the traffic across carefully maintained, even policed boundaries moves with often terrifying ease. But then such fluid ideas, full of ambiguity and skepticism about notions that we hold on to, scarcely furnish us with suitable, practical guidelines for situations such as the one we face now. Hence the altogether more reassuring battle orders (a crusade, good versus evil, freedom against fear, etc.) drawn out of Huntington's alleged opposition between Islam and the West, from which official discourse drew its vocabulary in the first days after the September 11 attacks. There's since been a noticeable de-escalation in that discourse, but to judge from the steady amount of hate speech and actions, plus reports of law enforcement efforts directed against Arabs, Muslims and Indians all over the country, the paradigm stays on.

One further reason for its persistence is the increased presence of Muslims all over Europe and the United States. Think of the populations today of France, Italy, Germany, Spain, Britain, America, even Sweden, and you must concede that Islam is no longer on the fringes of the West but at its center. But what is so threatening about that presence? Buried in the collective culture are memories of the first great Arab-Islamic conquests, which began in the seventh century and which, as the celebrated Belgian historian Henri Pirenne wrote in his landmark book *Mohammed and Charlemagne* (1939), shattered once and for all the ancient unity of the Mediterranean, destroyed the Christian-Roman synthesis and gave rise to a new civilization dominated by northern powers (Germany and Carolingian France) whose mission, he seemed to be saying, is to resume defense of the "West" against its historical-cultural enemies. What Pirenne left out, alas, is that in the creation of this new line of defense the West drew on the humanism, science, philosophy, sociology and historiography of Islam, which had already interposed itself between Charlemagne's world and classical antiquity. Islam is inside from the start, as even Dante, great enemy of Mohammed, had to concede when he placed the Prophet at the very heart of his *Inferno*.

Then there is the persisting legacy of monotheism itself, the Abrahamic religions, as Louis Massignon aptly called them. Beginning with Judaism and Christianity, each is a successor haunted by what came before; for Muslims, Islam fulfills and ends the line of prophecy. There is still no decent history or demystification of the many-sided contest among these three followers—not one of them by any means a monolithic, unified camp—of the most jealous of all gods, even though the bloody modern convergence on Palestine furnishes a rich secular instance of what has been so tragically irreconcilable about them. Not surprisingly, then, Muslims and Christians speak readily of crusades and *jihads,* both of them eliding the Judaic presence with often sublime insouciance. Such an agenda, says Eqbal Ahmad, is "very reassuring to the men and women who are stranded in the middle of the ford, between the deep waters of tradition and modernity."

But we are all swimming in those waters, Westerners and Muslims and others alike. And since the waters are part of the ocean of history, trying to plow or divide them with barriers is futile. These are tense times, but it is better to think in terms of powerful and powerless communities, the secular politics of reason and ignorance, and universal principles of justice and injustice, than to wander off in search of vast abstractions that may give momentary satisfaction but little self-knowledge or informed analysis. "The Clash of Civilizations" thesis is a gimmick like "The War of the Worlds," better for reinforcing defensive self-pride than for critical understanding of the bewildering interdependence of our time.

Edward W. Said, University Professor of English and Comparative Literature at Columbia University, is the author of more than twenty books, the most recent of which is Power, Politics, and Culture *(Pantheon). Copyright Edward W. Said, 2001.*

Article 4

Mr. Order Meets Mr. Chaos

We live in an era of unprecedented prosperity, but when the financial bubble bursts we'll plunge into a world depression. Nations no longer go to war, but civil wars are booming. Humanity has embraced the idea of environmental interdependence, but the global ecosystem is in terminal crisis. Depending on your perspective, we stand either on the verge of a golden age or at the brink of disaster. Robert Wright and Robert Kaplan, two of the United States' most perceptive observers of world affairs and the human condition, met recently in Washington, D.C., to offer conflicting views of the path of history.

My Minivan and World Peace

By Robert Wright

Anyone who knows me would be surprised to find me cast as an optimist, but when you're juxtaposed with Robert Kaplan, it's not hard to come off looking pretty chipper and upbeat about the world.

What is the basis for my relative optimism? My prescription and diagnosis are built upon the notion of the non-zero-sum game, which is a reference to game theory. A zero-sum game is what you see in an athletic event like tennis: Every point in the match is good for one player and bad for the other. So the fates of the players are inversely correlated. In a non-zero-sum game, the fortunes can be positively correlated; the outcome can be win-win or lose-lose, depending on how competitors play the game. And, in fact, in a tennis doubles match the players on the same team have a highly non-zero-sum relationship because they'll both win or they'll both lose.

Nowadays we're all embedded in lots of non-zero-sum relationships that we really don't even think about. For instance, when I bought my Honda minivan I was in a non-zero-sum relationship with workers in various countries. The deal was I paid a tiny hit of their wages and they built me a car. It is characteristic of globalization that it embeds us in these non-zero-sum relationships. It makes our fates more correlated with the fates of people at great distances. It's a subtle process that we usually don't think about, but every once in a while this correlation of fortunes becomes glaringly evident, as was the case with the Asian crisis when we realized that a financial downturn can instantly spread around the world; or when a virus spreads across the Internet and you realize that computer users on different continents are all vulnerable, their fates are correlated.

In theory, as globalization makes relations among nations more and more non-zero-sum, you would expect to see more in the way of institutionalized cooperation to address these problems. That is not a pathbreaking insight. For some time now, political scientists have been talking about the growing interdependence of nations and the growing logic behind cooperation. But I believe that this process is now moving so fast that, much sooner than most people expect, we're going to reach a system of institutionalized cooperation among nations that is so thorough it qualifies as world governance. I don't mean world government, a single centralized authority. I imagine a looser mix of global and regional organizations. But still I'm imagining some very significant sacrifices of national sovereignty to supranational bodies. We've already seen a little of this surrender of national sovereignty with the World Trade Organization, and I would argue there was a little bit of surrender (a well-advised surrender) when 174 nations signed the Chemical Weapons Convention.

Wright: "History is not just one damn thing after another, it's a process with a direction; it has an arrow."

I fully expect this trend toward global governance to continue, although I'm much more confident about it happening in the long run than in the short run. The zone of non-zero-sumness has been expanding for a very long time: You can go back to the Stone Age when the most complex polity on earth was a hunter-gatherer village and chart the evolution to the level of the chiefdom—a multivillage polity—and then to the level of the ancient state, and then to the system of modern nation-states, and so on. The key element that has driven the evolution of social complexity and of governance to higher levels is technology. Sometimes it is information technology, as when the invention of writing often accompanied the evolution of the first ancient states. Sometimes it is transportation technology and sometimes, ironically enough, it is weapons technology. Weapons technologies can make relations much more non-zero-sum—certainly nuclear weapons make war a very non-zero-sum endeavor in the sense of making it a lose-lose game, wherein the object of the game is never to play. Nuclear weapons thus strengthen the argument for a system of collective security pursued through some supranational institution such as the United Nations.

We don't know in detail what the future of technological evolution will be, but we have a pretty good idea. Information technologies will continue to evolve and enmesh people in webs of transactions, interactions, and interdependence. Weapons technologies will evolve, but perhaps more important, the information about how to build very lethal weapons of mass destruction will likely be accessible to more and more people. Thus, almost all nations share a common interest in controlling the development and use of these weapons. Technological evolution will continue doing what it has done for the broad sweep of history, which is expanding the realm of non-zero-sumness, making the fates of peoples and nations more correlated, and in the process driving governance to a higher level, to the global level.

Kaplan: "You're right... but neither is it on a direct, predetermined course... The course of history [is] just a gradual improvement, punctuated with a lot of ups and downs."

That the fates of the world's people have grown more and more correlated over time is not by itself especially good news. As you may have noticed, many examples of non-zero-sum dynamics are actually negative-sum games, lose-lose games, where the object of the game is to break even. Global warming is an example of such a negative-sum game—where we just want to fend off the bad outcome—that I think calls for institutionalized cooperation and some real, if small, sacrifice of national sovereignty.

So when I argue that history features more and more of this non-zero-sumness, that statement isn't by itself good or bad, it just is. It's just something we have to reckon with. But there is one feature of the direction of human history that is at least mildly upbeat, in some ways redeeming. It's what I call the expanding moral compass. Philosopher Peter Singer has written about this. If you go back to ancient Greece, there was a time when members of one Greek city-state considered members of another Greek city-state literally subhuman. They would slaughter and pillage without any compunction whatsoever. Then the Greeks underwent a process of enlightenment and they decided that actually other Greeks are humans, too. It's just the Persians who aren't humans. (Okay, it was limited progress, but it was progress.) And today I think we've made more progress, especially in economically developed nations. I think almost everyone in such countries would say that people everywhere, regardless of race, creed, or color, deserve at least minimal respect.

If you ask why that has happened, I argue that it gets back to this basic dynamic of history, this growth of non-zero-sumness. If you look at Greece at the time of their limited enlightenment, relations were growing more non-zero-sum among Greek city-states because they were fighting a war together against the Persians. They needed each other more, they were in the same boat, and to cooperate they had to accord each other at least minimal respect. And if you ask why an ethos of moral universalism now prevails in economically advanced, globally integrated nations, I would say it's the same answer. If you ask me why don't I think it's a good idea to bomb the Japanese, I'd say, "For one thing, because they built my minivan." I'm proud to say I have some more high-minded reasons as well, but I do think this basic, concrete interdependence forces people to accord one another at least minimal respect, to think a little about the welfare of people halfway around the world. I expect this dynamic to grow and persist in the future because in a world where disease can spread across borders in no time at all, it's in the interest of Americans to worry about the health of people in Africa or Asia. In a world where terrorists can wield unprecedentedly lethal technologies, it's in the interests of Americans to worry about political grievances before they fester to the point of terrorism. One feature of a globalized society is that disaster can happen at the global level, so we're now in this process where either we grasp the moral and political implications of this increasingly shared fate we have with other people or very bad things will happen.

The modern world is in many ways a disoriented and disturbing place. Things are changing very fast, but I think if you look at the broad sweep of the past it offers a way to orient ourselves. History is not just one damn thing after another, it's a process with a direction; it has an arrow. And I think if we use that arrow to orient ourselves then I would predict that the coming decades will not be characterized by chaos.

Robert Wright is author of Nonzero: The Logic of Human Destiny *(New York: Pantheon Books, 2000) and a visiting scholar at the University of Pennsylvania.*

Hope for the Best, Expect the Worst

Robert Kaplan

Well, Bob, while you've been looking ahead to discern the broad, cosmic sweep of history, I've been looking ahead just 10 or 15 years in terms of foreign policy—which is often most effective when it's conceived of in light of worst-case scenarios, in the hope that those scenarios don't occur. I should remind you that constructive pessimism is profoundly in the American tradition. It's the basis for the U.S. Constitution. If you read *The Federalist Papers*, you can see that Americans have become a country of optimists over 225 years precisely because we've had the good fortune of having our systems of government founded by pessimists. The French Revolution conversely was founded on optimism, on the belief that elites could engineer positive results from above, and it devolved into the guillotine and Napoleon's dictatorship. Alexander Hamilton, whom I consider the greatest of the Founding Fathers, said don't think there will be fewer wars in the world simply because there will be more democracies. In *Federalist Number Six* he said there are as many wars from commercial motives as from territorial aggrandizement. So it is in that spirit of *The Federalist Papers* that I'm going to present a scenario about what worries me over the next 10 or 15 years.

I wrote in 1994 that even as part of the globe was moving toward economic prosperity, another part—containing much of the population—was marching in another direction due to issues such as demography, resource scarcity and disease. So let me tell you how I see things now, seven years later. The European colonialists did a lot of terrible things, but they did bring a certain degree of order to much of sub-Saharan Africa, South Asia, and Central Asia. That colonial grid work of states started dissolving in the 1990s when we saw the weakening or outright collapse of several marginal places. I use the term "marginal" not because their well-being wasn't important, but because they had low populations, their economies were small, and they didn't really affect the region around them all that much. Somalia, Sierra Leone, Tajikistan, Haiti, and Rwanda were not core regional states in any sense, but look at how they disrupted the international community.

Wright: "We're going to reach a system of institutionalized cooperation among nations that is so thorough it qualifies as world governance."

I believe that, for a number of reasons, we're going to see the weakening, dilution, and perhaps even crackup of larger, more complex, modern societies in the next 10 or 15 years in places such as Nigeria, Ivory Coast, and Pakistan. And we're going to see severe crises in countries like Brazil and India. This dissolution of the colonial grid work is going to create the kind of crises where there will be no intervention scenarios, or the intervention scenarios will be far worse than they were in Bosnia or Sierra Leone. The problem is not that these places have particularly bad governments. They're coping as best as any could. The reasons are far more complex and intractable.

First of all, these societies are modernizing. Although history teaches us that modern democratic institutions provide stability, history also reveals that the process of creating and developing modern democratic institutions is very destabilizing. As free-market democracies develop, more and more people are brought into the political process. And all of these people are full of yearning, ambitions, and demands that governing institutions very often cannot keep pace with. So things start to break down here and there. It is economic growth that typically fuels political upheavals, not poverty.

The other challenge to the stability of the nation-state is demography. You hear a lot about how the world population is aging, but that's over the long term and throughout the world as a whole [see "The Population Implosion," FOREIGN POLICY, March/April 2001]. But when you look ahead at just 20 or 30 countries over the next 10 or 20 years, you see dramatic rises in the youth population (what demographers call "youth bulges"). When you watch your television and you see unrest or rioting in Indonesia, Ivory Coast, Gaza, and the West Bank, what's similar about all of them? All of the violence is typically conducted by young men, ages 15 to 29, who are unemployed and frustrated. The sector of the young male population within this age group is going to grow dramatically in the countries that already have tremendous unrest and are already on the edge. In other words, the places that will have a population pyramid that is bottom-heavy with the youngest members of society are the ones that can least afford it.

And if that isn't enough, you've got urbanization. The 21st century is going to be the first century in world history when more than half of humanity will live in cities. Even sub-Saharan Africa is almost 50 percent urban. Urban societies are much more challenging to govern than rural societies. In rural societies people can grow their own food, so they are less susceptible to price increases for basic commodities. Rural societies don't require the complex infrastructure of sewage, potable water, electricity, and other things that urban societies have. Urbanization widens the scope of error for leaders in the developing world while simultaneously narrowing the scope for success. It is harder to satisfy an urban population than a rural population, especially when that population is growing in such leaps and bounds that governing institutions simply cannot keep pace.

Then you have resource scarcity, particularly water. I spent the summer in a small village in Portugal where we only had running water about eight hours a week. We had to drive about half a mile to a local fountain to fill pitchers of water. Anyone who has not gone without water has no idea what it's like not to be able to flush your toilet or take a bath. There's been a drought for the last four years across a swath of South Asia from Afghanistan, Pakistan, and into India. Dams are low, so there is not enough water for drinking or generating electricity. So in these hot cities of the subcontinent you have less and less air conditioning in the summer. This kind of stuff doesn't necessarily cause political crises, but it's all part of the background noise that aggravates existing crises. This frustration worsens ethnic tension and makes social divides harder to resolve. In short, people get angry. There was a spate of riots in Karachi, Pakistan, not long ago that was preceded by an extended period when there was very little electricity due to water shortages.

Kaplan: "We're going to see the weakening, dilution, and perhaps even crackup of larger, more complex, modern societies in the next 10 or 15 years..."

Then there's the issue of climate change. Let's just say for the sake of argument that this whole global warming issue has been exaggerated, that it really doesn't exist, that it's not going to be a problem. Well, even if you factor out global warming, the normal climatic variations of the earth during the next few decades will still ensure devastating floods and other upheavals because, for the first time in world history, you have hundreds of millions of human beings living in environmentally fragile terrain—where perhaps human beings were never meant to live at all. So even without global warming you're going to have natural events that can spark political upheaval.

And finally, the other factor that's going to spark serious institutional crises in a lot of states is democracy. Everyone wants to be democratic, no use denying it. But democracy tends to emerge best when it emerges last. It should be the capstone to all other types of development, when you already have middle classes that pay income taxes, when you already have institutions run by literate bureaucrats, when the major issues of a society (such as territorial borders) are all resolved and you already have a functioning polity. Then, and only then, can a society cope with weak minority governments. Then, and only then, can democracy unleash a nation's full potential. Right now, we're seeing democracy evolve in many places around the earth accompanied by unemployment and inflation rates every bit as dire as Germany in the 1930s, when Hitler emerged under democratic conditions, and in Italy, when Mussolini came to power in the early 1920s. I'm not arguing against democracy, but I believe democracy will be another destabilizing factor.

If it seems like I'm deliberately cultivating a sense of the tragic it's because that's how you avoid tragedy in the first place. Remember that Klemens von Metternich was so brilliant in creating a post-Napoleonic order that Europe saw decades of peace and prosperity—so much so that politicians in France and England lost their sense of the tragic. All they saw ahead were optimistic scenarios and, as such, they stumbled and miscalculated their way into World War I. Take my concern in that spirit.

Robert Kaplan is author of The Coming Anarchy: Shattering the Dreams of the Post Cold War *(New York: Vintage Books, 2000) and a senior fellow at the New America Foundation.*

In the Long Run, We're All Interdependent

Robert Wright responds.

Well Bob, I'm actually something of a fan of pessimism myself. I think it focuses us on the problems that need our attention. I find it particularly heartening that your books have a sizable American readership, since that suggests that Americans increasingly realize their fates are intertwined with the fates of people around the world. But I don't want to overdo the pessimism. And in particular I don't want to make it sound like globalization and its attendant technological fluctuations are part of some kind of uniformly bad force. I'm actually something of a cheerleader for globalization. It has problems, but I think on balance it's a good thing.

You said that the world was increasingly dividing into two parts, echoing the common refrain that globalization exacerbates income inequality worldwide. But that conclusion actually depends on how you examine the data. If you look at the number of rich versus poor nations, then you can certainly make that argument. But if you look at the total number of people in the world, ignoring where the borders fall, then what's happening in absolute terms is that there are fewer poor people than there used to be. And even in relative terms, it's far from clear that income inequality is growing, and a number of people have argued that the income gap is actually shrinking worldwide. It turns out that many of the world's poor people are concentrated in a few very large countries (like China and India) that have seen more progress than some of the smaller countries (notably those in Africa). But even in Africa, globalization has seen a kind of vindication: The countries that have seen the most economic advancement are the ones that are most open to trade and investment.

Another virtue of globalization is that it is basically an antiwar activity. I think as peoples and nations become more economically intertwined, war becomes more of a lose-lose kind of non-zero-sum game that it doesn't make sense to play. There still are wars in the world, but there is a very interesting feature of the modern world that is insufficiently noted: We increasingly think of wars between nations as something that poor countries do. Nobody expects any of the most economically advanced nations to go to war with one another, which represents a real shift of mind-set. If you look back at most of history it was really standard procedure for the most powerful polities to go to war with one another. Nowadays, most interstate fighting breaks out in parts of the world that could be termed "underglobalized" areas. I don't mean that pejoratively. It's not their fault that they're underglobalized. There are various quirks of history or geographical circumstance that explain why some parts of the world have advanced faster economically than others. But the fact is that wars are mostly a threat in the poorest parts of the world.

Now, when you get to subnational conflict, war within nations, I agree, Bob, that's a problem that may grow more serious. You argue that conflict is often exacerbated by economic development. I'd add another way in which modernization has given rise to intranational conflict, and that is through the propagation of information technology. As I suggested earlier, information technology has certain globalizing effects, but it also has fragmenting effects because whenever you lower the cost of communication you make it easier for small groups with meager resources to organize. It's no coincidence that the Protestant Reformation roughly coincided with the invention of the printing press. After Martin Luther had tacked up his 95 Theses, printers took it upon themselves to start printing them in various cities. That is how Luther first organized the masses, because printing was suddenly so cheap.

You're seeing the same thing in the modern world thanks to the Internet. Inevitably, information technology is going to empower separatist groups such as Muslims in the west of China and Basques in Spain. But, in the long run, you can imagine this secessionist frenzy working itself out, because as some of these subnational groups choose to drop out of nations they can at the same time cement themselves into supranational bodies. In fact, the Quebec separatists have said they plan to join the North American Free Trade Agreement (NAFTA) as soon as they get out of Canada, and I would expect that European separatist groups would be strongly tempted to join the European Union. So, I certainly agree that globalization presents us with all kinds of short-term difficulties, but I do still think it's a process that is fundamentally beneficial and will lead to a new equilibrium in the long run.

Passion Play

Robert Kaplan responds.

Bob, let me draw some distinctions here, just in the spirit of argument. You tend to put a lot of emphasis on the ability of people to make good, rational choices. But if you think that people are always going to behave accord-

The Clash of Interpretations

Samuel Huntington, cofounder of FOREIGN POLICY *and one of the world's most influential political scientists, incited widespread debate during the 1990S with his "Clash of Civilizations" thesis, which maintained that cultural fault lines would dominate the post-Cold War world. How do Huntington's views fare when examined through the prisms of order and chaos?*

Robert Wright:
I thought Dr. Huntington somewhat overdid the fissures between civilizations. The world is full of examples where nations with very different cultural heritages are on very good and stable terms, the United States and Japan to name just one example. At the same time, I realize that cultural history matters and it can be a source of tension. But to the extent that he was right about that, what bothered me was his prescription that we should be true to our cultural spirit. He said, for instance, that Australia is not really an Asian nation, so it should not be in a trade bloc with Asian nations, it should be part of an expanded NAFTA. It seems to me that the moral of the story is exactly the opposite: If indeed fissures among civilizations are deep and threatening (and sometimes they are), then the effort should be to bridge them with supranational organizations like trade blocs.

Robert Kaplan:
I thought Sam Huntington's thesis was brilliant, which is proven by the fact that it got everybody angry. Just look at the three countries that were brought into NATO: Hungary, Poland, and the Czech Republic were all part of Western Christendom, and countries that were left out (Bulgaria and Romania) were part of the Eastern Orthodox world. When you look at the current borders of NATO, it's basically a variation of the Holy Roman Empire in the 11th century. If you travel through the Middle East you see increasing tensions in villages between Christians and Muslims. All the corporate mergers are between American and European companies. It's true they have different corporate cultures, but they're similar compared to corporate cultures in other parts of the world. And our main foreign-policy challenge of the next 20 years will be managing a relationship with China. Probably never before have we had a major adversary where there is such a great chance for cultural misunderstanding.

But it's important to recall that Huntington's scenario was a paradigm. It was just a big abstract argument that you judge on the basis of whether it is better than any other generalizing abstract argument. I think on that basis he succeeded very well, but I would agree with Bob that the solution is maybe to bring Romania into NATO, to bridge some of these gaps so that NATO doesn't evolve into a bastion of Western Christendom.

ing to their best, rational self-interest, read *Mein Kampf.* As Hamilton said, "the passions of men will not conform to the dictates of reason and justice, without constraint." The U.S. Constitution was established to slyly organize and control our passions. I'm not convinced that we're going to act any more rationally than we have in the past. It is true that there is a movement toward world governance, but a single, unifying thread is not necessarily a good thing. For instance, the European Union could readily devolve into a benign bureaucratic despotism that will ignore the interests of the lower middle classes. I think the nationalist movements popping up throughout Europe are already a reaction to this benign bureaucratic despotism from Brussels. If there is to be world governance, it has to be a kind that doesn't only appeal to the elites.

And those who feel marginalized have resources at their disposal that go way beyond the Internet. The Industrial Revolution was about bigness—big aircraft carriers, tanks, and railway grids—so that only large states could take advantage of the power the Industrial Revolution had to offer. But when you're talking about cyberwarfare, biological weapons, and this whole new gamut of weaponry in the post-Industrial Revolution, when you live in a world where just a telephone jack and a petri dish give you power, then it's not just large nations that can benefit. Nonstate actors who feel shut out can also magnify their power through this new technology. Power relationships are going to be more complex than ever. You were right when you said that technology drives history, but it doesn't necessarily do so in an orderly manner.

As for the moral universalism that you mention, I think we have to be a bit careful because the West is now using the term "global community" in the way we used to use the term "free world." We're trying to define the whole world in terms of our own moral outlook and what we want. There may be other powers and other cultures that have different views of how the world should be organized, so we have to be careful not to sound triumphalist.

And although inequality might be decreasing, I believe the most significant form of inequality is not what we see between the United States and sub-Saharan Africa, but the income gap you see between the wealthy coastal community and poor interior of a place such as Ghana. The biggest divides are between these globalized communities within the poorest countries—with their own electricity generators, their own water wells, and their own private security guards—that are hooked up to the world economy and surrounded by people with whom they have less and less in common.

You're right Bob, history is not one damn thing after another, but neither is it on a direct, predetermined course à la Karl Marx. The philosopher who captures it all best is Charles de Montesquieu who, in *The Spirit of the Laws*, sees the course of history as just a gradual improvement, punctuated with a lot of ups and downs.

But, lest I sound too contrarian, allow me to point out that I've been concentrating on the zero-sum games that occur within your vast non-zero-sum game. So, in that sense, there is no contradiction between us.

Coffee, Tea, or Apocalypse

Robert Wright responds.

I would hate to let stand the accusation that I think people behave rationally. I've long argued that people are really quite spotty on this particular front, and the saving grace of history has been that whenever people screwed up in one part of the world, there were people in another part of the world who picked up the torch. So when the Roman emperors messed up and began exhibiting the sort of increasingly autocratic rule that people are prone to given the opportunity, and the barbarian hordes did us the service of dismantling the Roman Empire, there were other empires that could continue to grow and thrive.

But I agree that once we reach the global level of organization, we face exactly the threat you describe in that there is no longer a plurality of experiments going on around the world. Increasingly it's one big experiment, and if it collapses that is bad news on a very large scale. That is one reason why I always say that history almost reads better than any novel. The protagonist of this story, that is to say the human species, has been driven more or less inexorably to a moment of fundamental moral and political choice. Making the right decision really depends on our level of moral enlightenment, an understanding of the commonality of all human beings. And if we fail to make the right moral choice, then apocalypse could well ensue. We live at a time of great drama and I absolutely acknowledge that chaos is one of the prospects we face.

A Whiff of Medievalism

Robert Kaplan responds.

Bob, I think chaos is more than a prospect. As divisions within societies and nation-states become greater, chaos might very well be inevitable. A new global community is taking root, but it is doing so at the top. Right now that community is so small that it's still a Potemkin village, but it's nor going to be that way forever. The middle and upper middle classes, what I call the "nouvelle cuisine classes," are merging together at the pinnacle. If you've ever been to the annual Davos conference, you are struck by how medieval it has become: You see the world's elites gathered together, just like the aristocrats of Germany, France, and England 200 or 300 years ago, who had more in common with each other than with their own peasants at home. Our sense of identity is being driven more by what economic class we belong to than what country we live in. The world is moving very slowly and inexorably out of the nation-state phase. That may ultimately lead to something better, but the process of leading to something better is very chaotic.

Want to Know More?

This debate is based on a dialogue between Robert Wright and Robert Kaplan that took place at the **Meridian International Center** in Washington, D.C., on March 13, 2001. Ambassador Walter Cutler moderated the event.

Robert Wright Recommends:
The great historian William McNeill's books ***The Rise of the West: A History of the Human Community*** (Chicago: University of Chicago Press, 1999) and ***A World History*** (New York: Oxford University Press,, 1999) convey the directional nature of history without sacrificing nuance. But seeing direction in history is so unpopular among historians that the task is often left to nonhistorians, such as political scientist Francis Fukuyama. His justly famous ***The End of History and the Last Man*** (New York: Free Press, 1992) differs from my ***Nonzero: The Logic of Human Destiny*** (New York: Pantheon Books, 2000) in that mine is a more materialist (in a somewhat Marxist sense) account of history's driving force. Peter Singer's ***The Expanding Circle: Ethics and Sociobiology*** (Oxford: Oxford University Press, 1981) acutely noted history's moral direction—the erratic movement over the last few millenniums toward moral universalism (though, again, my explanation is more materialist than his). Thomas Friedman's bestseller ***The Lexus and the Olive Tree: Understanding Globalization*** (New York: Farrar, Straus & Giroux, 1999) gives due weight to globalization's positive side without being Panglossian. His term the "superempowered angry man" captures the growing ability of small groups to wreak massive damage. For an abstract but fascinating account of how non-zero-sumness can beget more non-zero-sumness as the growth of cooperation strengthens the logic of further cooperation, see Robert Axelrod's classic ***The Evolution of Cooperation*** (New York: Penguin Books, 1990).

Robert Kaplan Recommends:
Paul Kennedy's ***Preparing for the 21st Century***. (New York: Random House, 1993) is the best primer available on how demography, the environment, technology, and other related factors will test humankind's political skills in the future. Martin van Creveld's ***The Transformation of War*** (New York: Free Press, 1991) is a brilliant work of sustained, abstract thinking (perhaps the greatest since Carl von Clausewitz's ***On War***) that shows how technology will be used toward primitive ends in future wars. In ***The Clash of Civilizations and the Remaking of World Order*** (New York: Simon & Schuster, 1996) Harvard professor Samuel Huntington—who, since the 1950s, has been a controversial but uncannily accurate forecaster—offers a prognosis of a future where tangible cultural divides will replace artificial, ideological ones. My own ***The Coming Anarchy: Shattering the Dreams of the Post Cold War*** (New York: Vintage Books, 2000) identifies the demographic, environmental, and political problems ahead while finding hope in ancient and modern philosophy.

Among the greatest works of philosophy that demonstrate how and why order must precede democracy—and how the search for order stems from the human need to be protected from others—is Thomas Hobbes' ***Leviathan*** (New York: W. W. Norton & Company, 1997). Arnold J. Toynbee's ***A Study of History*** (Oxford: Oxford University Press, 1987) presents an epic pageant explaining how culturally based states have arisen out of the ashes of preceding ones.

- For links to relevant Web sites, as well as a comprehensive index of related FOREIGN POLICY articles, access **www.foreignpolicy.com**.

UNIT 2

Population and Food Production

Unit Selections

5. **The Big Crunch**, Jeffrey Kluger
6. **Breaking *Out* or Breaking *Down***, Lester R. Brown and Brian Halweil
7. **Grains of Hope**, J. Madeleine Nash

Key Points to Consider

- What are the basic characteristics of the global population situation? How many people are there? How long do people typically live?
- How fast is the world's population growing? What are the reasons for this growth? How do population dynamics vary from one region to the next?
- How does rapid population growth affect the quality of the environment, social structures, and the ways in which humanity views itself?
- How does a rapidly growing population affect a poor country's ability to plan its economic development?
- How can economic and social policies be changed in order to reduce the impact of population growth on environmental quality?
- In an era of global interdependence, how much impact can individual governments have on demographic changes?

Links: www.dushkin.com/online/
These sites are annotated in the World Wide Web pages.

The Hunger Project
http://www.thp.org

Penn Library: Resources by Subject
http://www.library.upenn.edu/resources/websitest.html

World Health Organization
http://www.who.int

WWW Virtual Library: Demography & Population Studies
http://demography.anu.edu.au/VirtualLibrary/

After World War II, the world's population reached an estimated 2 billion people. It had taken 250 years to triple to that level. In the 55 years since the end of World War II, the population has tripled again to 6 billion. When the typical reader of this book reaches the age of 50, experts estimate that the global population will have reached 8 ½ billion! By 2050, or about 100 years after World War II, some experts forecast that the world may be populated by 10 to 12 billion people. A person born in 1946 (a so-called baby boomer) who lives to be 100 could see a six-fold increase in population.

Nothing like this has ever occurred before. To state this in a different way: In the next 50 years there will have to be twice as much food grown, twice as many schools and hospitals available, and twice as much of everything else just to maintain the current and rather uneven standard of living. We live in an unprecedented time in human history.

One of the most interesting aspects of this population growth is that there is little agreement about whether this situation is good or bad. The government of China, for example, has a policy that encourages couples to have only one child. In contrast, there are a few governments that use various financial incentives to promote large families.

Some experts view population growth as the major problem facing the world, while others see it as secondary to social, economic, and political problems. The theme of conflicting views, in short, has been carried forward from the introductory unit of this book to the more specific discussion of population.

As the world celebrates the new millennium, there are many population issues that transcend numerical or economic considerations. The disappearance of indigenous cultures is a good example of the pressures of population growth on people who live on the margins of modern society. Finally, while demogra-

phers develop various scenarios forecasting population growth, it is important to remember that there are circumstances that could lead not to growth but to a significant decline in global population. The spread of AIDS and other infectious diseases reveals that confidence in modern medicine's ability to control these scourges may be premature. Nature has its own checks and balances to the population dynamic that are not policy instruments of some international organization. This factor is often overlooked in an age of technological optimism.

The lead article in this section provides an overview of the general demographic trends of the contemporary world. The unit continues with a more focused discussion of a few regions in the world that are experiencing a sudden reversal in the general trend to longer life.

There is no greater check on population growth than the ability to produce an adequate food supply. Some experts question whether current technologies are sustainable over the long run. How much food are we going to need in the decades to come, and how are farmers and fishermen going to produce it?

Making predictions about the future of the world's population is a complicated task, for there are a variety of forces at work and considerable variation from region to region.

The danger of oversimplification must be overcome if governments and international organizations are going to respond with meaningful policies. Perhaps one could say that there is not a global population problem but rather many challenges that vary from country to country and region to region.

THE BIG CRUNCH

Birthrates are falling, but it may be a half-century before the number of people—and their impact—reaches a peak

By Jeffrey Kluger

ODDS ARE YOU'LL NEVER MEET ANY OF THE ESTIMATED 247 HUMAN BEINGS WHO WERE BORN IN THE PAST MINUTE. IN A POPULATION OF 6 BILLION, 247 IS A DEMOGRAPHIC HICCUP. IN THE MINUTE BEFORE LAST, HOWEVER, THERE WERE ANOTHER 247. IN THE MINUTES TO COME THERE WILL be another, then another, then another. By next year at this time, all those minutes will have produced nearly 130 million newcomers to the great human mosh pit. That kind of crowd is awfully hard to miss.

For folks inclined to fret that the earth is heading for the environmental abyss, the population problem has always been one of the biggest causes for worry—and with good reason. The last time humanity celebrated a new century there were 1.6 billion people here for the party—or a quarter as many as this time. In 1900 the average life expectancy was, in some places, as low as 23 years; now it's 65, meaning the extra billions are staying around longer and demanding more from the planet. The 130 million or so births registered annually—even after subtracting the 52 million deaths—is still the equivalent of adding nearly one new Germany to the world's population each year.

But things may not be as bleak as they seem. Lately demographers have come to the conclusion that the population locomotive—while still cannonballing ahead—may be chugging toward a stop. In country after country, birthrates are easing, and the population growth rate is falling.

To be sure, this kind of success is uneven. For every region in the world that has brought its population under control, there's another where things are still exploding. For every country that has figured out the art of sustainable agriculture, there are others that have worked their land to exhaustion. The population bomb may yet go off before governments can snuff the fuse, but for now, the news is better than it's been in a long time. "We could have an end in sight to population growth in the next century," says Carl Haub, a demographer with the nonprofit Population Research Bureau. "That's a major change."

Cheering as the population reports are becoming today, for much of the past 50 years, demographers were bearers of mostly bad tidings. In census after census, they reported that humanity was not just settling the planet but smothering it. It was not until the century was nearly two-thirds over that scientists and governments finally bestirred themselves to do something about it. The first great brake on population growth came in the early 1960s, with the development of the birth-control pill, a magic pharmacological bullet that made contraception easier—not to mention tidier—than it had ever been before. In 1969 the United Nations got in on the population game, creating the U.N. Population Fund, a global organization dedicated to bringing family-planning techniques to women who would not otherwise have them. In the decades that followed, the U.N. increased its commitment, sponsoring numerous global symposiums to address the population problem further. The most significant was the 1994 Cairo conference, where attendees pledged $5.7 billion to reduce birthrates in the developing world and acknowledged that giving women more education and reproductive freedom was the key to accomplishing that goal. Even a global calamity like AIDS has yielded unexpected dividends, with international campaigns to promote condom use and abstinence helping to prevent not only disease transmission but also conception.

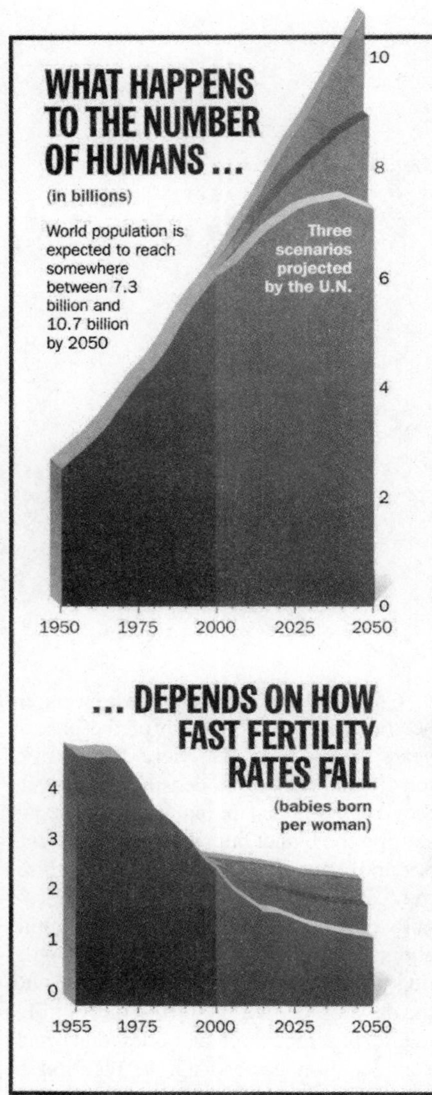

Source: United Nations

Such efforts have paid off in a big way. According to U.N. head counters, the average number of children produced per couple in the developing world—a figure that reached a whopping 4.9 earlier this century—has plunged to just 2.7. In many countries, including Spain, Slovenia, Greece and Germany, the fertility rate is well below 1.5, meaning parents are producing 25% fewer offspring than would be needed to replace themselves—in effect, throwing the census into reverse. A little more than 30 years ago, global population growth was 2.04% a year, the highest in human history. Today it's just 1.3%. "It was a remarkable century," says Joseph Chamie of the U.N. Population Division. "We quadrupled the population in 100 years, but that's not going to happen again."

Sunny as the global averages look, however, things get a lot darker when you break them down by region. Even the best family-planning programs do no good if there is neither the money nor governmental expertise to carry them out, and in less-developed countries—which currently account for a staggering 96% of the annual population increase—both are sorely lacking. In parts of the Middle East and Africa, the fertility rate exceeds seven babies per woman. In India, nearly 16 million births are registered each year, for a growth rate of 1.8%. While Europe's population was three times that of Africa in 1950, today the two continents have about the same count. At the current rate, Africa will triple Europe in another 50 years.

Many of the countries in the deepest demographic trouble have imposed aggressive family-planning programs, only to see them go badly—even criminally—awry. In the 1970s, Indian Prime Minister Indira Gandhi tried to reduce the national birthrate by offering men cash and transistor radios if they would undergo vasectomies. In the communities in which those sweeteners failed, the government resorted to coercion, putting millions of males—from teenage boys to elderly men—on the operating table. Amid the popular backlash that followed, Gandhi's government was turned out of office, and the public rejected family planning.

China's similarly notorious one-child policy has done a better job of slowing population growth but not without problems. In a country that values boys over girls, one-child rules have led to abandonments, abortions and infanticides, as couples limited to a single offspring keep spinning the reproductive wheel until it comes up male. "We've learned that there is no such thing as 'population control,'" says Alex Marshall of the U.N. Population Fund. "You don't control it. You allow people to make up their own mind."

That strategy has worked in many countries that once had runaway population growth. Mexico, one of Latin America's population success stories, has made government-subsidized contraception widely available and at the same time launched public-information campaigns to teach people the value of using it. A recent series of ads aimed at men makes the powerful point that there is more machismo in clothing and feeding offspring than in conceiving and leaving them. In the past 30 years, the average number of children born to a Mexican woman has plunged from seven to just 2.5. Many developing nations are starting to recognize the importance of educating women and letting them—not just their husbands—have a say in how many children they will have.

But bringing down birthrates loses some of its effectiveness as mortality rates also fall. At the same time Mexico reduced its children-per-mother figure, for example, it also boosted its average life expectancy from 50 years to 72—a wonderful accomplishment, but one that offsets part of the gain achieved by reducing the number of births.

When people live longer, populations grow not just bigger but also older and frailer. In the U.S. there has been no end of hand wringing over what will happen when baby boomers—who owe their very existence to the procreative free-for-all that followed World War II—retire, leaving themselves to be supported by the much smaller generation they produced. In Germany there are currently four workers for every retired person. Before long that ratio will be down to just 2 to 1.

> **STATE OF THE PLANET**
>
> **Humans already use 54% of Earth's rainfall, says the U.N. report, and 70% of that goes to agriculture**

For now, the only answer may be to tough things out for a while, waiting for the billions of people born during the great population booms to live out their long life, while at the same time continuing to reduce birthrates further so that things don't get thrown so far out of kilter again. But there's no telling if the earth—already worked to exhaustion feeding the 6 billion people currently here—can take much more. People in the richest countries consume a disproportionate share of the world's resources, and as poorer nations push to catch up, pressure on the planet will keep growing. "An ecologist looks at the population size relative to the carrying capacity of Earth," says Lester Brown, president of the Worldwatch Institute. "Looking at it that way, things are much worse than we expected them to be 20 years ago."

How much better they'll get will be decided in the next half-century (*see chart*). According to three scenarios published by the U.N., the global population in the year 2050 will be somewhere between 7.3 billion and 10.7 billion, depending on how fast the fertility rate falls. The difference between the high scenario and the low scenario? Just one child per couple. With the species poised on that kind of demographic knife edge, it pays for those couples to make their choices carefully.

—Reported by William Dowell/New York, Meenakshi Ganguly/New Delhi and Dick Thompson/Washington

Breaking *Out* or Breaking *Down*

In some parts of the world, the historic trend toward longer life has been abruptly reversed.

by Lester R. Brown and Brian Halweil

On October 12 of this year, the world's human population is projected to pass 6 billion. The day will be soberly observed by population and development experts, but media attention will do nothing to immediately slow the expansion. During that day, the global total will swell by another 214,000—enough people to fill two of the world's largest sports stadiums.

Even as world population continues to climb, it is becoming clear that the several billion additional people projected for the next half century are not likely to materialize. What is not clear is how the growth will be curtailed. Unfortunately, in some countries, a slowing of the growth is taking place only partly because of success in bringing birth rates down—and increasingly because of newly emergent conditions that are raising death rates.

Evidence of this shift became apparent in late October, 1998, when U.N. demographers released their biennial update of world population projections, revising the projected global population for 2050. Instead of rising in the next 50 years by more than half, to 9.4 billion (as computed in 1996), the 1998 projection rose only to 8.9 billion. The good news was that two-thirds of this anticipated slow-down was expected to be the result of falling fertility—of the decisions of more couples to have fewer children. But the other third was due to rising death rates, largely as a result of rising mortality from AIDS.

This rather sudden reversal in the human death rate trend marks a tragic new development in world demography, which is dividing the developing countries into two groups. When these countries embarked on the development journey a half century or so ago, they followed one of two paths. In the first, illustrated by the East Asian nations of South Korea, Taiwan, and Thailand, early efforts to shift to smaller families set in motion a positive cycle of rising living standards and falling fertility. Those countries are now moving toward population stability.

In the second category, which prevails in sub-Saharan Africa (770 million people) and the Indian subcontinent (1.3 billion), fertility has remained high or fallen very little, setting the stage for a vicious downward spiral in which rapid population growth reinforces poverty, and in which some segments of society eventually are deprived of the resources needed even to survive. In Ethiopia, Nigeria, and Pakistan, for example, demographers estimate that the next half-century will bring a doubling or near-tripling of populations. Even now, people in these regions each day awaken to a range of daunting conditions that threatens to drop their living standards below the level at which humans can survive.

We now see three clearly identifiable trends that either are already raising death rates or are likely to do so in these regions: the spread of the HIV virus that causes AIDS, the depletion of aquifers, and the shrinking amount of cropland available to support each person. The HIV epidemic is spiraling out of control in sub-Saharan Africa. The depletion of aquifers has become a major threat to India, where water tables are falling almost everywhere. The shrinkage in cropland per person threatens to force reductions in food consumed per person, increasing malnutrition—and threatening lives—in many parts of these regions.

Containing one-third of the world's people, these two regions now face a potentially dramatic shortening of life expectancy. In sub-Saharan Africa, mortality rates are already rising, and in the Indian subcontinent they could begin rising soon. Without clearly defined national strategies for quickly lowering birth rates in these countries, and without a commitment by the international community to support them in their efforts, one-third of humanity could slide into a demographic black hole.

Birth and Death

Since 1950, we have witnessed more growth in world population than during the preceding 4 million years since our human ancestors first stood upright. This post-1950 explosion can be attributed, in part, to several developments that reduced death rates throughout the developing world. The wider availability of safe drinking water, childhood immunization programs, antibiotics, and expanding food production sharply reduced the number of people dying of hunger and from infectious diseases. Together these trends dramatically lowered mortality levels.

But while death rates fell, birth rates remained high. As a result, in many countries, population growth rose to 3 percent or more per year—rates for which there was no historical precedent. A 3 percent annual increase in population leads to a twenty-fold increase within a century. Ecologists have long known that such rates of population growth—which have now been sustained for close to half a century in many countries—could not be sustained indefinitely. At some point, if birth rates did not come down, disease, hunger, or conflict would force death rates up.

Projected Population Growth in Selected Developing Countries, 1999 to 2050

	1999 (millions)	2050 (millions)	Growth From 1999 to 2050 (millions)	Growth From 1999 to 2050 (percent)
Developing Countries That Have Slowed Population Growth:				
South Korea	46	51	5	+11
Taiwan	22	25	3	+14
Thailand	61	74	13	+21
Developing Countries Where Rapid Population Growth Continues:				
Ethiopia	61	169	108	+177
Nigeria	109	244	135	+124
Pakistan	152	345	193	+127

Source: *United Nations, Global Population Projections, 1998.*

Although most of the world has succeeded in reducing birth rates to some degree, only some 32 countries—containing a mere 12 percent of the world's people—have achieved population stability. In these countries, growth rates range between 0.4 percent per year and minus 0.6 percent per year. With the exception of Japan, all of the 32 countries are in Europe, and all are industrial. Although other industrial countries, such as the United States, are still experiencing some population growth as a result of a persistent excess of births over deaths, the population of the industrial world as a whole is not projected to grow at all in the next century—unless, perhaps, through the arrival of migrants from more crowded regions.

Within the developing world, the most impressive progress in reducing fertility has come in East Asia. South Korea, Taiwan, and Thailand have all reduced their population growth rates to roughly one percent per year and are approaching stability. (See table, this page.) The biggest country in Latin America—Brazil—has reduced its population growth to 1.4 percent per year. Most other countries in Latin America are also making progress on this front. In contrast, the countries of sub-Saharan Africa and the Indian subcontinent have lagged in lowering growth rates, and populations are still rising ominously—at rates of 2 to 3 percent or more per year.

Graphically illustrating this contrast are Thailand and Ethiopia, each with 61 million people. Thailand is projected to add 13 million people over the next half century for a gain of 21 percent. Ethiopia, meanwhile, is projected to add 108 million for a gain of 177 percent. (The U.N.'s projections are based on such factors as the number of children per woman, infant mortality, and average life span in each country—factors that could change in time, but meanwhile differ sharply in the two countries.) The deep poverty among those living in sub-Saharan Africa and the Indian subcontinent has been a principal factor in their rapid population growth, as couples lack access to the kinds of basic social services and education that allow control over reproductive choices. Yet, the population growth, in turn, has only worsened their poverty—perpetuating a vicious cycle in which hopes of breaking out become dimmer with each passing year.

After several decades of rapid population growth, governments of many developing countries are simply being overwhelmed by their crowding—and are suffering from what we term "demographic fatigue." The simultaneous challenges of educating growing numbers of children, creating jobs for the swelling numbers of young people coming into the job market, and confronting such environmental consequences of rapid population growth as deforestation, soil erosion, and falling water tables, are undermining the capacity of governments to cope. When a major new threat arises, as has happened with the HIV virus, governments often cannot muster the leadership energy and fiscal resources to mobilize effectively. Social problems that are easily contained in industrial societies can become humanitarian disasters in many developing ones. As a result, some of the latter may soon see their population growth curves abruptly flattened, or even thrown into decline, not because of falling birth rates but because of fast-rising death rates. In some countries, that process has already begun.

Countries Where HIV Infection Rate Among Adults Is Greater Than Ten Percent

Country	Population	Share of Adult Population Infected
	(millions)	(percent)
Zimbabwe	11.7	26
Botswana	1.5	25
South Africa	43.3	22
Namibia	1.6	20
Zambia	8.5	19
Swaziland	0.9	18
Malawi	10.1	15
Mozambique	18.3	14
Rwanda	5.9	13
Kenya	28.4	12
Central African Republic	3.4	11
Cote d'Ivoire	14.3	10

Source: UNAIDS

Shades of the Black Death

Industrial countries have held HIV infection rates under 1 percent of the adult population, but in many sub-Saharan African countries, they are spiraling upward, out of control. In Zimbabwe, 26 percent of the adult population is infected; in Botswana, the rate is 25 percent. In South Africa, a country of 43 million people, 22 percent are infected. In Namibia, Swaziland, and Zambia, 18 to 20 percent are. (See table, this page.) In these countries, there is little to suggest that these rates will not continue to climb.

In other African nations, including some with large populations, the rates are lower but climbing fast. In both Tanzania, with 32 million people, and Ethiopia, with its 61 million, the race is now 9 percent. In Nigeria, the continent's largest country with 111 million people, the latest estimate now puts the infection rate also at 9 percent and rising.

What makes this picture even more disturbing is that most Africans carrying the virus do not yet know they are infected, which means the disease can gain enormous momentum in areas where it is still largely invisible. This, combined with the social taboo that surrounds HIV/AIDS in Africa, has made it extremely difficult to mount an effective control effort.

Barring a medical miracle, countries such as Zimbabwe, Botswana, and South Africa will lose at least 20 percent of their adult populations to AIDS within the next decade, simply because few of those now infected with the virus can afford treatment with the costly antiviral drugs now used in industrial countries. To find a precedent for such a devastating region-wide loss of life from an infectious disease, we have to go back to the decimation of Native American communities by the introduction of small pox in the sixteenth century from Europe or to the bubonic plaque that claimed roughly a third of Europe's population in the fourteenth century (see table, next page).

Reversing Progress

The burden of HIV is not limited to those infected, or even to their generation. Like a powerful storm or war that lays waste to a nation's physical infrastructure, a growing HIV epidemic damages a nation's social infrastructure, with lingering demographic and economic effects. A viral epidemic that grows out of control is likely to reinforce many of the very conditions—poverty, illiteracy, malnutrition—that gave it an opening in the first place.

Using life expectancy—the sentinel indicator of development—as a measure, we can see that the HIV virus is reversing the gains of the last several decades. For example, in Botswana life expectancy has fallen from 61 years in 1990 to 44 years in 1999. By 2010, it is projected to drop to 39 years—a life expectancy more characteristic of medieval times than of what we had hoped for in the twenty-first century.

Beyond its impact on mortality, HIV also reduced fertility. For women, who live on average scarcely 10 years after becoming infected, many will die long before they have reached the end of their reproductive years. As the symptoms of AIDS begin to develop, women are less likely to conceive. For those who do conceive, the likelihood of spontaneous abortion rises. And among the reduced number who do give birth, an estimated 30 percent of the infants born are infected and an additional 20 percent are likely to be infected before they are weaned. For babies born with the virus, life expectancy is less than 2 years. The rate of population growth falls, but not in the way any family-planning group wants to see.

One of the most disturbing social consequences of the HIV epidemic is the number of orphans that it produces. Conjugal sex is one of the surest ways to spread AIDS, so if one parent dies, there is a good change the other will as well. By the end of 1997, there were already 7.8 million AIDS orphans in Africa—a new and rapidly growing social subset. The burden of raising these AIDS orphans falls first on the extended family, and then on society at large. Mortality rates for these orphans are likely to be much higher than the rates for children whose parents are still with them.

As the epidemic progresses and the symptoms become visible, health care systems in developing countries are being overwhelmed. The estimated cost of providing an-

Profiles of Major Epidemics Throughout Human History

Epidemic and Date	Mode of Introduction and Spread	Description of Plague and Its Effects on Population
Black Death in Europe, 14th century	Originating in Asia, the plague bacteria moved westward via trade routes, entering Europe in 1347; transmitted via rats as well as coughing and sneezing.	One fourth of the population of Europe was wiped out (an estimated 25 million deaths); old, young, and poor hit hardest.
Smallpox in the New World, 16th century	Spanish conquistadors and European colonists introduced virus into the Americas, where it spread through respiratory channels and physical contact.	Decimated Aztec, Incan, and native American civilizations, killing 10 to 20 million.
HIV/AIDS, worldwide, 1980 to present	Thought to have originated in Africa; a primate virus that mutated and spread to infect humans; transmitted by the exchange of bodily fluids, including blood, semen, and breast milk.	More than 14 million deaths worldwide thus far; an additional 33 million infected; one-fifth of adult population infected in several African nations; strikes economically active populations hardest.

Source: Jared Diamond, *Guns, Germs, and Steel: The Fates of Human Societies*, 1997; UNAIDS.

tiviral treatment (the standard regimen used to reduce symptoms, improve life quality, and postpone death) to all infected individuals in Malawi, Mozambique, Uganda, and Tanzania would be larger than the GNPs of those countries. In some hospitals in South Africa, 70 percent of the beds are occupied by AIDS patients. In Zimbabwe, half the health care budget now goes to deal with AIDS. As AIDS patients increasingly monopolize nurses' and doctors' schedules, and drain funds from health care budgets, the capacity to provide basic health care to the general population—including the immunizations and treatments for routine illnesses that have underpinned the decline in mortality and the rise in life expectancy in developing countries—begins to falter.

Worldwide, more than half of all new HIV infections occur in people between the ages of 15 and 24—an atypical pattern for an infectious disease. Human scourges have historically spread through respiratory exposure to coughing or sneezing, or through physical contact via shaking hands, food handling, and so on. Since nearly everyone is vulnerable to such exposure, the victims of most infectious diseases are simply those among society at large who have the weakest immune systems—generally the very young and the elderly. But with HIV, because the primary means of transmission is unprotected sexual activity, the ones who are most vulnerable to infection are those who are most sexually active—young, healthy adults in the prime of their lives. According to a UNAIDS report, "the bulk of the increase in adult death is in the younger adult ages—a pattern that is common in wartime and has become a signature of the AIDS epidemic, but that is otherwise rarely seen."

One consequence of this adult die-off is an increase in the number of children and elderly who are dependent on each economically productive adult. This makes it more difficult for societies to save and, therefore, to make the investments needed to improve living conditions. To make matters worse, in Africa it is often the better educated, more socially mobile populations who have the highest infection rate. Africa is losing the agronomists, the engineers, and the teachers it needs to sustain its economic development. In South Africa, for example, at the University of Durban-Westville, where many of the country's future leaders are trained, 25 percent of the students are HIV positive.

Countries where labor forces have such high infection levels will find it increasingly difficult to attract foreign investment. Companies operating in countries with high infection rates face a doubling, tripling, or even quadrupling of their health insurance costs. Firms once operating in the black suddenly find themselves in the red. What has begun as an unprecedented social tragedy is beginning to translate into an economic disaster. Municipalities throughout South Africa have been hesitant to publicize the extent of their local epidemics or scale up control efforts for fear of deterring outside investment and tourism.

The feedback loops launched by AIDS may be quite predictable in some cases, but could also destabilize societies in unanticipated ways. For example, where levels of unemployment are already high—the present situation in most African nations—a growing population of orphans and displaced youths could exacerbate crime. Moreover, a country in which a substantial share of the population suffers from impaired immune systems as a result of

AIDS is much more vulnerable to the spread of other infectious diseases, such as tuberculosis, and waterborne illness. In Zimbabwe, the last few years have brought a rapid rise in deaths due to tuberculosis, malaria, and even the bubonic plague—even among those who are not HIV positive. Even without such synergies, in the early years of the next century, the HIV epidemic is poised to claim more lives than did World War II.

Sinking Water Tables

While AIDS is already raising death rates in sub-Saharan Africa, the emergence of acute water shortages could have the same effect in India. As population grows, so does the need for water. Home to only 358 million people in 1950, India will pass the one-billion mark later this year. It is projected to overtake China as the most populous nation around the year 2037, and to reach 1.5 billion by 2050.

As India's population has soared, its demand for water for irrigation, industry, and domestic use has climbed far beyond the sustainable yield of the country's aquifers. According to the International Water Management Institute (IWMI), water is being pumped from India's aquifers at twice the rate the aquifers are recharged by rainfall. As a result, water tables are falling by one to three meters per year almost everywhere in the country. In thousands of villages, wells are running dry.

In some cases, wells are simply drilled deeper—if there is a deeper aquifer within reach. But many villages now depend on trucks to bring in water for household use. Other villages cannot afford such deliveries, and have entered a purgatory of declining options—lacking enough water even for basic hygiene. In India's western state of Gujarat, water tables are falling by as much as five meters per year, and farmers now have to drill their wells down to between 700 and 1200 feet to reach the receding supply. Only the more affluent can afford to drill to such depths.

Although irrigation goes back some 6,000 years, aquifer depletion is a rather recent phenomenon. It is only within the last half century or so that the availability of powerful diesel and electric pumps has made it possible to extract water at rates that exceed recharge rates. Little is known about the total capacity of India's underground supply, but the unsustainability of the current consumption is clear. If the country is currently pumping water at double the rate at which its aquifers recharge, for example, we know that when the aquifers are eventually depleted, the rate of pumping will necessarily have to be reduced to the recharge rate—which would mean that the amount of water pumped would be cut in half. With at least 55 percent of India's grain production now coming from irrigated lands, IWMI speculates that aquifer depletion could reduce India's harvest by one-fourth. Such a massive cutback could prove catastrophic for a nation where 53 percent of the children are already undernourished and underweight.

Impending aquifer depletion is not unique to India. It is also evident in China, North Africa and the Middle East, as well as in large tracts of the United States. However, in wealthy Kuwait or Saudi Arabia, precariously low water availability per person is not life-threatening because these countries can easily afford to import the food that they cannot produce domestically. Since it takes 1,000 tons of water to produce a ton of grain, the ability to import food is in effect an ability to import water. But in poor nations, like India, where people are immediately dependent on the natural-resource base for subsistence and often lack money to buy food, they are limited to the water they can obtain from their immediate surroundings—and are much more endangered if it disappears.

In India—as in other nations—poorer farmers are thus disproportionately affected by water scarcity, since they often cannot get the capital or credit to obtain bigger pumps necessary to extract water from ever-greater depths. Those farmers who can no longer deepen their wells often shift their cropping patterns to include more water-efficient—but lower-yielding—crops, such as mustard, sorghum, or millet. Some have abandoned irrigated farming altogether, resigning themselves to the diminished productivity that comes with depending only on rainfall.

When production drops, of course, poverty deepens. When that happens, experience shows that most people, before succumbing to hunger or starvation, will migrate. On Gujarat's western coast, for example, the overpumping of underground water has led to rapid salt-water intrusion as seawater seeps in to fill the vacuum left by the freshwater. The groundwater has become so saline that farming with it is impossible, and this has driven a massive migration of farmers inland in search of work.

Village communities in India tend to be rather insular, so that these migrants—uprooted from their homes—cannot take advantage of the social safety net that comes with community and family bonds. Local housing restrictions force them to camp in the fields, and their access to village clinics, schools, and other social services is restricted. But while attempting to flee, the migrants also bring some of their troubles along with them. Navroz Dubash, a researcher at the World Resources Institute who examined some of the effects of the water scarcity in Gujarat, notes that the flood of migrants depresses the local labor markets, driving down wages and diminishing the bargaining power of all landless laborers in the region.

In the web of feedback loops linking health and water supply, another entanglement is that when the *quantity* of available water declines, the *quality* of the water, too, may decline, because shrinking bodies of water lose their efficacy in diluting salts or pollutants. In Gujarat, water pumped from more than 700 feet down tends to have an unhealthy concentration of some inorganic elements, such as fluoride. As villagers drink and irrigate with this contaminated water, the degeneration of teeth and bones known as fluorosis has emerged as a major health threat. Similarly, in both West Bengal, India and Bangladesh, receding water tables have exposed arsenic-laden sediments to oxygen, converting them to a water-soluble form. According to UNDP estimates, at least 30 million people are exposed to health-impairing levels of arsenic in their drinking water.

AIDS attacks whole communities, but unlike other scourges it takes its heaviest toll on teenagers and young adults—the people most needed to care for children and keep the economy productive.

As poverty deepens in the rural regions of India—and is driven deeper by mutually exacerbating health threats and water scarcities—migration from rural to urban areas is likely to increase. But for those who leave the farms, conditions in the cities may be no better. If water is scarce in the countryside, it is also likely to be scarce in the squatter settlements or other urban areas accessible to the poor. And where water is scarce, access to adequate sanitation and health services is poor. In most developing nations, the incidence of infectious diseases, including waterborne microbes, tuberculosis, and HIV/AIDS, is considerably higher in urban slums—where poverty and compromised health define the way of life—than in the rest of the city.

In India, with so many of the children undernourished, even a modest decline in the country's ability to produce or purchase food is likely to increase child mortality. With India's population expected to increase by 100 million people per decade over the next half century, the potential losses of irrigation water pose an ominous specter not only to the Indian people now living but to the hundreds of millions more yet to come.

Shrinking Cropland Per Person

The third threat that hangs over the future of nearly all the countries where rapid population growth continues is the steady decline in the amount of cropland remaining per person—a threat both of rising population and of the conversion of cropland to other uses. In this analysis, we use grainland per person as a surrogate for cropland, because in most developing countries the bulk of land is used to produce grain, and the data are much more reliable. Among the more populous countries where this trend threatens future food security are Nigeria, Ethiopia, and Pakistan—all countries with weak family-planning programs.

As a limited amount of arable land continues to be divided among larger numbers of people, the average amount of cropland available for each person inexorably shrinks. Eventually, it drops below the point where people can feed themselves. Below 600 square meters of grainland per person (about the area of a basketball court), nations typically begin to depend heavily on imported grain. Cropland scarcity, like, water scarcity, can easily be translated into increased food imports in countries that can afford to import grain. But in the poorer nations of sub-Saharan Africa and the Indian subcontinent, subsistence farmers may not have access to imports. For them, land scarcity readily translates into malnutrition, hunger, rising mortality, and migration—and sometimes conflict. While most experts agree that resource scarcity alone is rarely the cause of violent conflict, resource scarcity has often compounded socioeconomic and political disruptions enough to drive unstable situations over the edge.

Thomas Homer-Dixon, director of the Project on Environment, Population, and Security at the University of Toronto, notes that "environmental scarcity is, without doubt, a significant cause of today's unprecedented levels of internal and international migration around the world." He has examined two cases in South Asia—a region plagued by land and water scarcity—in which resource constraints were underlying factors in mass migration and resulting conflict.

In the first case, Homer-Dixon finds that over the last few decades, land scarcity has caused millions of Bangladeshis to migrate to the Indian states of Assam, Tripura, and West Bengal. These movements expanded in the late 1970s after several years of flooding in Bangladesh, when population growth had reduced the grainland per person in Bangladesh to less than 0.08 hectares. As the average person's share of cropland began to shrink below the survival level, the lure of somewhat less densely populated land across the border in the Indian state of Assam became irresistible. By 1990, more than 7 million Bangladeshis had crossed the border, pushing Assam's population from 15 million to 22 million. The new immigrants in turn exacerbated land shortages in the Indian states, setting off a string of ethnic conflicts that have so far killed more than 5,000 people.

In the second case, Homer-Dixon and a colleague, Peter Gizewski, studied the massive rural-to-urban migration that has taken place in recent years in Pakistan. This migration, combined with population growth within the cities, has resulted in staggering urban growth rates of roughly 15 percent a year. Karachi, Pakistan's coastal capital, has seen its population balloon to 11 million. Urban services have been unable to keep pace with growth, especially for low-income dwellers. Shortages of water, sanitation, health services and jobs have become especially acute, leading to deteriorating public health and growing impoverishment.

"This migration... aggravates tensions and violence among diverse ethnic groups," according to Homer-

Dixon and Gizewski. "This violence, in turn, threatens the general stability of Pakistani society." The cities of Karachi, Hyderabad, Islamabad, and Rawalpindi, in particular, have become highly volatile, so that "an isolated, seemingly chance incident—such as a traffic accident or short-term breakdown in services—ignites explosive violence." In 1994, water shortages in Islamabad provoked widespread protest and violent confrontation with police in hard-hit poorer districts.

When people of parenting age die, the elderly are often left alone to care for the children. Meanwhile, poverty worsens with the loss of wage-earners. In other situations, poverty is worsened by declines in the amounts of productive land or fresh water available to each person and here, too, death may take an unnatural toll.

Without efforts to step up family planning in Pakistan, these patterns are likely to be magnified. Population is projected to grow from 146 million today to 345 million in 2050, shrinking the grainland area per person in Pakistan to a miniscule 0.036 hectares by 2050—less than half of what it is today. A family of six will then have to produce its food on roughly one-fifth of a hectare, or half an acre—the equivalent of a small suburban building lot in the United States.

Similar prospects are in the offing for Nigeria, where population is projected to double to 244 million over the next half century, and in Ethiopia, where population is projected to nearly triple. In both, of course, the area of grainland per person will shrink dramatically. In Ethiopia, if the projected population growth materializes, it will cut the amount of cropland per person to one-third of its current 0.12 hectares per person—a level at which already more than half of the country's children are undernourished. And even as its per capita land shrinks, its long-term water supply is jeopardized by the demands of nine other rapidly growing, water-scarce nations throughout the Nile River basin. But even these projections may underestimate the problem, because they assume an equitable distribution of land among all people. In reality, the inequalities in land distribution that exist in many African and South Asian nations mean that as the competition for declining resources becomes more intense, the poorer and more marginal groups face even harsher deprivations than the averages imply.

Moreover, in these projections we have assumed that the total grainland area over the next half-century will not change. In reality this may be overly optimistic simply because of the ongoing conversion of cropland to nonfarm uses and the loss of cropland from degradation. A steadily growing population generates a need for more homes, schools, and factories, many of which will be built on once-productive farmland. Degradation, which may take the form of soil erosion or of the waterlogging and salinization of irrigated land, is also claiming cropland.

Epidemics, resource scarcity, and other societal stresses thus do not operate in isolation. Several disruptive trends will often intersect synergistically, compounding their effects on public health, the environment, the economy, and the society. Such combinations can happen anywhere, but the effects are likely to be especially pernicious—and sometimes dangerously unpredictable—in such places as Bombay and Lagos, where HIV prevalence is on the rise, and where fresh water and good land are increasingly beyond the reach of the poor.

Regaining Control of Our Destiny

The threats from HIV, aquifer depletion, and shrinking cropland are not new or unexpected. We have known for at least 15 years that the HIV virus could decimate human populations if it is not controlled. In each of the last 18 years, the annual number of new HIV infections has risen, climbing from an estimated 200,000 new infections in 1981 to nearly 6 million in 1998. Of the 47 million people infected thus far, 14 million have died. In the absence of a low-cost cure, most of the remaining 33 million will be dead by 2005.

It may seem hard to believe, given the advanced medical knowledge of the late twentieth century, that a controllable disease is decimating human populations in so many countries. Similarly, it is hard to understand how falling water tables, which may prove an even greater threat to future economic progress, could be so widely ignored.

The arithmetic of emerging resource shortages is not difficult. The mystery is not in the numbers, but in our failure to do what is needed to prevent such threats from spiraling out of control.

Today's political leaders show few signs of comprehending the long-term consequences of persistent environmental and social trends, or of the interconnectedness of these trends. Despite advances in our understanding of the complex—often chaotic—nature of biological, ecological, and climatological systems, political thought continues to be dominated by reductionist thinking that fails to target the root causes of problems. As a result, political action focuses on responses to crises rather than prevention.

Leaders who are prepared to meet the challenges of the next century will need to understand that universal access to family planning not only is essential to coping with resource scarcity and the spread of HIV/AIDS, but is likely to improve the quality of life for the citizens they serve. Family planning comprises wide availability of contraception and reproductive healthcare, as well as improved access to educational opportunities for young women and men. Lower birth rates generally allow greater investment in each child, as has occurred in East Asia.

Overwhelmed by multiple attacks on its health, the society falls deeper into poverty and as the cycle continues, more of its people die prematurely.

Leaders all over the world—not just in Africa and Asia—now need to realize that the adverse effects of global population growth will affect those living in nations such as the United States or Germany, that seem at first glance to be relatively protected from the ravages now looming in Zimbabwe or Ethiopia. Economist Herman Daly observes that whereas in the past surplus labor in one nation had the effect of driving down wages only in that nation, "global economic integration will be the means by which the consequences of overpopulation in the Third World are generalized to the globe as a whole." Large infusions of job-seekers into Brazil's or India's work force that may lower wages there may now also mean large infusions into the global workforce, with potentially similar consequences.

As the recent Asian economic downturn further demonstrates, "localized instability" is becoming an anachronistic concept. The consequences of social unrest in one nation, whether resulting from a currency crisis or an environmental crisis, can quickly cross national boundaries. Several nations, including the United States, now recognize world population growth as a national security issue. As the U.S. Department of State Strategic Plan, issued in September 1997, explains, "Stabilizing population growth is vital to U.S. interests.... Not only will early stabilization of the world's population promote environmentally sustainable economic development in other countries, but it will benefit the United States by improving trade opportunities and mitigating future global crises."

One of the keys to helping countries quickly slow population growth, before it becomes unmanageable, is expanded international assistance for reproductive health and family planning. At the United Nations Conference on Population and Development held in Cairo in 1994, it was estimated that the annual cost of providing quality reproductive health services to all those in need in developing countries would amount to $17 billion in the year 2000. By 2015, the cost would climb to $22 billion.

Industrial countries agreed to provide one-third of the funds, with the developing countries providing the remaining two-thirds. While developing countries have largely honored their commitments, the industrial countries—and most conspicuously, the United States—have reneged on theirs. And in late 1998, the U.S. Congress—mired in the quicksand of anti-abortion politics—withdrew all funding for the U.N. Population Fund, the principal source of international family planning assistance. Thus was thrown aside the kind of assistance that helps both to slow population growth and to check the spread of the HIV virus.

In most nations, stabilizing population will require mobilization of domestic resources that may now be tied up in defense expenditures, crony capitalism or government corruption. But without outside assistance, many nations many still struggle to provide universal family planning. For this reason, delegates at Cairo agreed that the immense resources and power found in the First World are indispensable in this effort. And as wealth further consolidates in the North and the number living in absolute poverty increases in the South, the argument for assistance grows more and more compelling. Given the social consequences of one-third of the world heading into a demographic nightmare, failure to provide such assistance is unconscionable.

Lester Brown is president of the Worldwatch Institute and Brian Halweil is a staff researcher at the Institute.

Article 7

GRAINS OF HOPE

GENETICALLY ENGINEERED CROPS could revolutionize farming. Protesters fear they could also destroy the ecosystem. You decide

By **J. MADELEINE NASH** ZURICH

At first, the grains of rice that Ingo Potrykus sifted through his fingers did not seem at all special, but that was because they were still encased in their dark, crinkly husks. Once those drab coverings were stripped away and the interiors polished to a glossy sheen, Potrykus and his colleagues would behold the seeds' golden secret. At their core, these grains were not pearly white, as ordinary rice is, but a very pale yellow—courtesy of beta-carotene, the nutrient that serves as a building block for vitamin A.

Potrykus was elated. For more than a decade he had dreamed of creating such a rice: a golden rice that would improve the lives of millions of the poorest people in the world. He'd visualized peasant farmers wading into paddies to set out the tender seedlings and winnowing the grain at harvest time in handwoven baskets. He'd pictured small children consuming the golden gruel their mothers would make, knowing that it would sharpen their eyesight and strengthen their resistance to infectious diseases.

And he saw his rice as the first modest start of a new green revolution, in which ancient food crops would acquire all manner of useful properties: bananas that wouldn't rot on the way to market; corn that could supply its own fertilizer; wheat that could thrive in drought-ridden soil.

But imagining a golden rice, Potrykus soon found, was one thing and bringing one into existence quite another. Year after year, he and his colleagues ran into one unexpected obstacle after another, beginning with the finicky growing habits of the rice they transplanted to a greenhouse near the foothills of the Swiss Alps. When success finally came, in the spring of 1999, Potrykus was 65 and about to retire as a full professor at the Swiss Federal Institute of Technology in Zurich. At that point, he tackled an even more formidable challenge.

Having created golden rice, Potrykus wanted to make sure it reached those for whom it was intended: malnourished children of the developing world. And that, he knew, was not likely to be easy. Why? Because in addition to a full complement of genes from Oryza sativa—the Latin name for the most commonly consumed species of rice—the golden grains also contained snippets of DNA borrowed from bacteria and daffodils. It was what some would call Frankenfood, a product of genetic engineering. As such, it was entangled in a web of hopes and fears and political baggage, not to mention a fistful of ironclad patents.

For about a year now—ever since Potrykus and his chief collaborator, Peter Beyer of the University of Freiburg in Germany, announced their achievement—their golden grain has illuminated an increasingly polarized public debate. At issue is the question of what genetically engineered crops represent. Are they,

HOW TO MAKE GOLDEN RICE

A four-step process to feed the poor

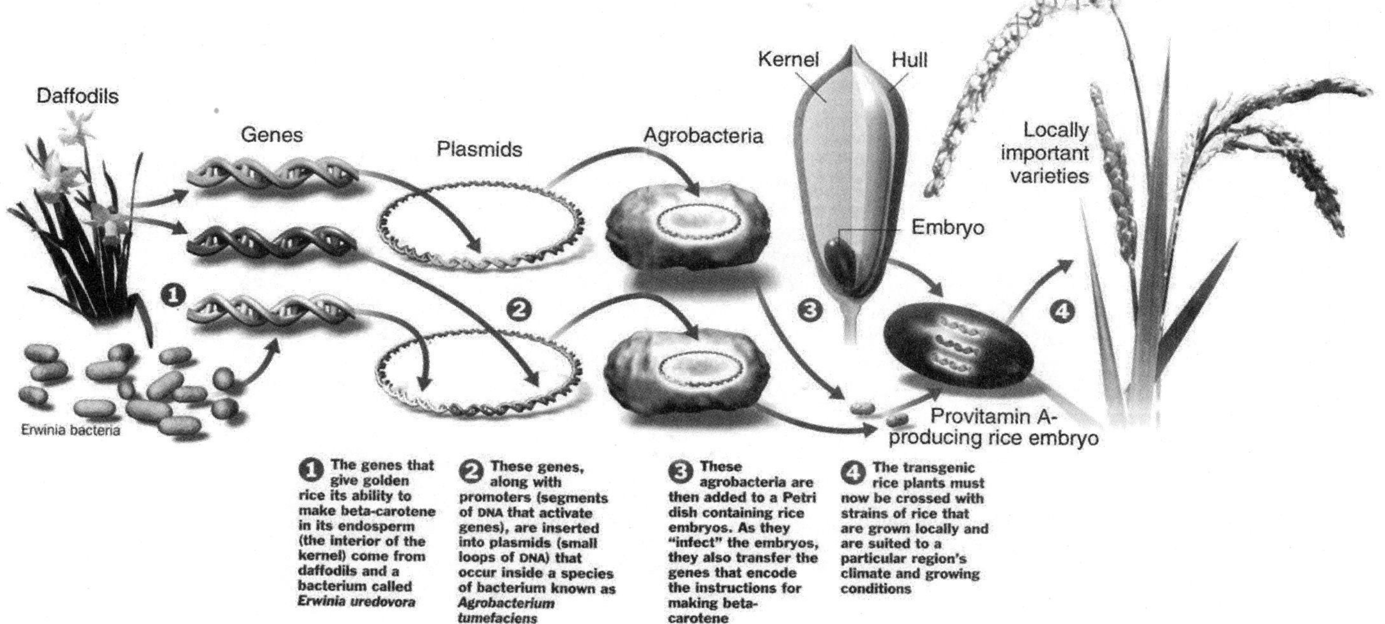

Source: Dr. Peter Beyer, Center for Applied Biosciences, University of Freiburg

as their proponents argue, a technological leap forward that will bestow incalculable benefits on the world and its people? Or do they represent a perilous step down a slippery slope that will lead to ecological and agricultural ruin? Is genetic engineering just a more efficient way to do the business of conventional crossbreeding? Or does the ability to mix the genes of any species—even plants and animals—give man more power than he should have?

The debate erupted the moment genetically engineered crops made their commercial debut in the mid-1990s, and it has escalated ever since. First to launch major protests against biotechnology were European environmentalists and consumer-advocacy groups. They were soon followed by their U.S. counterparts, who made a big splash at last fall's World Trade Organization meeting in Seattle and last week launched an offensive designed to target one company after another (see accompanying story). Over the coming months, charges that transgenic crops pose grave dangers will be raised in petitions, editorials, mass mailings and protest marches. As a result, golden rice, despite its humanitarian intent, will probably be subjected to the same kind of hostile scrutiny that has already led to curbs on the commercialization of these crops in Britain, Germany, Switzerland and Brazil.

The hostility is understandable. Most of the genetically engineered crops introduced so far represent minor variations on the same two themes: resistance to insect pests and to herbicides used to control the growth of weeds. And they are often marketed by large, multinational corporations that produce and sell the very agricultural chemicals farmers are spraying on their fields. So while many farmers have embraced such crops as Monsanto's Roundup Ready soybeans, with their genetically engineered resistance to Monsanto's Roundup-brand herbicide, that let them spray weed killer without harming crops, consumers have come to regard such things with mounting suspicion. Why resort to a strange new technology that might harm the biosphere, they ask, when the benefits of doing so seem small?

FROM THE TRANSGENIC GARDEN

COTTON
BEAUTIFUL BOLL: This plant has been given a bacterial gene to help it fight off worms that infest cotton crops

CORN
HEALTHY KERNEL: These corn seeds are protected by the same bacterial gene, one that ecologists fear could harm butterflies

PAPAYA
VIRAL RESISTANCE: Fruit carrying a gene from the ringspot virus are better able to withstand ringspot outbreaks

CANOLA
PROBLEM POLLEN: When transgenic seeds contaminated a non-transgenic shipment from Canada, European farmers cried foul

SOYBEANS
ROUNDUP READY: Will crops designed to take frequent spraying with Monsanto's top weed killer lead to Roundup-resistant weeds?

Taking It to Main Street

By **MARGOT ROOSEVELT** SAN FRANCISCO

IT WAS THE SORT OF KITSCHY STREET THEATER YOU EXPECT IN A city like San Francisco. A gaggle of protesters in front of a grocery store, some dressed as monarch butterflies, others as Frankenstein's monster. Signs reading HELL NO, WE WON'T GROW IT! People in white biohazard jumpsuits pitching Campbell's soup and Kellogg's cornflakes into a mock toxic-waste bin. The crowd shouting, "Hey, hey, ho, ho—GMO has got to go!" And, at the podium, Jesse Cool, a popular restaurant owner, wondering what would happen if she served a tomato spliced with an oyster gene and a customer got sick. "I could get sued," she says.

But just as the California activists were revving up last week, similar rants and chants were reverberating in such unlikely places as Grand Forks, N.D., Augusta, Maine, and Miami—19 U.S. cities in all. This was no frolicking radical fringe but the carefully coordinated start of a nationwide campaign to force the premarket safety testing and labeling of those GMOs, or genetically modified organisms. Seven organizations— including such media-savvy veterans as the Sierra Club, Friends of the Earth and the Public Interest Research Groups—were launching the Genetically Engineered Food Alert, a million-dollar, multiyear organizing effort to pressure Congress, the Food and Drug Administration and individual companies, one at a time, starting with Campbell's soup.

The offensive represents the seeds of what could grow into a serious problem for U.S. agribusiness, which had been betting that science-friendly American consumers would remain immune to any "Frankenfood" backlash cross-pollinating from Europe or Japan. After all, this is (mostly) U.S. technology, and it has spread so quickly and so quietly that the proportion of U.S. farmland planted in genetically altered corn now stands at nearly 25%. Some 70% of processed food in American supermarkets, from soup to sandwich meat, contains ingredients derived from transgenic corn, soybeans and other plants. Yet all of a sudden, activists are "yelling fire in a movie theater," says Dan Eramian, spokesman for the Biotechnology Industry Organization (BIO).

How widespread is this protest movement? And how deep are its roots? We may soon find out, for it's emergence is a study in the warp-speed politics of the age of the Internet. This is a time when a Web designer named Craig Winters can start an organization called the Campaign to Label Genetically Engineered Food with a staff of one (himself), mount a website and sell 160,000 "Take Action Packets" in nine weeks. Want to know what the Chileans are doing about transgenic grain shipments? How South Korean labeling laws work? Just subscribe to one of the four biotech e-mail lists of the Institute for Agriculture and Trade Policy, based in Minneapolis, Minn.

Even so-called ecoterrorists who have uprooted scores of university test plots across the country in the past year use the Net to organize their lawbreaking protests. In an Internet posting from Santa Cruz last week, Earth First! beckons, "You're all invited to sunny California for a weekend of workshops, training and fun! We also have plenty of [genetically engineered] crops waiting for your night time gardening efforts." Says Carl Pope, the Sierra Club's executive director: "I've never seen an issue go so quickly."

It started about two years ago, when the buzz from European antibiotech protest groups began to ricochet throughout the Net, reaching the community groups that were springing up across the U.S. Many were galvanized by proposed FDA regulations that would have allowed food certified as "organic" to contain genetically modified ingredients—an effort shouted down by angry consumers. Meanwhile, Greenpeace began to target U.S. companies such as Gerber, which quickly renounced the use of transgenic ingredients, and Kellogg's, which has yet to do so. With so-called Frankenfoods making headlines, several other companies cut back on biotech: McDonald's forswore genetically engineered potatoes, and Frito-Lay decreed it would buy no more genetically modified corn.

But the issue that is now on the front burner dates back to 1992, when the FDA decided that biotech ingredients did not materially alter food and therefore did not require labeling. Nor, the agency declared, was premarket safety testing required, because biotech additives were presumed to be benign. Last March the Center for Food Safety and 53 other groups, including the Union of Concerned Scientists, filed a petition to force the FDA to change its policy.

Meanwhile, the biotech issue is gathering steam in Congress, where safety and labeling bills have been introduced by Democratic Representative Dennis Kucinich of Ohio and 55 co-sponsors in the House, and by Daniel Patrick Moynihan and Barbara Boxer in the Senate. Similar statewide bills are pending in Maine, Colorado and Oregon. Shareholder resolutions demanding safety testing and labeling have targeted a score of companies from life-science giants to supermarket chains.

Surveys indicate that between two-thirds and three-quarters of Americans want biotech food to be labeled. Then why not do it? Because companies fear such disclosure could spell disaster. "Our data show that 60% of consumers would consider a mandatory biotech label as a warning that it is unsafe," says Gene Grabowski, spokesman for the Grocery Manufacturers of America. "It is easier," BIO's Eramian points out, "to scare people about biotechnology than to educate them."

The labeling threat finally spurred a hitherto complacent industry into action. Last April, Monsanto, Novartis and five other biotech companies rolled out a $50 million television advertising campaign, with soft-focus fields and smiling children, pitching "solutions that could improve our world tomorrow."

But by then the opposition was morphing from inchoate splinter groups into something that looks like a mainstream coalition. In July 1999, some 40 environmentalists, consumer advocates and organic-food activists met in Bolinas, Calif., to map a national campaign. Rather than endorse a total ban on genetically modified foods that Greenpeace was pushing, says Wendy Wendlandt, political director of the state Public Interest Research Groups, "it was more practical to call for a moratorium until the stuff is safety tested and labeled, and companies are held responsible for any harmful effects."

In May the FDA announced that in the fall it would propose new rules for genetically engineered crops and products. Instead of safety testing, it would require only that companies publicly disclose their new biotech crops before they are planted. Labeling would be voluntary.

The critics' response came last week: a campaign to muster public opposition to the FDA's new rules and to target individual companies and their previous trademarks. The mock advertisements for "Campbull's Experimental Vegetable Soup," with the advisory, "Warning: This Product Is Untested," is only the first salvo. Some 18 other brand-name U.S. companies are on a tentative hit list, including General Mills, Coca-Cola and Kraft.

Will the companies succumb to the pressure, as they have in Europe? As of last week, Campbell claimed to be unfazed, with few customers registering concern, despite the spotlight. Even at the San Francisco rally, there was some ambivalence. "I may not eat Campbell's soup as much," offered Shanae Walls, 19, a student at Contra Costa College who was there with her Environmental Science and Thought class. But as the protesters tossed products from Pepperidge Farm—a Campbell subsidiary—into the toxic-waste bin, she had second thoughts. "I love those cookies," she said wistfully. "That might take some time."

THE GLOBAL FOOD FIGHT

1 BRUSSELS, 1998 France, Italy, Greece, Denmark and Luxembourg team up to block introduction of all new GM products in the European Union—including those approved by E.U. scientific advisory committees and even a few developed in these five countries. Several E.U. countries have also banned the importation and use of 18 GM crops and foods approved before the blockade went into effect. New safety rules could eventually break this logjam.

2 SEATTLE, NOVEMBER 1999 Taking to the streets to protest the spread of "Frankenfoods," among other issues, demonstrators trying to disrupt the World Trade Organization summit are tear-gassed and beaten by police.

3 MIDWESTERN U.S., 1999 A coalition of agricultural groups calls for a freeze on government approval of new GM seeds in light of dwindling markets in anti-GM European countries. Planting of GM corn drops from 25 million acres (10 million hectares) in 1999 to 19.9 million acres (8 million hectares) in 2000.

4 MONTREAL, JANUARY 2000 130 nations, including Mexico, Australia and Japan, sign the Cartagena Protocol on Biosafety, which requires an exporting country to obtain permission from an importing country before shipping GM seeds and organisms and to label such shipments with warnings that they "may contain" GM products.

Key

- *Strongly in favor of GM foods*
- *Somewhat in favor of GM foods*
- *Opposed to GM foods*

Canada

POPULATION 31,147,000

ATTITUDE Generally pro, though consumers are wary

REASON Second biggest producer of GM products, after the U.S., and a major food exporter.

Grains make up 24.8% of diet

U.S.

POPULATION 278,357,000

ATTITUDE Cautiously pro

REASON As a major food exporter and home to giant agribiotech businesses, led by Monsanto, the country stands to reap huge profits from GM foods.

Grains make up 23.6% of diet

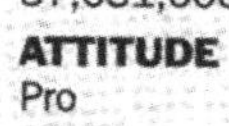

Argentina

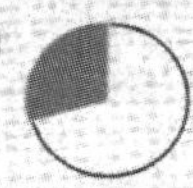

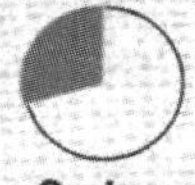

POPULATION 37,031,000

ATTITUDE Pro

REASON Third largest producer of biotech crops in the world, after the U.S. and Canada.

Grains make up 29.5% of diet

Brazil

POPULATION 170,116,000

ATTITUDE Very cautiously pro

REASON The country is eager to participate in the potentially profitable biotech revolution but is worried about alienating anti-GM customers in Europe.

Grains make up 30.9% of diet

Britain

POPULATION 58,830,000

ATTITUDE Strongly anti

REASON "Mad cow" disease in beef and a report that GM potatoes caused immune-system damage in rats have alarmed most Brits. Markets ban GM foods, and experiments are tightly controlled.

Grains make up 22.8% of diet

France

POPULATION 59,079,000

ATTITUDE Strongly anti

REASON Like Britain, France has been stung by incidents with tainted food. Its attitude is also colored by hostility to U.S. imports and a desire to protect French farmers.

Grains make up 24.3% of diet

—By Michael D. Lemonick. With reporting by Yudhijit Bhattacharjee and Max Rust/New York, with other bureaus

(CONTINUED)

(CONTINUED)

5 COLOMBO, SRI LANKA, FEBRUARY 2000
The government bans GM foods pending further research.
6 RIO DE JANEIRO, FEBRUARY 2000
A U.S. ship suspected of carrying GM corn is turned away by a Brazilian meat producer. The nation as a whole prohibits the importation of GM foods unless they've been proved safe; earlier this month, a federal court upheld that policy despite a statement from the Cabinet that Brazil "cannot be left out of this technology."
7 NEW DELHI, MAY 2000
The government approves large-scale field trials of Bollgard, Monsanto's pest-resistant GM cotton. Two years earlier, activists and angry farmers had burned fields planted with transgenic cotton.
8 BEIJING, JULY 2000
While still receptive to GM foods, the government passes a law requiring the labeling of GM seeds.
9 TOKYO, 2001
New rules will go into effect requiring GM foods to be labeled as such and tested for safety—although the government is also promoting the export of Japanese GM expertise and technology to Third-World nations. Meanwhile, a small anti-GM movement is growing stronger.
7
8
9
5
India
POPULATION
1,013,661,000
ATTITUDE
Cautiously pro
REASON
Needs to find the most efficient ways to feed and clothe its enormous, rapidly growing population.
Grains make up 62.6% of diet
China
POPULATION
1,277,558,000
ATTITUDE
Pro
REASON
Needs to feed and clothe a large population; rural hunger brought about a revolution 50 years ago, and leaders don't want another one.
Grains make up 54.7% of diet
Japan
POPULATION
126,714,000
ATTITUDE
Cautiously pro, but heading toward anti
REASON
Japan has a national obsession with food quality, enhanced by several recent food-poisoning incidents, and a tradition of protectionism for Japanese farmers.
Grains make up 40.7% of diet

Indeed, the benefits have seemed small—until golden rice came along to suggest otherwise. Golden rice is clearly not the moral equivalent of Roundup Ready beans. Quite the contrary, it is an example—the first compelling example—of a genetically engineered crop that may benefit not just the farmers who grow it but also the consumers who eat it. In this case, the consumers include at least a million children who die every year because they are weakened by vitamin-A deficiency and an additional 350,000 who go blind.

No wonder the biotech industry sees golden rice as a powerful ally in its struggle to win public acceptance. No wonder its critics see it as a cynical ploy. And no wonder so many of those concerned about the twin evils of poverty and hunger look at golden rice and see reflected in it their own passionate conviction that genetically engineered crops can be made to serve the greater public good—that in fact such crops have a critical role to play in feeding a world that is about to add to its present population of 6 billion. As former President Jimmy Carter put it, "Responsible biotechnology is not the enemy; starvation is."

Indeed, by the year 2020, the demand for grain, both for human consumption and for animal feed, is projected to go up by nearly half, while the amount of arable land available to satisfy that demand will not only grow much more slowly but also, in some areas, will probably dwindle. Add to that the need to conserve overstressed water resources and reduce the use of polluting chemicals, and the enormity of the challenge becomes apparent. In order to meet it, believes Gordon Conway, the agricultural ecologist who heads the Rockefeller Foundation, 21st century farmers will have to draw on every arrow in their agricultural quiver, including genetic engineering. And contrary to public perception, he says, those who have the least to lose and the most to gain are not well-fed Americans and Europeans but the hollow-bellied citizens of the developing world.

GOING FOR THE GOLD

IT WAS IN THE LATE 1980S, AFTER HE became a full professor of plant science at the Swiss Federal Institute of Technology, that Ingo Potrykus started to think about using genetic engineering to improve the nutritional qualities of rice. He knew that of some 3 billion people who depend on rice as their major staple, around 10% risk some degree of vitamin-A deficiency and the health problems that result. The reason, some alleged, was an overreliance on rice ushered in by the green revolution. Whatever its cause, the result was distressing: these people were so poor that they ate a few bowls of rice a day and almost nothing more.

The problem interested Potrykus for a number of reasons. For starters, he was attracted by the scientific challenge of transferring not just a single gene, as many had already done, but a group of genes that represented a key part of a biochemical pathway. He was also motivated by complex emotions, among them empathy. Potrykus knew more than most what it meant not to have enough to eat. As a child growing up in war-ravaged Germany, he and his brothers were often so desperately hungry that they ate what they could steal.

Around 1990, Potrykus hooked up with Gary Toenniessen, director of food security for the Rockefeller Foundation. Toenniessen had identified the lack of beta-carotene in polished rice grains as an appropriate target for gene scientists like Potrykus to tackle because it lay beyond the ability of traditional plant breeding to address. For while rice, like other green plants, contains light-trapping beta-carotene in its external tissues, no plant in the entire *Oryza* genus—as far as anyone knew—produced beta-carotene in its endosperm (the starchy interior part of the rice grain that is all most people eat).

It was at a Rockefeller-sponsored meeting that Potrykus met the University of Freiburg's Peter Beyer, an expert on the beta-carotene pathway in daffodils. By combining their expertise, the two scientists figured, they might be able to remedy this unfortunate oversight in nature. So in 1993, with some $100,000 in seed money from the Rockefeller Foundation, Potrykus and Beyer launched what turned into a seven-year, $2.6 million project, backed also by the Swiss government and the European Union. "I was in a privileged situation," reflects Potrykus, "because I was able to operate without industrial support. Only in that situation can you think of giving away your work free."

That indeed is what Potrykus announced he and Beyer planned to do. The two scientists soon discovered, however, that giving away golden rice was not going to be as easy as they thought. The genes they transferred and the bacteria they used to transfer those genes were all encumbered by patents and proprietary rights. Three months ago, the two scientists struck a deal with AstraZeneca, which is based in London and holds an exclusive license to one of the genes Potrykus and Beyer used to create golden rice. In exchange for commercial marketing rights in the U.S. and other affluent markets, AstraZeneca agreed to lend its financial muscle and legal expertise to the cause of putting the seeds into the hands of poor farmers at no charge.

No sooner had the deal been made than the critics of agricultural biotechnology erupted. "A rip-off of the public trust," grumbled the Rural Advancement Foundation International, an advocacy group based in Winnipeg, Canada. "Asian farmers get (unproved) genetically modified rice, and AstraZeneca gets the 'gold.'" Potrykus was dismayed by such negative reaction. "It would be irresponsible," he exclaimed, "not to say immoral, not to use biotechnology to try to solve this problem!" But such expressions of good intentions would not be enough to allay his opponents' fears.

WEIGHING THE PERILS

BENEATH THE HYPERBOLIC TALK OF Frankenfoods and Superweeds, even proponents of agricultural biotechnology agree, lie a number of real concerns. To begin with, all foods, including the transgenic foods created through genetic engineering, are potential sources of allergens. That's because the transferred genes contain instructions for making proteins, and not all proteins are equal. Some—those in peanuts, for example—are well known for causing allergic reactions. To many, the possibility that golden rice might cause such a problem seems farfetched, but it nonetheless needs to be considered.

Then there is the problem of "genetic pollution," as opponents of biotechnology term it. Pollen grains from such wind-pollinated plants as corn and canola, for instance, are carried far and wide. To farmers, this mainly poses a nuisance. Transgenic canola grown in one field, for example, can very easily pollinate nontransgenic plants grown in the next. Indeed this is the reason behind the furor that recently erupted in Europe when it was discovered that canola seeds from Canada—unwittingly planted by farmers in England, France, Germany and Sweden—contained transgenic contaminants.

The continuing flap over Bt corn and cotton—now grown not only in the U.S. but also in Argentina and China—has provided more fodder for debate. Bt stands for a common soil bacteria, *Bacillus thuringiensis*, different strains of which produce toxins that target specific insects. By transferring to corn and cotton the bacterial gene responsible for making this toxin, Monsanto and other companies have produced crops that are resistant to the European corn borer and the cotton bollworm. An immediate concern, raised by a number of ecologists, is whether or not widespread planting of these crops will spur the development of resistance to Bt among crop pests. That would be unfortunate, they point out, because Bt is a safe and effective natural insecticide that is popular with organic farmers.

SQUEEZE ME: Scientists turned off the gene that makes tomatoes soft and squishy

Even more worrisome are ecological concerns. In 1999 Cornell University entomologist John Losey performed a provocative, "seat-of-the-pants" laboratory experiment. He dusted Bt corn pollen on plants populated by monarch-butterfly caterpillars. Many of the caterpillars died. Could what happened in Losey's laboratory happen in cornfields across the Midwest? Were these lovely butterflies, already under pressure owing to human encroachment on their Mexican wintering grounds, about to face a new threat from high-tech farmers in the north?

The upshot: despite studies pro and con—and countless save-the-monarch protests acted out by children dressed in butterfly costumes—a conclusive answer to this question has yet to come. Losey himself is not yet convinced that Bt corn poses a grave danger to North America's monarch-butterfly population, but he does think the issue deserves attention. And others agree. "I'm not anti biotechnology per se," says biologist Rebecca Goldberg, a senior scientist with the Environmental Defense Fund, "but I would like to have a tougher regulatory regime. These crops should be subject to more careful screening before they are released."

Are there more potential pitfalls? There are. Among other things, there is the possibility that as transgenes in pollen drift, they will fertilize wild plants, and weeds will emerge that are hardier and even more difficult to control. No one knows how common the exchange of genes between domestic plants and their wild relatives really is, but Margaret Mellon, director of the Union of Concerned Scientists' agriculture and biotechnology program, is certainly not alone in thinking that it's high time we find out. Says she: "People should be responding to these concerns with experiments, not assurances."

And that is beginning to happen, although—contrary to expectations—the reports coming in are not necessarily that scary. For three years now, University of Arizona entomologist Bruce Tabashnik has been monitoring fields of Bt cotton that farmers have planted in his state. And in this instance at least, he says, "the environmental risks seem minimal, and the benefits seem great." First of all, cotton is self-pollinated rather than wind-pollinated, so that the spread of the Bt gene is of less concern. And because the Bt gene is so effective, he notes, Arizona farmers have reduced their use of chemical insecticides 75%. So far, the pink bollworm population has not rebounded, indicating that the feared resistance to Bt has not yet developed.

ASSESSING THE PROMISE

ARE THE CRITICS OF AGRICULTURAL biotechnology right? Is biotech's promise nothing more than overblown corporate hype? The papaya growers in Hawaii's Puna district clamor to disagree. In 1992 a wildfire epidemic of papaya ringspot virus threatened to destroy the state's papaya industry; by 1994, nearly half the state's papaya acreage had been infected, their owners forced to seek outside employment. But then help arrived, in the form of a virus-resistant transgenic papaya developed by Cornell University plant pathologist Dennis Gonsalves.

In 1995 a team of scientists set up a field trial of two transgenic lines—UH SunUP and UH Rainbow—and by 1996, the verdict had been rendered. As everyone could see, the nontransgenic plants in the field trial were a stunted mess, and the transgenic plants were healthy. In 1998, after negotiations with four patent holders, the papaya growers switched en masse to the transgenic seeds and reclaimed their orchards. "Consumer acceptance has been great," reports Rusty Perry, who runs a papaya farm near Puna. "We've found that customers are more concerned with how the fruits look and taste than with whether they are transgenic or not."

Viral diseases, along with insect infestations, are a major cause of crop loss in Africa, observes Kenyan plant scientist Florence Wambugu. African sweet-potato fields, for example, yield only 2.4 tons per acre, vs. more than double that in the rest of the world. Soon Wambugu hopes to start raising those yields by introducing a transgenic sweet potato that is resistant to the feathery mottle virus. There really is no other option, explains Wambugu, who currently directs the International Service for the Acquisition of Agri-biotech Applications in Nairobi. "You can't control the virus in the field, and you can't breed in resistance through conventional means."

To Wambugu, the flap in the U.S. and Europe over genetically engineered crops seems almost ludicrous. In Africa, she notes, nearly half the fruit and vegetable harvest is lost because it rots on the way to market. "If we had a transgenic banana that ripened more slowly," she says, "we could have 40% more bananas than now." Wambugu also dreams of getting access to herbicide-resistant crops. Says she: "We could liberate so many people if our crops were resistant to herbicides that we could then spray on the surrounding weeds. Weeding enslaves Africans; it keeps children from school."

In Wambugu's view, there are more benefits to be derived from agricultural biotechnology in Africa than practically anywhere else on the planet—and this may be so. Among the genetic-engineering projects funded by the Rockefeller Foundation is one aimed at controlling striga, a weed that parasitizes the roots of African corn plants. At present there is little farmers can do about striga infestation, so tightly intertwined are the weed's roots with the roots of the corn plants it targets. But scientists have come to understand the source of the problem: corn roots exude chemicals that attract striga. So it may prove possible to identify the genes that are responsible and turn them off.

The widespread perception that agricultural biotechnology is intrinsically inimical to the environment perplexes the Rockefeller Foundation's Conway, who views genetic engineering as an important tool for achieving what he has termed a "doubly green revolution." If the technology can marshal a plant's natural defenses against weeds and viruses, if it can induce crops to flourish with minimal application of chemical fertilizers, if it can make dryland agriculture more productive without straining local water supplies, then what's wrong with it?

Of course, these particular breakthroughs have not happened yet. But as the genomes of major crops are ever more finely mapped, and as the tools for transferring genes become ever more precise, the possibility for tinkering with complex biochemical pathways can be expected to expand rapidly. As Potrykus sees it, there is no question that agricultural biotechnology can be harnessed for the good of humankind. The only question is whether there is the collective will to do so. And the answer may well emerge as the people of the world weigh the future of golden rice.

—With reporting by Simon Robinson/Nairobi

UNIT 3

The Global Environment and Natural Resources Utilization

Unit Selections

8. **The Global Challenge**, Michael H. Glantz
9. **The Energy Question, Again**, Vaclav Smil
10. **Invasive Species: Pathogens of Globalization**, Christopher Bright
11. **We *Can* Build a Sustainable Economy**, Lester R. Brown

Key Points to Consider

- How is the availability of natural resources affected by population growth?
- Do you think that the international community has adequately responded to problems of pollution and threats to our common natural heritage? Why or why not?
- What is the natural resource picture going to look like 30 years from now?
- How is society, in general, likely to respond to the conflicts between economic necessity and resource conservation?
- What is the likely future of energy supplies in both the industrial and the developing world?
- What transformations will societies that are heavy users of fossil fuels have to undergo in order to meet future energy needs?
- Can a sustainable economy be organized and what changes in behavior and values are necessary to accomplish this?

Links: www.dushkin.com/online/
These sites are annotated in the World Wide Web pages.

Friends of the Earth
http://www.foe.co.uk/index.html

National Geographic Society
http://www.nationalgeographic.com

National Oceanic and Atmospheric Administration (NOAA)
http://www.noaa.gov

Public Utilities Commission of Ohio (PUCO)
http://www.puc.state.oh.us/consumer/gcc/index.html

SocioSite: Sociological Subject Areas
http://www.pscw.uva.nl/sociosite/TOPICS/

United Nations Environment Programme (UNEP)
http://www.unep.ch

Beginning in the eighteenth century, the concept of the modern nation-state was initially conceived, and over many generations it evolved to the point where it is now difficult to imagine a world without national governments. These legal entities have been viewed as separate, self-contained units that independently pursue their "national interests." Scholars often described the world as a political community of independent units that interact with each other (a concept that has been described as a billiard ball model).

This perspective of the international community as comprised of self-contained and self-directed units has undergone major rethinking in the past 30 years. One of the reasons for this is the international dimensions of the demands being placed on natural resources. The Middle East, for example, contains a majority of the world's oil reserves. The United States, Western Europe, and Japan are very dependent on this vital source of energy. This unbalanced supply and demand equation has created an unprecedented lack of self-sufficiency for the world's major economic powers.

The increased interdependence of countries is further illustrated by the fact that air and water pollution often do not respect political boundaries. One country's smoke is often another country's acid rain. The concept that independent political units control their own destiny, in short, makes less sense than it may have 100 years ago. In order to more fully understand why this is so, one must first look at how Earth's natural resources are being utilized and how this may be affecting the global environment.

The initial articles in the unit examine the broad dimensions of the uses and abuses of natural resources. The central theme in these articles is whether or not human activity is in fact bringing about fundamental changes in the functioning of Earth's self-regulating ecological systems. In many cases an unsustainable rate of usage is under way, and, as a consequence, an alarming decline in the quality of the natural resource base is taking place.

An important conclusion resulting from this analysis is that contemporary methods of resource utilization often create problems that transcend national boundaries. Global climate changes, for example, will affect everyone, and if these changes are to be successfully addressed, international collaboration will be required. The consequences of basic human activities such as growing and cooking food are profound when multiplied billions of times every day. A single country or even a few countries working together cannot have a significant impact on redressing these problems. Solutions will have to be conceived that are truly global in scope. Just as there are shortages of natural resources, there are also shortages of new ideas for solving many of these problems.

Unit 3 continues by examining specific natural resources. These case studies explore in greater detail new technologies, potential new economic incentives, and the impact that traditional power politics has on how natural resources are developed and for whose benefit.

The unit concludes with a discussion of the issues involved in moving from a perspective of the environment as simply an economic resource to be consumed to a perspective that has been defined as "sustainable development." This change is easily called for, but in fact it goes to the core of social values and basic economic activities. Developing sustainable practices, therefore, is a challenge of unprecedented magnitude.

Nature is not some object "out there" to be visited at a national park. It is the food we eat and the energy we consume. Human beings are joined in the most intimate of relationships with the natural world in order to survive from one day to the next. It is ironic how little time is spent thinking about this relationship. This lack of attention, however, is not likely to continue, for rapidly growing numbers of people and the increased use of energy-consuming technologies are placing unprecedented pressures on Earth's carrying capacity.

Article 8

The Global Challenge

Circulating freely around the planet, the atmosphere and oceans are shared resources whose resiliency is being tested by ever-growing human demands.

MICHAEL H. GLANTZ

The atmosphere and the oceans are fluids that encircle the globe. Their movements can be described in physical and mathematical terms, or even by some popular adages: "what goes up, must come down" and "what goes around, comes around."

The atmosphere and oceans are two of Earth's truly global commons. In cycles that vary from days to centuries to millions of years, air and water circulate interactively around the globe irrespective of national boundaries and territorial claims.

With regard to the first adage, pollutants emitted into the atmosphere must come down somewhere on Earth's surface—unless, like the chlorofluorocarbons (CFCs), they can escape into the stratosphere until they are broken down by the Sun's rays. Depending on the form of the pollutant (gaseous or particulate), its size, or the height at which it has been ejected into the atmosphere, it can stay airborne for short or long periods. So, pollutants expelled into the air in one country and on one continent may make their way to other countries and continents. The same can be said of the various pollutants that are cast into the ocean. "What goes around, comes around" clearly applies to the global commons.

As human demands on the atmosphere and oceans escalate, the pressures on the commons are clearly increasing. Defining the boundaries between acceptable human impacts and crisis impacts is a demanding and rather subjective task.

The Atmosphere

The atmosphere is owned by no nation, but in a sense it belongs to all nations. Several types of human activity interact with geophysical processes to affect the atmosphere in ways that engender crisis situations. The most obvious example of local effects is urban air pollution resulting from automobile emissions, home heating and cooling, and industrial processes. The Denver "brown cloud" is a case in point, as is the extreme pollution in Mexico City. Such pollution can occur within one political jurisdiction or across state, provincial, or international borders. Air pollution is one of those problems to which almost everyone in the urban area contributes.

Acid rain is an example of pollution of a regional atmospheric commons. Industrial processes release pollutants, which can then interact with the atmosphere and be washed out by rainfall. Acid rain has caused the health of forest ecosystems to deteriorate in such locations as the northeastern part of North America, central Europe, and Scandinavia. The trajectories of airborne industrial pollutants moving from highly industrialized areas across these regions have been studied. The data tend to support the contention that while acid rain is a regional commons problem, it is also a problem of global interest.

A nation can put any chemical effluents it deems necessary for its well-being into its own airspace. But then the atmosphere's fluid motion can move those effluents across international borders. The purpose of the tall smokestack, for example, was to put effluents higher into the air, so they would be carried away and dispersed farther from their source. The tall stacks, in essence, turned local air pollution problems into regional ones. In many instances, they converted national pollution into an international problem.

Climate as a Global Commons

There is a difference between the atmosphere as a commons and the climate as a commons. Various societies have emitted a wide range of chemicals into the atmosphere, with little understanding of their potential effects on climate. For example, are industrial processes that produce large amounts of carbon dioxide (which contributes to atmospheric warming) or sulfur dioxide (which contributes to atmospheric cooling and acid rain) altering global climate? There seems to be a growing consensus among scientists that these alterations manifest themselves as regional changes in the frequencies, intensities, and even the location of extreme events such as droughts and floods.

Not all pollutants emitted in the air have an impact on the global climate system. But scientists have long known that some gases can affect global climate patterns by interacting with sunlight or the heat radiated from Earth's surface. Emission of such gases, especially CO_2, can result from human activities such as the burning of fossil fuels, tropical deforestation, and food production processes. The amount of CO_2 in the atmosphere has increased considerably since the mid 1700s and is likely to double the preindustrial level by the year 2050. Carbon dioxide is a highly effective greenhouse gas. Other greenhouse gases emitted to the atmosphere as a result of human activities include CFCs (used as refrigerants, foam-blowing agents, and cleansers for electronic components), nitrous oxide (used in fertilizers), and methane (emitted during rice production). Of these trace gases, the CFCs are produced by industrial processes alone; and others are produced by both industrial and natural processes.

The increase in greenhouse gases during the past two centuries has resulted primarily from industrial processes in which fossil fuels are burned. Thus, a large proportion of the greenhouse gases produced by human activity has resulted from economic development in the industrialized countries (a fact that developing countries are not reluctant to mention when discussing the global warming issue).

National leaders around the globe are concerned about the issue of climate change. Mandatory international limits on the emissions of greenhouse gases could substantially affect their own energy policies. Today, there are scientific and diplomatic efforts to better understand and deal with the prospects of global atmospheric warming and its possible impacts on society. Many countries have, for a variety of motives, agreed that there are reasons to limit greenhouse gas emissions worldwide. National representatives of the Conference of Parties meet each year to address this concern. In the meantime, few countries, if any, want to forgo economic development to avoid a global environmental problem that is still surrounded by scientific uncertainty.

The Oceans

The oceans represent another truly global commons. Most governments have accepted this as fact by supporting the Law of the Sea Treaty, which notes that the seas, which cover almost 70 percent of Earth's surface, are "the common heritage of mankind." In the early 1940s, Athelstan Spilhaus made a projection map that clearly shows that the world's oceans are really subcomponents of one global ocean.

There are at least three commons-related issues concerning the oceans: pollution, fisheries, and sea level. Problems and possible crises have been identified in each area.

The oceans are the ultimate sink for pollutants. Whether they come from the land or the atmosphere, they are likely to end up in the oceans. But no one really owns the oceans, and coastal countries supervise only bits and pieces of the planet's coastal waters. This becomes a truly global commons problem, as currents carry pollutants from the waters of one country into the waters of others. While there are many rules and regulations governing pollution of the oceans, enforcement is quite difficult. Outside a country's 200-mile exclusive economic zone are the high seas, which are under the jurisdiction of no single country.

Bound Together by Air and Water

- "What goes up must come down" describes the fate of most pollutants ejected into the atmosphere. Taller smokestacks were used to assure that the pollutants did not come down "in my backyard."
- Fish stocks that naturally straddle the boundary between a country's protected zone and the open seas are a global resource requiring international protection measures.
- Sea level in all parts of the world would quickly rise some 8 meters (26 feet) if the vast West Antarctic ice sheet broke away and slid into the sea.
- Scientific controversy still surrounds the notion that human activities can produce enough greenhouse gases to warm the global atmosphere.

In many parts of the world, fisheries represent a common property resource. The oceans provide many countries with protein for domestic food consumption or export. Obtaining the same amount of protein from the land would require that an enormous additional amount of the land's surface be put into agricultural production. Whether under the jurisdiction of one country, several countries, or no country at all, fish populations have often been exploited with incomplete understanding of the causes of variability in their numbers. As a result, most fish

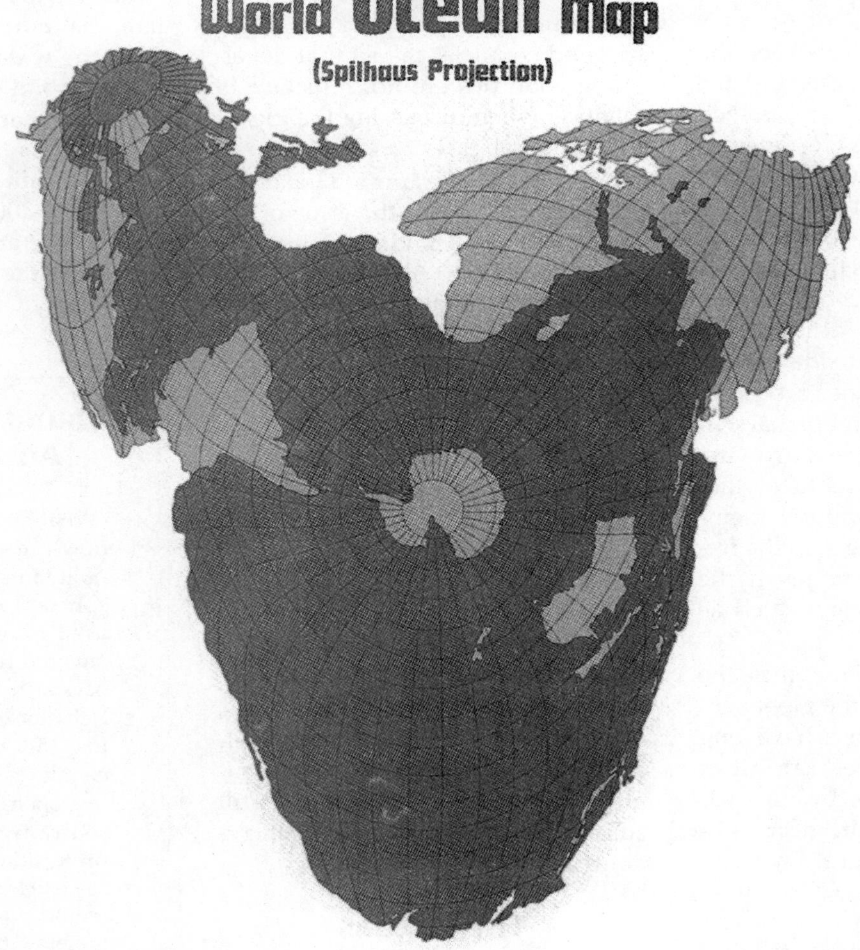

ATHELSTAN SPILHAUS/COURTESY OF CELESTIAL PRODUCTS, PHILMONT, VA.

Our one-ocean world: The oceans are but one body of water, as highlighted by the World Ocean Map developed more than 50 years ago by oceanographer Athelstan Spilhaus.

stocks that have been commercially sought after have collapsed under the combined pressures of natural variability in the physical environment, population dynamics, and fish catches. This is clearly a serious problem; many perceive it to be a crisis.

For example, an area in the Bering Sea known as the "Donut Hole" had, until recently, also been suffering from overexploitation of pollack stocks. In the midst of the Bering Sea, outside the coastal zones and jurisdictions of the United States and Russia, there is an open-access area that is subject to laws related to the high seas, a truly global commons. Fishermen from Japan and other countries were overexploiting the pollack in this area. But these stocks were part of the same population that also lived in the protected coastal waters of the United States and Russia. In other words, the pollack population was a straddling stock—it straddled the border between the controlled coastal waters and the high seas.

To protect pollack throughout the sea by limiting its exploitation, the two coastal states took responsibility for protecting the commons (namely, the Donut Hole) without having to nationalize it. They did so by threatening to close the Bering Sea to "outsiders," if the outsiders were unable to control their own exploitation of the commonly shared pollack stock. There are several other examples of the overexploitation of straddling stocks, such as the recent collapse of the cod fishery along the Georges Bank in the North Atlantic.

Another commons-related issue is the sea level rise that could result from global warming of the atmosphere. Whereas global warming, if it were to occur, could change rainfall and temperature patterns in yet-unknown ways both locally and regionally, sea level rise will occur everywhere, endangering low-lying coastal areas worldwide. Compounding the problem is the fact that the sea is also an attractor of human populations. For example, about 60 percent of the U.S. population lives within a hundred miles of the coast.

In many parts of the world, fisheries represent a common property resource.

This would truly be a global commons problem because *all* coastal areas and adjoining estuaries would suffer from the consequences of global warming. Concern about sea level rise is highest among the world's small island states, many of which (e.g., the Maldives) are at risk of becoming submerged even with a modest increase in sea level. In sum, there are no winners among coastal states if sea level rises.

Antarctica always appears on the list of global commons. Although it is outside the jurisdiction of any country, some people have questioned its classification as a global commons. It is a fixed piece of territory with no indigenous human population, aside from scientific visitors. It does have a clear link to the oceans as a global commons, however. One key concern about global warming is the possible disintegration of the West Antarctic ice sheet. Unlike Arctic sea ice, which sits in water, the West Antarctic ice sheet would cause sea level to rise an estimated eight meters if it broke away and fell into the Southern Ocean. Viewed from this perspective, the continent clearly belongs on the list of global commons. It is up to the global community to protect it from the adverse influences of human activities occurring elsewhere on the globe.

What's the Problem?

Are the changes in the atmosphere and oceans really problems? And if so, are they serious enough to be considered crises?

The consequences of the greenhouse effect are matters that scientists speculate about. But changes in the environment are taking place *now*. These changes are mostly incremental: low-grade, slow-onset, long-term, but gradually accumulating. They can be referred to as "creeping environmental problems." Daily changes in the environment are not noticed, and today's environment is not much different from yesterday's. In 5 or 10 years, however, those incremental changes can mount into a major environmental crisis [see "Creeping Environmental Problems," THE WORLD & I, June 1994, p. 218].

Just about every environmental change featuring human involvement is of the creeping kind. Examples include air pollution, acid rain, global warming, ozone depletion, tropical deforestation, water pollution, and nuclear waste accumulation. For many such changes, the threshold of irreversible damage is difficult to identify until it has been crossed. It seems that we can recognize the threshold only by the consequences that become manifest after we have crossed it. With regard to increasing amounts of atmospheric carbon dioxide, what is the critical threshold beyond which major changes in the global climate system might be expected? Although scientists regularly refer to a doubling of CO_2 from preindustrial levels, the truth of the matter is that a doubling really has little scientific significance except that it has been selected as some sort of marker or milestone.

In 5 or 10 years incremental changes can mount into a major environmental crisis.

Policymakers in industrialized and developing countries alike lack a good process for dealing with creeping environmental changes. As a result, they often delay action on such changes in favor of dealing with issues that seem more pressing. Creeping environmental problems tend to be put on the back burner; that is, they are ignored until they have emerged as full-blown crises. The ways that individuals and societies deal with slow-onset, incremental adverse changes in the environment are at the root of coping effectively with deterioration and destruction of local to global commons.

Societal concerns about human impacts on commonly owned or commonly exploited resources have been recorded for at least 2,500 years. Aristotle, for example, observed "that which is common to the greatest number has the least care bestowed upon it." How to manage a common property resource, whether it is a piece of land, a fish population, a body of water, the atmosphere, or outer space, will likely confound decisionmakers well into the future.

Michael H. Glantz is program director of the Environmental and Societal Impacts Group at the National Center for Atmospheric Research (NCAR) in Boulder, Colorado. NCAR is sponsored by the National Science Foundation.

This article originally appeared in *The World & I*, April 1997, pp. 24-31. Reprinted by permission of *The World & I*, a publication of The Washington Times Corporation.

The Energy Question, Again

"Abundant, inexpensive, and reliable energy is taken for granted, and the citizens of rich countries seem to expect this to continue indefinitely. Reality is different: this veritable fairytale is threatened by many changes—some of which are already upon us, others that are discernible on the horizon."

VACLAV SMIL

The twentieth century was the first era dominated by fossil fuels and electricity, and their vastly expanded supply, lower cost, increasing flexibility of use, and ease of control have created the first high-energy civilization in history. This remarkable increase in power at our fingertips has transformed our world. Mechanization and chemization of agriculture have given us a plentiful and varied food supply: more than a fourfold increase in crop productivity during the twentieth century has been made possible by a roughly 150-fold increase of fossil fuels and electricity used directly and indirectly in global cropping.

Increased energy usage also undergirds longer life expectancies (in excess of 70 years throughout the affluent world), the result of better nutrition and medical advances whose dependence on energy inputs, ranging from food pasteurization to vaccine refrigeration, is little noticed. A reliable electricity supply has also created the first instantaneously interconnected global civilization. And inexpensive energy has allowed an unprecedented degree of personal mobility through mass ownership of cars and frequent air travel.

Although our societies are dependent on incessant flows of commercial energies, provision of these critical inputs is not commensurately valued by the supposedly rational markets. Some days the stockmarket value of corporations such as Microsoft or Oracle can reach levels higher than the entire capitalization of such giant energy-supply companies as PG&E or Consolidated Edison—yet the former enterprises cannot exist without the latter.

If the markets work this way, it is hardly surprising that our dependence on massive energy flows goes largely unnoticed. Abundant, inexpensive, and reliable energy is taken for granted, and the citizens of rich countries seem to expect this to continue indefinitely. Reality is different: this veritable fairytale is threatened by many changes—some of which are already upon us, others that are discernible on the horizon. Consequently, any appraisal of a civilization's outlook must include a closer examination of its changing energy affairs.

THE REVOLUTION IN ENERGY USE

At the beginning of the twentieth century, most people did not use fossil fuels, although in the United States average per capita primary consumption of coal and oil (and some hydroelectricity) already amounted to about 2.5 tons of oil equivalent (TOE). Yet much of this energy was wasted. After subtracting conversion losses—over 99 percent in early carbon-filament lightbulbs, 95 percent in steam locomotives, and about 80 percent in coal stoves—useful energy providing the desired services (light, locomotion, and heat) was less than 0.5 TOE.

At the century's end, the global consumption of primary commercial energies (coal, oil, natural gas, and hydro and nuclear electricity) has increased sixteenfold, with average annual per capita supply of commercial energy more than quadrupling to about 1.4 TOE. The flow of useful energy has increased dramatically because of higher efficiencies in traditional energy converters and new machines and devices introduced during the century. Today's best lighting is almost 20 percent efficient, while converters ranging from large electric motors to natural gas-fired furnaces have efficiencies in excess of 90 percent.

Consequently, affluent countries have experienced eight- to twelvefold increases in the per capita supply of useful energy during the twentieth century, and the gain has been twenty- or even thirtyfold in many low-income countries undergoing rapid modernization. This conservative calculation indicates that the world now has at its disposal about 25 times more useful commercial energy than it did in 1900, or more than eight times as much in per capita terms. And this energy now derives mostly from forms that are much more convenient to use than wood or coal, with hydrocarbons (crude oils and natural gases) supplying roughly two-thirds of the total. In rich countries coal now has just two markets: a small one for the production of metallurgical coke, and a large one for electricity generation.

The expanding use of electricity has been another key mark of twentieth-century progress. In 1900 less than 2 percent of the world's fossil-fuel output was converted to electricity; in 2000 the share surpassed 30 percent. Electricity is the preferred form of energy because of its high efficiency, instant and effortless access, perfect and easily adjustable flow, cleanliness, and silence at the point of use. In addition to revolutionizing industrial production and services, electricity has helped implement profound social changes by easing household chores through mass ownership of various appliances and by allowing instant global communication. And it has become an incredible bargain: after factoring in higher disposable incomes and improved conversion efficiencies, a unit of useful electrical service in the United States is as much as 600 times more affordable than it was a century ago.

Contrasts between energy flows that are now routinely controlled by millions of individuals, especially when compared to the experiences of their great-grandparents, provide more stunning illustrations of the expanded use of energy. In 1900 a fairly affluent American urban housewife could turn on inefficient, low-power bulbs whose power totaled less than 500 watts. Today's all-electric suburban house has scores of lights and appliances whose installed power capacity can exceed 30 kilowatts, a seventy- to eightyfold increase from 1900.

At the beginning of the twentieth century, a farmer holding the reins of two good horses and perched on a steel seat while plowing his field controlled a sustained delivery of no more than 2 horsepower. A hundred years later his grandson driving a large tractor while sitting in an upholstered, elevated, and air-conditioned cabin effortlessly controls more than 300 horsepower. Moreover, in 1900 an engineer operating a transcontinental locomotive controlled no more than about 1 megawatt, or roughly 1,340 horsepower, of steam power as the machine traveled at 60 miles an hour (100 km/h). Today a pilot of a Boeing 747 on the same route merely watches a computerized discharge of about 120 megawatts (more than 160,000 horsepower) as the jumbo jet cruises at 560 miles an hour (900 km/h) some 9 miles (11 km) above the ground.

Reasons for Concern

As the twenty-first century dawns, the last century's focus on achieving greater and more efficient use of energy will give way to heightened concern about global energy matters, especially in the next 10 to 20 years. First is the challenge of rising energy demand, particularly for hydrocarbons and electricity. The 1990s showed that consumption appears to be insatiable even in those rich nations that are already by far the largest users and importers of energy. Between 1989 and 1999, energy consumption rose about 15 percent in the United States, 17 percent in France, and 19 percent in Australia; despite a stagnating, even declining, economy, it expanded 24 percent in Japan. This trend has been driven almost completely by private consumption: industries and services have generally reduced energy use per dollar of their final products, but increased travel, larger homes equipped with more appliances, and higher consumer spending have pushed energy use to record levels.

Although nearly all these countries have low population growth, other realities—including mass immigration to both North America and Europe; profligate, debt-driven spending; and widespread emotional attachment to cars as extensions of personality—will promote higher demand for fuels and electricity. In most of the populous low-income countries whose potential energy demands amount to large multiples of current use, growth in energy consumption has recently been at least as high as, or higher than, that of the richer nations, although they remain far behind in relative consumption. Nothing indicates this better than international comparisons: North America's energy consumption mean is now about 8 TOE per capita, and the European average is approximately 4 TOE—but China's mean is 0.6, India's less than 0.3, and Bangladesh's not even 0.1 TOE. Long-term forecasts of energy use have been notoriously poor, but even conservative predictions see a 50 percent increase in the global primary energy consumption by 2020.

Satisfying the world's energy demand thus will be more challenging than in the past—and the task may become more difficult because of a widely anticipated decline in global crude oil production during the next 20 years, and because unequivocal indications of potentially serious global warming may become apparent. The first scenario would likely lead the Organization of Petroleum Exporting Countries (OPEC) to once again take control of the world oil market, a momentous change with implications ranging from much higher energy prices to the possibility of a dangerous escalation of geopolitical contests in the Middle East. Consequences of planetary climate change attributable largely to the generation of greenhouse gases from the combustion of fossil fuels can be foreseen only in qualitative terms: confident quantification of numerous impacts remains elusive.

Another concern is the absence of any commercially available and effective technical fixes to deal with these challenges: the dual task of securing expanded energy needs while reducing fossil-fuel dependence has no simple solution. Finally, there appears to be both an incomprehensible lack of urgency on the part of policymakers and the public in dealing with these realities and an institutional incapacity to make effective, no-regret decisions and to pursue long-range energy policies.

The affluent, high-energy nations and the low-income, low-energy modernizing countries thus appear to be at major, and very messy, energy crossroads: we obviously cannot proceed as we have for generations, but this retrospection does not point to any obvious, all-embracing solution. Unsure of what combination of new goals to follow, both governments and individuals prefer the delusions of an indefinite extension of the status quo to the pursuit of many effective, readily available measures that could help with the truly global task of ensuring adequate energy supply while minimizing its environmental impacts.

The Coming Oil Crisis

Recent forecasts of an imminent decline of global oil extraction are just the latest additions to a long list of predictions of the end of the oil era. Previous forecasts proved wrong because the timing of this event depends not only on the little-known quantity of ultimately recoverable crude oil resources but also on the future rates of demand growth, which are determined by a complex interplay of energy substitutions, technical advances, government policies, and environmental considerations. For example, excessive concern about supply would be unnecessary if the gradual decline in production following the not-too distant peak of the global oil output would be more than compensated by cheap natural gas and a rapid diffusion of photovoltaics, which directly convert solar radiation to electricity. But natural gas may not be available for all desired substitutions, its prices are bound to increase, and photovoltaics are still far from being in the mainstream of commercial energy supply.

Unfortunately, several trends point to high probability of yet another oil crisis whose impact may be even greater than that of the oil crisis of 1973–1974 (OPEC's quintupling of prices from about $2 a barrel to just over $11 a barrel) and 1979–1980 (when the Iranian monarchy's 1979 collapse drove average prices up to $35 a barrel by 1981). OPEC's powers eventually were undercut by reduced energy consumption in rich countries and by the development of new, non-OPEC supplies. The cartel produced about 56 percent of all crude oil in 1973—but only 29 percent by 1985. Both these trends have changed. Global crude oil demand rose nearly 12 percent during the 1990s, and modernizing countries currently are putting a new strain on the export market. China, for decades self-sufficient in oil (and even a small oil exporter), became a net importer of petroleum and refined products in 1993; its imports in 2000 nearly doubled to 70 million tons, and conservative forecasts see purchases of 100 million tons by 2005 (only the United States and Japan would be larger oil importers).

Not surprisingly, OPEC's share of global crude oil output is back to over 40 percent, and increased extraction aimed at a temporary stabilization of rising prices, the absence of any major new non-OPEC supplies ready for immediate production, and the collapse of extraction in the countries of the former Soviet Union (by 2000 their 20 percent share of the world output had been halved) make it very likely that OPEC's share of the world oil market will once again rise above 50 percent before 2010 (the cartel expects at least 46 percent by that time). Of even greater concern is the increasing share of OPEC exports that will be coming from its Middle Eastern member states, all Muslim and most either overtly anti-Western or only opportunistically friendly.[1] The stage thus is being set for a third round of sudden oil price increases and their unpredictable economic and geopolitical consequences. Recent increases in crude oil to almost $40 a barrel can be seen as a mere trial run of developments to come.

A No-Regret Strategy

It now appears increasingly unlikely that even an unlimited flow of cheap oil or inexpensive natural gas would allow the multiplication of future fossil-fuel use comparable to twentieth-century expansion. Although the complexities of global climate change preclude any confident quantitative forecasts, rising atmospheric levels of anthropogenic greenhouse gases may already be changing the earth's climate—and global warming conceivably could increase at an unprecedented rate during the twenty-first century, resulting in an unpredictable range of biospheric, economic, social, and political impacts.

These inherent uncertainties have made it easy to turn the debate about global climate change into pointless arguments about the actual extent and rate of future warming and about the magnitude of net losses (or even benefits) arising from that change. This is a counterproductive approach. Faced with such uncertainties, the only responsible way to act is as risk minimizers and to take bold steps to reduce greenhouse gas emissions: such a course makes perfect sense even if global warming eventually did not to occur, or if it proved to be a tolerable change. The no-regret strategy of reduced energy consumption in production and households, more efficient fossil-fuel use, the substitution of coal with natural gases, and the introduction of appropriate nonfossil-fuel conversions would cut greenhouse gas emissions and reduce photochemical smog, acid deposition, water pollution, and land degradation.

The high frequency and high levels of photochemical smog that now prevail in all the world's large cities—Atlanta or Athens, Bangkok or Beijing, Taipei or Toronto—have effects that have spilled to surrounding regions. High levels of ozone, the most aggressive oxidant in photochemical smog, have contributed to the worldwide epidemic of asthma and to higher respiratory mortality; ozone also has reduced crop yields, especially in the United States and China.

During the past two decades, emissions of acidifying sulfur and nitrogen oxides have been reduced (but far from eliminated) in North America and Europe, but they are increasing in Asia. Growing tanker shipments of crude oil, drilling for and refining hydrocarbons, coal mining, and thermal-electricity generation all result in water pollution. Surface extraction of coal, and infrastructures of fossil-fuel transportation and processing (tanker ports, oil storages, pipelines, refineries, power plants, high-voltage lines) also claim a great deal of land.

A no-regret strategy of reducing our fossil-fuel dependence would ease all these burdens. But despite the potentially immense and long-lasting consequences of global climate change and regardless of the undeniable benefits of reduced smog, acid deposition, and water and land degradation, inadequate progress has been made in this direction. The United States, the world's largest energy consumer, will not meet its Kyoto Treaty obligations requiring it to cut its carbon dioxide output to 7 percent below the 1990 level (this treaty requires the wealthy nations to cut their carbon dioxide emissions below their 1990 levels by 2007). And China, with its modernizing aspirations, refuses to sign any agreement limiting its expansion of fossil-fuel consumption. Two reasons explain this lack of commitment. First, there is no simple, single solution to this challenge of reducing emissions; and there has been an inexplicable absence of determination and commitment to pursue even those obviously effective steps that rely on well-known techniques, proper pricing (heavy subsidies have been common), and effective legislative measures.

IS THERE A FIX?

None of the alternatives to fossil fuels that were extolled during the second half of the twentieth century as perfect solutions to our future energy needs has fulfilled its early promise. Most notably, between the mid-1950s and the early 1970s, many experts were convinced that by 2000 the world's energy use would be dominated by inexpensive nuclear electricity. The nuclear power industry, however, has undergone a dramatic devolution in all but one of the countries that pioneered its rise. Weaker post-1975 demand for electricity, runaway construction costs, safety concerns, and the unresolved problem of long-term disposal of radioactive wastes gradually ended the industry's growth. Public perception of intolerable risks was sealed by the core meltdown and the release of radioactivity during the 1986 disaster at the nuclear power plant in Chernobyl in the former Soviet Union. Although nuclear fission produced about 17 percent of global electricity by 2000 (22 percent in the United States, 70 percent in France), prospects for any major expansion outside China, and perhaps Japan, are very unlikely.

Nor have the "soft" energy sources—small-scale, decentralized conversions of solar radiation (mostly by using photovoltaic cells), biomass (into both liquid and gaseous fuels), and wind, ocean wave, and water flows—made the decisive difference promised by their advocates, who were opposed to nuclear power and fossil fuels. In the United States, these renewable, small-scale energy conversions (excluding large-scale hydro generation) supplied less than 4 percent of all primary energy use during the late 1990s. It is difficult to envisage a scenario where their share would go up four- or fivefold to 15–20 percent during the next two decades.

The United States now imports more than 20 percent of its total primary energy use, and almost 60 percent of all liquid fuels.

Prospects for major contributions by soft-energy sources in populous low-income countries are no brighter as rapid urbanization and industrialization of those nations require much-expanded large-scale supplies for the still-growing megacities of 10 to 20 million people, be they Beijing and Cairo, or Mexico City and New Delhi. And it remains highly uncertain how much and how fast large cities will be able to relieve their most pressing environmental problem—high levels of photochemical smog, which causes higher morbidities and mortalities and increases damage to crops and materials—through mass diffusion of low- or non-polluting vehicles.

This technical fix, too, has been tantalizingly close on the approximately ten-year—but always receding—horizon. At least one thing now appears clear: electric cars, promoted as the best solution just a few years ago, have fallen out of favor, and fuel-cell vehicles are now seen as the better option. Although various fuels are under consideration (gasoline, methanol, and hydrogen fuel cells), the initial operating costs of hydrogen-based transportation will be very high, and it is unclear how competitive these cars will be with the already available high-efficiency hybrid drives.

NOT ACTING WITH FORESIGHT

Nearly 30 years ago, the Nixon administration came up with Project Independence, which aimed to make the United States self-sufficient in energy by the 1980s. Unrealistic as that plan was (the United States now imports more than 20 percent of its total primary energy use, and almost 60 percent of all liquid fuels), its framers at least tried to look well ahead. Higher energy prices were the main driving force, but legislative changes of the 1970s were not insignificant. These included better building codes reduced energy consumption in housing, and mandated limits of minimum car-fleet performance—corporate automotive fuel efficiency (CAFE) standards—that more than doubled the average United States rate from just 13.4 miles per gallon (MPG) in 1973 to 27.5 MPG in 1985.

These measures helped break OPEC's power, but the resulting slide in crude oil prices almost instantly stopped any serious effort to shape long-range American energy consumption. CAFE has remained at 27.5 MPG for the past 15 years—and that rate does not apply to sport utility vehicles (SUVs), which are classified as light trucks and commonly get less than 20 MPG. Why is SUV-obsessed America surprised when its falling oil output (down about 15 percent during the 1990s) and the rising gasoline demand (up about 7 percent since 1989) has, as it had to, bumped into OPEC's production ceiling and led to more than a 50 percent increase in gasoline prices in a matter of months?

Perhaps the most touching outcome of this situation was seeing President Bill Clinton beg "friendly" OPEC nations to boost their oil output, and hearing assorted members of Congress talk about the need for long-term energy policy—after the huge SUVs were allowed to gain more than half of the new car market. This absence of any rational policymaking is particularly regrettable in view of what could have been accomplished. Continuation of the 1973–1985 CAFE trend would have by now lifted the rate above 40 MPG—and this performance would still be far below the best technical capacity: the hybrid Honda Insight now delivers 61 MPG in the city and 70 MPG on the highway. Incremental progress to about 40 MPG would have been enough to halve United States crude oil imports and save at least $30 billion annually while greatly reducing photochemical smog and lowering carbon dioxide emissions.

Constructing catastrophic scenarios is easy, and, unfortunately, a combination of relatively rapid anthropogenic global warming, declining global crude oil production, rising rivalry over access to Middle Eastern hydrocarbons, the inability of new energy conversions to fill the growing oil gap, and the continuing refusal to pursue rational long-term solutions makes global warming an uncomfortably high probability. Fortunately, the outcome is still open. Will we act only when energy prices are soaring (as we did between 1973 and 1985), or when an acutely demonstrable environmental risk arises (as we did after the discovery of Antarctic ozone hole when we banned the use of chlorofluorocarbons)? Can only such drastic realities stimulate action—or will we adopt all those readily available, common-sense solutions as a matter of determined, long-range, no-regret energy policy? The fortunes of modern civilization will depend on this choice.

NOTE

1. OPEC states include Saudi Arabia, Kuwait, Iraq, Iran, Qatar, the United Arab Emirates, Libya, Algeria, Nigeria, Venezuela, and Indonesia.

VACLAV SMIL *is Distinguished Professor at the University of Manitoba and the author, most recently, of* Energies *(Cambridge, Mass.: MIT Press, 1997) and* Feeding the World *(Cambridge, Mass.: MIT Press, 2000).*

Invasive Species: Pathogens of Globalization

by Christopher Bright

World trade has become the primary driver of one of the most dangerous and least visible forms of environmental decline: Thousands of foreign, invasive species are hitch-hiking through the global trading network aboard ships, planes, and railroad cars, while hundreds of others are traveling as commodities. The impact of these bioinvasions can now be seen on every landmass, in nearly all coastal waters (which comprise the most biologically productive parts of the oceans), and probably in most major rivers and lakes. This "biological pollution" is degrading ecosystems, threatening public health, and costing billions of dollars annually. Confronting the problem may now be as critical an environmental challenge as reducing global carbon emissions.

Despite such dangers, policies aimed at stopping the spread of invasive "exotic" species have so far been largely ineffective. Not only do they run up against far more powerful policies and interests that in one way or another encourage invasion, but the national and international mechanisms needed to control the spread of non-native species are still relatively undeveloped. Unlike chemical pollution, for instance, bioinvasion is not yet a working category of environmental decline within the legal culture of most countries and international institutions.

In part, this conceptual blindness can be explained by the fact that even badly invaded landscapes can still look healthy. It is also a consequence of the ancient and widespread practice of introducing exotic species for some tangible benefit: A bigger fish makes for better fishing, a faster-growing tree means more wood. It can be difficult to think of these activities as a form of ecological corrosion—even if the fish or the tree ends up demolishing the original natural community.

The increasing integration of the world's economies is rapidly making a bad situation even worse. The continual expansion of world trade—in ways that are not shaped by any real understanding of their environmental effects—is causing a degree of ecological mixing that appears to have no evolutionary precedent. Under more or less natural conditions, the arrival of an entirely new organism was a rare event in most times and places. Today it can happen any time a ship comes into port or an airplane lands. The real problem, in other words, does not lie with the exotic species themselves, but with the economic system that is continually showering them over the Earth's surface. Bioinvasion has become a kind of globalization disease.

They Came, They Bred, They Conquered

Bioinvasion occurs when a species finds its way into an ecosystem where it did not evolve. Most of the time when this happens, conditions are not suitable for the new arrival, and it enjoys only a brief career. But in a small percentage of cases, the exotic finds everything it needs—and nothing capable of controlling it. At the very least, the invading organism is liable to suppress some native species by consuming resources that they would have used instead. At worst, the invader may rewrite some basic ecosystem "rules"—checks and balances that have developed between native species, usually over many millennia.

Although it is not always easy to discern the full extent of havoc that invasive species can wreak upon an ecosystem, the resulting financial damage is becoming increasingly difficult to ignore. Worldwide, the losses to agriculture might be anywhere from $55 billion to nearly $248 billion annually. Researchers at Cornell University recently concluded that bioinvasion might be costing the United States alone as much as $123 billion per year. In South and Central America, the growth of specialty export crops—upscale vegetables and fruits—has spurred the spread of whiteflies, which are capable of transmitting at least 60 plant viruses. The spread of these viruses has forced the abandonment of more than 1 million hectares of cropland in South America. In the wetlands of northern Nigeria, an exotic cattail is strangling rice paddies, ruining fish habitats, and slowly choking off the Hadejia-Nguru river system. In southern India, a tropical American shrub, the bush morning glory, is causing similar chaos throughout the basin of the Cauvery, one of the region's biggest rivers. In the late 1980s, the accidental release into the Black Sea of *Mnemiopsis leidyi*—a comb jelly native to the east coast of the Americas—provoked the collapse of the already highly stressed Black Sea fisheries, with estimated financial losses as high as $350 million.

Controlling invasive species is difficult enough, but the bigger problem is preventing the machinery of the world trading system from releasing them in the first place.

Controlling such exotics in the field is difficult enough, but the bigger problem is preventing the machinery of the world trading system from releasing them in the first place. That task is becoming steadily more formidable as the trading system continues to grow. Since 1950, world trade has expanded sixfold in terms of value. More important in terms of potential invasions is the vast increase in the volume of goods traded. Look, for instance, at the ship, the primary mechanism of trade—80 percent of the world's goods travel by ship for at least part of their journey from manufacturer to consumer. From 1970 to 1996, the volume of seaborne trade nearly doubled.

Ships, of course, have always carried species from place to place. In the days of sail, shipworms bored into the wooden hulls, while barnacles and seaweeds attached themselves to the sides. A small menagerie of other creatures usually took up residence within these "fouling communities." Today, special paints and rapid crossing times have greatly reduced hull fouling, but each of the 28,700 ships in the world's major merchant fleets represents a honeycomb of potential habitats for all sorts of life, both terrestrial and aquatic.

The most important of these habitats lies deep within a modern ship's plumbing, in the ballast tanks. The ballast tanks of a really big ship—say, a supertanker—may contain more than 200,000 cubic meters of water—equivalent to 2,000 Olympic-sized swimming pools. When those tanks are filled, any little creatures in the nearby water or sediment may suddenly become inadvertent passengers. A few days or weeks later, when the tanks are discharged at journey's end, they may become residents of a coastal community on the other side of the world. Every year, these artificial ballast currents move some 10 billion cubic meters of water from port to port. Every day, some 3,000 to 10,000 different species are thought to be riding the ballast currents. The result is a creeping homogenization of estuary and bay life. The same creatures come to dominate one coastline after another, eroding the biological diversity of the planet's coastal zones—and jeopardizing their ecological stability.

Some pathways of invasion extend far beyond ships. Another prime mechanism of trade is the container: the metal box that has revolutionized the transportation of just about every good not shipped in bulk. The container's effect on invasion ecology has been just as profound. For centuries, shipborne exotics were largely confined to port areas—but no longer. Containers move from ship to harbor crane to the flatbed of a truck or railroad car and then on to wherever a road or railroad leads. As a result, all sorts of stowaways that creep aboard containers often wind up far inland. Take the Asian tiger mosquito, for example, which can carry dengue fever, yellow fever, and encephalitis. The huge global trade in containers of used tires—which are, under the right conditions, an ideal mosquito habitat—has dispersed this species from Asia and the Indo-Pacific into Australia, Brazil, the eastern United States, Mozambique, New Zealand, Nigeria, and southern Europe. Even packing material within containers can be a conduit for exotic species. Untreated wood pallets, for example, are to forest pests what tires are to mosquitoes. One creature currently moving along this pathway is the Asian long-horn beetle, a wood-boring insect from China with a lethal appetite for deciduous trees. It has turned up at more than 30 locations around the United States and has also been detected in Great Britain. The only known way to eradicate it is to cut every tree suspected of harboring it, chip all the wood, and burn all the chips.

As other conduits for global trade expand, so does the potential for new invasions. Air cargo service, for example, is building a global network of virtual canals that have great potential for transporting tiny, short-lived creatures such as microbes and insects. In 1989, only three airports received more than 1 million tons of cargo; by 1996, there were 13 such airports. Virtually everywhere you look, the newly constructed infrastructure of the global economy is forming the groundwork for an ever-greater volume of biological pollution.

The Global Supermarket

Bioinvasion cannot simply be attributed to trade in general, since not all trade is "biologically dirty." The natural resource industries—especially agriculture, aquaculture, and forestry—are causing a disproportionate share of the problem. Certain trends within each of these industries are liable to exacerbate the invasion pressure. The migration of crop pests can be attributed, in part, to a global agricultural system that has become increasingly uniform and integrated. (In China, for example, there were about 10,000 varieties of wheat being grown at mid-century; by

1970 there were only about 1,000.) Any new pest—or any new form of an old pest—that emerges in one field may eventually wind up in another.

The key reason that South America has suffered so badly from white-flies, for instance, is because a pesticide-resistant biotype of that fly emerged in California in the 1980s and rapidly became one of the world's most virulent crop pests. The fly's career illustrates a common dynamic: A pest can enter the system, disperse throughout it, and then develop new strains that reinvade other parts of the system. The displacement of traditional developing-world crop varieties by commercial, homogenous varieties that require more pesticide, and the increasing development of pesticide resistance among all the major pest categories—insects, weeds, and fungi—are likely to boost this trend.

Similar problems pertain to aquaculture—the farming and exporting of fish, shellfish, and shrimp. Partly because of the progressive depletion of the world's most productive fishing grounds, aquaculture is a booming business. Farmed fish production exceeded 23 million tons by 1996, more than triple the volume just 12 years before. Developing countries in particular see aquaculture as a way of increasing protein supply.

But many aquaculture "crops" have proved very invasive. In much of the developing world, it is still common to release exotic fish directly into natural waterways. It is hardly surprising, then, that some of the most popular aquaculture fish have become true cosmopolitans. The Mozambique tilapia, for example, is now established in virtually every tropical and subtropical country. Many of these introductions—not just tilapia, but bass, carp, trout, and other types of fish—are implicated in the decline of native species. The constant flow of new introductions catalogued with such enthusiasm in the industry's publications are a virtual guarantee that tropical freshwater ecosystems are unraveling beneath the surface.

Aquaculture is also a spectacularly efficient conduit of disease. Perhaps the most virulent set of wildlife epidemics circling the Earth today involves shrimp production in the developing world. Unlike fish, shrimp are not a subsistence crop: They are an extremely lucrative export business that has led to the bulldozing of many tropical coasts to make way for shrimp ponds. One of the biggest current developments is an Indonesian operation that may eventually cover 200,000 hectares. A horde of shrimp pathogens—everything from viruses to protozoa—is chasing these operations, knocking out ponds, and occasionally ruining entire national shrimp industries: in Taiwan in 1987, in China in 1993, and in India in 1994. Shrimp farming has become, in effect, a form of "managed invasion." Since shrimp are important components of both marine and freshwater ecosystems worldwide, it is anybody's guess at this point what impact shrimpborne pathogens will ultimately have.

Managed invasion is an increasingly common procedure in another big biopolluting industry: forestry. Industrial roundwood production (basically, the cutting of logs for uses other than fuel) currently hovers at around 1.5 billion cubic meters annually, which is more than twice the level of the 1950s. An increasing amount of wood and wood pulp is coming out of tree plantations (not inherently a bad idea, given the rate at which the world is losing natural forests). In North America and Europe, plantation forestry generally uses native species, so the gradation from natural forest to plantation is not usually as stark as it is in developing countries, where exotics are the rule in industrial-plantation development.

For the most part, these developing-country plantations bear about as much resemblance to natural forests as corn fields do to undisturbed prairies. And like corn fields, they are maintained with heavy doses of pesticides and subjected to a level of disturbance—in particular, the use of heavy equipment to harvest the trees—that tends to degrade soil. Some plantation trees have launched careers as king-sized weeds. At least 19 species of exotic pine, for example, have invaded various regions in the Southern Hemisphere, where they have displaced native vegetation and, in some areas, apparently lowered the water tables by "drinking" more water than the native vegetation would consume. Even where the trees have not proved invasive, the exotic plantations themselves are displacing natural forest and traditional forest peoples. This type of tree plantation is almost entirely designed to feed wood to the industrialized world, where 77 percent of industrial roundwood is consumed. As with shrimp production, local ecological health is being sacrificed for foreign currency.

There is another, more poignant motive for the introduction of large numbers of exotic trees into the developing world. In many countries severely affected by forest loss, reforestation is recognized as an important social imperative. But the goal is often nothing more than increasing tree cover. Little distinction is made between plantation and forest or between foreign and native species. Surayya Khatoon, a botanist at the University of Karachi, observes that "awareness of the dangers associated with invasive species is almost nonexistent in Pakistan, where alien species are being planted on a large scale in so-called afforestation drives."

Even international agreements that focus specifically on ecological problems have generally given bioinvasion short shrift.

The industrial sources of biological pollution are very diverse, but they reflect a common mindset. Whether it is a tree plantation, a shrimp farm, or even a bit of landscaping in the back yard, the Earth has become a sort of "species supermarket"; if a species looks good for whatever it is that you have in mind, pull it off the shelf and take it home. The problem is that many of the traits you want the most—adaptability, rapid growth, and easy reproduction—also tend to make the organism a good candidate for invasion.

Launching a Counter-Attack

Since the processes of invasion are deeply embedded in the globalizing economy, any serious effort to root them out will run the risk of exhausting itself. Most industries and policymakers are striving to open borders, not erect new barriers to trade. Moreover, because bioinvasion is not yet an established policy category, jurisdiction over it is generally badly fragmented—or even absent—on both the national and international levels. Most countries have some relevant legislation—laws intended to discourage the movement of crop pests, for example—but very few have any overall legislative authority for dealing with the problem. (New Zealand is the noteworthy exception: Its Biosecurity Act of 1993 and its Hazardous Substances and New Organisms Act of 1996 do establish such an authority.) Although it is true that there are many treaties that bear on the problem in one way or another—23 at least count—there is no such thing as a bioinvasion treaty.

Even agreements that focus specifically on ecological problems have generally given bioinvasion short shrift. Agenda 21, for example—the blueprint for sustainable development that emerged from the 1992 Earth Summit in Rio de Janeiro—reflects little awareness of the dangers of exotic forestry and aquaculture. Among international agencies, only certain types of invasion seem to get much attention. There are treaties—such as the 1951 International Plant Protection Convention—that limit the movement of agricultural pests, but there is currently no clear international mechanism for dealing with ballast water releases. Obviously, in such a context, you need to pick your fights carefully. They have to be important, winnable, and capable of yielding major opportunities elsewhere. The following three-point agenda offers some hope of slowing invasion over the near term.

The first item: Plug the ballast water pathway. As a technical problem, this objective is probably just on the horizon of feasibility, making it an excellent policy target. Strong national and international action could push technologies ahead rapidly. At present, the most effective technique is ballast water exchange, in which the tanks of a ship are pumped out and refilled in the open sea. (Coastal organisms, pumped into the tanks at the ship's last port of call, usually will not survive in the open ocean; organisms that enter the tanks in mid-ocean probably will not survive in the next port of call.) But it can take several days to exchange the water in all of a ship's ballast tanks, so the procedure may not be feasible for every leg of a journey, and the tanks never empty completely. In bad weather, the process can be too dangerous to perform at all. Consequently, other options will be necessary—filters or even toxins (that may not sound very appealing, but some common water treatment compounds may be environmentally sound). It might even be possible to build port-side ballast water treatment plants. Such a mixture of technologies already exists as the standard means of controlling chemical pollution.

This objective is drifting into the realm of legal possibility as well. As of July 1 this year, all ships entering U.S. waters must keep a record of their ballast water management. The United States has also issued voluntary guidelines on where those ships can release ballast water. These measures are a loose extension of the regulations that the United States and Canada have imposed on ship traffic in the Great Lakes, where foreign ballast water release is now explicitly forbidden. In California, the State Water Resources Control Board has declared San Francisco Bay "impaired" because it is so badly invaded—a move that may allow authorities to use regulations written for chemical pollution as a way of controlling ballast water. Australia now levies a small tax on all incoming ships to support ballast water research.

Internationally, the problem has acquired a high profile at the UN International Maritime Organization (IMO), which is studying the possibility of developing a ballast management protocol that would have the force of international law. No decision has been made on the legal mechanism for such an agreement, although the most likely possibility is an annex to MARPOL, the International Convention for the Prevention of Pollution from Ships.

Within the shipping industry, the responses to such proposals have been mixed. Although industry officials concede the problem in the abstract, the prospect of specific regulations has tended to provoke unfavorable comment. After an IMO meeting last year on ballast water management, a spokesperson for the International Chamber of Shipping argued that rigorous ballast exchange would cost the industry millions of dollars a year—and that internationally binding regulations should be avoided in favor of local regulation, wherever particular jurisdictions decide to address the problem. Earlier this year in California, a proposed bill that would have essentially prohibited foreign ballast water release in the state's ports provoked outcries from local port representatives, who argued that such regulations might encourage ship traffic to bypass California ports in favor of the Pacific Northwest or Mexico. Of course, any management strategy is bound to cost something, but the important question is: What impact will this additional cost have? It may not have much impact at all. In Canada, for example, the Vancouver Port Authority reported that its ballast water program has had no detectable effect on port revenues.

The second item on the agenda: Fix the World Trade Organization (WTO) Agreement on the Application of Sanitary and Phytosanitary Measures. This agreement, known as the SPS, was part of the diplomatic package that created the WTO in 1994. The SPS is supposed to promote a common set of procedures for evaluating risks of contamination in internationally traded commodities. The contaminants can be chemical (pesticide residues in food) or they can be living things (Asian longhorn beetles in raw wood).

One of the procedures required by the SPS is a risk assessment, which is supposed to be done before any trade-constricting barriers are imposed to prevent a contaminated good from entering a country. If you want to understand the fundamental flaw in this approach as it applies to bioinvasion, all you have to do is recall the famous observation by the eminent biologist E. O. Wilson: "We dwell on a largely unexplored planet." When it comes to the largest categories of living things—insects, fungi, bacteria, and so on—we have managed to name only a tiny fraction of them, let alone figure out what damage they can cause. Consider, for example, the rough, aggregate risk assessments done by the United States Department of Agriculture (USDA) for wood imported into the United States from Chile, Mexico, and New Zealand. The USDA found dozens of "moderate" and "high" risk pests and pathogens that have the potential for doing economic damage on the order of hundreds of millions of dollars at least—and ecological damage that is incalculable. But even with wide-open thoroughfares of invasion such as these, the SPS requirement in its current form is likely to make preemptive action vulnerable to trade complaints before the WTO.

Another SPS requirement intended to insure a consistent application of standards is that a country must not set up barriers against an organism that is already living within its borders unless it has an "official control program" for that species. This approach is unrealistic for both biological and financial reasons. Thousands of exotic species are likely to have invaded most of the world's countries and not even the wealthiest country could possibly afford to fight them all. Yet it certainly is possible to exacerbate a problem by introducing additional infestations of a pest, or by boosting the size of existing infestations, or even by increasing the genetic vigor of a pest population by adding more "breeding stock." The SPS does not like "inconsistencies"—if you are not controlling a pest, you have no right to object to more of it; if you try to block one pathway of invasion, you had better be trying to block all the equivalent pathways. Such an approach may be theoretically neat, but in the practical matter of dealing with exotics, it is a prescription for paralysis.

In the near term, however, any effort to repair the SPS is likely to be difficult. The support of the United States, a key member of the WTO, will be critical for such reforms. And although the United States has demonstrated a heightened awareness of the problem—as evidenced by President Bill Clinton's executive order to create an Invasive Species Council—it is not clear whether that commitment will be reflected in the administration's trade policy. During recent testimony before Congress, the U.S. Trade Representative's special trade negotiator for agricultural issues warned that the United States was becoming impatient with the "increasing use of SPS barriers as the 'trade barrier of choice.'" In the developing world, it is reasonable to assume that any country with a strong export sector in a natural resource industry would not welcome tougher regulations. Some developed countries, however, may be sympathetic to change. The European Union (EU) has sought very strict standards in its disputes with the United States over bans on beef from cattle fed with growth hormones and on genetically altered foods. It is possible that the EU might be willing to entertain a stricter SPS. The same might be true of Japan, which has attempted to secure stricter testing of U.S. fruit imports.

The third item: Build a global invasion database. Currently, the study of bioinvasion is an obscure and rather fractured enterprise. It can be difficult to locate critical information or relevant expertise. The full magnitude of the issue is still not registering on the public radar screen. A global database would consolidate existing information, presumably into some sort of central research institution with a major presence on the World Wide Web. One could "go" to such a place—either physically or through cyberspace—to learn about everything from the National Ballast Water Information Clearinghouse that the U.S. Coast Guard is setting up, to the database on invasive woody plants in the tropics that is being assembled at the University of Wales. The database would also stimulate the production of new media to encourage additional research and synthesis. It is a telling indication of how fragmented this field is that, after more than 40 years of formal study, it is just now getting its first comprehensive journal: *Biological Invasions*.

Better information should have a number of practical effects. The best way to control an invasion—when it cannot be prevented outright—is to go after the exotic as soon as it is detected. An emergency response capability will only work if officials know what to look for and what to do when they find it. But beyond such obvious applications, the database could help bring the big picture into focus. In the struggle with exotics, you can see the free-trade ideal colliding with some hard ecological realities. Put simply: It may never be safe to ship certain goods to certain places—raw wood from Siberia, for instance, to North America. The notion of real, permanent limits to economic activity will for many politicians (and probably some economists) come as a strange and unpalatable idea. But the global economy is badly in need of a large dose of ecological realism. Ecosystems are very diverse and very different from each other. They need to stay that way if they are going to continue to function.

WANT TO KNOW MORE?

Although the scientific literature on bioinvasion is enormous and growing rapidly, most of it is too technical to attract a readership outside the field. For a nontechnical, broad overview of the problem, readers should consult Robert Devine's ***Alien Invasion: America's Battle with Non-Native Animals and Plants*** (Washington: National Geographic Society, 1998) or Christopher Bright's ***Life Out of Bounds: Bioinvasion in a Borderless World*** (New York: W.W. Norton & Company, 1998).

If you have a long-term interest in bioinvasion, you will want to get acquainted with the book that founded the field: Charles Elton's ***The Ecology of Invasions by Animals and Plants*** (London: Methuen, 1958). A historical overview of bioinvasions can be found in Alfred Crosby's book ***Ecological Imperialism: The Biological Expansion of Europe, 900–1900*** (Cambridge: Cambridge University Press, 1986).

Many studies focus on invasion of particular regions. The focus can be very broad, as in P. S. Ramakrishnan, ed., ***Ecology of Biological Invasions in the Tropics***, proceedings of an international workshop held at Nainital, India, (New Delhi: International Scientific Publications, 1989). Generally, however, the coverage is much narrower, as in Daniel Simberloff, Don Schmitz, and Tom Brown, eds., ***Strangers in Paradise: Impact***

and Management of Nonindigenous Species in Florida (Washington: Island Press, 1997). The other standard research tack has been to look at a particular type of invader. The most accessible results of this exercise are encyclopedic surveys such as Christopher Lever's ***Naturalized Mammals of the World*** (London: Longman, 1985) and his companion volumes on naturalized birds and fish. In the plant kingdom, the genre is represented by Leroy Holm, et al., ***World Weeds: Natural Histories and Distribution*** (New York: John Wiley and Sons, 1997).

There are many worthwhile documents available for anyone who is interested not just in the ecology of invasion, but also in its economic, social, and epidemiological implications. Just about every aspect of the problem is discussed in Odd Terje Sandlund, Peter Johan Schei, and Aslaug Viken, eds., ***Proceedings of the Norway/UN Conference on Alien Species*** (Trondheim: Directorate for Nature Management and Norwegian Institute for Nature Research, 1996). A groundbreaking study of invasion in the United States, with particular emphasis on economic effects, is ***Harmful Nonindigenous Species in the United States*** (Washington: Office of Technology Assessment, September 1993). An assessment of the ballast water problem is available from the National Research Council's Commission on Ships' Ballast Operations' ***Stemming the Tide: Controlling Introductions of Nonindigenous Species by Ships' Ballast Water*** (Washington: National Academy Press, 1996). Readers who are interested in exotic tree plantations as a form of "managed invasion" might look through Ricardo Carrere and Larry Lohmann's ***Pulping the South: Industrial Tree Plantations and the World Paper Economy*** (London: Zed Books, 1996) and the World Rainforest Movement's ***Tree Plantations: Impacts and Struggles*** (Montevideo: WRM, 1999). Unfortunately, there are no analogous studies of shrimp farms.

For links to relevant Web sites, as well as a comprehensive index of related FOREIGN POLICY articles, access **www.foreignpolicy.com.**

Christopher Bright is a research associate at the Worldwatch Institute in Washington, DC, and author of *Life Out of Bounds: Bioinvasion in a Borderless World (New York: W.W. Norton & Company, 1998).*

We *Can* Build a Sustainable Economy

The keys to securing the planet's future lie in stabilizing both human population and climate. The challenges are great, but several trends look promising.

by Lester R. Brown

The world economy is growing faster than ever, but the benefits of this rapid growth have not been evenly distributed. As population has doubled since mid-century and the global economy has nearly quintupled, the demand for natural resources has grown at a phenomenal rate.

Since 1950, the need for grain has nearly tripled. Consumption of seafood has increased more than four times. Water use has tripled. Demand for beef and mutton has tripled. Firewood demand has tripled, lumber demand has more than doubled, and paper demand has gone up sixfold. The burning of fossil fuels has increased nearly fourfold, and carbon emissions have risen accordingly.

These spiraling human demands for resources are beginning to outgrow the earth's natural systems. As this happens, the global economy is damaging the foundation on which it rests.

To build an environmentally sustainable global economy, there are many obstacles, but there are also several promising trends and factors in our favor. One is that we know what an environmentally sustainable economy would look like. In a sustainable economy:

- Human births and deaths are in balance.
- Soil erosion does not exceed the natural rate of new soil formation.
- Tree cutting does not exceed tree planting.
- The fish catch does not exceed the sustainable yield of fisheries.
- The number of cattle on a range does not exceed the range's carrying capacity.
- Water pumping does not exceed aquifer recharge.
- Carbon emissions and carbon fixation are in balance.
- The number of plant and animal species lost does not exceed the rate at which new species evolve.

We know how to build an economic system that will meet our needs without jeopardizing prospects for future generations. And with some trends already headed in the right direction, we have the cornerstones on which to build such an economy.

Stabilizing Population

With population, the challenge is to complete the demographic transition, to reestablish the balance between births and deaths that characterizes a sustainable society. Since populations are rarely ever precisely stable, a stable population is defined here as one with a growth rate below 0.3%. Populations are effectively stable if they fluctuate narrowly around zero.

Thirty countries now have stable populations, including most of those in Europe plus Japan. They provide the solid base for building a world population stabilization effort. Included in the 30 are all the larger industrialized countries of Europe—France, Germany, Italy, Russia, and the United Kingdom. Collectively, these 30 countries contain 819 million people or 14% of humanity. For this goal, one-seventh of humanity is already there.

The challenge is for the countries with the remaining 86% of the world's people to reach stability. The two large nations that could make the biggest difference in this effort are China and the United States. In both, population growth is now roughly 1% per year. If the global food situation becomes desperate, both could reach stability in a decade or two if they decided it were important to do so.

The world rate of population growth, which peaked around 2% in 1970, dropped below 1.6% in 1995. Although the rate is declining, the annual addition is still close to 90 million people per year. Unless populations can be stabilized with demand below the sustainable yield of local ecosystems, these systems will be destroyed. Slowing growth may delay the eventual collapse of ecosystems, but it will not save them.

The European Union, consisting of some 15 countries and containing 360 million people, provides a model for the rest of the world of an environmentally sustainable food/population balance. At the same time that the region has reached zero population growth, movement up the food chain has come to a halt as diets have become saturated with livestock products. The result is that Europe's grain consumption has been stable for close to two decades at just under 160 million tons—a level that is within the region's carrying capacity. Indeed, there is a potential for a small but sustainable export surplus of grain that can help countries where the demand for food has surpassed the carrying capacity of their croplands.

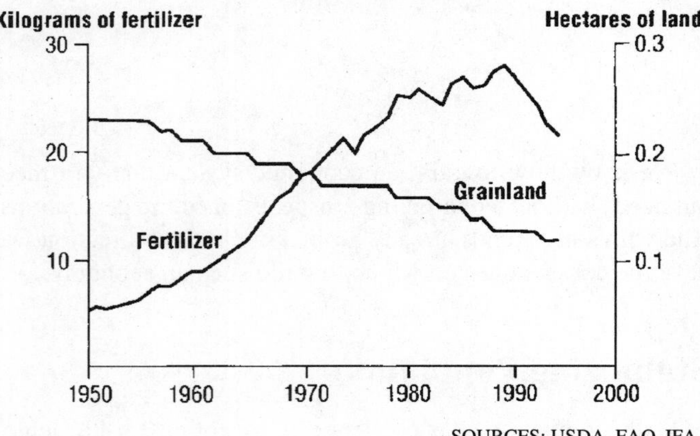

SOURCES: USDA, FAO, IFA

As other countries realize that continuing on their current population trajectory will prevent them from achieving a similar food/ population balance, more and more may decide to do what China has done—launch an all-out campaign to stabilize population. Like China, other governments will have to carefully balance the reproductive rights of the current generation with the survival rights of the next generation.

Very few of the group of 30 countries with stable populations had stability as an explicit policy goal. In those that reached population stability first, such as Belgium, Germany, Sweden, and the United Kingdom, it came with rising living standards and expanding employment opportunities for women. In some of the countries where population has stabilized more recently, such as Russia and other former Soviet republics, the deep economic depression accompanying economic reform has substantially lowered birth rates, much as the Great Depression did in the United States. In addition, with the rising number of infants born with birth defects and deformities since Chernobyl, many women are simply afraid to bear children. The natural decrease of population (excluding migration) in Russia of 0.6% a year—leading to an annual population loss of 890,000—is the most rapid on record.

Not all countries are achieving population stability for the right reasons. This is true today and it may well be true in the future. As food deficits in densely populated countries expand, governments may find that there is not enough food available to import. Between fiscal year 1993 and 1996, food aid dropped from an all-time high of 15.2 million tons of grain to 7.6 million tons. This cut of exactly half in three years reflects primarily fiscal stringencies in donor countries, but also, to a lesser degree, higher grain prices in fiscal 1996. If governments fail to establish a humane balance between their people and food supplies, hunger and malnutrition may raise death rates, eventually slowing population growth.

Some developing countries are beginning to adopt social policies that will encourage smaller families. Iran, facing both land hunger and water scarcity, now limits public subsidies for housing, health care, and insurance to three children per family. In Peru, President Alberto Fujimori, who was elected overwhelmingly to his second five-year term in a predominantly Catholic country, said in his inaugural address in August 1995 that he wanted to provide better access to family-planning services for poor women. "It is only fair," he said, "to disseminate thoroughly the methods of family planning to everyone."

Stabilizing Climate

With climate, as with population, there is disagreement on the need to stabilize. Evidence that atmospheric carbon-dioxide levels are rising is clear-cut. So, too, is the greenhouse effect that these gases produce in the atmosphere. That is a matter of basic physics. What is debatable is the rate at which global temperatures will rise and what the precise local effects will be. Nonetheless, the consensus of the mainstream scientific community is that there is no alternative to reducing carbon emissions.

How would we phase out fossil fuels? There is now a highly successful "phase out" model in the case of chlorofluorocarbons (CFC's). After two British scientists discovered the "hole" in the ozone layer over Antarctica and published their findings in *Nature* in May 1985, the international community convened a conference in Montreal to draft an agreement designed to reduce CFC production sharply. Subsequent meetings in London in 1990 and Copenhagen in 1992 further advanced the goals set in Montreal. After peaking in 1988 at 1.26 million tons, the manufacture of CFCs dropped to an estimated 295,000 tons in 1994—a decline of 77% in just six years.

As public understanding of the costs associated with global warming increases, and as evidence of the effects of higher temperatures accumulates, support for reducing dependence on fossil fuels is building. At the March 1995 U.N. Climate Convention in Berlin, environmental groups were joined in lobbying for a reduction in carbon emissions by a group of 36 island communities and insurance industry representatives.

The island nations are beginning to realize that rising sea levels would, at a minimum, reduce their land area and displace people. For some low-lying island countries, it could actually threaten their survival. And the insurance industry is beginning to realize that increasing storm intensity can threaten the survival of insurance companies as well. When Hurricane Andrew tore through Florida in 1992, it took down not only thousands of buildings, but also eight insurance firms.

In September 1995, the U.S. Department of Agriculture reported a sharp drop in the estimated world grain harvest because of crop-withering heat waves in the northern tier of industrial countries. Intense late-summer heat had damaged harvests in Canada and the United States, across Europe, and in Russia. If farmers begin to see that the productivity of their land is threatened by global warming, they, too, may begin to press for a shift to renewable sources of energy.

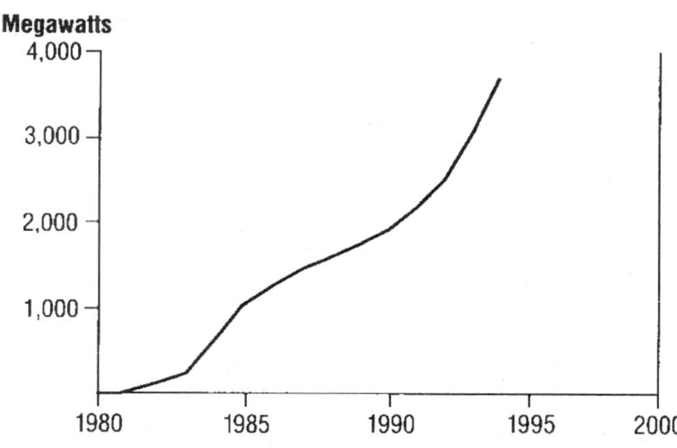

SOURCES: Gipe and Asociates, BTM Consulting

As with CFCs, there are alternatives to fossil fuels that do not alter climate. Several solar-based energy sources, including wind power, solar cells, and solar thermal power plants, are advancing rapidly in technological sophistication, resulting in steadily falling costs. The cost of photovoltaic cells has fallen precipitously over the last few decades. In some villages in developing countries where a central grid does not yet exist, it is now cheaper to install an array of photovoltaic cells than to build a centralized power plant plus the grid needed to deliver the power.

Wind power, using the new, highly efficient wind turbines to convert wind into electricity, is poised for explosive growth in the years ahead. In California, wind farms already supply enough electricity to meet the equivalent of San Francisco's residential needs.

The potential for wind energy is enormous, dwarfing that of hydropower, which provides a fifth of the world's electricity. In the United States, the harnessable wind potential in North Dakota, South Dakota, and Texas could easily meet national electricity needs. In Europe, wind power could theoretically satisfy all the continent's electricity needs. With scores of national governments planning to tap this vast resource, rapid growth in the years ahead appears inevitable.

A Bicycle Economy

Another trend to build on is the growing production of bicycles. Human mobility can be increased by investing in public transportation, bicycles, and automobiles. Of these, the first two are by far the most promising environmentally. Although China has announced plans to move toward an automobile-centered transportation system, and car production in India is expected to double by the end of the decade, there simply may not be enough land in these countries to support such a system and to meet the food needs of their expanding populations.

Against this backdrop, the creation of bicycle-friendly transportation systems, particularly in cities, shows great promise. Market forces alone have pushed bicycle production to an estimated 111 million in 1994, three times the level of automobile production. It is in the interest of societies everywhere to foster the use of bicycles and public transportation—to accelerate the growth in bicycle manufacturing while restricting that of automobiles. Not only will this help save cropland, but this technology can greatly increase human mobility without destabilizing climate. If food becomes increasingly scarce in the years ahead, as now seems likely, the land-saving, climate-stabilizing nature of bicycles will further tip the scales in their favor and away from automobiles.

The stabilization of population in some 30 countries, the stabilization of food/people balance in Europe, the reduction in CFC production, the dramatic growth in the world's wind power generating capacity, and the extraordinary growth in bicycle use are all trends for the world to build on. These cornerstones of an environmentally sustainable global economy provide glimpses of a sustainable future.

Regaining Control of Our Destiny

Avoiding catastrophe is going to take a far greater effort than is now being contemplated by the world's political leaders. We know what needs to be done, but politically we are unable to do it because of inertia and the investment of powerful interests in the status quo. Securing food supplies for the next generation depends on an all-out effort to stabilize population and climate, but we resist changing our reproductive behavior, and we refrain from converting our climate-destabilizing, fossil-fuel-based economy to a solar/hydrogen-based one.

As we move to the end of this century and beyond, food security may well come to dominate international affairs, national economic policy making, and—for much of humanity —personal concerns about survival. There is now evidence from enough countries that the old formula of substituting fertilizer for land is no longer working, so we need to search urgently for alternative formulas for humanly balancing our numbers with available food supplies.

Unfortunately, most national political leaders do not even seem to be aware of the fundamental shifts occurring in the world food economy, largely because the official projections by the World Bank and the U.N. Food and Agriculture Organization are essentially extrapolations of past trends.

If we are to understand the challenges facing us, the teams of economists responsible for world food supply-and-demand projections at these two organizations need to be replaced with an interdisciplinary team of analysts, including, for example, an agronomist, hydrologist, biologist, and meteorologist, along with an economist. Such a team could assess and incorporate into projections such things as the effect of soil erosion on land productivity, the effects of aquifer depletion on future irrigation water supplies, and the effect of increasingly intense heat waves on future harvests.

The World Bank team of economists argues that, because the past is the only guide we have to the future, simple extrapolations of past trends are the only reasonable way to make projections. But the past is also filled with a body of scientific literature on growth in finite environments, and it shows that biological growth trends typically conform to an S-shaped curve over time.

The risk of relying on these extrapolative projections is that they are essentially "no problem" projections. For example, the most recent World Bank projections, which use 1990 as a base and which were published in late 1993, are departing further and further from reality with each passing year. They show the world grain harvest climbing from 1.78 billion tons in 1990 to 1.97 billion tons in the year 2000. But instead of the projected gain of nearly 100 million tons since 1990, world grain production has not grown at all. Indeed, the 1995 harvest, at 1.69 billion tons, is 90 million tons below the 1990 harvest.

One of the most obvious needs today is for a set of country-by-country carrying-capacity assessments. Assessments using an interdisciplinary team can help provide information needed to face the new realities and formulate policies to respond to them.

Setting Priorities

The world today is faced with an enormous need for change in a period of time that is all too short. Human behavior and values, and the national priorities that reflect them, change in response to either new information or new experiences. The effort now needed to reverse the environmental degradation of the planet and ensure a sustainable future for the next generation will require mobilization on a scale comparable to World War II.

Regaining control of our destiny depends on stabilizing population as well as climate. These are both key to the achievement of a wide array of social goals ranging from the restoration of a rise in food consumption per person to protection of the diversity of plant and animal species. And neither will be easy. The first depends on a revolution in human reproductive behavior; the second, on a restructuring of the global energy system.

Serving as a catalyst for these gargantuan efforts is the knowledge that if we fail our future will spiral out of control as the acceleration of history overwhelms political institutions. It will almost guarantee a future of starvation, economic insecurity, and political instability. It will bring political conflict between societies and among ethnic and religious groups within societies. As these forces are unleashed, they will leave social disintegration in their wake.

Offsetting the dimensions of this challenge, including the opposition to change that is coming from vested interests and the momentum of trends now headed in the wrong direction, are some valuable assets. These include a well-developed global communications network, a growing body of scientific knowledge, and the possibility of using fiscal policy—a potentially powerful instrument for change—to build an environmentally sustainable economy.

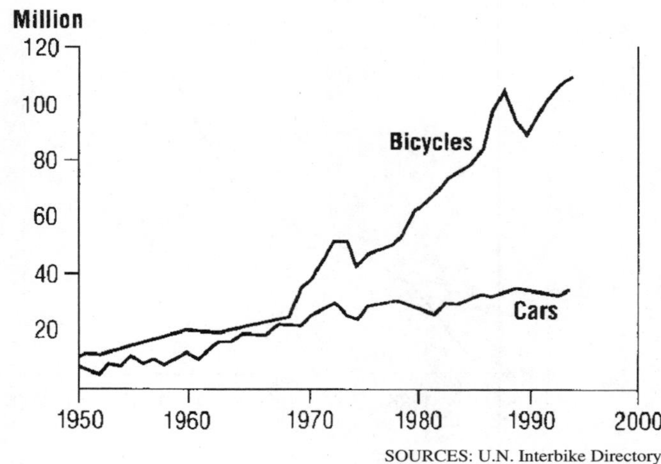

Policies for Progress

Satisfying the conditions of sustainability—whether it be reversing the deforestation of the planet, converting a throwaway economy into a reuse-recycle one, or stabilizing climate—will require new investment. Probably the single most useful instrument for converting an unsustainable world economy into one that is sustainable is fiscal policy. Here are a few proposals:

• **Eliminate subsidies for unsustainable activities**. At present, governments subsidize many of the very activities that threaten the sustainability of the economy. They support fishing fleets to the extent of some $54 billion a year, for example, even though existing fishing capacity already greatly exceeds the sustainable yield of oceanic fisheries. In Germany, coal production is subsidized even though the country's scientific community has been outspoken in its calls for reducing carbon emissions.

• **Institute a carbon tax**. With alternative sources of energy such as wind power, photovoltaics, and solar thermal power plants becoming competitive or nearly so, a carbon tax that would reflect the cost to society of burning fossil fuels—the costs, that is, of air pollution, acid rain, and global warming—could quickly tip the scales away from further investment in fossil fuel production to investment in wind and solar energy.

Today's fossil-fuel-based energy economy can be replaced with a solar/hydrogen economy that can meet all the energy needs of a modern industrial society without causing disruptive temperature rises.

• **Replace income taxes with environmental taxes**. Income taxes discourage work and savings, which are both positive activities that should be encouraged. Taxing environmentally destructive activities instead would help steer the global economy in an environmentally sustainable direction. Among the activities to be taxed are the use of pesticides, the generation of toxic wastes, the use of virgin raw materials, the conversion of cropland to nonfarm uses, and carbon emissions.

The time may have come also to limit tax deductions for children to two per couple: It may not make sense to subsidize childbearing beyond replacement level when the most pressing need facing humanity is to stabilize population.

The challenge for humanity is a profound one. We have the information, the technology, and the knowledge of what needs to be done. The question is, Can we do it? Can a species that is capable of formulating a theory that explains the birth of the universe now implement a strategy to build an environmentally sustainable economic system?

About the Author Lester R. Brown is president of the Worldwatch Institute, 1776 Massachusetts Avenue, N.W., Washington, D.C. 20036. Telephone 202/452-1999; fax 202/296-7365.

UNIT 4

Political Economy

Unit Selections

Key Points to Consider

- Are those who argue that there is in fact a process of globalization overly optimistic? Why or why not?
- What are some of the impediments to a truly global political economy?
- How are the political economies of traditional societies different from those of the consumer-oriented societies?
- How are the nonindustrial countries dependent on the industrialized countries?
- What are some of the barriers that make it difficult for nonindustrial countries to develop?
- How are China and other emerging countries trying to alter their ways of doing business in order to meet the challenges of globalization? Are they likely to succeed?
- What is the nature of the debate surrounding the practices of international organizations like the IMF and WTO?

Links: www.dushkin.com/online/
These sites are annotated in the World Wide Web pages.

Belfer Center for Science and International Affairs (BCSIA)
http://ksgwww.harvard.edu/csia/

Communications for a Sustainable Future
http://csf.colorado.edu

U.S. Agency for International Development
http://www.info.usaid.gov

Virtual Seminar in Global Political Economy/Global Cities & Social Movements
http://csf.colorado.edu/gpe/gpe95b/resources.html

World Bank
http://www.worldbank.org

A defining characteristic of the twentieth century's social history was the contest between two dramatically opposing views about how economic systems should be organized. The focus of the debate was on what role government should play in the management of a country's economy. For some the dominant capitalist economic system appeared to be organized primarily for the benefit of the few. From their perspective, the masses were trapped in poverty, supplying cheap labor to further enrich the wealthy. These critics argued that the capitalist system could be changed only by gaining control of the political system and radically changing the ownership of the means of production. In striking contrast to this perspective, others argued that the best way to create wealth and eliminate poverty was through the profit motive, which encouraged entrepreneurs to innovate. An open and competitive marketplace that minimized government interference was the best system for making decisions about production, wages, and the distribution of goods and services.

The debate between socialism/communism on the one hand and capitalism on the other (with variations in between) has been characterized by both abstract theorizing and very pragmatic and often violent political conflict. The Russian and Chinese revolutions overthrew the old social order and created radical changes in the political and economic systems in these two important countries. The political structures that were created to support new systems of agricultural and industrial production (along with the centralized planning of virtually all aspects of economic activity) eliminated most private ownership of property. These two revolutions were, in short, unparalleled experiments in social engineering.

The collapse of the Soviet Union and the dramatic reforms that have taken place in China have recast the debate about how to best structure contemporary economic systems. Some believe that with the end of communism and the resulting participation of hundreds of millions of new consumers in the global market, an unprecedented era has been entered. Many have noted that this process of "globalization" is being accelerated by the revolution in communication and computer technologies. Proponents of this view argue that a new global economy is emerging that will ultimately eliminate national economic systems.

Others are less optimistic about the prospects of globalization. They argue that the creation of a single economic system where there are no boundaries to impede the flow of capital does not mean a closing of the gap between the world's rich and poor. Rather, they argue that giant corporations will have fewer legal constraints on their behavior, and this will lead to greater exploitation of workers and the accelerated destruction of the environment.

The use of the term "political economy" for the title of this unit is a recognition that economic and political systems are not separate. All economic systems have some type of marketplace where goods and services are bought and sold. Government (either national or international) regulates these transactions to some degree; that is, government sets the rules that regulate the marketplace.

One of the most important concepts in assessing the contemporary political economy is "development." For the purposes of this unit, the term "development" is defined as an improvement in the basic aspects of life: lower infant mortality rates, longer life expectancy, lower disease rates, higher rates of literacy, healthier diets, and improved sanitation. Judged by these standards, some countries are more "developed" than others. A fundamental question that a thoughtful reader must consider is whether globalization is resulting in increased development not only for a few people but for all of those participating in the global political economy.

The unit is organized into two subsections. The first is a general discussion of the concept of globalization. How do various experts define the term, and what are their differing perspectives on it? For example, is the idea of a global economy merely wishful thinking by those who sit on top of the power hierarchy, self-deluded into believing that globalization is an inexorable force that will evolve in its own way, following its own rules? Or will there continue to be the traditional tensions of power politics; that is, between the powerful and those who are either ascending or descending in power?

The second subsection is a selection of case studies that focus on specific countries or economic sectors (e.g., agriculture). These case studies have been selected to challenge the reader to develop his or her own conclusions about the positive and negative consequences of the globalization process. Does the contemporary global political economy result in an age-old system of winners and losers, or can everyone positively benefit from its system of wealth creation and distribution?

The Complexities and Contradictions of Globalization

Globalization, we are told, is what every business should be pursuing, and what every nation should welcome. But what, exactly, is it? James Rosenau offers a nuanced understanding of a process that is much more real, and transforming, than the language of the marketplace expresses.

JAMES N. ROSENAU

The mall at Singapore's airport has a food court with 15 food outlets, all but one of which offering menus that cater to local tastes; the lone standout, McDonald's, is also the only one crowded with customers. In New York City, experts in *feng shui*, an ancient Chinese craft aimed at harmonizing the placement of man-made structures in nature, are sought after by real estate developers in order to attract a growing influx of Asian buyers who would not be interested in purchasing buildings unless their structures were properly harmonized.

Most people confronted with these examples would probably not be surprised by them. They might even view them as commonplace features of day-to-day life late in the twentieth century, instances in which local practices have spread to new and distant sites. In the first case the spread is from West to East and in the second it is from East to West, but both share a process in which practices spread and become established in profoundly different cultures. And what immediately comes to mind when contemplating this process? The answer can be summed up in one word: globalization, a label that is presently in vogue to account for peoples, activities, norms, ideas, goods, services, and currencies that are decreasingly confined to a particular geographic space and its local and established practices.

Indeed, some might contend that "globalization" is the latest buzzword to which observers resort when things seem different and they cannot otherwise readily account for them. That is why, it is reasoned, a great variety of activities are labeled as globalization, with the result that no widely accepted formulation of the concept has evolved. Different observers use it to describe different phenomena, and often there is little overlap among the various usages. Even worse, the elusiveness of the concept of globalization is seen as underlying the use of a variety of other, similar terms—world society, interdependence, centralizing tendencies, world system, globalism, universalism, internationalization, globality—that come into play when efforts are made to grasp why public affairs today seem significantly different from those of the past.

Such reasoning is misleading. The proliferation of diverse and loose definitions of globalization as well as the readiness to use a variety of seemingly comparable labels are not so much a reflection of evasive confusion as they are an early stage in a profound ontological shift, a restless search for new ways of understanding unfamiliar phenomena. The lack of precise formulations may suggest the presence of buzzwords for the inexplicable, but a more convincing interpretation is that such words are voiced in so many different contexts because of a shared sense that the human condition is presently undergoing profound transformations in all of its aspects.

WHAT IS GLOBALIZATION?

Let us first make clear where globalization fits among the many buzzwords that indicate something new in world affairs that is moving important activities and concerns beyond the national seats of power that have long served as the foundations of economic, political, and social life. While all the buzzwords seem to cluster around the same dimension of the present human condition, useful distinctions can be drawn among them.

Most notably, if it is presumed that the prime characteristic of this dimension is change—a transformation of practices and norms—then the term "globalization" seems appropriate to denote the "something" that is changing humankind's preoccupation with territoriality and the traditional arrangements of the state system. It is a term that directly implies change, and thus differentiates the phenomenon as a process rather than as a prevailing condition or a desirable end state.

Conceived as an underlying process, in other words, globalization is not the same as globalism, which points to aspirations for a state of affairs where values are shared by or pertinent to all the world's more than 5 billion people, their environment, and their role as citizens, consumers, or producers with an interest in collective action to solve common problems. And it can also be distinguished from universalism, which refers to those values that embrace all of humanity (such as the values that science or religion draws on), at any time or place. Nor is it coterminous with complex interdependence, which signifies structures that link people and communities in various parts of the world.

Although related to these other concepts, the idea of globalization developed here is narrower in scope. It refers neither to values nor to structures, but to sequences that unfold either in the mind or in behavior, to processes that evolve as people and organizations go about their daily tasks and seek to realize their particular goals. What distinguishes globalizing processes is that they are not hindered or prevented by territorial or jurisdictional barriers. As indicated by the two examples presented at the outset, such processes can readily spread in many directions across national boundaries, and are capable of reaching into any community anywhere in the world. They consist of all those forces that impel individuals, groups, and institutions to engage in similar forms of behavior or to participate in more encompassing and coherent processes, organizations, or systems.

Contrariwise, localization derives from all those pressures that lead individuals, groups, and institutions to narrow their horizons, participate in dissimilar forms of behavior, and withdraw to less encompassing processes, organizations, or systems. In other words, any technological, psychological, social, economic, or political developments that foster the expansion of interests and practices beyond established boundaries are both sources and expressions of the processes of globalization, just as any developments in these realms that limit or reduce interests are both sources and expressions of localizing processes.

Note that the processes of globalization are conceived as only capable of being worldwide in scale. In fact, the activities of no group, government, society, or company have never been planetary in magnitude, and few cascading sequences actually encircle and encompass the entire globe. Televised events such as civil wars and famines in Africa or protests against governments in Eastern Europe may sustain a spread that is worldwide in scope, but such a scope is not viewed as a prerequisite of globalizing dynamics. As long as it has the potential of an unlimited spread that can readily transgress national jurisdictions, any interaction sequence is considered to reflect the operation of globalization.

Obviously, the differences between globalizing and localizing forces give rise to contrary conceptions of territoriality. Globalization is rendering boundaries and identity with the land less salient while localization, being driven by pressures to narrow and withdraw, is highlighting borders and intensifying the deep attachments to land that can dominate emotion and reasoning.

In short, globalization is boundary-broadening and localization is boundary-heightening. The former allows people, goods, information, norms, practices, and institutions to move about oblivious to despite boundaries. The boundary-heightening processes of localization are designed to inhibit or prevent the movement of people, goods, information, norms, practices, and institutions. Efforts along this line, however, can be only partially successful. Community and state boundaries can be heightened to a considerable extent, but they cannot be rendered impervious. Authoritarian governments try to make them so, but their policies are bound to be undermined in a shrinking world with increasingly interdependent economies and communications technologies that are not easily monitored. Thus it is hardly surprising that some of the world's most durable tensions flow from the fact that no geographic borders can be made so airtight to prevent the infiltration of ideas and goods. Stated more emphatically, some globalizing dynamics are bound, at least in the long run, to prevail.

The boundary-expanding dynamics of globalization have become highly salient precisely because recent decades have witnessed a mushrooming of the facilities, interests, and markets through which a potential for worldwide spread can be realized. Likewise, the boundary-contracting dynamics of localization have also become increasingly significant, not least because some people and cultures feel threatened by the incursions of globalization. Their jobs, their icons, their belief systems, and their communities seem at risk as the boundaries that have sealed them off from the outside world in the past no longer assure protection. And there is, of course, a basis of truth in these fears. Globalization does intrude; its processes do shift jobs elsewhere; its norms do undermine traditional mores. Responses to these threats can vary considerably. At one extreme are adaptations that accept the boundary-broadening processes and make the best of them by integrating them into local customs and practices. At the other extreme are responses intended to ward off the globalizing processes by resort to ideological purities, closed borders, and economic isolation.

THE DYNAMICS OF FRAGMEGRATION

The core of world affairs today thus consists of tensions between the dynamics of globalization and localization. Moreover, the two sets of dynamics are causally linked, almost as if every increment of globalization gives rise to an increment of localization, and vice versa. To account for these tensions I have long used the term "fragmegration," an awkward and perhaps even grating label that has the virtue of capturing the pervasive interactions between the fragmenting forces of localization and the integrative forces of globalization.1 One can readily observe the unfolding of fragmegrative dynamics in the struggle of the European Union to cope with proposals for monetary unification or in the electoral campaigns and successes of Jean-Marie Le Pen in France, Patrick Buchanan in the United States, and Pauline Hanson in Australia—to mention only three examples.

It is important to keep in mind that fragmegration is not a single dynamic. Both globalization and localization are clusters of forces that, as they interact in different ways and through different channels, contribute to more encompassing processes in the case of globalization and to less encompassing processes in the case of localization. These various dynamics, moreover, operate in all realms of human activity, from the cultural and social to the economic and political.

In the political realm, globalizing dynamics underlie any developments that facilitate the expansion of authority, policies, and interests beyond existing socially constructed territorial boundaries, whereas the politics of localization involves any trends in which the scope of authority and policies undergoes contraction and reverts to concerns, issues, groups, and institutions that are less extensive than the prevailing socially constructed territorial boundaries. In the economic realm, globalization encompasses the expansion of production, trade, and investments beyond their prior locales, while localizing dynamics are at work when the activities of producers and consumers are constricted to narrower boundaries. In the social and cultural realms, globalization operates to extend ideas, norms, and practices beyond the settings in which they originated, while localization highlights or compresses the original settings and thereby inhibits the inroad of new ideas, norms, and practices.

It must be stressed that the dynamics unfolding in all these realms are long-term processes. They involve fundamental human needs and thus span all of human history. Globalizing dynamics derive from peoples' need to enlarge the scope of their self-created orders so as to increase the goods, services, and ideas available for their well-being. The agricultural revolution, followed by the industrial and postindustrial transformations, are among the major sources that have sustained globalization. Yet even as these forces have been operating, so have contrary tendencies toward contraction been continuously at work. Localizing dynamics derive from people's need for the psychic comforts of close-at-hand, reliable support—for the family and neighborhood, for local cultural practices, for a sense of "us" that is distinguished from "them." Put differently, globalizing dynamics have long fostered large-scale order, whereas localizing dynamics have long created pressure for small-scale order. Fragmegration, in short, has always been an integral part of the human condition.

Globalization's Eventual Predominance

Notwithstanding the complexities inherent in the emergent structures of world affairs, observers have not hesitated to anticipate what lies beyond fragmegration as global history unfolds. All agree that while the contest between globalizing and localizing dynamics is bound to be marked by fluctuating surges in both directions, the underlying tendency is for the former to prevail over the latter. Eventually, that is, the dynamics of globalization are expected to serve as the bases around which the course of events is organized.

Consensus along these lines breaks down, however, over whether the predominance of globalization is likely to have desirable or noxious consequences. Those who welcome globalizing processes stress the power of economic variables. In this view the globalization of national economies through the diffusion of technology and consumer products, the rapid transfer of financial resources, and the efforts of transnational companies to extend their market shares is seen as so forceful and durable as to withstand and eventually surmount any and all pressures toward fragmentation. This line acknowledges that the diffusion that sustains the processes of globalization is a centuries-old dynamic, but the difference is that the present era has achieved a level of economic development in which it is possible for innovations occurring in any sector of any country's economy to be instantaneously transferred to and adapted in any other country or sector. As a consequence,

> when this process of diffusion collides with cultural or political protectionism, it is culture and protectionism that wind up in the shop for repairs. Innovation accelerates. Productivity increases. Standards of living improve. There are setbacks, of course. The newspaper headlines are full of them. But we believe that the time required to override these setbacks has shortened dramatically in the developed world. Indeed, recent experience suggests that, in most cases, economic factors prevail in less than a generation....
>
> Thus understood, globalization—the spread of economic innovations around the world and the political and cultural adjustments that accompany this diffusion—cannot be stopped.... As history teaches, the political organizations and ideologies that yield superior economic performance survive, flourish, and replace those that are less productive.[2]

While it is surely the case that robust economic incentives sustain and quicken the processes of globalization, this line of theorizing nevertheless suffers from not allowing for its own negation. The theory offers no alternative interpretations as to how the interaction of economic, political, and social dynamics will play out. One cannot demonstrate the falsity—if falsity it is—of the theory because any contrary evidence is seen merely as "setbacks," as expectable but temporary deviations from the predicted course. The day may come, of course, when event so perfectly conform to the predicted patterns of globalization that one is inclined to conclude that the theory has been affirmed. But in the absence of alternative scenarios, the theory offers little guidance as to how to interpret intervening events, especially those that highlight the tendencies toward fragmentation. Viewed in this way, it is less a theory and more an article of faith to which one can cling.

Other observers are much less sanguine about the future development of fragmegration. They highlight a litany of noxious consequences that they see as following from the eventual predominance of globalization: "its economism; its economic reductionism; its technological determinism; its political cynicism, defeatism, and immobilism; its de-socialization of the subject and resocialization of risk; its teleological subtext of inexorable global 'logic' driven exclusively by capital accumulation and the market; and its ritual exclusion of factors, causes, or goals other than capital accumulation and the market from the priority of values to be pursued by social action."[3]

Still another approach, allowing for either desirable or noxious outcomes, has been developed by Michael Zurn. He identifies a mismatch between the rapid extension of boundary-crossing activities and the scope of effective governance. Consequently, states are undergoing what is labeled "uneven denationalization," a primary process in which "the rise of international governance is still remarkable, but not accompanied by mechanisms for… democratic control; people, in addition, become alienated from the remote political process.… The democratic state in the Western world is confronted with a situation in which it is undermined by the process of globalization and overarched by the rise of international institutions."[4]

There is no inherent contradiction between localizing and globalizing tendencies.

While readily acknowledging the difficulties of anticipating where the process of uneven denationalization is driving the world, Zurn is able to derive two scenarios that may unfold: "Whereas the pessimistic scenario points to instances of fragmentation and emphasizes the disruption caused by the transition, the optimistic scenario predicts, at least in the long run, the triumph of centralization." The latter scenario rests on the presumption that the increased interdependence of societies will propel them to develop ever more effective democratic controls over the very complex arrangements on which international institutions must be founded.

UNEVEN FRAGMEGRATION

My own approach to theorizing about the fragmegrative process builds on these other perspectives and a key presumption of my own—that there is no inherent contradiction between localizing and globalizing tendencies—to develop an overall hypothesis that anticipates fragmegrative outcomes and that allows for its own negation: the more pervasive globalizing tendencies become, the less resistant localizing reactions will be to further globalization. In other words, globalization and localization will coexist, but the former will continue to set the context for the latter. Since the degree of coexistence will vary from situation to situation (depending on the salience of the global economy and the extent to which ethnic and other noneconomic factors actively contribute to localization), I refer, borrowing from Zurn, to the processes depicted by the hypothesis as uneven fragmegration. The hypothesis allows for continuing pockets of antagonism between globalizing and localizing tendencies even as increasingly (but unevenly) the two accommodate each other. It does not deny the pessimistic scenario wherein fragmentation disrupts globalizing tendencies; rather it treats fragmentation as more and more confined to particular situations that may eventually be led by the opportunities and requirements of greater interdependence to conform to globalization.

For globalizing and localizing tendencies to accommodate each other, individuals have to come to appreciate that they can achieve psychic comfort in collectivities through multiple memberships and multiple loyalties, that they can advance both local and global values without either detracting from the other. The hypothesis of uneven fragmegration anticipates a growing appreciation along these lines because the contrary premise, that psychic comfort can only be realized by having a highest loyalty, is becoming increasingly antiquated. To be sure, people have long been accustomed to presuming that, in order to derive the psychic comfort they need through collective identities, they had to have a hierarchy of loyalties and that, consequently, they had to have a highest loyalty that could only be attached to a single collectivity. Such reasoning, however, is a legacy of the state system, of centuries of crises that made people feel they had to place nation-state loyalties above all others. It is a logic that long served to reinforce the predominance of the state as the "natural" unit of political organization and that probably reached new heights during the intense years of the cold war.

But if it is the case, as the foregoing analysis stresses, that conceptions of territoriality are in flux and that the failure of states to solve pressing problems has led to a decline in their capabilities and a loss of legitimacy, it follows that the notion that people must have a "highest loyalty" will also decline and give way to the development of multiple loyalties and an understanding that local, national, and transnational affiliations need not be mutually exclusive. For the reality is that human affairs are organized at all these levels for good reasons; people have needs that can only be filled by close-at-hand organizations and other needs that are best served by distant entities at the national or transnational level.

In addition, not only is an appreciation of the reality that allows for multiple loyalties and memberships likely to grow as the effectiveness of states and the salience of national loyalties diminish, but it also seems likely to widen as the benefits of the global economy expand and people become increasingly aware of the extent to which their well-being is dependent on events and trends elsewhere in the world. At the same time, the distant economic processes serving their needs are impersonal and hardly capable of advancing the need to share with others in a collective affiliation. This need was long served by the nation-state, but with fragmegrative dynamics having undermined the national level as a source of psychic comfort and with transnational entities seeming too distant to provide the psychic benefits of affiliation, the satisfactions to be gained through more close-at-hand affiliations are likely to seem ever more attractive.

THE STAKES

It seems clear that fragmegration has become an enduring feature of global life; it is also evident that globalization is not merely a buzzword, that it encompasses pervasive complexities and contradictions that have the potential both to enlarge and to degrade our humanity. In order to ensure that the enlargement is more prevalent than the degradation, it is important that people and their institutions become accustomed to the multiple dimensions and nuances as our world undergoes profound and enduring transformations. To deny the complexities and contradictions in order to cling to a singular conception of what globalization involves is to risk the many dangers that accompany oversimplification.

NOTES

1. For an extensive discussion of the dynamics of fragmegration, see James N. Rosenau, *Along the Domestic-Foreign Frontier: Exploring Governance in a Turbulent World* (Cambridge: Cambridge University Press, 1997), ch. 6.
2. William W. Lewis and Marvin Harris, "Why Globalization Must Prevail," *The McKinsey Quarterly*, no. 2 (1992), p. 115.
3. Barry K. Gills, "Editorial: 'Globalization' and the 'Politics of Resistance,'" *New Political Economy*, vol. 2 (March 1997), p. 12.
4. Michael Zurn, "What Has Changed in Europe? The Challenge of Globalization and Individualization," paper presented at a meeting on What Has Changed? Competing Perspectives on World Order (Copenhagen, May 14–16, 1993), p. 40.

JAMES N. ROSENAU *is University Professor of International Affairs at George Washington University. His latest book is* Along the Domestic-Foreign Frontier: Exploring Governance in a Turbulent World *(Cambridge: Cambridge University Press, 1997). This article draws on the author's "New Dimensions of Security: The Interaction of Globalizing and Localizing Dynamics,"* Security Dialogue, *September 1994, and "The Dynamics of Globalization: Toward an Operational Formulation,"* Security Dialogue, *September 1996).*

Article 13

The Great Divide in the Global Village

Bruce R. Scott

INCOMES ARE DIVERGING

MAINSTREAM economic thought promises that globalization will lead to a widespread improvement in average incomes. Firms will reap increased economies of scale in a larger market, and incomes will converge as poor countries grow more rapidly than rich ones. In this "win-win" perspective, the importance of nation-states fades as the "global village" grows and market integration and prosperity take hold.

But the evidence paints a different picture. Average incomes have indeed been growing, but so has the income gap between rich and poor countries. Both trends have been evident for more than 200 years, but improved global communications have led to an increased awareness among the poor of income inequalities and heightened the pressure to emigrate to richer countries. In response, the industrialized nations have erected higher barriers against immigration, making the world economy seem more like a gated community than a global village. And although international markets for goods and capital have opened up since World War II and multilateral organizations now articulate rules and monitor the world economy, economic inequality among countries continues to increase. Some two billion people earn less than $2 per day.

At first glance, there are two causes of this divergence between economic theory and reality. First, the rich countries insist on barriers to immigration and agricultural imports. Second, most poor nations have been unable to attract much foreign capital due to their own government failings. These two issues are fundamentally linked: by forcing poor people to remain in badly governed states, immigration barriers deny those most in need the opportunity to "move up" by "moving out." In turn, that immobility eliminates a potential source of pressure on ineffective governments, thus facilitating their survival.

Since the rich countries are unlikely to lower their agricultural and immigration barriers significantly, they must recognize that politics is a key cause of economic inequality. And since most developing countries receive little foreign investment, the wealthy nations must also acknowledge that the "Washington consensus," which assumes that free markets will bring about economic convergence, is mistaken. If they at least admit these realities, they will abandon the notion that their own particular strategies are the best for all countries. In turn, they should allow poorer countries considerable freedom to tailor development strategies to their own circumstances. In this more pragmatic view, the role of the state becomes pivotal.

Why have economists and policymakers not come to these conclusions sooner? Since the barriers erected by rich countries are seen as vital to political stability, leaders of those countries find it convenient to overlook them and focus instead on the part of the global economy that has been liberalized. The rich countries' political power in multilateral organizations makes it difficult for developing nations to challenge this self-serving world-view. And standard academic solutions may do as much harm as good, given their focus on economic stability and growth rather than on the institutions that underpin markets. Economic theory has ignored the political issues at stake in modernizing institutions, incorrectly assuming that market-based prices can allocate resources appropriately.

The fiasco of reform in Russia has forced a belated reappraisal of this blind trust in markets. Many observers now admit that the transition economies needed appropriate property rights and an effective state to enforce those rights as much as they needed the liberalization of prices. Indeed, liberalization without property rights turned out to be the path to gangsterism, not capitalism. China, with a more effective state, achieved much greater success in its transition than did Russia, even though Beijing proceeded much more slowly with liberalization and privatization.

Economic development requires the transformation of institutions as well as the freeing of prices, which in turn requires political and social modernization as well as economic reform. The state plays a key role in this process; without it, developmental strategies have little hope of succeeding. The creation of effective states in the developing world will not be driven by familiar market forces, even if pressures from capital markets can force fiscal and monetary discipline. And in a world still governed by "states rights," real progress in achieving accountable governments will require reforms beyond the mandates of multilateral institutions.

GO WITH THE FLOW

IN THEORY, globalization provides an opportunity to raise incomes through increased specialization and trade. This opportunity is conditioned by the size of the markets in question, which in turn depends on geography, transportation costs, communication networks, and the institutions that underpin markets. Free trade increases both the size of the market and the pressure to improve economic performance. Those who are most competitive take advantage of the enhanced market opportunities to survive and prosper.

Neoclassical economic theory predicts that poor countries should grow faster than rich ones in a free global market. Capital from rich nations in search of cheaper labor should flow to poorer economies, and labor should migrate from low-income areas toward those with higher wages. As a result, labor and capital costs—and eventually income—in rich and poor areas should eventually converge.

The U.S. economy demonstrates how this theory can work in a free market with the appropriate institutions. Since the 1880s, a remarkable convergence of incomes among the country's regions has occurred. The European Union has witnessed a similar phenomenon, with the exceptions of Greece and Italy's southern half, the *Mezzogiorno*. What is important, however, is that both America and the EU enjoy labor and capital mobility as well as free internal trade.

But the rest of the world does not fit this pattern. The most recent *World Development Report* shows that real per capita incomes for the richest one-third of countries rose by an annual 1.9 percent between 1970 and 1995, whereas the middle third went up by only 0.7 percent and the bottom third showed no increase at all. In the Western industrial nations and Japan alone, average real incomes have been rising about 2.5 percent annually since 1950—a fact that further accentuates the divergence of global income. These rich countries account for about 60 percent of world GDP but only 15 percent of world population.

Why is it that the poor countries continue to fall further behind? One key reason is that most rich countries have largely excluded the international flow of labor into their markets since the interwar period. As a result, low-skilled labor is not free to flow across international boundaries in search of more lucrative jobs. From an American or European perspective, immigration appears to have risen in recent years, even approaching its previous peak of a century ago in the United States. Although true, this comparison misses the central point. Billions of poor people could improve their standard of living by migrating to rich countries. But in 1997, the United States allowed in only 737,000 immigrants from developing nations, while Europe admitted about 665,000. Taken together, these flows are only 0.04 percent of all potential immigrants.

> Global markets offer opportunities for all, but opportunities do not guarantee results

The point is not that the rich countries should permit unfettered immigration. A huge influx of cheap labor would no doubt be politically explosive; many European countries have already curtailed immigration from poor countries for fear of a severe backlash. But the more salient issue is that rich nations who laud liberalism and free markets are rejecting those very principles when they restrict freedom of movement. The same goes for agricultural imports. Both Europe and Japan have high trade barriers in agriculture, while the United States remains modestly protectionist.

Mainstream economic theory does provide a partial rationalization for rich-country protectionism: Immigration barriers need not be a major handicap to poor nations because they can be offset by capital flows from industrialized economies to developing ones. In other words, poor people need not demand space in rich countries because the rich will send their capital to help develop the poor countries. This was indeed the case before World War I, but it has not been so since World War II.

But the question of direct investment, which typically brings technologies and know-how as well as financial capital, is more complicated than theories would predict. The total stock of foreign direct investment did rise almost sevenfold from 1980 to 1997, increasing from 4 percent to 12 percent of world GDP during that period. But very little has gone to the poorest countries. In 1997, about 70 percent went from one rich country to another, 8 developing countries received about 20 percent, and the remainder was divided among more than 100 poor nations. According to the World Bank, the truly poor countries received less than 7 percent of the foreign direct investment to all developing countries in 1992–98. At the same time, the unrestricted opening of capital markets in developing countries gives larger firms from rich countries the opportunity for takeovers that are reminiscent of colonialism. It is not accidental that rich countries insist on open markets where they have an advantage and barriers in agriculture and immigration, where they would be at a disadvantage.

As for the Asian "tigers," their strong growth is due largely to their high savings rate, not foreign capital. Singapore stands out because it has enjoyed a great deal of foreign investment, but it has also achieved one of the highest domestic-savings rates in the world, and its government has been a leading influence on the use of these funds. China is now repeating this pattern, with a savings rate of almost 40 percent of GDP. This factor, along with domestic credit creation, has been its key motor of economic growth. China now holds more than $100 billion in low-yielding foreign-exchange reserves, the second largest reserves in the world.

In short, global markets offer opportunities for all, but opportunities do not guarantee results. Most poor countries have been unable to avail themselves of much foreign capital or to take advantage of increased market access. True, these countries have raised their trade ratios (exports plus imports) from about 35 percent of their GDP in 1981 to almost 50 percent in 1997. But without the Asian tigers, developing-country exports remain less than 25 percent of world exports.

Part of the problem is that the traditional advantages of poor countries have been in primary commodities (agriculture and minerals), and these categories have shrunk from about 70 percent of world trade in 1900 to about 20 percent at the end of the century. Opportunities for growth in the world market have shifted from raw or semiprocessed commodities toward manufactured goods and services—and, within these categories, toward more knowledge-intensive segments. This trend obviously favors rich countries over poor ones, since most of the latter are still peripheral players in the knowledge economy. (Again, the Asian tigers are the exception. In 1995, they exported as much in high-technology goods as did France, Germany, Italy, and Britain combined—which together have three times the population of the tigers.)

ONE COUNTRY, TWO SYSTEMS

WHY is the performance of poor countries so uneven and out of sync with theoretical forecasts? Systemic barriers at home and abroad inhibit the economic potential of poorer nations, the most formidable of these obstacles being their own domestic political and administrative problems. These factors, of course, lie outside the framework of mainstream economic analysis. A useful analogy is the antebellum economy of the United States, which experienced a similar set of impediments.

Like today's "global village," the U.S. economy before the Civil War saw incomes diverge as the South fell behind the North. One reason for the Confederacy's secession and the resulting civil war was Southern recognition that it was falling behind in both economic and political power, while the richer and more populous North was attracting more immigrants. Half of the U.S. population lived in the North in 1780; by 1860, this share had climbed to two-thirds. In 1775, incomes in the five original Southern states equaled those in New England, even though wealth (including slaves) was disproportionately concentrated in the South. By 1840, incomes in the northeast were about 50 percent higher than those in the original Southern states; the North's railroad mileage was about 40 percent greater (and manufacturing investment four times higher) than the South's. As the economist Robert Fogel has pointed out, the South was not poor—in 1860 it was richer than all European states except England—but Northern incomes were still much higher and increasing.

Why had Southern incomes diverged from those in the North under the same government, laws, and economy? Almost from their inception, the Southern colonies followed a different path from the North—specializing in plantation agriculture rather than small farms with diversified crops—due to geography and slavery. Thanks to slave labor, Southerners were gaining economies of scale and building comparative advantage in agriculture, exporting their goods to world markets and the North. Gang labor outproduced "free" (paid) labor. But the North was building even greater advantages by developing a middle class, a manufacturing sector, and a more modern social and political culture. With plans to complete transcontinental railroads pending, the North was on the verge of achieving economic and political dominance and the capacity to shut off further expansion of slavery in the West. The South chose war over Northern domination—and modernization.

Although the Constitution guaranteed free trade and free movement of capital and labor, the institution of slavery meant that the South had much less factor mobility than the North. It also ensured less development of its human resources, a less equal distribution of income, a smaller market for manufactures, and a less dynamic economy. It was less attractive to both European immigrants and external capital. With stagnant incomes in the older states, it was falling behind. In these respects, it was a forerunner of many of today's poor countries, especially those in Latin America.

What finally put the South on the path to economic convergence? Four years of civil war with a total of 600,000 deaths and vast destruction of property were only a start. Three constitutional amendments and twelve years of military "reconstruction" were designed to bring equal rights and due process to the South. But the reestablishment of racial segregation following Reconstruction led to sharecropping as former slaves refused to return to the work gangs. Labor productivity dropped so much that Southern incomes fell to about half of the North's in 1880. In fact, income convergence did not take off until the 1940s, when a wartime boom in the North's industrial cities attracted Southern migrants in search of better jobs. At the same time, the South began drawing capital as firms sought lower wages, an anti-union environment, and military contracts in important congressional districts. But this process did not fully succeed until the 1960s, as new federal laws and federal troops brought full civil rights to the South and ensured that the region could finally modernize.

THE GREAT DIVIDE

ALTHOUGH slavery is a rarity today, the traditional U.S. divide between North and South provides a good model for understanding contemporary circumstances in many developing countries. In the American South, voter intimidation, segregated housing, and very unequal schooling were the rule, not the exception—and such tactics are repeated today by the elites in today's poor countries. Brazil, Mexico, and Peru had abundant land relative to population when the Europeans arrived, and their incomes roughly approximated those in North America, at least until 1700. The economists Stanley Engerman and Kenneth Sokoloff have pointed out that these states, like the Confederacy, developed agricultural systems based on vast landholdings for the production of export crops such as sugar and coffee. Brazil and many Caribbean islands also adopted slavery, while Peru and Mexico relied on forced indigenous labor rather than African slaves.

History shows that the political development of North America and developing nations—most of which were colonized by Europeans at some point—was heavily influenced by mortality. In colonies with tolerable death rates (Australia, Canada, New Zealand, and the United States), the colonists soon exerted pressure for British-style protections of persons and property. But elsewhere (most of Africa, Latin America, Indonesia, and to a lesser degree, India), disease caused such high mortality rates that the few resident Europeans were permitted to exploit a disenfranchised laboring class, whether slave or free. When the colonial era ended in these regions, it was followed by "liberationist" regimes (often authoritarian and incompetent) that maintained the previous system of exploitation for the advantage of a small domestic elite. Existing inequalities within poor countries continued; policies and institutions rarely protected individual rights or private initiative for the bulk of the population and allowed elites to skim off rents from any sectors that could bear it. The economist Hernando de Soto has shown how governments in the developing world fail to recognize poor citizens' legal titles to their homes and businesses, thereby depriving them of the use of their assets for collateral. The losses in potential capital to these countries have dwarfed the cumulative capital inflows going to these economies in the last century.

The legacy of these colonial systems also tends to perpetuate the unequal distribution of income, wealth, and political power while limiting capital mobility. Thus major developing nations such as Brazil, China, India, Indonesia, and Mexico are experiencing a divergence of incomes by province within their economies, as labor and capital fail to find better opportunities. Even in recent times, local elites have fought to maintain oppressive conditions in Brazil, El Salvador, Guatemala, Mexico, Nicaragua, and Peru. Faced with violent intimidation, poor people in these countries have suffered from unjust law enforcement similar to what was once experienced by black sharecroppers in the American South.

Modernization and economic development inevitably threaten the existing distribution of power and income, and powerful elites continue to protect the status quo—even if it means that their society as a whole falls further behind. It takes more than a constitution, universal suffrage, and regular elections to achieve governmental accountability and the rule of law. It may well be that only the right of exit—emigration—can peacefully bring accountability to corrupt and repressive regimes. Unlike the U.S. federal government, multilateral institutions lack the legitimacy to intervene in the internal affairs of most countries. Europe's economic takeoff in the second half of the nineteenth century was aided by the emigration of 60 million people to North America, Argentina, Brazil, and Australia. This emigration—about 10 percent of the labor force—helped raise European wages while depressing inflated wages in labor-scarce areas such as Australia and the United States. A comparable out-migration of labor from today's poor countries would involve hundreds of millions of people.

Of course, Latin America has seen some success. Chile has received the most attention for its free market initiatives, but its reforms were implemented by a brutally repressive military regime—hardly a model for achieving economic reform through democratic processes. Costa Rica would seem to be a much better model for establishing accountability, but its economic performance has not been as striking as Chile's.

Italy, like the United States in an earlier era, is another good example of "one country, two systems." Italy's per capita income has largely caught up with that of its European neighbors over the past 20 years, even exceeding Britain's and equaling France's in 1990, but its *Mezzogiorno* has failed to keep up. Whereas overall Italian incomes have been converging toward those of the EU, *Mezzogiorno* incomes have been diverging from those in the north. Southern incomes fell from 65 percent of the northern average in 1975 to 56 percent 20 years later; in Calabria, they fell to 47 percent of the northern average. Southern unemployment rose from 8 percent in 1975 to 19 percent in 1995—almost three times the northern average. In short, 50 years of subsidies from Rome and the EU have failed to stop the *Mezzogiorno* from falling further behind. Instead, they have yielded local regimes characterized by greatly increased public-sector employment, patronage, dependency, and corruption—not unlike the results of foreign aid for developing countries. And the continuing existence of the Mafia further challenges modernization.

> Democracy is not enough to ensure that the governed reap the gains of their own efforts.

Democracy, then, is not enough to ensure that the governed are allowed to reap the gains of their own efforts. An effective state requires good laws as well as law enforcement that is timely, evenhanded, and accessible to the poor. In many countries, achieving objective law enforcement means reducing the extralegal powers of vested interests. When this is not possible, the only recourse usually available is emigration. But if the educated elite manages to emigrate while the masses remain trapped in a society that is short of leaders, the latter will face even more formidable odds as they try to create effective institutions and policies. Although Italians still emigrate from south to north, the size of this flow is declining, thanks in part to generous transfer payments that allow them to consume almost as much as northerners. In addition, policymaking for the *Mezzogiorno* is still concentrated in Rome.

The immigration barriers in rich countries not only foreclose opportunities in the global village to billions of poor people, they help support repressive, pseudodemocratic governments by denying the citizens of these countries the right to vote against the regime with their feet. In effect, the strict dictates of sovereignty allow wealthy nations to continue to set the rules in their own favor while allowing badly governed poor nations to continue to abuse their own citizens and retard economic development. Hence the remedy for income divergence must be political as well as economic.

GETTING INSTITUTIONS RIGHT

According to economic theory, developing nations will create and modernize the institutions needed to underpin their markets so that their markets and firms can gradually match the performance of rich countries. But reality is much more complex than theory. For example, de Soto's analysis makes clear that effectively mobilizing domestic resources offers a much more potent source of capital for most developing nations than foreign inflows do. Yet mainstream economists and their formal models largely ignore these resources. Western economic advisers in Russia were similarly blindsided by their reliance on an economic model that had no institutional context and no historical perspective. Economists have scrambled in recent years to correct some of these shortcomings, and the Washington consensus now requires the "right" institutions as well as the "right" prices. But little useful theory exists to guide policy when it comes to institutional analysis, and gaps in the institutional foundations in most developing countries leave economic models pursuing unrealistic solutions or worse.

The adjustment of institutions inevitably favors certain actors and disadvantages others. As a result, modernization causes conflict that must be resolved through politics as well as economics. At a minimum, successful development signifies that the forces for institutional change have won out over the status quo. Achieving a "level playing field" signifies that regulatory and political competition is well governed.

Economists who suggest that all countries must adopt Western institutions to achieve Western levels of income often fail to consider the changes and political risks involved. The experts who recommended that formerly communist countries apply "shock therapy" to markets and democracy disregarded the political and regulatory issues involved. Each change requires a victory in the "legislative market" and successful persuasion within the state bureaucracy for political approval. Countries with lower incomes and fewer educated people than Russia face even more significant developmental challenges just to achieve economic stability, let alone attract foreign investment or make effective use of it. Institutional deficiencies, not capital shortages, are the major impediment to development, and as such they must be addressed before foreign investors will be willing to send in capital.

Although price liberalization can be undertaken rapidly, no rapid process (aside from revolution) exists for an economy modernizing its institutions. Boris Yeltsin may be credited with a remarkable turnover, if not a coup d'état, but his erratic management style and the lack of parliamentary support ensured that his government would never be strong. In these circumstances, helping the new Russian regime improve law enforcement should have come ahead of mass privatization. Launching capitalism in a country where no one other than apparatchiks had access to significant amounts of capital was an open invitation to gangsterism and a discredited system. Naive economic models made for naive policy recommendations.

HOW THE WEST WON

THE STATE'S crucial role is evident in the West's economic development. European economic supremacy was forged not by actors who followed a "Washington consensus" model but by strong states. In the fifteenth century, European incomes were not much higher than those in China, India, or Japan. The nation-state was a European innovation that replaced feudalism and established the rule of law; in turn, a legal framework was formed for effective markets. Once these countries were in the lead, they were able to continuously increase their edge through technological advances. In addition, European settlers took their civilization with them to North America and the South Pacific, rapidly raising these areas to rich-country status as well. Thus Europe's early lead became the basis for accumulating further advantages with far- reaching implications.

Europe's rise to economic leadership was not rapid at first. According to the economist Angus Maddison, Europe's economy grew around 0.07 percent a year until 1700; only after 1820 did it reach one percent. But the pace of technological and institutional innovation accelerated thereafter. Meanwhile, discovery of new markets in Africa, Asia, and the Americas created new economic opportunities. Secular political forces overthrew the hegemony of the Catholic Church. Feudalism was eroded by rising incomes and replaced by a system that financed government through taxes, freeing up land and labor to be traded in markets. Markets permitted a more efficient reallocation of land and labor, allowing further rises in incomes. Effective property rights allowed individuals to keep the fruits of their own labor, thereby encouraging additional work. And privatization of common land facilitated the clearing of additional acreage.

The nation-state helped forge all these improvements. It opened up markets by expanding territory; reduced transaction costs; standardized weights, measures, and monetary units; and cut transport costs by improving roads, harbors, and canals. In addition, it was the state that established effective property rights. The European state system thrived on flexible alliances, which constantly changed to maintain a balance of power. Military and economic rivalries prompted states to promote development in agriculture and commerce as well as technological innovation in areas such as shipping and weaponry. Absent the hegemony of a single church or state, technology was diffused and secularized. Clocks, for instance, transferred timekeeping from the monastery to the village clock tower; the printing press did much the same for the production and distribution of books.

Europe's development contrasts sharply with Asia's. In the early modern era, China saw itself as the center of the world, without real rivals. It had a much larger population than Europe and a far bigger market as well. But though the Chinese pioneered the development of clocks, the printing press, gunpowder, and iron, they did not have the external competitive stimulus to promote economic development. Meanwhile, Japan sealed itself off from external influences for more than 200 years, while India, which had continuous competition within the subcontinent, never developed an effective national state prior to the colonial era.

The Europeans also led in establishing accountable government, even though it was achieved neither easily nor peacefully. Most European states developed the notion that the sovereign (whether a monarch or a parliament) had a duty to protect subjects and property in return for taxes and service in the army. Rulers in the Qing, Mughal, and Ottoman Empires, in contrast, never recognized a comparable responsibility to their subjects. During the Middle Ages, Italy produced a number of quasi-democratic city-states, and in the seventeenth century Holland created the first modern republic after a century of rebellion and warfare with Spain. Britain achieved constitutional monarchy in 1689, following two revolutions. After a bloody revolution and then dictatorship, France achieved accountable government in the nineteenth century.

Europe led in establishing accountable government, although it was not easy or peaceful.

Europe led the way in separating church and state—an essential precursor to free inquiry and adoption of the scientific method—after the Thirty Years' War. The secular state in turn paved the way for capitalism and its "creative destruction." Creative destruction could hardly become the norm until organized religion lost its power to execute as heretics those entrepreneurs who would upset the status quo. After the Reformation, Europeans soon recognized another fundamental tenet of capitalism: the role of interest as a return for the use of capital. Capitalism required that political leaders allow private hands to hold power as well as wealth; in turn, power flowed from the rural nobility to merchants in cities. European states also permitted banks, insurance firms, and stock markets to develop. The "yeast" in this recipe lay in the notion that private as well as state organizations could mobilize and reallocate society's resources—an idea with profound social, political, and economic implications today.

Most of Europe's leading powers did not rely on private initiative alone but adopted mercantilism to promote their development. This strategy used state power to create a trading system that would raise national income, permitting the government to enhance its own power through additional taxes. Even though corruption was sometimes a side effect, the system generally worked well. Venice was the early leader, from about 1000 to 1500; the Dutch followed in the sixteenth and seventeenth centuries; Britain became dominant in the eighteenth century. In Britain, as in the other cases, mercantilist export promotion was associated with a dramatic rise in state spending and employment (especially in the navy), as well as "crony capitalism." After World War II, export-promotion regimes were adopted by Japan, South Korea, Singapore, and Taiwan with similar success. Today, of course, such strategies are condemned as violations of global trade rules, even for poor countries.

Finally, geography played a pivotal role in Europe's rise, providing a temperate climate, navigable rivers, accessible coastline, and defensible boundaries for future states. In addition, Europe lacked the conditions for the production of labor-intensive commodities such as coffee, cotton, sugar, or tobacco—production that might have induced the establishment of slavery. Like in the American North, European agriculture was largely rain-fed, diversified, and small-scale.

Europe's rise, then, was partly due to the creation and diffusion of technological innovations and the gradual accumulation of capital. But the underlying causes were political and social. The creation of the nation-state and institutionalized state rivalry fostered government accountability. Scientific enlightenment and upward social mobility, spurred by healthy competition, also helped Europe achieve such transformations. But many of today's developing countries still lack these factors crucial for economic transformation.

PLAYING CATCH-UP

GLOBALIZATION offers opportunities for all nations, but most developing countries are very poorly positioned to capitalize on them. Malarial climates, limited access to navigable water, long distances to major markets, and unchecked population growth are only part of the problem. Such countries also have very unequal income structures inherited from colonial regimes, and these patterns of income distribution are hard to change unless prompted by a major upheaval such as a war or a revolution. But as serious as these disadvantages are, the greatest disadvantage has been the poor quality of government.

If today's global opportunities are far greater and potentially more accessible than at any other time in world history, developing countries are also further behind than ever before. Realistic political logic suggests that weak governments need to show that they can manage their affairs much better before they pretend to have strategic ambitions. So what kind of catch-up models could they adopt?

Substituting domestic goods for imports was the most popular route to economic development prior to the 1980s. But its inward orientation made those who adopted it unable to take advantage of the new global opportunities and ultimately it led to a dead end. Although the United States enjoyed success with such a strategy from 1790 until 1940, no developing country has a home market large enough to support a modern economy today. The other successful early growth model was European mercantilism, namely export promotion, as pioneered by Venice, the Dutch republic, Britain, and Germany. Almost all of the East Asian success stories, China included, are modern versions of the export-oriented form of mercantilism.

For its part, free trade remains the right model for rich countries because it provides decentralized initiatives to search for tomorrow's market opportunities. But it does not necessarily promote development. Britain did not adopt free trade until the 1840s, long after it had become the world's leading industrial power. The prescription of lower trade barriers may help avoid even worse strategies at the hands of bad governments, but the Washington-consensus model remains best suited for those who are ahead rather than behind.

Today's shareholder capitalism brings additional threats to poor countries, first by elevating compensation for successful executives, and second by subordinating all activities to those that maximize shareholder value. Since 1970, the estimated earnings of an American chief executive have gone from 30 times to 450 times that of the average worker. In the leading developing countries, this ratio is still less than 50. Applying a similar "market-friendly" rise in executive compensation within the developing world would therefore only aggravate the income gap, providing new ammunition for populist politicians. In addition, shareholder capitalism calls for narrowing the managerial focus to the interests of shareholders, even if this means dropping activities that offset local market imperfections. A leading South African bank has shed almost a million small accounts—mostly held by blacks—to raise its earnings per share. Should this bank, like its American counterparts, have an obligation to serve its community, including its black members, in return for its banking license?

Poor nations must improve the effectiveness of their institutions and bureaucracies in spite of entrenched opposition and poorly paid civil servants. As the journalist Thomas Friedman has pointed out, it is true that foreign-exchange traders can dump the currencies of poorly managed countries, thereby helping discipline governments to restrain their fiscal deficits and lax monetary policies. But currency pressures will not influence the feudal systems in Pakistan and Saudi Arabia, the theocracies in Afghanistan and Iran, or the kleptocracies in Kenya or southern Mexico. The forces of capital markets will not restrain Brazilian squatters as they take possession of "public lands" or the slums of Rio de Janeiro or São Paulo, nor will they help discipline landlords and vigilantes in India's Bihar as they fight for control of their state. Only strong, accountable government can do that.

LOOKING AHEAD

INCREASED TRADE and investment have indeed brought great improvements in some countries, but the global economy is hardly a win-win situation. Roughly one billion people earn less than $1 per day, and their numbers are growing. Economic resources to ameliorate such problems exist, but the political and administrative will to realize the potential of these resources in poor areas is lacking. Developing-nation governments need both the pressure to reform their administrations and institutions, and the access to help in doing so. But sovereignty removes much of the external pressure, while immigration barriers reduce key internal motivation. And the Washington consensus on the universality of the rich-country model is both simplistic and self-serving.

The world needs a more pragmatic, country-by-country approach, with room for neomercantilist regimes until such countries are firmly on the convergence track. Poor nations should be allowed to do what today's rich countries did to get ahead, not be forced to adopt the laissez-faire approach. Insisting on the merits of comparative advantage in low-wage, low-growth industries is a sure way to stay poor. And continued poverty will lead to rising levels of illegal immigration and low-level violence, such as kidnappings and vigilante justice, as the poor take the only options that remain. Over time, the rich countries will be forced to pay more attention to the fortunes of the poor—if only to enjoy their own prosperity and safety.

Still, the key initiatives must come from the poor countries, not the rich. In the last 50 years, China, India, and Indonesia have led the world in reducing poverty. In China, it took civil war and revolution, with tens of millions of deaths, to create a strong state and economic stability; a de facto coup d'état in 1978 brought about a very fortunate change of management. The basic forces behind Chinese reform were political and domestic, and their success depended as much on better using resources as opening up markets. Meanwhile, the former Soviet Union and Africa lie at the other extreme. Their economic decline stems from their failure to maintain effective states and ensure the rule of law.

It will not be surprising if some of today's states experience failure and economic decline in the new century. Argentina, Colombia, Indonesia, and Pakistan will be obvious cases to watch, but other nations could also suffer from internal regional failures—for example, the Indian state of Bihar. Income growth depends heavily on the legal, administrative, and political capabilities of public actors in sovereign states. That is why, in the end, external economic advice and aid must go beyond formal models and conform to each country's unique political and social context.

BRUCE R. SCOTT is Paul W. Cherington Professor of Business Administration at Harvard Business School.

Article 14

Dueling Globalizations:

A Debate Between Thomas L. Friedman and Ignacio Ramonet

DOSCAPITAL

by Thomas L. Friedman

If there can be a statute of limitations on crimes, then surely there must be a statute of limitations on foreign-policy clichés. With that in mind, I hereby declare the "post–Cold War world" over.

For the last ten years, we have talked about this "post–Cold War world." That is, we have defined the world by what it wasn't because we didn't know what it was. But a new international system has now clearly replaced the Cold War: globalization. That's right, globalization—the integration of markets, finance, and technologies in a way that is shrinking the world from a size medium to a size small and enabling each of us to reach around the world farther, faster, and cheaper than ever before. It's not just an economic trend, and it's not just some fad. Like all previous international systems, it is directly or indirectly shaping the domestic politics, economic policies, and foreign relations of virtually every country.

As an international system, the Cold War had its own structure of power: the balance between the United States and the USSR, including their respective allies. The Cold War had its own rules: In foreign affairs, neither superpower would encroach on the other's core sphere of influence, while in economics, underdeveloped countries would focus on nurturing their own national industries, developing countries on export-led growth, communist countries on autarky, and Western economies on regulated trade. The Cold War had its own dominant ideas: the clash between communism and capitalism, as well as détente, nonalignment, and perestroika. The Cold War had its own demographic trends: The movement of peoples from East to West was largely frozen by the Iron Curtain; the movement from South to North was a more steady flow. The Cold War had its own defining technologies: Nuclear weapons and the Second Industrial Revolution were dominant, but for many developing countries, the hammer and sickle were still relevant tools. Finally, the Cold War had its own defining anxiety: nuclear annihilation. When taken all together, this Cold War system didn't shape everything, but it shaped many things.

Today's globalization system has some very different attributes, rules, incentives, and characteristics, but it is equally influential. The Cold War system was characterized by one overarching feature: division. The world was chopped up, and both threats and opportunities tended to grow out of whom you were divided from. Appropriately, that Cold War system was symbolized by a single image: the Wall. The globalization system also has one overarching characteristic: integration. Today, both the threats and opportunities facing a country increasingly grow from whom it is connected to. This system is also captured by a single symbol: the World Wide Web. So in the broadest sense, we have gone from a system built around walls to a system increasingly built around networks.

Once a country makes the leap into the system of globalization, its élite begin to internalize this perspective of integration and try to locate themselves within a global context. I was visiting Amman, Jordan, in the summer of 1998 when I met my friend, Rami Khouri, the country's leading political columnist, for coffee at the Hotel Inter-Continental. We sat down, and I asked him what was new. The first thing he said to me was "Jordan was just added to CNN's worldwide weather highlights." What Rami was saying was that it is important for Jordan to know that those institutions that think globally believe it is now worth knowing what the weather is like in Amman. It makes Jordanians feel more important and holds out the hope that they will profit by having more tourists or global investors visiting. The day after seeing Rami I happened to interview Jacob Frenkel, governor of the Bank of Israel and a University of Chicago-trained economist. He remarked to me: "Before, when we talked about macroeconomics, we started by looking at the local markets, local financial system, and the interrelationship between them, and then, as an afterthought, we looked at the international economy. There was a feeling that what we do is primarily our own business and then there are some outlets where we will sell abroad. Now, we reverse the perspective. Let's not ask what markets we should export to after having decided what to produce; rather, let's first study the global framework within which we operate and then decide what to produce. It changes your whole perspective."

Integration has been driven in large part by globalization's defining technologies: computerization, miniaturization, digitization, satellite communications, fiber optics, and the Internet. And that integration, in turn, has led to many other differences between the Cold War and globalization systems.

Unlike the Cold War system, globalization has its own dominant culture, which is why integration tends to be homogenizing. In previous eras, cultural homogenization happened on a regional scale—the Romanization of Western Europe and the Mediterranean world, the Islamization of Central Asia, the Middle East, North Africa, and Spain by the Arabs, or the Russification of Eastern and Central Europe, and parts of Eurasia, under the Soviets. Culturally speaking, globalization is largely the spread (for better and for worse) of Americanization—from Big Macs and iMacs to Mickey Mouse.

Whereas the defining measurement of the Cold War was weight, particularly the throw-weight of missiles, the defining measurement of the globalization system is speed—the speed of commerce, travel, communication, and innovation. The Cold War was about Einstein's mass-energy equation, $e=mc^2$. Globalization is about Moore's Law, which states that the performance power of microprocessors will double every 18 months. The defining document of the Cold War system was "the treaty." The defining document of the globalization system is "the deal." If the defining anxiety of the Cold War was fear of annihilation from an enemy you knew all too well in a world struggle that was fixed and stable, the defining anxiety in globalization is fear of rapid change from an enemy you cannot see, touch, or feel—a sense that your job, community, or workplace can be changed at any moment by anonymous economic and technological forces that are anything but stable.

If the defining economists of the Cold War system were Karl Marx and John Maynard Keynes, each of whom wanted to tame capitalism, the defining economists of the globalization system are Joseph Schumpeter and Intel chairman Andy Grove, who prefer to unleash capitalism. Schumpeter, a former Austrian minister of finance and Harvard University professor, expressed the view in his classic work *Capitalism, Socialism, and Democracy* (1942) that the essence of capitalism is the process of "creative destruction"—the perpetual cycle of destroying old and less efficient products or services and replacing them with new, more efficient ones. Grove took Schumpeter's insight that only the paranoid survive for the title of his book about life in Silicon Valley and made it in many ways the business model of globalization capitalism. Grove helped popularize the view that dramatic, industry-transforming innovations are taking place today faster and faster. Thanks to these technological breakthroughs, the speed at which your latest invention can be made obsolete or turned into a commodity is now lightening quick. Therefore, only the paranoid will survive—only those who constantly look over their shoulders to see who is creating something new that could destroy them and then do what they must to stay one step ahead. There will be fewer and fewer walls to protect us.

If the Cold War were a sport, it would be sumo wrestling, says Johns Hopkins University professor Michael Mandelbaum. "It would be two big fat guys in a ring, with all sorts of posturing and rituals and stomping of feet, but actually very little contact until the end of the match, when there is a brief moment of shoving and the loser gets pushed out of the ring, but nobody gets killed." By contrast, if globalization were a sport, it would be the 100-meter dash, over and over and over. No matter how many times you win, you have to race again the next day. And if you lose by just one-hundredth of a second, it can be as if you lost by an hour.

Last, and most important, globalization has its own defining structure of power, which is much more complex than the Cold War structure. The Cold War system was built exclusively around nation-states, and it was balanced at the center by two superpowers. The globalization system, by contrast, is built around three balances, which overlap and affect one another.

The first is the traditional balance between nation-states. In the globalization system, this balance still matters. It can still explain a lot of the news you read on the front page of the paper, be it the containment of Iraq in

A Tale of Two Systems	Cold War	Globalization
"The Cold War had its own dominant ideas: the clash between communism and capitalism.... The driving idea behind globalization is free-market capitalism."	In 1961, dressed in military fatigues, Cuban president Fidel Castro made his famous declaration: "I shall be a Marxist-Leninist for the rest of my life." In February 1972, President Richard Nixon traveled to China to discuss a strategic alliance between the two countries against the USSR.	This January, Castro donned a business suit for a conference on globalization in Havana. Financier George Soros and conservative economist Milton Friedman were invited. In April 1999, Chinese premier Zhu Rongji came to Washington to discuss China's admission to the World Trade Organization.
"These countries that are most willing to let capitalism quickly destroy inefficient companies, so that money can be freed up and directed to more innovative ones, will thrive in the era of globalization. Those which rely on governments to protect them from such creative destruction will fall behind."	Many countries raised trade barriers and tried import substitution industrialization, nationalization, price controls, and interventionist policies. The International Monetary Fund (IMF) and the World Bank were always present but rarely heeded. **Result**: Hyperinflation, overwhelming external debt, corruption, and inefficient industries ruled the day. Only 8 percent of countries had liberal capital regimes in 1975 and foreign direct investment was at a low of $23 billion.	Economic development relies on private-sector ownership, transparency and accountability, as well as investments in human capital and social infrastructure. The IMF plays a critical role, but must be enmeshed in a web of other organizations that support social welfare and the environment while promoting economic growth. **Result**: Foreign direct investment increased five-fold between 1990 and 1997, jumping into $644 billion, and the number of countries with liberal regimes tripled to 28 percent.
"The balance between individuals and nation-states [has changed].... So you have today not only a superpower, not only Supermarkets, but... Super-empowered individuals."	In 1956, there were 973 international nongovernmental organizations (NGOs) in the world. In 1972, the total volume of world trade was only a fraction larger than the gross national product of the USSR. In 1970, there were only 7,000 transnational corporations (TNCs) in the world.	In 1996, there were 5,472 international NGOs in the world. The estimated annual revenue of transnational organized crime as of 1997, $750 billion, is larger than the gross domestic product of Russia. By 1994 the number of TNCs grew to 37,000 parent companies with 200,000 affiliates worldwide—controlling 33 percent of the world's productive assets.

SOURCE: Quotes taken from *The Lexus and the Olive Tree*, by Thomas Friedman (New York: Farrar, Straus, and Giroux, 1999).

the Middle East or the expansion of NATO against Russia in Central Europe.

The second critical balance is between nation-states and global markets. These global markets are made up of millions of investors moving money around the world with the click of a mouse. I call them the "Electronic herd." They gather in key global financial centers, such as Frankfurt, Hong Kong, London, and New York—the "supermarkets." The United States can destroy you by dropping bombs and the supermarkets can destroy you by downgrading your bonds. Who ousted President Suharto in Indonesia? It was not another superpower, it was the supermarkets.

The third balance in the globalization system—the one that is really the newest of all—is the balance between individuals and nation-states. Because globalization has brought down many of the walls that limited the movement and reach of people, and because it has simultaneously wired the world into networks, it gives more direct power to individuals than at any time in history. So we have today not only a superpower, not only supermarkets, but also super-empowered individuals. Some of these super-empowered individuals are quite angry, some of them quite constructive—but all are now able to act directly on the world stage without the traditional mediation of governments or even corporations.

Jody Williams won the Nobel Peace Prize in 1997 for her contribution to the International Campaign to Ban Landmines. She managed to build an international coalition in favor of a landmine ban without much government help and in the face of opposition from the major powers. What did she say was her secret weapon for organizing 1,000 different human rights and arms control groups on six continents? "E-mail."

By contrast, Ramzi Ahmed Yousef, the mastermind of the February 26, 1993, World Trade Center bombing in New York, is the quintessential "super-empowered angry man." Think about him for a minute. What was his program? What was his ideology? After all, he tried to blow up two of the tallest buildings in America. Did he want an Islamic state in Brooklyn? Did he want a Palestinian state in New Jersey? No. He just wanted to blow up two of the tallest buildings in America. He told the Federal District Court in Manhattan that his goal was to set off an explosion that would cause one World Trade Center tower to fall onto the other and kill 250,000 civilians. Yousef's message was that he had no message, other than to rip up the message coming from the all-powerful America to his society. Globalization (and Americanization) had gotten in his face and, at the same time, had empowered him as an individual to do something about it. A big part of the U.S. government's conspiracy case against Yousef (besides trying to blow up the World Trade Center in 1993, he planned to blow up a dozen American airliners in Asia in January 1995) relied on files found in the off-white Toshiba laptop computer that Philippine police say Yousef abandoned as he fled his Manila apartment in January 1995, shortly before his arrest. When investigators got hold of Yousef's laptop and broke into its files, they found flight schedules, projected detonation times, and sample identification documents bearing photographs of some of his co-conspirators. I loved that—Ramzi Yousef kept all his plots on the C drive of his Toshiba laptop! One should have no illusions, though. The super-empowered angry men are out there, and they present the most immediate threat today to the United States and the stability of the new globalization system. It's not because Ramzi Yousef can ever be a superpower. It's because in today's world, so many people can be Ramzi Yousef.

So, we are no longer in some messy, incoherent "post–Cold War world." We are in a new international system, defined by globalization, with its own moving parts and characteristics. We are still a long way from fully understanding how this system is going to work. Indeed, if this were the Cold War, the year would be about 1946. That is, we understand as much about how this new system is going to work as we understood about how the Cold War would work in the year Churchill gave his "Iron Curtain" speech.

Nevertheless, it's time we recognize that there is a new system emerging, start trying to analyze events within it, and give it its own name. I will start the bidding. I propose that we call it "DOScapital."

THOMAS L. FRIEDMAN *is a foreign affairs columnist for the* New York Times *and author of* The Lexus and the Olive Tree *(New York: Farrar, Straus, and Giroux, 1999).*

A NEW TOTALITARIANISM

by Ignacio Ramonet

We have known for at least ten years that globalization is the dominant phenomenon of this century. No one has been waiting around for Thomas Friedman to discover this fact. Since the end of the 1980s, dozens of authors have identified, described, and analyzed globalization inside and out. What is new in Friedman's work—and debatable—is the dichotomy he establishes between globalization and the Cold War: He presents them as opposing, interchangeable "systems." His constant repetition of this gross oversimplification reaches the height of annoyance.

Just because the Cold War and globalization are dominant phenomena in their times does not mean that they are both systems. A system is a set of practices and institutions that provides the world with a practical and theoretical framework. By this fight, the Cold War never constituted a system—Friedman makes a gross error by suggesting otherwise. The term "Cold War," coined by the media, is shorthand for a period of contemporary history (1946–89) characterized by the predominance of geopolitical and geostrategic concerns. However, it does not explain a vast number of unrelated events that also shaped that era: the expansion of multinational corporations, the development of air transportation, the worldwide extension of the United Nations, the decolonization of Africa, apartheid in South Africa, the advancement of environmentalism, or the development of computers and high-tech industries such as genetic engineering. And the list goes on.

Furthermore, tension between the West and the Soviet Union, contrary to Friedman's ideas, dates from before the Cold War. In fact, that very tension was formative in shaping the way democratic states understood Italian fascism in the 1920s, Japanese militarism in the 1930s, German rearmament after the rise of Adolf Hitler in 1933, and the Spanish Civil War between 1936 and 1939.

Friedman is right, however, to argue that globalization has a systemic bent. Step by step, this two-headed monster of technology and finance throws everything into confusion. Friedman, by contrast, tells a tale of globalization fit for Walt Disney. But the chaos that seems to delight our author so much is hardly good for the whole of humanity.

Friedman notes, and rightly so, that everything is now interdependent and that, at the same time, everything is in conflict. He also observes that globalization embodies (or infects) every trend and phenomenon at work in the world today—whether political, economic, social, cultural, or ecological. But he forgets to remark that there are groups from every nationality, religion, and ethnicity that vigorously oppose the idea of global unification and homogenization.

Furthermore, our author appears incapable of observing that globalization imposes the force of two powerful and contradictory dynamics on the world: fusion and fission. On the one hand, many states seek out alliances. They pursue fusion with others to build institutions, especially economic ones, that provide strength—or safety—in numbers. Like the European Union, groups of countries in Asia, Eastern Europe, North Africa, North America, and South America are signing free-trade agreements and reducing tariff barriers to stimulate commerce, as well as reinforcing political and security alliances.

But set against the backdrop of this integration, several multinational communities are falling victim to fission, cracking or imploding into fragments before the astounded eyes of their neighbors. When the three federal states of the Eastern bloc—Czechoslovakia, the USSR, and Yugoslavia—broke apart, they gave birth to some 22 independent states! A veritable sixth continent!

The political consequences have been ghastly. Almost everywhere, the fractures provoked by globalization have reopened old wounds. Borders are increasingly contested, and pockets of minorities give rise to dreams of annexation, secession, and ethnic cleansing. In the Balkans and the Caucasus, these tensions unleashed wars (in Abkhazia, Bosnia, Croatia, Kosovo, Moldova, Nagorno-Karabakh, Slovenia, and South Ossetia).

The social consequences have been no kinder. In the 1980s, accelerating globalization went hand in hand with the relentless ultraliberalism of British prime minister Margaret Thatcher and U.S. president Ronald Reagan. Quickly, globalization became associated with increased inequality, hikes in unemployment, deindustrialization, and deteriorated public services and goods.

Now, accidents, uncertainty, and chaos have become the parameters by which we measure the intensity of globalization. If we sized up our globalizing world today, what would we find? Poverty, illiteracy, violence, and illness are on the rise. The richest fifth of the world's population owns 80 percent of the world's resources, while the poorest fifth owns barely .5 percent. Out of a global population of 5.9 billion, barely 500 million people live comfortably, while 4.5 billion remain in need. Even in the European Union, there are 16 million people unemployed and 50 million living in poverty. And the combined fortune of the 358 richest people in the world (billionaires, in dollars) equals more than the annual revenue of 45 percent of the poorest in the world, or 2.6 billion people. That, it seems, is the brave new world of globalization.

Dazzled by the glimmer of fast profits, the champions of globalization are incapable of taking stock of the future.

Beware of Dogma

Globalization has little to do with people or progress and everything to do with money. Dazzled by the glimmer of fast profits, the champions of globalization are incapable of taking stock of the future, anticipating the needs of humanity and the environment, planning for the expansion of cities, or slowly reducing inequalities and healing social fractures.

According to Friedman, all of these problems will be resolved by the "invisible hand of the market" and by macroeconomic growth—so goes the strange and insidious logic of what we in France call the *pensée unique*. The *pensée unique*, or "single thought," represents the interests of a group of economic forces—in particular, free-flowing international capital. The arrogance of the *pensée unique* has reached such an extreme that one can, without exaggerating, call it modern dogmatism. Like a cancer, this vicious doctrine imperceptibly surrounds any rebellious logic, then inhibits it, disturbs it, paralyzes it, and finally kills it. This doctrine, this *pensée unique*, is the only ideology authorized by the invisible and omnipresent opinion police.

The *pensée unique* was born in 1944, at the time of the Bretton Woods Agreement. The doctrine sprang from the world's large economic and monetary institutions—the Banque de France, Bundesbank, European Commission, International Monetary Fund, Organisation for Economic Cooperation and Development, World Bank, and World Trade Organization—which tap their deep coffers to enlist research centers, universities, and foundations around the planet to spread the good word.

Almost everywhere, university economics departments, journalists (such as Friedman), writers, and political leaders take up the principal commandments of these new tablets of law and, through the mass media, repeat them until they are blue in the face. Their dogma is echoed dutifully by the mouthpieces of economic information and notably by the "bibles" of investors and stockbrokers—the *Economist, Far Eastern Economic Review,* Reuters, and *Wall Street Journal,* for starters—which are often owned by large industrial or financial groups. And of course, in our media-mad society, repetition is as good as proof.

So what are we told to believe? The most basic principle is so strong that even a Marxist, caught offguard, would agree: The economic prevails over the political. Or as the writer Alain Minc put it, "Capitalism cannot collapse, it is the natural state of society. Democracy is not the natural state of society. The market, yes." Only an economy disencumbered of social speed bumps and other "inefficiencies" can steer clear of regression and crisis.

The remaining key commandments of the *pensée unique* build upon the first. For instance, the market's "invisible hand corrects the unevenness and malfunctions of capitalism" and, in particular, financial markets, whose "signals orient and determine the general movement of the economy." Competition and competitiveness "stimulate and develop businesses, bringing them permanent and beneficial modernization." Free trade without barriers is "a factor of the uninterrupted development of commerce and therefore of societies." Globalization of manufactured production and especially financial flows should be encouraged at all costs. The international division of labor "moderates labor demands and lowers labor costs." A strong currency is a must, as is deregulation and privatization at every turn. There is always "less of the state" and a constant bias toward the interests of capital to the detriment of the interests of labor, not to mention a callous indifference to ecological costs. The constant repetition of this catechism in the media by almost all political decision makers, Right and Left alike (think of British and German prime ministers Tony Blair and Gerhard Schroder's "Third Way" and "New Middle"), gives it such an intimidating power that it snuffs out every tentative free thought.

Magnates and Misfits

Globalization rests upon two pillars, or paradigms, which influence the way globalizers such as Friedman think. The first pillar is communication. It has tended to replace, little by little, a major driver of the last two centuries: progress. From schools to businesses, from families and law to government, there is now one command: Communicate.

The second pillar is the market. It replaces social cohesion, the idea that a democratic society must function like a clock. In a clock, no piece is unnecessary and all pieces are unified. From this eighteenth-century mechanical metaphor, we can derive a modern economic and financial version. From now on, everything must operate according to the criteria of the "master market." Which of our new values are most fundamental? Windfall profits, efficiency, and competitiveness.

In this market-driven, interconnected world, only the strongest survive. Life is a fight, a jungle. Economic and social Darwinism, with its constant calls for competition, natural selection, and adaptation, forces itself on everyone and everything. In this new social order, individuals are divided into "solvent" or "nonsolvent"—i.e., apt to integrate into the market or not. The market offers protection to the solvents only. In this new order, where human solidarity is no longer an imperative, the rest are misfits and outcasts.

Thanks to globalization, only activities possessing four principal attributes thrive—those that are planetary, permanent, immediate, and immaterial in nature. These four characteristics recall the four principal attributes of God Himself. And in truth, globalization is set up to be a kind of modern divine critic, requiring submission, faith, worship, and new rites. The market dictates the Truth, the Beautiful, the Good, and the Just. The "laws" of the market have become a new stone tablet to revere.

Friedman warns us that straying from these laws will bring us to ruin and decay. Thus, like other propagandists of the New Faith, Friedman attempts to convince us that there is one way, and one way alone—the ultraliberal way—to manage economic affairs and, as a consequence, political affairs. For Friedman, the political is in effect the economic, the economic is finance, and finances are markets. The Bolsheviks said, "All power to the Soviets!" Supporters of globalization, such as Friedman, demand, "All power to the market!" The assertion is so peremptory that globalization has become, with its dogma and high priests, a kind of new totalitarianism.

IGNACIO RAMONET *is editor of* Le Monde *diplomatique.*

DOSCAPITAL 2.0

by Thomas L. Friedman

Ignacio Ramonet makes several points in his provocative and impassioned anti-globalization screed. Let me try to respond to what I see as the main ones.

Ramonet argues that the Cold War was not an international system. I simply disagree. To say that the Cold War was not an international system because it could not explain everything that happened during the years 1946 to 1989—such as aerial transport or apartheid—is simply wrong. An international system doesn't explain everything that happens in a particular era. It is, though, a dominant set of ideas, power structures, economic patterns, and rules that shape the domestic politics and international relations of more countries in more places than anything else.

Diplomacy then: Soviet premier Nikita Khrushev and U.S. vice president Richard Nixon argue over the merits of capitalism in 1959's "Kitchen Debate"...

Not only was the Cold War such an international system, but France had a very comfortable, unique, and, at times, constructive niche in that system, bridging the two superpower camps. Now that this old order is gone, it is obvious France is looking for a new, singular, and equally comfortable niche in today's system of globalization. Just as in the Cold War, France, like every other country, will have to define itself in relation to this new system. The obsession with globalization in the pages of *Le Monde diplomatique* is eloquent testimony to the fact that this search is alive and well in France.

Ramonet says that I "forget to remark that there are groups from every nationality, religion, ethnicity, etc., who vigorously oppose... globalization." In my book *The Lexus and the Olive Tree*, however, I have five separate chapters dealing with different aspects of that backlash. The penultimate chapter, in fact, lays out why I believe that globalization is not irreversible and identifies the five major threats to it: Globalization may be "just too hard" for too many people; it may be "just too connected" so that small numbers of people can disrupt the whole wired world today; it may be "just too intrusive" into people's lives; it may be "just too unfair to too many people"; and lastly, it may be "just too dehumanizing." My approach could hardly be called the Walt Disney version of globalization.

Frankly, I can and do make a much stronger case for the downsides of globalization than Ramonet does. I know that globalization is hardly all good, but unlike Ramonet I am not utterly blind to the new opportunities it creates for people—and I am not just talking about the wealthy few. Ask the high-tech workers in Bangalore, India, or Taiwan, or the Bordeaux region of France, or Finland, or coastal China, or Idaho what they think of the opportunities created by globalization. They are huge beneficiaries of the very market forces that Ramonet decries. Don't they count? What about all the human rights and environmental nongovernmental organizations that have been empowered by the Internet and globalization? Don't they count? Or do only French truck drivers count?

Ramonet says I am "incapable of observing that globalization imposes the force of two powerful contradictory dynamics on the world: fusion and fission." Say what? Why does he think I called my book *The Lexus and the Olive Tree?* It is all about the interaction between what is old and inbred—the quest for community, nation, family, tribe, identity, and one's own olive tree—and the economic pressures of globalization that these aspirations must interact with today, represented by the Lexus. These age-old passions are bumping up against, being squashed by, ripping through, or simply learning to live in balance with globalization.

What Ramonet can accuse me of is a belief that for the moment, the globalization system has been dominating the olive-tree impulses in most places. Many critics have pointed out that my observation that no two countries have ever fought a war against each other while they both had a McDonald's was totally disproved by the war in Kosovo. This is utter nonsense. Kosovo was only a temporary exception that in the end proved my rule. Why did airpower work to bring the Balkan war to a close after only 78 days? Because NATO bombed the Serbian tanks and troops out of Kosovo? No way. Airpower alone worked because NATO bombed the electricity stations, water system, bridges, and economic infrastructure in Belgrade—a modern European city, a majority of whose citizens wanted to be integrated with Europe and the globalization system. The war was won on the power grids of Belgrade, not in the trenches of Kosovo. One of the first things to be reopened in Belgrade was the McDonald's. It turns out in the end the Serbs wanted to wait in line for burgers, not for Kosovo.

The wretched of the earth want to go to Disneyworld, not to barricades. They want the Magic Kingdom, not Les Misérables. Just ask them.

Ramonet falls into a trap that often ensnares French intellectuals, and others, who rail against globalization. They assume that the rest of the world hates it as much as they do, and so they are always surprised in the end when the so-called little people are ready to stick with it. My dear Mr. Ramonet, with all due respect to you and Franz Fanon, the fact is the wretched of the earth want to go to Disneyworld, not to the barricades. They want the Magic Kingdom, not *Les Misérables.* Just ask them.

Finally, Ramonet says that I believe all the problems of globalization will be solved by the "invisible hand of the market." I have no idea where these quotation marks came from, let alone the thought. It certainly is not from anything I have written. The whole last chapter of my book lays out in broad strokes what I believe governments—the American government in particular—must do to "democratize" globalization, both economically and politically. Do I believe that market forces and the Electronic Herd are very powerful today and can, at times, rival governments? Absolutely. But do I believe that market forces will solve everything? Absolutely not. Ramonet, who clearly doesn't know a hedge fund from a hedge hog, demonizes markets to an absurd degree. He may think governments are powerless against such monsters, but I do not.

I appreciate the passion of Ramonet's argument, but he confuses my analysis for advocacy. My book is not a tract for or against globalization, and any careful reader will see that. It is a book of reporting about the world we now live in and the dominant international system that is shaping it—a system driven largely by forces of technology that I did not start and cannot stop. Ramonet treats globalization as a choice, and he implicitly wants us to choose something different. That is his politics. I view globalization as a reality, and I want us first to understand that reality and then, by understanding it, figure out how we can get the best out of it and cushion the worst. That is my politics.

. . . and now: Microsoft boss Bill Gates gives Russia's former first deputy premier Anatoly Chubais a crash course on the new economy in Moscow, 1997.

Let me share a secret with Ramonet. I am actually rooting for France. I hope that it can preserve all that is good and unique in its culture and way of life from the brutalizing, homogenizing forces of globalization. There is certainly room for a different path between the United States and North Korea, and good luck to France in finding it. But the readers of *Le Monde diplomatique* will get a lot better idea of how to find that middle path by reading my book than by reading Ramonet's critique.

Unfortunately, his readers will have to read *The Lexus and the Olive Tree* in a language other than French. The book is coming out in Arabic, Chinese, German, Japanese, and Spanish. There is only one major country where my American publisher could not find a local publisher to print it: France.

LET THEM EAT BIG MACS

by Ignacio Ramonet

It is truly touching when Thomas Friedman says, "The wretched of the earth want to go to Disneyworld, not to the barricades." Such a sentence deserves a place in posterity alongside Queen Marie-Antoinette's declaration in 1789, when she learned that the people of Paris were revolting and demanding bread: "Let them eat cake!"

My dear Mr. Friedman, do reread the 1999 *Human Development Report* from the United Nations Development Programme. It confirms that 1.3 billion people (or one-quarter of humanity) live on less than one dollar a day. Going to Disneyworld would probably not displease them, but I suspect they would prefer, first off, to eat well, to have a decent home and decent clothes, to be better educated, and to have a job. To obtain these basic needs, millions of people around the world (their numbers grow more numerous each day) are without a doubt ready to erect barricades and resort to violence.

I deplore this kind of solution as much as Friedman does. But if we are wise, it should never come to that. Rather, why not allocate a miniscule part of the world's wealth to the "wretched of the earth"? If we assigned just 1 percent of this wealth for 20 years to the development of the most unhappy of our human brothers, extreme misery might disappear, and with it, risks of endemic violence.

But globalization is deaf and blind to such considerations—and Friedman knows it. On the contrary, it worsens differences and divides and polarizes societies. In 1960, before globalization, the most fortunate 20 percent of the planet's population were 30 times richer than the poorest 20 percent. In 1997, at the height of globalization, the most fortunate were 74 times richer than the world's poorest! And this gap grows each day. Today, if you add up the gross national products of all the world's underdeveloped countries (with their 600 million inhabitants) they still will not equal the total wealth of the three richest people in the world. I am sure, my dear Mr. Friedman, that those 600 million people have only one thing on their minds: Disneyworld!

It is true that there is more to globalization than just the downsides, but how can we overlook the fact that during the last 15 years of globalization, per capita income has decreased in more than 80 countries, or in almost half the states of the world? Or that since the fall of communism, when the West supposedly arranged an economic miracle cure for the former Soviet Union—more or less, as Friedman would put it, new McDonald's restaurants—more than 150 million ex-Soviets (out of a population of approximately 290 million) have fallen into poverty?

If you would agree to come down out of the clouds, my dear Mr. Friedman, you could perhaps understand that globalization is a symptom of the end of a cycle. It is not only the end of the industrial era (with today's new technology), not only the end of the first capitalist revolution (with the financial revolution), but also the end of an intellectual cycle—the one driven by reason, as the philosophers of the eighteenth century defined it. Reason gave birth to modern politics and sparked the American and French Revolutions. But almost all that modern reason constructed—the state, society, industry, nationalism, socialism—has been profoundly changed. In terms of political philosophy, this transformation captures the enormous significance of globalization. Since ancient times, humanity has known two great organizing principles: the gods, and then reason. From here on out, the market succeeds them both.

Now the triumph of the market and the irresistible expansion of globalization cause me to fear an inevitable showdown between capitalism and democracy. Capitalism inexorably leads to the concentration of wealth and economic power in the hands of a small group. And this in turn leads to a fundamental question: How much redistribution will it take to make the domination of the rich minority acceptable to the majority of the world's population? The problem, my dear Mr. Friedman, is that the market is incapable of responding. All over the world, globalization is destroying the welfare state.

What can we do? How do we keep half of humanity from revolting and choosing violence? I know your response, dear Mr. Friedman: Give them all Big Macs and send them to Disneyworld!

Want to Know More?

An insightful overview of the social transformations that globalization has ushered in can be found in Malcolm Waters' ***Globalization*** (New York: Routledge, 1995). In ***Capitalism, Socialism, and Democracy*** (London: Harper, 1942), Joseph Schumpeter argues that only innovation can compensate for the destructive forces of the market. Benjamin Barber looks at culture clash in his book ***Jihad versus McWorld*** (New York: Times Books, 1995). William Greider argues for more managed globalization in ***One World Ready or Not: The Manic Logic of Global Capitalism*** (New York: Simon & Schuster, 1997). In his book, ***The Post-Corporate World: Life after Capitalism*** (San Francisco: Berrett-Koehler, 1999), David Korten stipulates that corporate capitalism could unravel the cohesion of society. Robert Reich considers how international labor markets will react to a shrinking world in ***The Work of Nations: Preparing Ourselves for the 21st Century*** (New York: Alfred A. Knopf, 1991). For a view on how information technology has changed the world economy, see Frances Cairncross' ***The Death of Distance*** (Cambridge: Harvard Business School Press, 1997). For a provocative advocate of Americanization, see David Rothkopf's **"In Praise of Cultural Imperialism"** (FOREIGN POLICY, Summer 1997). Refraining from taking sides, Dani Rodrik reexamines some of the faulty assumptions made on both sides of the globalization debate in ***"Sense and Nonsense in the Globalization Debate"*** (FOREIGN POLICY, Summer 1997). Ignacio Ramonet's wide-ranging commentary can be found in back issues of ***Le Monde diplomatique***, archived online. Rigorous critiques of Thomas Friedman's new book, ***The Lexus and the Olive Tree*** (New York: Farrar Straus and Giroux, 1999) can be found in the ***New Yorker*** (May 10, 1999), ***Nation*** (June 14, 1999), ***Financial Times*** (May 15, 1999) and ***New Statesman*** (July 5,1999).

For links to relevant Web sites, as well as a comprehensive index of related FOREIGN POLICY articles, access **www.foreignpolicy.com**.

Will Globalization Go Bankrupt?

Global integration is driven not by politics or the Internet or the World Trade Organization or even—believe it or not—McDonald's. No, throughout history, globalization has been driven primarily by monetary expansions. Credit booms spark periods of economic integration, while credit contractions quickly squelch them. Is today's world on the verge of another globalization bust?

By Michael Pettis

Only the young generation which has had a college education is capable of comprehending the exigencies of the times," wrote Alphonse, a third-generation Rothschild, in a letter to a family member in 1865. At the time the world was in the midst of a technological boom that seemed to be changing the globe beyond recognition, and certainly beyond the ability of his elders to understand. As part of that boom, capital flowed into remote corners of the earth, dragging isolated societies into modernity. Progress seemed unstoppable.

Eight years later, however markets around the world collapsed. Suddenly, investors turned away from foreign adventures and new technologies. In the depression that ensued, many of the changes eagerly embraced by the educated young—free markets, deregulated banks, immigration—seemed too painful to continue. The process of globalization, it seems, was neither inevitable nor irreversible.

What today we call economic globalization—a combination of rapid technological progress, large-scale capital flows, and burgeoning international trade—has happened many times before in the last 200 years. During each of these periods (including our own), engineers and entrepreneurs became folk heroes and made vast fortunes while transforming the world around them. They exploited scientific advances, applied a succession of innovations to older discoveries, and spread the commercial application of these technologies throughout the developed world [see box]. Communications and transportation were usually among the most affected areas, with each technological surge causing the globe to "shrink" further.

But in spite of the enthusiasm for science that accompanied each wave of globalization, as a historical rule it was primarily commerce and finance that drove globalization, not science or technology, and certainly not politics or culture. It is no accident that each of the major periods of technological progress coincided with an era of financial market expansion and vast growth in international commerce. Specifically, a sudden expansion of financial liquidity in the world's leading banking centers—whether an increase in British gold reserves in the 1820s or the massive transformation in the 1980s of illiquid mortgage loans into very liquid mortgage securities, or some other structural change in the financial markets—has been the catalyst behind every period of globalization.

If liquidity expansions historically have pushed global integration forward, subsequent liquidity contractions have brought globalization to an unexpected halt. Easy money had allowed investors to earn fortunes for their willingness to take risks, and the wealth generated by rising asset values and new investments made the liberal ideology behind the rapid market expansion seem unassailable. When conditions changed, however, the outflow of money from the financial centers was reversed. Investors rushed to pull their money out of risky ventures and into safer assets. Banks tightened up their lending requirements and refused to make new loans. Asset values collapsed. The costs of globalization, in the form of social disruption, rising income inequality, and domination by foreign elites, became unacceptable. The political and intellectual underpinnings of globalization, which had once seemed so secure, were exposed as fragile, and the popular counterattack against the logic of globalization grew irresistible.

THE BIG BANG

The process through which monetary expansions lead to economic globalization has remained consistent over the last two centuries. Typically, every few decades, a large shift in income, money supply, saving patterns, or the structure of financial markets results in a major liquidity expansion in the rich-country financial centers. The initial expansion can take a variety of forms. In England, for example, the development of joint-stock banking (limited liability corporations that issued currency) in the 1820s and 1830s—and later during the 1860s and 1870s—produced a rapid expansion of money, deposits, and bank credit, which quickly spilled over into speculative investing and international lending. Other monetary expansions were sparked by large increases in U.S. gold reserves in the early 1920s, or by major capital recyclings, such as the massive French indemnity payment after the Franco-Prussian War of 1870, the petrodollar recycling of the 1970s, or the recycling of Japan's huge trade surplus in the 1980s and 1990s. Monetary expansions also can result from the conversion of assets into more liquid instruments, such as with the explosion in U.S. speculative real-estate lending in the 1830s or the creation of the mortgage securities market in the 1980s.

The expansion initially causes local stock markets to boom and real interest rates to drop. Investors, hungry for high yields, pour money into new, nontraditional investments, including ventures aimed at exploiting emerging technologies. Financing becomes available for risky new projects such as railways, telegraph cables, textile looms, fiber optics, or personal computers, and the strong business climate that usually accompanies the liquidity expansion quickly makes these investments profitable. In turn, these new technologies enhance productivity and slash transportation costs, thus speeding up economic growth and boosting business profits. The cycle is self-reinforcing: Success breeds success, and soon the impact of rapidly expanding transportation and communication technology begins to cause a noticeable impact on social behavior, which adapts to these new technologies.

But it is not just new technology ventures that attract risk capital. Financing also begins flowing to the "peripheral" economies around the world, which, because of their small size, are quick to respond. These countries then begin to experience currency strength and real economic growth, which only reinforce the initial investment decision. As more money flows in, local markets begin to grow. As a consequence of the sudden growth in both asset values and gross domestic product, political leaders in developing countries often move to reform government policies in these countries—whether reform consists of expelling a backward Spanish monarch in the 1820s, expanding railroad transportation across the Andes in the 1860s, transforming the professionalism of the Mexican bureaucracy in the 1890s, deregulating markets in the 1920s, or privatizing bloated state-owned firms in the 1990s. By providing the government with the resources needed to overcome the resistance of local elites, capital inflows enable economic-policy reforms.

This relationship between capital and reform is frequently misunderstood: Capital inflows do not simply respond to successful economic reforms, as is commonly thought; rather, they create the conditions for reforms to take place. They permit easy financing of fiscal deficits, provide industrialists who might oppose free trade with low-cost capital, build new infrastructure, and generate so much asset-based wealth as to mollify most members of the economic and political elite who might ordinarily oppose the reforms. Policymakers tend to design such reforms to appeal to foreign investors, since policies that encourage foreign investment seem to be quickly and richly rewarded during periods of liquidity. In reality, however, capital is just as likely to flow into countries that have failed to introduce reforms. It is not a coincidence that the most famous "money doctors"—Western-trained thinkers like French economist Jean-Gustave Courcelle-Seneuil in the 1860s, financial historian Charles Conant in the 1890s, and Princeton University economist Edwin Kemmerer in the 1920s, under whose influence many developing countries undertook major liberal reforms—all exerted their maximum influence during these periods. During the 1990s, their modern counterparts advised Argentina on its currency board, brought "shock therapy" to Russia, convinced China of the benefits of membership in the World Trade Organization, and everywhere spread the ideology of free trade.

Globalization takes place largely because sudden monetary expansions encourage investors to embrace new risks.

The pattern is clear: Globalization is primarily a monetary phenomenon in which expanding liquidity induces investors to take more risks. This greater risk appetite translates into the financing of new technologies and investment in less developed markets. The combination of the two causes a "shrinking" of the globe as communications and transportation technologies improve and investment capital flows to every part of the globe. Foreign trade, made easier by the technological advances, expands to accommodate these flows. Globalization takes place, in other words, largely because investors are suddenly eager to embrace risk.

THE BIG CRUNCH

As is often forgotten during credit and investment booms, however, monetary conditions contract as well as expand. In fact, the contraction is usually the inevitable outcome of the very conditions that prompted the expansion. In times of growth, financial institutions often overextend themselves, creating distortions in financial markets and leaving themselves vulnerable to external shocks that can force a sudden retrenchment in credit and investment. In a period of rising asset prices, for example, it is often easy for even weak borrowers to obtain collateral-based loans, which of course increases the risk to the banking system of a fall in the value of the collateral. For example, property loans in the 1980s dominated and ultimately brought down the Japanese banking system. As was evident in Japan, if the financial structure has become sufficiently fragile, a retrenchment can lead to a collapse that quickly spreads throughout the economy.

Since globalization is mainly a monetary phenomenon, and since monetary conditions eventually must contract, then the process of globalization can stop and even reverse itself. Historically, such reversals have proved extraordinarily disruptive. In each of the globalization periods before the 1990s, monetary contractions usually occurred when bankers and financial authorities began to pull back from market excesses. If liquidity contracts—in the context of a perilously overextended financial system—the likelihood of bank defaults and stock market instability is high. In 1837, for example, the U.S. and British banking systems, overdependent on real estate and commodity loans, collapsed in a series of crashes that left Europe's financial sector in tatters and the United States in the midst of bank failures and state government defaults.

The same process occurred a few decades later. Alphonse Rothschild's globalizing cycle of the 1860s ended with the stock market crashes that began in Vienna in May 1873 and spread around the world during the next four months, leading, among other things, to the closing of the New York Stock Exchange (NYSE) that September amid the near-collapse of American railway securities. Conditions were so bad that the rest of the decade after 1873 was popularly referred to in the United States as the Great Depression. Nearly 60 years later, that name was reassigned to a similar episode—the one that ended the Roaring Twenties and began with the near-breakdown of the U.S. banking system in 1930–31. The expansion of the 1960s was somewhat different in that it began to unravel during the early and mid-1970s when, thanks partly to the OPEC oil price hikes and subsequent petrodollar recycling, a second liquidity boom occurred, and lending to sovereign borrowers in the developing world continued through the end of the decade. However, the cycle finally broke down altogether when rising interest rates and contracting money engineered by then Federal Reserve Chairman Paul Volcker helped precipitate the Third World debt crisis of the 1980s. Indeed, with the exception of the globalization period of the early 1900s, which ended with the advent of World War I, each of these eras of international integration concluded with sharp monetary contractions that led to a banking system collapse or retrenchment, declining asset values, and a sharp reduction in both investor risk appetite and international lending.

Following most such market crashes, the public comes to see prevalent financial market practices as more sinister, and criticism of the excesses of bankers becomes a popular sport among politicians and the press in the advanced economies. Once capital stops flowing into the less developed, capital-hungry countries, the domestic consensus in favor of economic reform and international integration begins to disintegrate. When capital inflows no longer suffice to cover the short-term costs to the local elites and middle classes of increased international integration-including psychic costs such as feelings of wounded national pride-support for globalization quickly wanes. Populist movements, never completely dormant, become reinvigorated. Countries turn inward. Arguments in favor of protectionism suddenly start to sound appealing. Investment flows quickly become capital flight.

Following market crashes, the public comes to see financial markets as more sinister, and criticism of bankers becomes a popular sport among politicians and the press.

This pattern emerged in the aftermath of the 1830s crash, when confidence in free markets nose-dived and the subsequent populist and nationalist backlash endured until the failure of the muchdreaded European liberal uprisings of 1848, which saw the earliest stirrings of communism and the publication of the *Communist Manifesto*. Later, in the 1870s, the economic depression that followed the mass bank closings in Europe, the United States, and Latin America was accompanied by an upsurge of political radicalism and populist outrage, along with bouts of protectionism throughout Europe and the United States by the end of the decade. Similarly, the Great Depression of the 1930s also fostered political instability and a popular revulsion toward the excesses of financial capitalism, culminating in burgeoning left-wing movements, the passage of anti-bank legislation, and even the jailing of the president of the NYSE.

PROFITS OF DOOM

Will these patterns manifest themselves again? Indeed, a new global monetary contraction already may be under way. In each of the previous contractions, stock markets fell, led by the collapse of the once-high-flying technology sector; lending to emerging markets dried up, bringing with it a series of sovereign defaults; and investors clamored for safety and security. Consider the crash of 1873, a typical case: Then, the equivalent of today's high-tech sector was the market for railway stocks and bonds, and the previous decade had seen a rush of new stock and bond offerings that reached near-manic proportions in the early 1870s. The period also saw rapid growth of lending to

Latin America, southern and eastern Europe, and the Middle East. Wall Street veterans had expressed nervousness about market excesses for years leading up to the crash, but the exuberance of investors who believed in the infinite promise of the railroads, at home and abroad, coupled with the rising prominence of bull-market speculators like Jay Gould and Diamond Jim Brady, swept them aside. When the market collapsed in 1873, railway securities were the worst hit, with many companies going bankrupt and closing their doors. Major borrowers from the developing world were unable to find new financing, and a series of defaults spread from the Middle East to Latin America in a matter of months. In the United States, the Congress and press became furious with the actions of stock market speculators and pursued financial scandals all the way to President Ulysses S. Grant's cabinet. Even Grant's brother-in-law was accused of being in cahoots with a notorious group that attempted a brutal gold squeeze.

Today, we see many of the same things. The technology sector is in shambles, and popular sentiment has turned strongly against many of the Wall Street heroes who profited most from the boom. Lending to emerging markets has all but dried up. As of this writing, the most sophisticated analysts predict that a debt default in Argentina is almost certain—and would unleash a series of other sovereign defaults in Latin America and around the world. The yield differences between risky assets and the safest and most liquid assets are at historical highs. In short, investors seem far more reluctant to take on risk than they were just a few years ago.

This lower risk tolerance does not bode well for poor nations. Historically, many developing countries only seem to experience economic growth during periods of heavy capital inflow, which in turn tend to last only as long as the liquidity-inspired asset booms in rich-country financial markets. Will the international consensus that supports globalization last when capital stops flowing? The outlook is not very positive. While there is still broad support in many circles for free trade, economic liberalization, technological advances, and free capital flows—even when the social and psychic costs are acknowledged—we already are witnessing a strong political reaction against globalization. This backlash is evident in the return of populist movements in Latin America; street clashes in Seattle, Prague, and Quebec; and the growing disenchantment in some quarters with the disruptions and uncertainties that follow in the wake of globalization.

The leaders now gathered in opposition to globalization—from President Hugo Chávez in Venezuela to Malaysian Prime Minister Mahathir bin Mohamad to anti-trade activist Lori Wallach in the United States—should not be dismissed too easily, no matter how dubious or fragile some of their arguments may seem. The logic of their arguments may not win the day, but rather a global monetary contraction may reverse the political consensus that was necessary to support the broad and sometimes disruptive social changes that accompany globalization. When that occurs, policy debates will be influenced by the less emotional and more thoughtful attacks on globalization by the likes of Robert Wade, a professor of political economy at the London School of Economics, who argues forcefully that globalization has actually resulted in greater global income inequality and worse conditions for the poor.

Investing in the Future

In past periods of monetary expansion and globalization, Western societies have experienced the rapid development and commercial application of new technologies.

1822–37: expansion of canal building, first railway boom, application of steam power to the manufacturing process, advances in machine tool design, invention of McCormick's reaper, first gas-lighting enterprises, and development of the telegraph

1851–73: advances in mining, second railway boom, developments in shipping, and rapid growth in the number of corporations in continental Europe

1881–1914: explosive productivity growth in Europe and the United States, improvement in steel production and heavy chemical manufacturing, first power station, spread of electricity, development of the internal combustion engine, another railway boom, innovation in newspaper practice and technology, and developments in canning and refrigeration

1922–30: commercialization of automobiles and aircraft, new forms of mass media, rising popularity of cinema and radio broadcasting, spread of artificial fibers and plastics, widespread use of electricity in U.S. factories, the creation and sale of a variety of new electric appliances, and expanded telephone ownership

1960–73: development and application of transistor technology, advances in commercial flying and shipping, and the spread of telecommunications and software

1985–present: ubiquity of information processing, explosion in computer memory, advances in biotechnology and medical technologies, and commercial application of the Internet

If a global liquidity contraction is under way, antiglobalization arguments will resonate more strongly as many of the warnings about the greed of Wall Street and the dangers of liberal reform will seem to come true. Supposedly irreversible trends will suddenly reverse themselves. Further attempts to deepen economic reform, spread free trade, and increase capital and labor mobility may face political opposition that will be very difficult to overcome, particularly since bankers, the most committed supporters of globalization, may lose much of their prestige and become the target of populist attacks following a serious stock market decline. Because bankers are so identified with globalization, any criticism of Wall Street will also implicitly be a criticism of globalizing markets.

Financiers, after all, were not the popular heroes in the 1930s that they were during the 1920s, and current events seem to mirror past backlashes. Already the U.S. Securities and Exchange Commission, which was created during the Great Depression of the 1930s, is investigating the role of bankers and analysts in misleading the public on the market excesses of the 1990s. In June 2001, the industry's lobby group, the Securities Industry Association, proposed a voluntary code, euphemized as "a compilation of best practices... to ensure the ongoing integrity of securities research and analysis," largely to head off an expansion of external regulation. Increasingly, experts bewail the conflicts of interest inherent among the mega-banks that dominate U.S. and global finance.

Globalization itself always will wax and wane with global liquidity. For those committed to further international integration within a liberal economic framework, the successes of the recent past should not breed complacency since the conditions will change and the mandate for liberal expansion will wither. For those who seek to reverse the socioeconomic changes that globalization has wrought, the future may bring far more progress than they hoped. If global liquidity contracts and if markets around the world pull back, our imaginations will once again turn to the increasingly visible costs of globalization and away from the potential for all peoples to prosper. The reaction against globalization will suddenly seem unstoppable.

Michael Pettis is an investment banker and professor of finance at Columbia University He is author of The Volatility Machine: Emerging Economies and the Threat of Financial Collapse *(New York: Oxford University Press, 2001).*

Want to Know More?

Charles P. Kindleberger's ***A Financial History of Western Europe***, 2nd ed. (New York: Oxford University Press, 1993) is probably the best single volume for anyone interested in understanding the financial history of globalization. For a discussion of how structural changes in financial systems can lead to overextension and banking crises, consult Hyman P. Minsky's ***Can "It" Happen Again? Essays on Instability and Finance*** (Armonk: M.E. Sharpe, 1982). Also see Paul W. Drake's, ed., ***Money Doctors, Foreign Debts, and Economic Reforms in Latin America from the 1890s to the Present*** (Wilmington: SR Books, 1994) and Christian Suter's ***Debt Cycles in the World Economy: Foreign Loans, Financial Crises, and Debt Settlements, 1820–1990*** (Boulder: Westview Press, 1992). Michael Pettis's ***The Volatility Machine: Emerging Economies and the Threat of Financial Collapse*** (New York: Oxford University Press, 2001) identifies the specific events that set off liquidity booms in prior periods of global integration.

Frank Griffith Dawson's ***The First Latin American Debt Crisis: The City of London and the 1822–25 Loan Bubble*** (New Haven: Yale University Press, 1990) offers a wonderful account of an early era of globalization, although his description of events 180 years ago is too familiar for comfort. Matthew Josephson's famous ***The Robber Barons: The Great American Capitalists, 1861–1901*** (New York: Harcourt, Brace & World, 1962) is as good a place as any to start reading up on the railway booms of the late 19th century. Harold James's ***The End of Globalization: Lessons from the Great Depression*** (Cambridge: Harvard University Press, 2001) is one of the best recent books on economic history and discusses the globalizing period of the 1920s and the subsequent backlash.

Kevin H. O'Rourke and Jeffrey G. Williamson recently completed a major work on globalization at the end of the 19th century and the backlash against it in ***Globalization and History: The Evolution of a Nineteenth-Century Atlantic Economy*** (Cambridge: MIT Press, 1999). Finally, Niall Ferguson's ***The House of Rothschild: Money's Prophets, 1798–1848*** (New York: Viking Press, 1998) and ***The World's Banker: The History of the House of Rothschild*** (London: Weidenfeld & Nicolson, 1998) tell the story of a family intimately involved with every aspect of globalization.

• For links to relevant Web sites, as well as a comprehensive index of related FOREIGN POLICY articles, access **www.foreignpolicy.com**.

Article 16

America's Two-Front Economic Conflict

C. Fred Bergsten

DOUBLE TROUBLE

SINCE THE END of the Cold War, the perceived threats to U.S. security have been mainly from "rogue states" such as Iraq and North Korea—none of which are superpowers or likely allies of each other in confronting the United States. But the United States now faces the real possibility of economic conflict with both Europe and East Asia—the commercial and financial equivalent of two-front combat. In this domain, both potential rivals are superpowers. Moreover, they have already demonstrated their ability to coalesce against the United States, as they did to help torpedo the Seattle ministerial meeting of the World Trade Organization (WTO) in December 1999.

Peaceful and effective resolution of these potential conflicts is one of the most important and difficult issues facing the new U.S. administration and the world. The American and global economies are slowing sharply, and their futures may be heavily affected by the outcomes. In a post–Cold War world in which economic issues are central to international relations, those outcomes will also be crucial for U.S. foreign policy and global stability. Compounding the complexity of the situation is the fact European and East Asian nations are not only the United States' economic competitors but also its economic partners—and many of them are close security allies as well.

CONTINENTAL DIVIDE

THE UNITED STATES and the European Union (EU) are on the brink of a major trade and economic conflict. Washington has already retaliated against European import restrictions on American beef and bananas—each retaliation accounting for a hundred million dollars or so of annual trade—and has rejected all European efforts to resolve these disputes. Europe in turn threatens to retaliate against several billion dollars of U.S. export subsidies, as well as new U.S. trade laws that would channel the proceeds of antidumping penalties from the Treasury Department to the complaining industries and would force the president to continually change the products being retaliated against, thus intensifying the impact of U.S. punitive sanctions.

Still larger trade clashes loom. The troubled U.S. steel industry will likely file additional antidumping cases against European firms or even an industry-wide safeguard action that would restrict all European imports. In addition, a major dispute over commercial aircraft is brewing as the two sides quarrel over whether direct European governmental subsidies for Airbus or indirect Pentagon subsidies for Boeing are more egregious. Europe's outcry over U.S. sanctions against European firms that deal with American adversaries such as Cuba and Iran has only been swept under the rug. And just over the horizon lies the biggest battle of all: the debates over farm subsidies, genetically modified products, and overall agricultural trade that will explode in 2003, when the U.S.-EU "peace clause" (a moratorium on new complaints in the agricultural sector) expires.

The United States and Europe also differ on global trade issues for which they share leadership responsibility. They remain divided, for example, on whether to include competition policy and investment issues in new WTO negotiations. It was their opposing views on issues such as these that scuttled any prospect of launching a new round of trade talks at Seattle.

Furthermore, the United States and Europe are divided on energy and environmental issues. As energy prices soared and riots erupted on European roadways last fall, European resentment flared anew over Americans' penchant for cheap fuel and their profligate energy consumption. The recent Hague conference that sought to devise operational plans to check global warming broke up over fundamental disagreements about who bears responsibility for greenhouse gas emissions, how they should be cut back, and who should pay for doing so.

Financial relations are another potential land mine. When the European Central Bank intervened to halt the slide of the euro last September, the United States provided only grudging support. But now that the euro has rebounded, the shoe may soon be on the other foot as the dollar risks a sharp decline in the wake of a domestic economic slowdown and an annual trade deficit approaching $500 billion. Europe should be willing to help in such a circumstance, since it would not want to see the euro soar to levels that would jeopardize the price competitiveness of its exports. But it might be less enthusiastic to bolster the dollar if the net effect were to finance massive tax cuts à la President George W. Bush that would further reduce U.S. national savings and hence increase America's draw on foreign capital.

The accumulation of such potential conflicts poses high risks for both American and European economies. Moreover, the global impact of a commercial clash between these two titans could be severe including systemic damage to the WTO, especially its crucial but fragile dispute settlement mechanism. A transatlantic economic conflict may also exacerbate potential security tensions over issues such as a future policy toward the Balkans, American concern over European plans for an autonomous military force, and European anxieties that American proposals for a missile defense system will renew tensions with Russia and trigger another global arms race. All this calls for new basic strategies for managing globalization, especially in light of the developments simultaneously arising on the other side of the world.

ASIAN FUSION

THE POTENTIAL economic confrontation between the United States and East Asia is quite different from the transatlantic one. The sector-specific conflicts that have traditionally burdened U.S.-Asian trade relations (and that now burden U.S.-European ones) have diminished sharply. The problem now is that East Asia, for the first time in history, is creating its own economic bloc, which could include preferential trade arrangements and an Asian Monetary Fund (AMF).

Asian countries will shortly complete a Network of Bilateral Swap Arrangements, which will provide initially up to $50 billion and eventually as much as $100 billion in mutual currency supports among the "ASEAN + 3": the ten members of the Association of Southeast Asian Nations (ASEAN), plus Japan, China, and South Korea. In addition, they are contemplating cooperative exchange-rate systems to shield themselves from the huge fluctuations in the currencies of the major industrial countries—similar to Europe's moves toward monetary integration in the 1970s to defend itself against wide fluctuations of the dollar. These countries are also devising new "early warning systems" to help prevent future regional economic crises. Building on the 1998 Miyazawa Plan, under which Japan offered $30 billion to support the recovery of the nations hit hardest by the 1997–98 financial crisis, these countries are clearly headed toward creating their own monetary arrangements.

On the trade side, fundamental changes in the trade policies of the three main East Asian powers—Japan, South Korea, and China—have initiated a spate of subregional and bilateral free trade negotiations. Japan, which has traditionally relied on the multilateral frameworks of the General Agreement on Trade and Tariffs (GATT) and now the WTO, has begun to pursue bilateral trade agreements with Singapore, Mexico, and South Korea over the past two years. South Korea has made a similar policy shift and is now actively negotiating with Chile, as well. China, which had also previously eschewed regional approaches, stunned everyone at the fourth annual ASEAN + 3 summit in late 2000 by proposing a China-ASEAN free trade area—which the Southeast Asians, fearing Chinese domination, immediately broadened to include Japan and South Korea.

Thus a study of a possible East Asian free trade area, which would be a world-shaking development, was launched at the summit. The new study will build on the one already underway for the creation of a Northeast Asia free trade area comprising China, Japan, and South Korea, which itself is of major significance. In short, the East Asia Economic Group proposed a decade ago by Malaysian Prime Minister Mahathir bin Mohammed is beginning to take shape, albeit slowly and in subregional stages. ASEAN, for example, has already developed detailed plans to complete its own free trade area and currency network. No overarching political strategy drives Asian integration, as it did for the EU, and little coordination exists between the current financial and trade initiatives. But there can be little doubt that these new movements will result in the evolution of an East Asian economic bloc.

East Asian integration is not necessarily a bad thing and could in fact prompt new trade liberalization on the multilateral level. But an East Asian free trade area could also erect new discrimination against U.S. exports of at least $20 billion per year. And a unified East Asia could be an even more formidable competitor than Japan was in the past or China is today, though it should also be a more attractive market for both exports and investment from the United States.

On the financial side, the members of the AMF would hold monetary reserves of almost $1 trillion—the largest in the world and far larger than those of the United States or the countries of the eurozone. Japan and China would support each other's currencies with the two largest dollar hoards in the world, totaling more than $500 billion. The AMF could clearly rival the International Monetary Fund (IMF) and raise potential conflicts, including disputes over the conditions of country rescue packages.

As with Europe, the new economic developments in Asia carry foreign policy and security implications as well. A truly united East Asia could sharply reduce the risk of conflict in the region and hence be very much in the U.S. interest. On the other hand, a sense that America was being shunted aside by both Asia and Europe could reinforce isolationist tendencies within the United States.

A CHANGING GLOBAL SCENE

THE MAIN HISTORICAL underpinning of America's potential two-front economic conflict is the increasing multipolarization of the world economy. Despite America's prodigious economic performance in the 1990s, the EU is now the largest economic entity on the globe, and its lead will grow further as it expands its membership over the next few years. The euro, although still suffering numerous growing pains, has completed the region's economic integration.

East Asia has achieved an economic weight comparable to those of the United States and the EU, but it has learned that its disunity has precluded it from achieving equal status on the global scene. Its inferior position was made clear during the 1997–98 financial crisis, when the region became dependent on the international financial institutions directed by the Atlantic powers. The image of IMF Managing Director Michel Camdessus dictating terms to Indonesian President Suharto is bitterly seared into Asian memories, especially now that prominent Western economists argue that IMF programs actually made the crisis worse and point to how Malaysia has recovered effectively without IMF assistance. Under such circumstances, Asia's gross under-representation in the IMF and other key international institutions has suddenly attained great salience. The Asians have vowed to never again be in such thrall to the West.

In addition, the creation of the euro has prompted Asian countries to consider moving toward their own currency unit, albeit over a long period of time. More broadly, the traditional Asian repugnance toward "the huge bureaucracy in Brussels" has turned into widespread contemplation of emulating the basic European strategy of economic cooperation, despite recognition of the differences between the two regions and thus doubts about deep integration. Through biannual Asia-Europe Meetings, Asia is in fact seeking and receiving extensive European advice for its own coordination efforts.

The end of the Cold War has also contributed to the potential for a two-front economic conflict. The disappearance of the Soviet threat has reduced the importance of the American military umbrella over Europe and Asia. The security glue that traditionally encouraged the postwar allies to resolve their economic differences no longer exists. The semiannual U.S.-EU summits have been pitiful failures, and the Asia-Pacific Economic Cooperation forum (APEC), which seeks to prevent U.S.-Asia conflict by providing an institutional link across the Pacific, has only begun to address the issues posed by East Asian regionalism.

These changes in the global scene—Europe's and East Asia's achievement of rough economic parity with the United States, and the end of the Cold War—require a restructuring of global economic arrangements. Further delays in such reform will only heighten the risk of costly conflicts.

FOLLOW THE LEADER

A MORE SUBTLE CAUSE of the present crisis is the decline of effective U.S. leadership in the global economic system. This in turn stems from a domestic popular backlash against globalization and the resulting political stalemate in Washington.

America's international posture has been hurt by domestic backlash against globalization.

During the postwar period, the pervasive tension between regionalism and multilateralism (mainly as a result of increasing European integration) was generally resolved in favor of multilateralism due to steady American leadership in that direction. The United States insisted on a new round of global trade liberalization after each major step in the European integration process, which otherwise would have created additional trade discrimination and likely emulation around the world. Thus the primacy of GATT was maintained. Indeed, a positive dynamic between regional and global trade liberalization remained consistent for more than four decades. Even when the United States itself began to embrace regionalism—from bilateral free trade with Canada to the North American Free Trade Agreement to the proposed Free Trade Area of the Americas (FTAA)—it was careful to simultaneously pursue new multilateral initiatives to ensure an umbrella of global trade liberalization.

Washington's ability to maintain such leadership has been severely curtailed over the past five years, however.

Despite the strength of America's economy and the reduction of its unemployment rate to a 30-year low, the popular backlash against globalization has produced a political stalemate on most international economic issues. As a result, the president has had no effective authority to negotiate new trade agreements since 1994. Legislation to replenish the IMF languished for a year in the midst of the Asian crisis, until it was rescued fortuitously by the farm community's interest in restoring its exports to Asia. Even relatively straightforward issues—such as extending permanent normal trade relations to China or offering enhanced market access to Africa and the Caribbean—required lengthy, all-out presidential and business campaigns to persuade Congress.

Largely as a result of this domestic standstill, America's international economic posture has been compromised. The United States' initial refusal in 1997 to contribute to the IMF support package for Thailand for fear of further riling Congress, for example, earned lasting enmity throughout Asia. The main reason for the debacle at Seattle was the United States' inability to propose a new round of trade negotiations that would meet the legitimate interests of other major players. Lacking the domestic authority to lower its own trade barriers, Washington was forced to offer an agenda that sought to reduce protection only in other countries—a prospect that was understandably unappealing to the rest of the world. Similarly, in 1997–98 APEC negotiations, the United States unsuccessfully pushed a program of sector-specific liberalization that focused almost wholly on U.S. export interests. And six years after the idea of the FTAA was launched in Miami, little progress has been made toward hemispheric trade liberalization.

This international leadership vacuum has had two subtle but profound effects on the world economy. Like a bicycle on a hill, the global trading system tends to slip backwards in the absence of continual progress forward. Now, with no serious multilateral trade negotiations taking place anywhere in the world, the backsliding has come in the form of intensified regionalism (which is inherently discriminatory), as well as mercantilist and protectionist disputes across the Atlantic. An East Asian free trade area—and along with it, a three-bloc world—will likely emerge if the United States remains on the sidelines of international trade for another five years. Such U.S. impotence would also mean that the traditionally positive impact of regional liberalization on the multilateral process would give way to increasing antagonism and even hostility between the regional blocs.

The other chief effect of the leadership vacuum is increased international disregard of, or even hostility toward, the United States on the economic front. Because of its weight in the world economy, its dynamic growth, and its traditional leadership role, the United States remains the most important player in the global economic system. The other economic powers generally seek to avoid confronting it directly. The EU, for example, has tried to avoid overt battles, despite its escalating range of disputes with the United States. East Asian governments are careful to assure Washington that their new regional initiatives are fully consistent with existing global norms and institutions—a conciliatory stance that is in sharp contrast to Mahathir's shrill rhetoric of a decade ago and Japanese Vice Minister of Finance Eisuke Sakakibara's aggressive 1997 promotion of the AMF.

In reality, however, the United States is perceived as wanting to call the shots without putting up much of its own money or making changes in its own laws and practices. These specific economic complaints fuse with and feed on more general anti-American sentiments throughout the world. Hence, the two other economic superpowers are proceeding on their own. The EU has launched the euro, a new association agreement with Mexico, and negotiations with Mercosur (the trade bloc comprising Argentina, Brazil, Paraguay, and Uruguay); East Asia is pursuing the AMF and the East Asian free trade area. The result is a clear and steady erosion of both the United States' position on the global economic scene and the multilateral rules and institutions that it has traditionally championed. If not checked soon, this erosion could deteriorate into severe international conflicts and the disintegration of global economic links.

ALTERNATIVE MEDICINE

THE REMEDIES for this risky situation are intellectually straightforward but politically difficult. The cardinal requirement is to subsume the current bilateral disputes and evolving regional initiatives within a reinvigorated multilateral system that rests on an internationally shared vision of how to manage globalization. Such a system will have to restart the momentum of multilateral trade liberalization, provide a global umbrella that effectively reconciles the inevitable regional groupings, and negotiate rather than litigate the most politically sensitive disputes among the major powers. This remedy will require the restoration of a domestic consensus on globalization in the United States and considerable trade and financial reforms in Europe and East Asia.

The United States faces two tempting responses to the current tensions, each of which would be a mistake. One is to resurrect the mid-1990s proposal for a transatlantic free trade area (TAFTA) between the United States and the EU. TAFTA would erect new trade discrimination against East Asia and thus assure the acceleration of both its regional integration and its anti-Western orientation. In addition, TAFTA would discriminate against all developing countries—"the richest ganging up on the poorest"—and would end any prospect of their constructive participation in the WTO and other global institutions.

The second bad idea is for the United States to pursue the FTAA without simultaneously working toward a new round of multilateral negotiations at the WTO. The new

Bush administration has indicated interest in the FTAA and will have an early opportunity to pursue it at the third Summit of the Americas in Québec in late April. Absent a parallel multilateral effort, however, such an initiative would validate the regional emphases of both Europe and Asia and spark new trade discrimination.

Although President Bush will not have enough time to obtain fast-track negotiating authority before going to Québec, he must work out enough congressional support to provide credibility for any pledges he makes at the hemispheric summit. While doing so, he could also seek congressional blessing for a broad-based initiative in the WTO to get the multilateral process back on track. Such an initiative would ideally move toward global free trade in which all regional trade preferences would be eliminated. The United States could then begin working with Europe and Asia to launch a new round at the WTO ministerial conference later this year, while still proceeding with inter-American integration at Québec. To buy time for this strategy to be implemented, the United States and the EU should broaden their "peace clause" on agriculture by declaring a three-year freeze on all retaliatory actions and complaints in additional sectors.

America must adopt stronger safety nets to cushion the blows of globalization.

A useful adjunct to this strategy of renewed multilateralism would be cross-regional free trade agreements (CRFTAs) that cut across East Asia, Europe, and the Americas. Such pacts are already being pursued at the bilateral level, such as the U.S.-Singapore and Japan-Mexico initiatives, and at the super-regional level, as with APEC and the EU-Mercosur talks. Although these arrangements still create new discrimination and potential trade conflict and are thus decidedly inferior to multilateral liberalization, they could nevertheless dilute the regional groupings that may otherwise solidify into rigid blocs. Thus CRFTAs represent a useful addition to renewed multilateral efforts, or at least a second-best fallback if that preferred course turns out to be unobtainable in the near term.

A renewal of multilateral efforts is also required on the financial side. The IMF has already made significant policy changes but must now take additional steps to buttress its ability to prevent and quickly respond to crises. The main institutional change needed at the IMF is to accord East Asia more voting shares and leadership assignments to account for its greatly increased economic weight—mostly at the expense of Europe, which is over-represented. The IMF also needs to address the costly instability and prolonged misalignments among the dollar, the euro, and the yen, which contribute to the need felt by the Asians to create their own monetary zone.

The success of these remedies rests on the ability of the United States to overcome its crippling domestic resistance to globalization. This will be a difficult task for the new administration, but the potential threats to U.S. economic prosperity, its international leadership, and global stability should be enough to convince both the White House and Congress to agree on a new approach to the international economy.

This agreement should rest on several key elements. It must start from a clear consensus that globalization brings substantial net benefits to the American economy, including intensified competition that holds down inflation and thus permits the creation of millions of additional jobs. At the same time, Washington must acknowledge that globalization causes job and income losses in certain sectors, which exact significant psychological tolls. The government, therefore, has a responsibility to channel help from the winners to the losers, for humanitarian and equity reasons as well as to maintain political support for continued globalization efforts.

To fulfill that obligation, the country must adopt stronger safety nets, including more generous unemployment insurance eligibility criteria and compensation levels, portable health insurance and pensions, and perhaps a new program of wage insurance. Even more important, government and business leaders need to work together to provide better education and training programs to enable all Americans to benefit from globalization rather than feel victimized by it.

At the international level, the White House and Congress need to reassert American leadership in negotiating new agreements on both trade and finance, as described above, that will place the current conflicts into a broader global and strategic context. These agreements should, among other things, promote international labor and environmental standards that will avoid distorting either global competition or normal trade flows.

If Washington does not adopt such a strategy early on, the current situation could become much worse. The U.S. economy has slowed sharply, the unemployment rate will soon rise, and the annual trade deficit is approaching $500 billion (about five percent of GDP). Blame for such economic troubles will inevitably focus on foreign competition—especially if European and Asian countries raise new barriers against U.S. exports. Washington will feel intense pressure to retaliate against Europe and to thwart the rise of even tougher rivals in East Asia. It will also be tempted to adopt new unilateralist measures, such as withdrawal from international monetary cooperation and multilateral trade efforts.

Both the prospective global slowdown and any such U.S. reactions to it could accelerate the current trends in Europe and Asia. Tougher economic times will make it harder for Europe to resist its own protectionists, especially as French elections approach in 2002. Economic troubles will prod East Asians to speed their integration plans, as their financial crisis has already done. Any new protectionist or unilateralist steps taken by the United States would trigger parallel responses elsewhere. And any significant American slowdown would further embolden the Europeans and the Asians to overcome their humiliations over the initial fall of the euro and the shattering of the "economic miracle," respectively, and go their own ways.

This potential two-front economic conflict could severely threaten international prosperity and even global security. Restoration of both an effective global economic order and renewed U.S. leadership should be a top priority for the new administration and Congress.

C. FRED BERGSTEN is Director of the Institute for International Economics and former Assistant Secretary of the Treasury (1977–81) and Assistant for International Economic Affairs to the National Security Council (1969–71).

What's Wrong With This Picture?

THE RISE OF THE MEDIA CARTEL HAS BEEN A LONG TIME COMING. THE CULTURAL EFFECTS ARE NOT NEW IN KIND, BUT THE PROBLEM HAS BECOME CONSIDERABLY LARGER.

MARK CRISPIN MILLER

For all their economic clout and cultural sway, the ten great multinationals—AOL Time Warner, Disney, General Electric, News Corporation, Viacom, Vivendi, Sony, Bertelsmann, AT&T and Liberty Media—rule the cosmos only at the moment. The media cartel that keeps us fully entertained and permanently half-informed is always growing here and shriveling there, with certain of its members bulking up while others slowly fall apart or get digested whole. But while the players tend to come and go—always with a few exceptions—the overall Leviathan itself keeps getting bigger, louder, brighter, forever taking up more time and space, in every street, in countless homes, in every other head.

The rise of the cartel has been a long time coming (and it still has some way to go). It represents the grand convergence of the previously disparate US culture industries—many of them vertically monopolized already—into one global superindustry providing most of our imaginary "content." The movie business had been largely dominated by the major studios in Hollywood; TV, like radio before it, by the triune axis of the networks headquartered in New York; magazines, primarily by Henry Luce (with many independent others on the scene); and music, from the 1960s, mostly by the major record labels. Now all those separate fields are one, the whole terrain divided up among the giants—which, in league with Barnes & Noble, Borders and the big distributors, also control the book business. (Even with its leading houses, book publishing was once a cottage industry at both the editorial and retail levels.) For all the democratic promise of the Internet, moreover, much of cyberspace has now been occupied, its erstwhile wildernesses swiftly paved and lighted over by the same colossi. The only industry not yet absorbed into this new world order is the newsprint sector of the Fourth Estate—a business that was heavily shadowed to begin with by the likes of Hearst and other, regional grandees, flush with the ill-gotten gains of oil, mining and utilities—and such absorption is, as we shall see, about to happen.

Thus what we have today is not a problem wholly new in kind but rather the disastrous upshot of an evolutionary process whereby that old problem has become considerably larger—and that great quantitative change, with just a few huge players now co-directing all the nation's media, has brought about enormous qualitative changes. For one thing, the cartel's rise has made extremely rare the sort of marvelous exception that has always popped up, unexpectedly, to startle and revivify the culture—the genuine independents among record labels, radio stations, movie theaters, newspapers, book publishers and so on. Those that don't fail nowadays are so remarkable that they inspire not emulation but amazement. Otherwise, the monoculture, endlessly and noisily triumphant, offers, by and large, a lot of nothing, whether packaged as "the news" or "entertainment."

Of all the cartel's dangerous consequences for American society and culture, the worst is its corrosive influence on journalism. Under AOL Time Warner, GE, Viacom et al., the news is, with a few exceptions, yet another version of the entertainment that the cartel also vends nonstop. This is also nothing new—consider the newsreels of yesteryear—but the gigantic scale and thoroughness of the corporate concentration has made a world of difference, and so has made this world a very different place.

Let us start to grasp the situation by comparing this new centerfold with our first outline of the National Entertainment State, published in the spring of 1996. Back then, the national TV news appeared to be a tidy tetrarchy: two network news divisions owned by large appliance makers/weapons manufacturers (CBS by Westinghouse, NBC by General Electric), and the other two bought lately by the nation's top purveyors of Big Fun (ABC by Disney, CNN by Time Warner). Cable was still relatively immature, so that, of its many enterprises, only CNN competed with the broadcast networks' short-staffed newsrooms; and its buccaneering founder, Ted Turner, still seemed to call the shots from his new aerie at Time Warner headquarters.

Today the telejournalistic firmament includes the meteoric Fox News Channel, as well as twenty-six television stations owned outright by Rupert Murdoch's News Corporation (which holds majority ownership in a further seven). Although ultimately thwarted in his bid to buy DirecTV and thereby dominate the US satellite television market, Murdoch wields a pervasive influence on the news—and not just in New York, where he has two TV stations, a major daily (the faltering *New York Post*) *and* the Fox News Channel, whose inexhaustible platoons of shouting heads attracts a fierce plurality of cable-viewers. Meanwhile, Time Warner has now merged with AOL—so as to own the cyberworks through which to market its floodtide of movies, ball games, TV shows, rock videos, cartoons, standup routines and (not least) bits from CNN, CNN Headline News, CNNfn (devised to counter GE's CNBC) and CNN/Sports Illustrated (a would-be rival to Disney's ESPN franchise). While busily cloning CNN, the parent company has also taken quiet steps to make it more like Fox, with Walter Isaacson, the new head honcho, even visiting the Capitol to seek advice from certain rightist pols on how, presumably, to make the network even shallower and more obnoxious. (He also courted Rush Himself.) All this has occurred since the abrupt defenestration of Ted Turner, who now belatedly laments the overconcentration of the cable business: "It's sad we're losing so much diversity of thought," he confesses, sounding vaguely like a writer for this magazine.

Whereas five years ago the clueless Westinghouse owned CBS, today the network is a property of the voracious Viacom—matchless cable occupier (UPN, MTV, MTV2, VH1, Nickelodeon, the Movie Channel, TNN, CMT, BET, 50 percent of Comedy Central, etc.), radio colossus (its Infinity Broadcasting—home to Howard Stern and Don Imus—owns 184 stations), movie titan (Paramount Pictures), copious publisher (Simon & Schuster, Free Press, Scribner), a big deal on the web and one of the largest US outdoor advertising firms. Under Viacom, CBS News has been obliged to help sell Viacom's product—in 2000, for example, devoting epic stretches of *The Early Show* to what lately happened on *Survivor* (CBS). Of course, such synergistic bilge is commonplace, as is the tendency to dummy up on any topic that the parent company (or any of its advertisers) might want stifled. These journalistic sins have been as frequent under "longtime" owners Disney and GE as under Viacom and Fox [see Janine Jaquet, "The Wages of Synergy"]. They may also abound beneath Vivendi, whose recent purchase of the film and TV units of USA Networks and new stake in the satellite TV giant EchoStar—could soon mean lots of oblique self-promotion on *USAM News*, in *L'Express* and *L'Expansion*, and through whatever other news-machines the parent buys.

Such is the telejournalistic landscape at the moment—and soon it will mutate again, if Bush's FCC delivers for its giant clients. On September 13, when the minds of the American people were on something else, the commission's GOP majority voted to "review" the last few rules preventing perfect oligopoly. They thus prepared the ground for allowing a single outfit to own both a daily paper and a TV station in the same market—an advantage that was outlawed in 1975. (Even then, pre-existing cases of such ownership were grandfathered in, and any would-be owner could get that rule waived.) That furtive FCC "review" also portended the elimination of the cap on the percentage of US households that a single owner might reach through its TV stations. Since the passage of the Telecommunications Act of 1996, the limit had been 35 percent. Although that most indulgent bill was dictated by the media giants themselves, its restrictions are too heavy for this FCC, whose chairman, Michael Powell, has called regulation per se "the oppressor."

And so, unless there's some effective opposition, the several-headed vendor that now sells us nearly all our movies, TV, radio, magazines, books, music and web services will soon be selling us our daily papers, too—for the major dailies have, collectively, been lobbying energetically for that big waiver, which stands to make their owners even richer (an expectation that has no doubt had a sweetening effect on coverage of the Bush Administration). Thus the largest US newspaper conglomerates—the New York Times, the Washington Post, Gannett, Knight-Ridder and the Tribune Co.—will soon be formal partners with, say, GE, Murdoch, Disney and/or AT&T; and then the lesser nationwide chains (and the last few independents) will be ingested, too, going the way of most US radio stations. America's cities could turn into informational "company towns," with one behemoth owning all the local print organs—daily paper(s), alternative weekly, city magazine—as well as the TV and radio stations, the multiplexes and the cable system. (Recently a federal appeals court told the FCC to drop its rule preventing any one company from serving more than 30 percent of US cable subscribers; and in December, the Supreme Court refused to hear the case.) While such a setup may make economic sense, as anticompetitive arrangements tend to do, it has no place in a democracy, where the people have to know more than their masters want to tell them.

That imperative demands reaffirmation at this risky moment, when much of what the media cartel purveys to us is propaganda, commercial or political, while no one in authority makes mention of "the public interest"—except to laugh it off. "I have no idea," Powell cheerily replied at his first press conference as chairman, when asked for his own definition of that crucial concept. "It's an empty vessel in which people pour in whatever their preconceived views or biases are." Such blithe obtuseness has marked all his public musings on the subject. In a speech before the American Bar Association in April 1998, Powell offered an ironic little riff about how thoroughly he doesn't get it: "The night after I was sworn in [as a commissioner], I waited for a visit from the angel of the public interest. I waited all night, but she did not come." On the other hand, Powell has never sounded glib about his sacred obligation to the corporate interest. Of his decision to move forward with the FCC vote just two days after 9/11, Powell spoke as if that sneaky move had been a gesture in the spirit of Patrick Henry: "The flame of the American ideal may flicker, but it will never be extinguished. We will do our small part and press on with our business, solemnly, but resolutely."

Certainly the FCC has never been a democratic force, whichever party has been dominant. Bill Clinton championed the disastrous Telecom Act of 1996 and otherwise did almost nothing to impede the drift toward oligopoly. (As *Newsweek* reported in 2000, Al Gore was Rupert Murdoch's personal choice for President. The mogul apparently sensed that Gore would happily play ball with him, and also thought—correctly—that the Democrat would win.)

What is unique to Michael Powell, however, is the showy superciliousness with which he treats his civic obligation to address the needs of people other than the very rich. That spirit has shone forth many times—as when the chairman genially compared the "digital divide" between the information haves and have-nots to a "Mercedes divide" between the lucky few who can afford great cars and those (like him) who can't. In the intensity of his pro-business bias, Powell recalls Mark Fowler, head of Reagan's FCC, who famously denied his social obligations by asserting that TV is merely "an appliance," "a toaster with pictures." And yet such Reaganite *bons mots*, fraught with the anti-Communist fanaticism of the late cold war, evinced a deadly earnestness that's less apparent in General Powell's son. He is a blithe, postmodern sort of ideologue, attuned to the complacent smirk of Bush the Younger—and, of course, just perfect for the cool and snickering culture of TV.

Although such flippancies are hard to take, they're also easy to refute, for there is no rationale for such an attitude. Take "the public interest"—an ideal that really isn't hard to understand. A media system that enlightens us, that tells us everything we need to know pertaining to our lives and liberty and happiness, would be a system dedicated to the public interest. Such a system would not be controlled by a cartel of giant corporations, because those entities are ultimately hostile to the welfare of the people. Whereas we need to know the truth about such corporations, they often have an interest in suppressing it (as do their advertisers). And while it takes much time and money to find out the truth, the parent companies prefer to cut the necessary costs of journalism, much preferring the sort of lurid fare that can drive endless hours of agitated jabbering. (Prior to 9/11, it was Monica, then *Survivor* and Chandra Levy, whereas, since the fatal day, we have had mostly anthrax, plus much heroic footage from the Pentagon.) The cartel's favored audience, moreover, is that stratum of the population most desirable to advertisers—which has meant the media's complete abandonment of working people and the poor. And while the press must help protect us against those who would abuse the powers of government, the oligopoly is far too cozy with the White House and the Pentagon, whose faults, and crimes, it is unwilling to expose. The media's big bosses want big favors from the state, while the reporters are afraid to risk annoying their best sources. Because of such politeness (and, of course, the current panic in the air), the US coverage of this government is just a bit more edifying than the local newscasts in Riyadh.

Against the daily combination of those corporate tendencies—conflict of interest, endless cutbacks, endless trivial pursuits, class bias, deference to the king and all his men—the public interest doesn't stand a chance. Despite the stubborn fiction of their "liberal" prejudice, the corporate media have helped deliver a stupendous one-two punch to this democracy. (That double whammy followed their uncritical participation in the long, irrelevant *jihad* against those moderate Republicans, the Clintons.) Last year, they helped subvert the presidential race, first by prematurely calling it for Bush, regardless of the vote—a move begun by Fox, then seconded by NBC, at the personal insistence of Jack Welch, CEO of General Electric. Since the coup, the corporate media have hidden or misrepresented the true story of the theft of that election.

And having justified Bush/Cheney's coup, the media continue to betray American democracy. Media devoted to the public interest would investigate the poor performance by the CIA, the FBI, the FAA and the CDC, so that those agencies might be improved for our protection—but the news teams (just like Congress) haven't bothered to look into it. So, too, in the public interest, should the media report on all the current threats to our security—including those far-rightists targeting abortion clinics and, apparently, conducting bioterrorism; but the telejournalists are unconcerned (just like John Ashcroft). So should the media highlight, not play down, this government's attack on civil liberties—the mass detentions, secret evidence, increased surveillance, suspension of attorney-client privilege, the encouragements to spy, the warnings not to disagree, the censored images, sequestered public papers, unexpected visits from the Secret Service and so on. And so should the media not parrot what the Pentagon says about the current war, because such prettified accounts make us complacent and preserve us in our fatal ignorance of what people really think of us—and why—beyond our borders. And there's much more—about the stunning exploitation of the tragedy, especially by the Republicans; about the links between the Bush and the bin Laden families; about the ongoing shenanigans in Florida—that the media would let the people know, if they were not (like Michael Powell) indifferent to the public interest.

In short, the news divisions of the media cartel appear to work *against* the public interest—and *for* their parent companies, their advertisers and the Bush Administration. The situation is completely un-American. It is the purpose of the press to help us run the state, and not the other way around. As citizens of a democracy, we have the right and obligation to be well aware of what is happening, both in "the homeland" and the wider world. Without such knowledge we cannot be both secure and free. We therefore must take steps to liberate the media from oligopoly, so as to make the government our own.

Mark Crispin Miller is a professor of media studies at New York University, where he directs the Project on Media Ownership. He is the author of The Bush Dyslexicon: Observations on a National Disorder *(Norton).*

Where Have All the Farmers Gone?

The globalization of industry and trade is bringing more and more uniformity to the management of the world's land, and a spreading threat to the diversity of crops, ecosystems, and cultures. As Big Ag takes over, farmers who have a stake in their land—and who often are the most knowledgeable stewards of the land—are being forced into servitude or driven out.

by Brian Halweil

Since 1992, the U.S. Army Corps of Engineers has been developing plans to expand the network of locks and dams along the Mississippi River. The Mississippi is the primary conduit for shipping American soybeans into global commerce—about 35,000 tons a day. The Corps' plan would mean hauling in up to 1.2 million metric tons of concrete to lengthen ten of the locks from 180 meters to 360 meters each, as well as to bolster several major wing dams which narrow the river to keep the soybean barges moving and the sediment from settling. This construction would supplement the existing dredges which are already sucking 85 million cubic meters of sand and mud from the river's bank and bottom each year. Several different levels of "upgrade" for the river have been considered, but the most ambitious of them would purportedly reduce the cost of shipping soybeans by 4 to 8 cents per bushel. Some independent analysts think this is a pipe dream.

Around the same time the Mississippi plan was announced, the five governments of South America's La Plata Basin—Bolivia, Brazil, Paraguay, Argentina, and Uruguay—announced plans to dredge 13 million cubic meters of sand, mud, and rock from 233 sites along the Paraguay-Paraná River. That would be enough to fill a convoy of dump trucks 10,000 miles long. Here, the plan is to straighten natural river meanders in at least seven places, build dozens of locks, and construct a major port in the heart of the Pantanal—the world's largest wetland. The Paraguay-Paraná flows through the center of Brazil's burgeoning soybean heartland—second only to the United States in production and exports. According to statements from the Brazilian State of Mato Grasso, this "Hidrovía" (water highway) will give a further boost to the region's soybean export capacity.

Lobbyists for both these projects argue that expanding the barge capacity of these rivers is necessary in order to improve competitiveness, grab world market share, and rescue farmers (either U.S. or Brazilian, depending on whom the lobbyists are addressing) from their worst financial crisis since the Great Depression. Chris Brescia, president of the Midwest River Coalition 2000, an alliance of commodity shippers that forms the primary lobbying force for the Mississippi plan, says, "The sooner we provide the waterway infrastructure, the sooner our family farmers will benefit." Some of his fellow lobbyists have even argued that these projects are essential to feeding the world (since the barges can then more easily speed the soybeans to the world's hungry masses) and to saving the environment (since the hungry masses will not have to clear rainforest to scratch out their own subsistence).

Probably very few people have had an opportunity to hear both pitches and compare them. But anyone who has may find something amiss with the argument that U.S. farmers will become more competitive versus their Brazilian counterparts, at the same time that Brazilian farmers will, for the same reasons, become more competitive with their U.S. counterparts. A more likely outcome is that farmers of these two nations will be pitted against each other in a costly race to maximize production, resulting in short-cut practices that essentially strip-mine their soil and throw long-term investments in the land to the wind. Farmers in Iowa will have stronger incentives to plow up land along stream banks, triggering faster erosion of topsoil. Their brethren in Brazil will find themselves needing to cut deeper into the savanna, also accelerating erosion. That will increase the flow of soybeans, all right—both north and south. But it will also further depress prices, so that even as the farmers are shipping more, they're getting less income per ton shipped. And in any case, increasing volume can't help the farmers survive in the long run, because sooner or later they will be swallowed by larger, corporate, farms that can make up for the smaller per-ton margins by producing even larger volumes.

So, how can the supporters of these river projects, who profess to be acting in the farmer's best interests, not notice the illogic of this form of competition? One explanation is that from the advocates' (as opposed to the farmers') standpoint, this competition isn't illogical at all—because the lobbyists aren't really representing farmers. They're working for the commodity processing, shipping, and trading firms who want the price of soybeans to fall, because these are the firms that buy the crops from the farmers. In fact, it is the same three agribusiness conglomerates—Archer Daniels Midland (ADM), Cargill, and Bunge—that are the top soybean processors and traders along both rivers.

Welcome to the global economy. The more brutally the U.S. and Brazilian farmers can batter each-other's prices (and standards of living) down, the greater the margin of profit these three giants gain. Meanwhile, another handful of companies controls the markets for genetically modified seeds, fertilizers, and herbicides used by the farmers—charging oligopolistically high prices both north and south of the equator.

In assessing what this proposed digging-up and reconfiguring of two of the world's great river basins really means, keep in mind that these projects will not be the activities of private businesses operating inside their own private property. These are proposed public works, to be undertaken at huge public expense. The motive is neither the plight of the family farmer nor any moral obligation to feed the world, but the opportunity to exploit poorly informed public sentiments about farmers' plights or hungry masses as a means of usurping public policies to benefit private interests. What gets thoroughly Big Muddied, in this usurping process, is that in addition to subjecting farmers to a gladiator-like attrition, these projects will likely bring a cascade of damaging economic, social, and ecological impacts to the very river basins being so expensively remodeled.

What's likely to happen if the lock and dam system along the Mississippi is expanded as proposed? The most obvious effect will be increased barge traffic, which will accelerate a less obvious cascade of events that has been underway for some time, according to Mike Davis of the Minnesota Department of Natural Resources. Much of the Mississippi River ecosystem involves aquatic rooted plants, like bullrush, arrowhead, and wild celery. Increased barge traffic will kick up more sediment, obscuring sunlight and reducing the depth to which plants can survive. Already, since the 1970s, the number of aquatic plant species found in some of the river has been cut from 23 to about half that, with just a handful thriving under the cloudier conditions. "Areas of the river have reached an ecological turning point," warns Davis. "This decline in plant diversity has triggered a drop in the invertebrate communities that live on these plants, as well as a drop in the fish, mollusk, and bird communities that depend on the diversity of insects and plants." On May 18, 2000, the U.S. Fish and Wildlife Service released a study saying that the Corps of Engineers project would threaten the 300 species of migratory birds and 12 species of fish in the Mississippi watershed, and could ultimately push some into extinction. "The least tern, the pallid sturgeon, and other species that evolved with the ebbs and flows, sandbars and depths, of the river are progressively eliminated or forced away as the diversity of the river's natural habitats is removed to maximize the barge habitat," says Davis.

The outlook for the Hidrovía project is similar. Mark Robbins, an ornithologist at the Natural History Museum at the University of Kansas, calls it "a key step in creating a Florida Everglades-like scenario of destruction in the Pantanal, and an American Great Plains-like scenario in the Cerrado in southern Brazil." The Paraguay-Paraná feeds the Pantanal wetlands, one of the most diverse habitats on the planet, with its populations of woodstorks, snailkites, limpkins, jabirus, and more than 650 other species of birds, as well as more than 400 species of fish and hundreds of other less-studied plants, mussels, and marshland organisms. As the river is dredged and the banks are built up to funnel the surrounding wetlands water into the navigation path, bird nesting habitat and fish spawning grounds will be eliminated, damaging the indigenous and other traditional societies that depend on these resources. Increased barge traffic will suppress river species here just as it will on the Mississippi. Meanwhile, herbicide-intensive soybean monocultures—on farms so enormous that they dwarf even the biggest operations in the U.S. Midwest—are rapidly replacing diverse grasslands in the fragile Cerrado. The heavy plowing and periodic absence of ground cover associated with such farming erodes 100 million tons of soil per year. Robbins notes that "compared to the Mississippi, this southern river system and surrounding grassland is several orders of magnitude more diverse and has suffered considerably less, so there is much more at stake."

Supporters of such massive disruption argue that it is justified because it is the most "efficient" way to do business. The perceived efficiency of such farming might be compared to the perceived efficiency of an energy system based on coal. Burning coal looks very efficient if you ignore its long-term impact on air quality and climate stability. Similarly, large farms look more efficient than small farms if you don't count some of their largest costs—the loss of the genetic diversity that underpins agriculture, the pollution caused by agro-chemicals, and the dislocation of rural cultures. The simultaneous demise of small, independent farmers and rise of multinational food giants is troubling not just for those who empathize with dislocated farmers, but for anyone who eats.

An Endangered Species

Nowadays most of us in the industrialized countries don't farm, so we may no longer really understand that way of life. I was born in the apple orchard and dairy country of Dutchess County, New York, but since age five have spent most of my life in New York City—while most of the farms back in Dutchess County have given way to spreading subdivisions. It's also hard for those of us who get our food from supermarket shelves or drive-thru windows to know how dependent we are on the viability of rural communities.

Whether in the industrial world, where farm communities are growing older and emptier, or in developing nations where population growth is pushing the number of farmers continually higher and each generation is inheriting smaller family plots, it is becoming harder and harder to make a living as a farmer. A combination of falling incomes, rising debt, and worsening rural poverty is forcing more people to either abandon farming as their primary activity or to leave the countryside altogether—a bewildering juncture, considering that farmers produce perhaps the only good that the human race cannot do without.

Since 1950, the number of people employed in agriculture has plummeted in all industrial nations, in some regions by more than 80 percent. Look at the numbers, and you might think farmers are being singled out by some kind of virus:

- In Japan, more than half of all farmers are over 65 years old; in the United States, farmers over 65 outnumber those under 35 by three to one. (Upon retirement or death, many will pass the farm on to children who live in the city and have no interest in farming themselves.)
- In New Zealand, officials estimate that up to 6,000 dairy farms will disappear during the next 10 to 15 years—dropping the total number by nearly 40 percent.
- In Poland, 1.8 million farms could disappear as the country is absorbed into the European Union—dropping the total number by 90 percent.
- In Sweden, the number of farms going out of business in the next decade is expected to reach about 50 percent.
- In the Philippines, Oxfam estimates that over the next few years the number of farm households in the corn–producing region of Mindanao could fall by some 500,000—a 50 percent loss.
- In the United States, where the vast majority of people were farmers at the time of the American Revolution, fewer people are now full-time farmers (less than 1 percent of the population) than are full-time prisoners.
- In the U.S. states of Nebraska and Iowa, between a fifth and a third of farmers are expected to be out of business within two years.

Of course, the declining numbers of farmers in industrial nations does not imply a decline in the importance of the farming sector. The world still has to eat (and 80 million more mouths to feed each year than the year before), so smaller numbers of farmers mean larger farms and greater concentration of ownership. Despite a precipitous plunge in the number of people employed in farming in North America, Europe, and East Asia, half the world's people still make their living from the land. In sub-Saharan Africa and South Asia, more than 70 percent do. In these regions, agriculture accounts, on average, for half of total economic activity.

Some might argue that the decline of farmers is harmless, even a blessing, particularly for less developed nations that have not yet experienced the modernization that moves peasants out of backwater rural areas into the more advanced economies of the cities. For most of the past two centuries, the shift toward fewer farmers has generally been assumed to be a kind of progress. The substitution of high-powered diesel tractors for slow-moving women and men with hoes, or of large mechanized industrial farms for clusters of small "old fashioned" farms, is typically seen as the way to a more abundant and affordable food supply. Our urban-centered society has even come to view rural life, especially in the form of small family-owned businesses, as backwards or boring, fit only for people who wear overalls and go to bed early—far from the sophistication and dynamism of the city.

Urban life does offer a wide array of opportunities, attractions, and hopes—some of them falsely created by urban-oriented commercial media—that many farm families decide to pursue willingly. But city life often turns out to be a disappointment, as displaced farmers find themselves lodged in crowded slums, where unemployment and ill-health are the norm and where they are worse off than they were back home. Much evidence suggests that farmers aren't so much being lured to the city as they are being driven off their farms by a variety of structural changes in the way the global food chain operates. Bob Long, a rancher in McPherson County, Nebraska, stated in a recent *New York Times* article that passing the farm onto his son would be nothing less than "child abuse."

As long as cities are under the pressure of population growth (a situation expected to continue at least for the next three or four decades), there will always be pressure for a large share of humanity to subsist in the countryside. Even in highly urbanized North America and Europe, roughly 25 percent of the population—275 million people—still reside in rural areas. Meanwhile, for the 3 billion Africans, Asians, and Latin Americans who remain in the countryside—and who will be there for the foreseeable future—the marginalization of farmers has set up a vicious cycle of low educational achievement, rising infant mortality, and deepening mental distress.

Hired Hands on Their Own Land

In the 18th and 19th centuries, farmers weren't so trapped. Most weren't wealthy, but they generally enjoyed stable incomes and strong community ties. Diversified farms yielded a range of raw and processed goods that the farmer could typically sell in a local market. Production costs tended to be much lower than now, as many of the needed inputs were home-grown: the farmer planted seed that he or she had saved from the previous year, the farm's cows or pigs provided fertilizer, and the diversity of crops—usually a large range of grains, tubers, vegetables, herbs, flowers, and fruits for home use as well as for sale—effectively functioned as pest control.

Things have changed, especially in the past half-century, according to Iowa State agricultural economist Mike Duffy. "The end of World War II was a watershed period," he says. "The widespread introduction of chemical fertilizers and synthetic pesticides, produced as part of the war effort, set in motion dramatic changes in how we farm—and a dramatic decline in the number of farmers." In the post-war period, along with increasing mechanization, there was an increasing tendency to "outsource" pieces of the work that the farmers had previously done themselves—from producing their own fertilizer to cleaning and packaging their harvest. That outsourcing, which may have seemed like a welcome convenience at the time, eventually boomeranged: at first it enabled the farmer to increase output, and thus profits, but when all the other farmers were doing it too, crop prices began to fall.

Before long, the processing and packaging businesses were adding more "value" to the purchased product than the farmer, and it was those businesses that became the

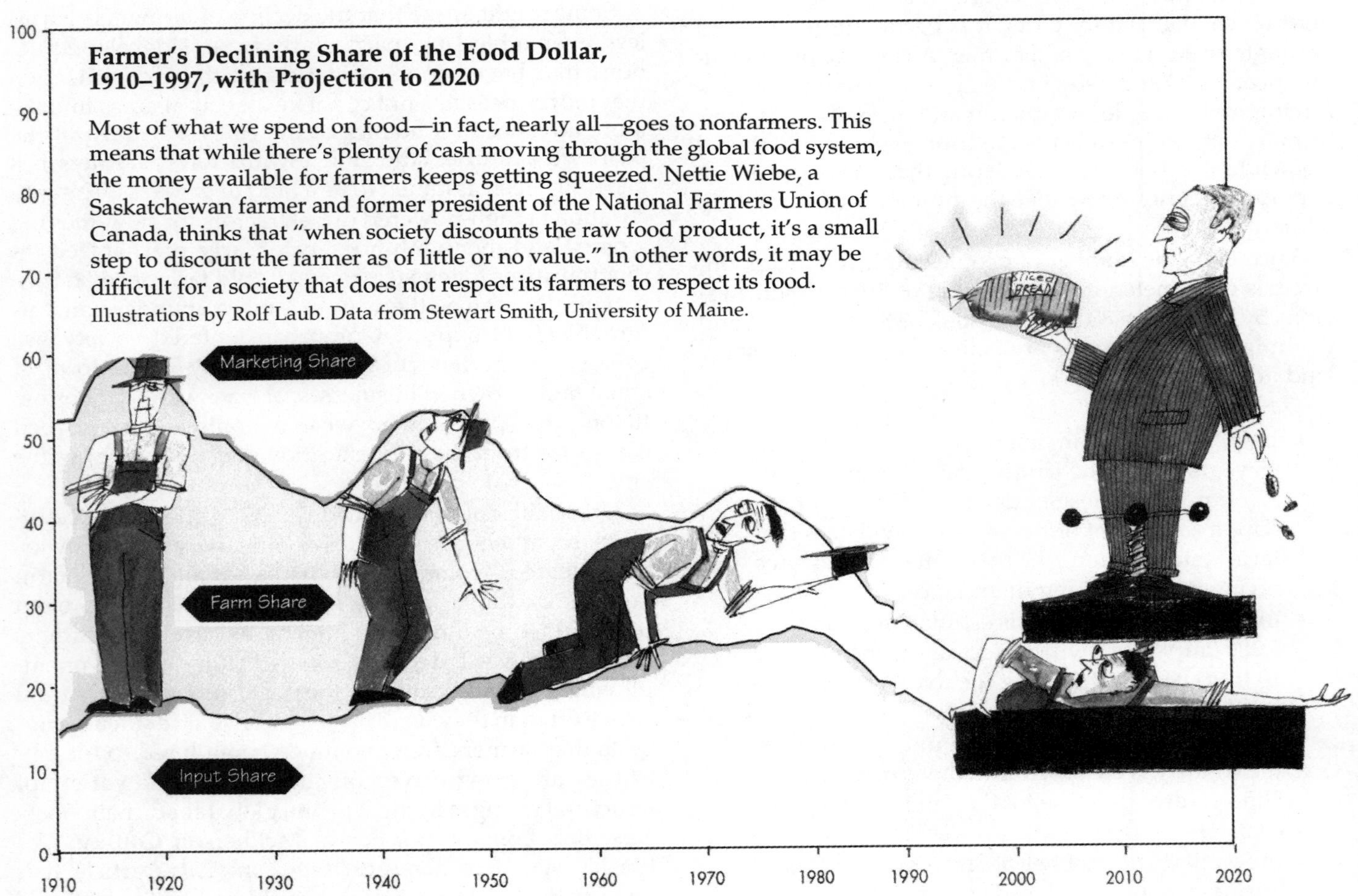

Farmer's Declining Share of the Food Dollar, 1910–1997, with Projection to 2020

Most of what we spend on food—in fact, nearly all—goes to nonfarmers. This means that while there's plenty of cash moving through the global food system, the money available for farmers keeps getting squeezed. Nettie Wiebe, a Saskatchewan farmer and former president of the National Farmers Union of Canada, thinks that "when society discounts the raw food product, it's a small step to discount the farmer as of little or no value." In other words, it may be difficult for a society that does not respect its farmers to respect its food.

Illustrations by Rolf Laub. Data from Stewart Smith, University of Maine.

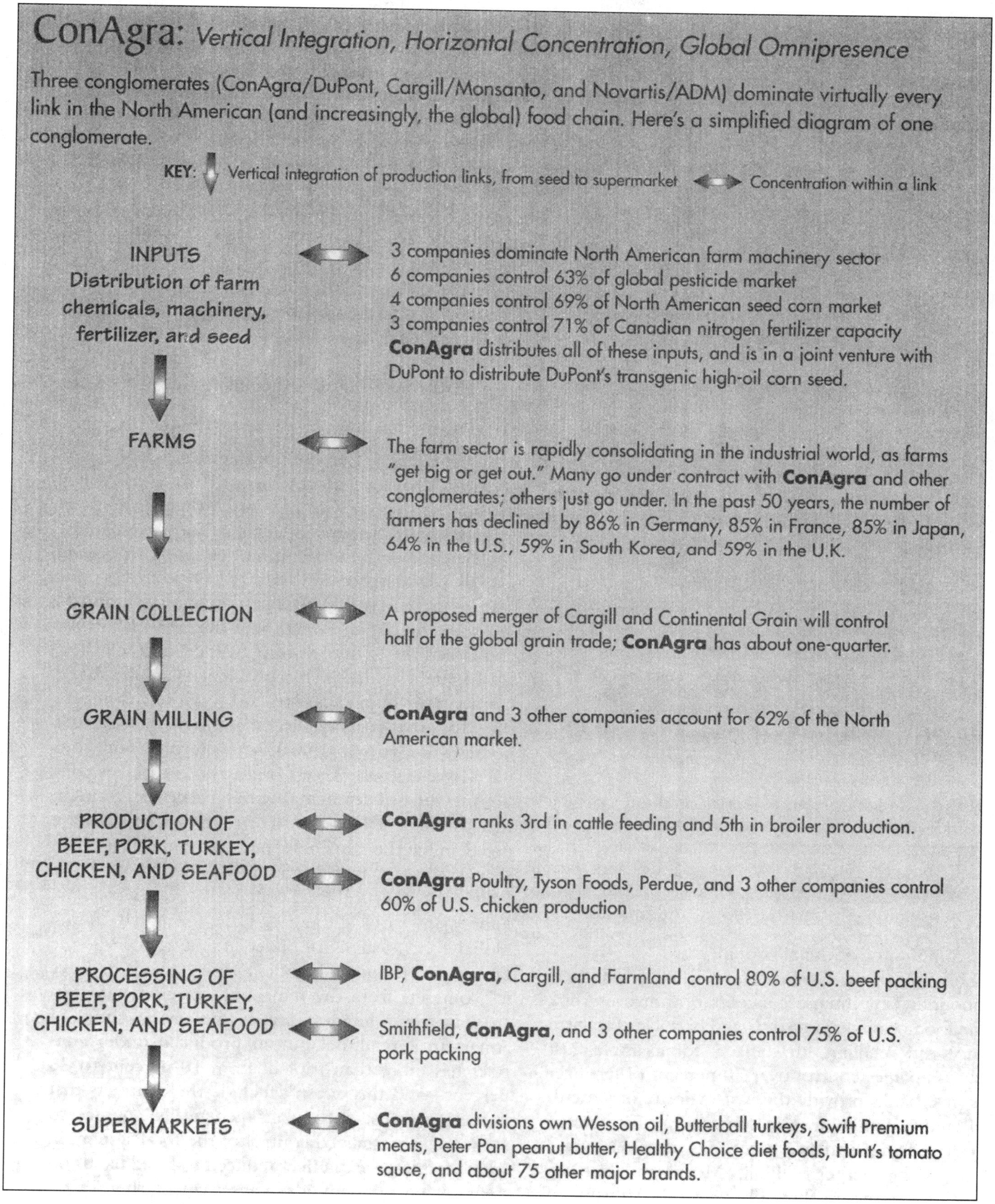

ConAgra: *Vertical Integration, Horizontal Concentration, Global Omnipresence*

Three conglomerates (ConAgra/DuPont, Cargill/Monsanto, and Novartis/ADM) dominate virtually every link in the North American (and increasingly, the global) food chain. Here's a simplified diagram of one conglomerate.

KEY: ↓ Vertical integration of production links, from seed to supermarket ↔ Concentration within a link

Link	Concentration within a link
INPUTS Distribution of farm chemicals, machinery, fertilizer, and seed	3 companies dominate North American farm machinery sector 6 companies control 63% of global pesticide market 4 companies control 69% of North American seed corn market 3 companies control 71% of Canadian nitrogen fertilizer capacity **ConAgra** distributes all of these inputs, and is in a joint venture with DuPont to distribute DuPont's transgenic high-oil corn seed.
↓ FARMS	The farm sector is rapidly consolidating in the industrial world, as farms "get big or get out." Many go under contract with **ConAgra** and other conglomerates; others just go under. In the past 50 years, the number of farmers has declined by 86% in Germany, 85% in France, 85% in Japan, 64% in the U.S., 59% in South Korea, and 59% in the U.K.
↓ GRAIN COLLECTION	A proposed merger of Cargill and Continental Grain will control half of the global grain trade; **ConAgra** has about one-quarter.
↓ GRAIN MILLING	**ConAgra** and 3 other companies account for 62% of the North American market.
↓ PRODUCTION OF BEEF, PORK, TURKEY, CHICKEN, AND SEAFOOD	**ConAgra** ranks 3rd in cattle feeding and 5th in broiler production. **ConAgra** Poultry, Tyson Foods, Perdue, and 3 other companies control 60% of U.S. chicken production
↓ PROCESSING OF BEEF, PORK, TURKEY, CHICKEN, AND SEAFOOD	IBP, **ConAgra,** Cargill, and Farmland control 80% of U.S. beef packing Smithfield, **ConAgra**, and 3 other companies control 75% of U.S. pork packing
↓ SUPERMARKETS	**ConAgra** divisions own Wesson oil, Butterball turkeys, Swift Premium meats, Peter Pan peanut butter, Healthy Choice diet foods, Hunt's tomato sauce, and about 75 other major brands.

dominant players in the food industry. Instead of farmers outsourcing to contractors, it became a matter of large food processors buying raw materials from farmers, on the processors' terms. Today, most of the money is in the work the farmer no longer does—or even controls. In the United States, the share of the consumer's food dollar that trickles back to the farmer has plunged from nearly 40 cents in 1910 to just above 7 cents in 1997, while the shares going to input (machinery, agrochemicals, and seeds) and marketing (processing, shipping, brokerage, advertising, and retailing) firms have continued to expand. (See graph "Farmer's Declining Share of the Food Dollar") The typical U.S. wheat farmer, for instance, gets just 6 cents of the dollar spent on a loaf of bread—so when you buy that loaf, you're paying about as much for the wrapper as for the wheat.

Ironically, then, as U.S. farms became more mechanized and more "productive," a self-destructive feedback loop was set in motion: over-supply and declining crop prices cut into farmers' profits, fueling a demand for more technology aimed at making up for shrinking margins by increasing volume still more. Output increased dramatically, but expenses (for tractors, combines, fertilizer, and seed) also ballooned—while the commodity prices stagnated or declined. Even as they were looking more and more modernized, the farmers were becoming less and less the masters of their own domain.

On the typical Iowa farm, the farmer's profit margin has dropped from 35 percent in 1950 to 9 percent today. In order to generate the same income, this farm would need to be roughly four times as large today as in 1950—or the farmer would need to get a night job. And that's precisely what we've seen in most industrialized nations: fewer farmers on bigger tracts of land producing a greater share of the total food supply. The farmer with declining margins buys out his neighbor and expands or risks being cannibalized himself.

There is an alternative to this huge scaling up, which is to buck the trend and bring some of the input-supplying and post-harvest processing—and the related profits—back onto the farm. But more self-sufficient farming would be highly unpopular with the industries that now make lucrative profits from inputs and processing. And since these industries have much more political clout than the farmers do, there is little support for rescuing farmers from their increasingly servile condition—and the idea has been largely forgotten. Farmers continue to get the message that the only way to succeed is to get big.

The traditional explanation for this constant pressure to "get big or get out" has been that it improves the efficiency of the food system—bigger farms replace smaller farms, because the bigger farms operate at lower costs. In some respects, this is quite true. Scaling up may allow a farmer to spread a tractor's cost over greater acreage, for example. Greater size also means greater leverage in purchasing inputs or negotiating loan rates—increasingly important as satellite-guided combines and other equipment make farming more and more capital-intensive. But these economies of scale typically level off. Data for a wide range of crops produced in the United States show that the lowest production costs are generally achieved on farms that are much smaller than the typical farm now is. But large farms can tolerate lower margins, so while they may not *produce* at lower cost, they can afford to *sell* their crops at lower cost, if forced to do so—as indeed they are by the food processors who buy from them. In short, to the extent that a giant farm has a financial benefit over a small one, it's a benefit that goes only to the processor—not to the farmer, the farm community, or the environment.

This shift of the food dollar away from farmers is compounded by intense concentration in every link of the food chain—from seeds and herbicides to farm finance and retailing. In Canada, for example, just three companies control over 70 percent of fertilizer sales, five banks provide the vast majority of agricultural credit, two companies control over 70 percent of beef packing, and five companies dominate food retailing. The merger of Philip Morris and Nabisco will create an empire that collects nearly 10 cents of every dollar a U.S. consumer spends on food, according to a company spokesperson. Such high concentration can be deadly for the bottom line, allowing agribusiness firms to extract higher prices for the products farmers buy from them, while offering lower prices for the crop they buy from the farmers.

An even more worrisome form of concentration, according to Bill Heffernan, a rural sociologist at the University of Missouri, is the emergence of several clusters of firms that—through mergers, takeovers, and alliances with other links in the food chain—now possess "a seamless and fully vertically integrated control of the food system from gene to supermarket shelf." (See diagram "ConAgra") Consider the recent partnership between Monsanto and Cargill, which controls seeds, fertilizers, pesticides, farm finance, grain collection, grain processing, livestock feed processing, livestock production, and slaughtering, as well as some well-known processed food brands. From the standpoint of a company like Cargill, such alliances yield tremendous control over costs and can therefore be extremely profitable.

But suppose you're the farmer. Want to buy seed to grow corn? If Cargill is the only buyer of corn in a hundred mile radius, and Cargill is only buying a particular Monsanto corn variety for its mills or elevators or feedlots, then if you don't plant Monsanto's seed you won't have a market for your corn. Need a loan to buy the seed? Go to Cargill-owned Bank of Ellsworth, but be sure to let them know which seed you'll be buying. Also mention that you'll be buying Cargill's Saskferco brand fertilizer. OK, but once the corn is grown, you don't like the idea of having to sell to Cargill at the prices it dictates? Well, maybe you'll feed the corn to your pigs, then, and sell them to the highest bidder. No problem—Cargill's Excel Corporation buys pigs, too. OK, you're moving to the city, and renouncing the farm life! No more home-made grits for breakfast, you're buying corn flakes. Well, good news: Cargill Foods supplies corn flour to the top cereal makers. You'll notice, though, that all the big brands of corn flakes seem to have pretty much the same hefty price per ounce. After all, they're all made by the agricultural oligopoly.

As these vertical food conglomerates consolidate, Heffernan warns, "there is little room left in the global food system for independent farmers"—the farmers being increasingly left with "take it or leave it" contracts from the remaining conglomerates. In the last two decades, for example, the share of American agricultural output produced under contract has more than tripled, from 10 percent to 35 percent—and this doesn't include the contracts that farmers must sign to plant genetically engineered seed. Such centralized control of the food system, in which farmers are in effect reduced to hired hands on their own land, reminds Heffernan of the Soviet-style state farms, but with the Big Brother role now being played by agribusiness executives. It is also reminiscent of the "company store" which once dominated small American mining or factory towns, except that if you move out of town now, the store is still with you. The company store has gone global.

With the conglomerates who own the food dollar also owning the political clout, it's no surprise that agricultural policies—including subsidies, tax breaks, and environmental legislation at both the national and international levels—do not generally favor the farms. For example, the conglomerates command growing influence over both private and public agricultural research priorities, which might explain why the U.S. Department of Agriculture (USDA), an agency ostensibly beholden to farmers, would help to develop the seed-sterilizing Terminator technology—a biotechnology that offers farmers only greater dependence on seed companies. In some cases the influence is indirect, as manifested in government funding decisions, while in others it is more blatant. When Novartis provided $25 million to fund a research partnership with the plant biology department of the University of California at Berkeley, one of the conditions was that Novartis has the first right of refusal for any patentable inventions. Under those circumstances, of course, the UC officials—mindful of where their funding comes from—have strong incentives to give more attention to technologies like the Terminator seed, which shifts profit away from the farmer, than to technologies that directly benefit the farmer or the public at large.

Even policies that are touted to be in the best interest of farmers, like liberalized trade in agricultural products, are increasingly shaped by non-farmers. Food traders, processors, and distributors, for example, were some of the principal architects of recent revisions to the General Agreement on Trade and Tariffs (GATT)—the World Trade Organization's predecessor—that paved the way for greater trade flows in agricultural commodities. Before these revisions, many countries had mechanisms for assuring that their farmers wouldn't be driven out of their own domestic markets by predatory global traders. The traders, however, were able to do away with those protections.

The ability of agribusiness to slide around the planet, buying at the lowest possible price and selling at the highest, has tended to tighten the squeeze already put in place by economic marginalization, throwing every farmer on the planet into direct competition with every other farmer. A recent UN Food and Agriculture Organization assessment of the experience of 16 developing nations in implementing the latest phase of the GATT concluded that "a common reported concern was with a general trend towards the concentration of farms," a process that tends to further marginalize small producers and exacerbate rural poverty and unemployment. The sad irony, according to Thomas Reardon, of Michigan State University, is that while small farmers in all reaches of the world are increasingly affected by cheap, heavily subsidized imports of foods from outside of their traditional rural markets, they are nonetheless often excluded from opportunities to participate in food exports themselves. To keep down transaction costs and to keep processing standardized, exporters and other downstream players prefer to buy from a few large producers, as opposed to many small producers.

As the global food system becomes increasingly dominated by a handful of vertically integrated, international corporations, the servitude of the farmer points to a broader society-wide servitude that OPEC-like food cartels could impose, through their control over food prices and food quality. Agricultural economists have already noted that the widening gap between retail food prices and farm prices in the 1990s was due almost exclusively to exploitation of market power, and not to extra services provided by processors and retailers. It's questionable whether we should pay as much for a bread wrapper as we do for the nutrients it contains. But beyond this, there's a more fundamental question. Farmers are professionals, with extensive knowledge of their local soils, weather, native plants, sources of fertilizer or mulch, native pollinators, ecology, and community. If we are to have a world where the land is no longer managed by such professionals, but is instead managed by distant corporate bureaucracies interested in extracting maximum output at minimum cost, what kind of food will we have, and at what price?

Agrarian Services

No question, large industrial farms can produce lots of food. Indeed, they're designed to maximize quantity. But when the farmer becomes little more than the lowest-cost producer of raw materials, more than his own welfare will suffer. Though the farm sector has lost power and profit, it is still the one link in the agrifood chain accounting for the largest share of agriculture's public goods—including half the world's jobs, many of its most vital communities, and many of its most diverse landscapes. And in providing many of these goods, small farms clearly have the advantage.

Local economic and social stability: Over half a century ago, William Goldschmidt, an anthropologist working at the USDA, tried to assess how farm structure and size affect the health of rural communities. In California's San Joaquin Valley, a region then considered to be at the cutting edge of agricultural industrialization, he identified two small towns that were alike in all basic economic and geographic dimensions, including value of agricultural production, except in farm size. Comparing the two, he found an inverse correlation between the sizes of the farms and the well-being of the communities they were a part of.

The small-farm community, Dinuba, supported about 20 percent more people, and at a considerably higher level of living—including lower poverty rates, lower levels of economic and social class distinctions, and a lower crime rate—than the large-farm community of Arvin. The majority of Dinuba's residents were independent entrepreneurs, whereas fewer than 20 percent of Arvin's residents were—most of the others being agricultural laborers. Dinuba had twice as many business establishments as Arvin, and did 61 percent more retail business. It had more schools, parks, newspapers, civic organizations, and churches, as well as better physical infrastructure—paved streets, sidewalks, garbage disposal, sewage disposal and other public services. Dinuba also had more institutions for democratic decision making, and a much broader participation by its citizens. Political scientists have long recognized that a broad base of independent entrepreneurs and property owners is one of the keys to a healthy democracy.

The distinctions between Dinuba and Arvin suggest that industrial agriculture may be limited in what it can do for a community. Fewer (and less meaningful) jobs, less local spending, and a hemorrhagic flow of profits to absentee landowners and distant suppliers means that industrial farms can actually be a net drain on the local economy. That hypothesis has been corroborated by Dick Levins, an agricultural economist at the University of Minnesota. Levins studied the economic receipts from Swift County, Iowa, a typical Midwestern corn and soybean community, and found that although total farm sales are near an all-time high, farm income there has been dismally low—and that many of those who were once the financial stalwarts of the community are now deeply in debt. "Most of the U.S. Corn Belt, like Swift County, is a colony, owned and operated by people who don't live there and for the benefit of those who don't live there," says Levin. In fact, most of the land in Swift County is rented, much of it from absentee landlords.

This new calculus of farming may be eliminating the traditional role of small farms in anchoring rural economies—the kind of tradition, for example, that we saw in the emphasis given to the support of small farms by Japan, South Korea, and Taiwan following World War II. That emphasis, which brought radical land reforms and targeted investment in rural areas, is widely cited as having been a major stimulus to the dramatic economic boom those countries enjoyed.

Not surprisingly, when the economic prospects of small farms decline, the social fabric of rural communities begins to tear. In the United States, farming families are more than twice as likely as others to live in poverty. They have less education and lower rates of medical protection, along with higher rates of infant mortality, alcoholism, child abuse, spousal abuse, and mental stress. Across Europe, a similar pattern is evident. And in sub-Saharan Africa, sociologist Deborah Bryceson of the Netherlands-based African Studies Centre has studied the dislocation of small farmers and found that "as de-agrarianization proceeds, signs of social dysfunction associated with urban areas [including petty crime and breakdowns of family ties] are surfacing in villages."

People without meaningful work often become frustrated, but farmers may be a special case. "More so than other occupations, farming represents a way of life and defines who you are," says Mike Rosemann, a psychologist who runs a farmer counseling network in Iowa. "Losing the family farm, or the prospect of losing the family farm, can generate tremendous guilt and anxiety, as if one has failed to protect the heritage that his ancestors worked to hold onto." One measure of the despair has been a worldwide surge in the number of farmers committing suicide. In 1998, over 300 cotton farmers in Andhra Pradesh, India, took their lives by swallowing pesticides that they had gone into debt to purchase but that had nonetheless failed to save their crops. In Britain, farm workers are two-and-a-half times more likely to commit suicide than the rest of the population. In the United States, official statistics say farmers are now five times as likely to commit suicide as to die from farm accidents, which have been traditionally the most frequent cause of unnatural death for them. The true number may be even higher, as suicide hotlines report that they often receive calls from farmers who want to know which sorts of accidents (Falling into the blades of a combine? Getting shot while hunting?) are least likely to be investigated by insurance companies that don't pay claims for suicides.

Whether from despair or from anger, farmers seem increasingly ready to rise up, sometimes violently, against government, wealthy landholders, or agribusiness giants. In recent years we've witnessed the Zapatista revolution in Chiapas, the seizing of white-owned farms by landless blacks in Zimbabwe, and the attacks of European farmers on warehouses storing genetically engineered seed. In the book *Harvest of Rage*, journalist Joel Dyer links the 1995 Oklahoma City bombing that killed nearly 200 people—

In the Developing World, an Even Deeper Farm Crisis

"One would have to multiply the threats facing family farmers in the United States or Europe five, ten, or twenty times to get a sense of the handicaps of peasant farmers in less developed nations," says Deborah Bryceson, a senior research fellow at the African Studies Centre in the Netherlands. Those handicaps include insufficient access to credit and financing, lack of roads and other infrastructure in rural areas, insecure land tenure, and land shortages where population is dense.

Three forces stand out as particularly challenging to these peasant farmers:

Structural adjustment requirements, imposed on indebted nations by international lending institutions, have led to privatization of "public commodity procurement boards" that were responsible for providing public protections for rural economies. "The newly privatized entities are under no obligation to service marginal rural areas," says Rafael Mariano, chairman of a Filipino farmers' union. Under the new rules, state protections against such practices as dumping of cheap imported goods (with which local farmers can't compete) were abandoned at the same time that state provision of health care, education, and other social services was being reduced.

Trade liberalization policies associated with structural adjustment have reduced the ability of nations to protect their agricultural economies even if they want to. For example, the World Trade Organization's Agreement on Agriculture will forbid domestic price support mechanisms and tariffs on imported goods—some of the primary means by which a country can shield its own farmers from overproduction and foreign competition.

The growing emphasis on agricultural grades and standards—the standardizing of crops and products so they can be processed and marketed more "efficiently"—has tended to favor large producers, and to marginalize smaller ones. Food manufacturers and supermarkets have emerged as the dominant entities in the global agri-food chain, and with their focus on brand consistency, ingredient uniformity, and high volume, smaller producers often are unable to deliver—or aren't even invited to bid.

Despite these daunting conditions, many peasant farmers tend to hold on long after it has become clear that they can't compete. One reason, says Peter Rosset of the Institute for Food and Development Policy, is that "even when it gets really bad, they will cling to agriculture because of the fact that it at least offers some degree of food security—that you can feed yourself." But with the pressures now mounting, particularly as export crop production swallows more land, even that fallback is lost.

as well as the rise of radical right and antigovernment militias in the U.S. heartland—to a spreading despair and anger stemming from the ongoing farm crisis. Thomas Homer-Dixon, director of the Project on Environment, Population, and Security at the University of Toronto, regards farmer dislocation, and the resulting rural unemployment and poverty, as one of the major security threats for the coming decades. Such dislocation is responsible for roughly half of the growth of urban populations across the Third World, and such growth often occurs in volatile shantytowns that are already straining to meet the basic needs of their residents. "What was an extremely traumatic transition for Europe and North America from a rural society to an urban one is now proceeding at two to three times that speed in developing nations," says Homer-Dixon. And, these nations have considerably less industrialization to absorb the labor. Such an accelerated transition poses enormous adjustment challenges for India and China, where perhaps a billion and a half people still make their living from the land.

Ecological stability: In the Andean highlands, a single farm may include as many as 30 to 40 distinct varieties of potato (along with numerous other native plants), each having slightly different optimal soil, water, light, and temperature regimes, which the farmer—given enough time—can manage. (In comparison, in the United States, just four closely related varieties account for about 99 percent of all the potatoes produced.) But, according to Karl Zimmerer, a University of Wisconsin sociologist, declining farm incomes in the Andes force more and more growers into migrant labor forces for part of the year, with serious effects on farm ecology. As time becomes constrained, the farmer manages the system more homogenously—cutting back on the number of traditional varieties (a small home garden of favorite culinary varieties may be the last refuge of diversity), and scaling up production of a few commercial varieties. Much of the traditional crop diversity is lost.

Complex farm systems require a highly sophisticated and intimate knowledge of the land—something small-scale, full-time farmers are more able to provide. Two or three different crops that have different root depths, for example, can often be planted on the same piece of land, or crops requiring different drainage can be planted in close proximity on a tract that has variegated topography. But these kinds of cultivation can't be done with heavy tractors moving at high speed. Highly site-specific and management-intensive cultivation demands ingenuity and awareness of local ecology, and can't be achieved by heavy equipment and heavy applications of agrochemicals. That isn't to say that being small is always sufficient to ensure ecologically sound food production, because economic adversity can drive small farms, as well as big ones, to compromise sustainable food production by transmogrifying the craft of land stewardship into the crude labor of commodity production. But a large-scale, highly mechanized farm is simply not equipped to preserve landscape complexity. Instead, its normal modus is to use blunt management tools, like crops that have been genetically engineered to churn out insecticides, which obviate the need to scout the field to see if spraying is necessary at all.

In the U.S. Midwest, as farm size has increased, cropping systems have gotten more simplified. Since 1972, the number of counties with more than 55 percent of their acreage planted in corn and soybeans has nearly tripled, from 97 to 267. As farms scaled up, the great simplicity of managing the corn-soybean rotation—an 800 acre farm, for instance, may require no more than a couple of weeks planting in the spring and a few weeks harvesting in the fall—became its big selling point. The various arms of the agricultural economy in the region, from extension services to grain elevators to seed suppliers, began to solidify around this corn-soybean rotation, reinforcing the farmers' movement away from other crops. Fewer and fewer farmers kept livestock, as beef and hog production became "economical" only in other parts of the country where it was becoming more concentrated. Giving up livestock meant eliminating clover, pasture mixtures, and a key source of fertilizer in the Midwest, while creating tremendous manure concentrations in other places.

But the corn and soybean rotation—one monoculture followed by another—is extremely inefficient or "leaky" in its use of applied fertilizer, since low levels of biodiversity tend to leave a range of vacant niches in the field, including different root depths and different nutrient preferences. Moreover, the Midwest's shift to monoculture has subjected the country to a double hit of nitrogen pollution, since not only does the removal and concentration of livestock tend to dump inordinate amounts of feces in the places (such as Utah and North Carolina) where the livestock operations are now located, but the monocultures that remain in the Midwest have much poorer nitrogen retention than they would if their cropping were more complex. (The addition of just a winter rye crop to the corn-soy rotation has been shown to reduce nitrogen runoff by nearly 50 percent.) And maybe this disaster-in-the-making should really be regarded as a triple hit, because in addition to contaminating Midwestern water supplies, the runoff ends up in the Gulf of Mexico, where the nitrogen feeds massive algae blooms. When the algae die, they are decomposed by bacteria, whose respiration depletes the water's oxygen—suffocating fish, shellfish, and all other life that doesn't escape. This process periodically leaves 20,000 square kilometers of water off the coast of Louisiana biologically dead. Thus the act of simplifying the ecology of a field in Iowa can contribute to severe pollution in Utah, North Carolina, Louisiana, *and* Iowa.

The world's agricultural biodiversity—the ultimate insurance policy against climate variations, pest outbreaks, and other unforeseen threats to food security—depends largely on the millions of small farmers who use this diversity in their local growing environments. But the marginalization of farmers who have developed or inherited complex farming systems over generations means more than just the loss of specific crop varieties and the knowledge of how they best grow. "We forever lose the best available knowledge and experience of place, including what to do with marginal lands not suited for industrial production," says Steve Gleissman, an agroecologist at the University of California at Santa Cruz. The 12 million hogs produced by Smithfield Foods Inc., the largest hog producer and processor in the world and a pioneer in vertical integration, are nearly genetically identical and raised under identical conditions—regardless of whether they are in a Smithfield feedlot in Virginia or Mexico.

As farmers become increasingly integrated into the agribusiness food chain, they have fewer and fewer controls over the totality of the production process—shifting more and more to the role of "technology applicators," as opposed to managers making informed and independent decisions. Recent USDA surveys of contract poultry farmers in the United States found that in seeking outside advice on their operations, these farmers now turn first to bankers and then to the corporations that hold their contracts. If the contracting corporation is also the same company that is selling the farm its seed and fertilizer, as is often the case, there's a strong likelihood that the company's procedures will be followed. That corporation, as a global enterprise with no compelling local ties, is also less likely to be concerned about the pollution and resource degradation created by those procedures, at least compared with a farmer who is rooted in that community. Grower contracts generally disavow any environmental liability.

And then there is the ecological fallout unique to large-scale, industrial agriculture. Colossal confined animal feeding operations (CAFOs)—those "other places" where livestock are concentrated when they are no longer present on Midwestern soy/corn farms—constitute perhaps the most egregious example of agriculture that has, like a garbage barge in a goldfish pond, overwhelmed the scale at which an ecosystem can cope. CAFOs are increasingly the norm in livestock production, because, like crop monocultures, they allow the production of huge populations of animals which can be slaughtered and marketed at rock-bottom costs. But the disconnection between the livestock and the land used to produce their feed means that such CAFOs generate gargantuan amounts of waste, which the surrounding soil cannot possibly absorb. (One farm in Utah will raise over five million hogs in a year, producing as much waste each day as the city of Los Angeles.) The waste is generally stored in large lagoons, which are prone to leak and even spill over during heavy storms. From North Carolina to South Korea, the overwhelming stench of these lagoons—a combination of hydrogen sulfide, ammonia, and methane gas that smells like rotten eggs—renders miles of surrounding land uninhabitable.

A different form of ecological disruption results from the conditions under which these animals are raised. Because massive numbers of closely confined livestock are highly susceptible to infection, and because a steady diet of antibiotics can modestly boost animal growth, overuse of antibiotics has become the norm in industrial animal production. In recent months, both the Centers for Disease Control and Prevention in the United States and the World Health Organization have identified such industrial feeding operations as principal causes of the growing antibiotic resistance in food-borne bacteria like *salmonella* and *campylobacter*. And as decisionmaking in the food chain grows ever more concentrated—confined behind fewer corporate doors—there may be other food safety issues that you won't even hear about, particularly in the burgeoning field of genetically modified organisms (GMOs). In reaction to growing public concern over GMOs, a coalition that ingenuously calls itself the "Alliance for Better Foods"—actually made up of large food retailers, food processors, biotech companies and corporate-financed farm organizations—has launched a $50 million public "educational" campaign, in addition to giving over $676,000 to U.S. lawmakers and political parties in 1999, to head off the mandatory labeling of such foods.

Perhaps most surprising, to people who have only casually followed the debate about small-farm values versus factory-farm "efficiency," is the fact that a wide body of evidence shows that small farms are actually more productive than large ones—by as much as 200 to 1,000 percent greater output per unit of area. How does this jive with the often-mentioned productivity advantages of large-scale mechanized operations? The answer is simply that those big-farm advantages are always calculated on the basis of how much of *one crop* the land will yield per acre. The greater productivity of a smaller, more complex farm, however, is calculated on the basis of how much food *overall* is produced per acre. The smaller farm can grow several crops utilizing different root depths, plant heights, or nutrients, on the same piece of land simultaneously. It is this "polyculture" that offers the small farm's productivity advantage.

To illustrate the difference between these two kinds of measurement, consider a large Midwestern corn farm. That farm may produce more corn per acre than a small farm in which the corn is grown as part of a polyculture that also includes beans, squash, potato, and "weeds" that serve as fodder. But in overall output, the polycrop—under close supervision by a knowledgeable farmer—produces much more food overall, whether you measure in weight, volume, bushels, calories, or dollars.

The inverse relationship between farm size and output can be attributed to the more efficient use of land, water, and other agricultural resources that small operations afford, including the efficiencies of intercropping various plants in the same field, planting multiple times during the year, targeting irrigation, and integrating crops and livestock. So in terms of converting inputs into outputs, society would be better off with small-scale farmers. And as population continues to grow in many nations, and the agricultural resources per person continue to shrink, a small farm structure for agriculture may be central to meeting future food needs.

Rebuilding Foodsheds

Look at the range of pressures squeezing farmers, and it's not hard to understand the growing desperation. The situation has become explosive, and if stabilizing the erosion of farm culture and ecology is now critical not just to farmers but to everyone who eats, there's still a very challenging question as to what strategy can work. The agribusiness giants are deeply entrenched now, and scattered protests could have as little effect on them as a mosquito bite on a tractor. The prospects for farmers gaining political strength on their own seem dim, as their numbers—at least in the industrial countries—continue to shrink.

A much greater hope for change may lie in a joining of forces between farmers and the much larger numbers of other segments of society that now see the dangers, to their own particular interests, of continued restructuring of the countryside. There are a couple of prominent models for such coalitions, in the constituencies that have joined forces to fight the Mississippi River Barge Capacity and Hidrovía Barge Capacity projects being pushed forward in the name of global soybean productivity.

The American group has brought together at least the following riverbedfellows:

- National environmental groups, including the Sierra Club and National Audubon Society, which are alarmed at the prospect of a public commons being damaged for the profit of a small commercial interest group;
- Farmers and farmer advocacy organizations, concerned about the inordinate power being wielded by the agribusiness oligopoly;
- Taxpayer groups outraged at the prospect of a corporate welfare payout that will drain more than $1 billion from public coffers;
- Hunters and fishermen worried about the loss of habitat;

- Biologists, ecologists, and birders concerned about the numerous threatened species of birds, fish, amphibians, and plants;
- Local-empowerment groups concerned about the impacts of economic globalization on communities;
- Agricultural economists concerned that the project will further entrench farmers in a dependence on the export of low-cost, bulk commodities, thereby missing valuable opportunities to keep money in the community through local milling, canning, baking, and processing.

A parallel coalition of environmental groups and farmer advocates has formed in the Southern hemisphere to resist the Hidrovía expansion. There too, the river campaign is part of a larger campaign to challenge the hegemony of industrial agriculture. For example, a coalition has formed around the Landless Workers Movement, a grassroots organization in Brazil that helps landless laborers to organize occupations of idle land belonging to wealthy landlords. This coalition includes 57 farm advocacy organizations based in 23 nations. It has also brought together environmental groups in Latin America concerned about the related ventures of logging and cattle ranching favored by large landlords; the mayors of rural towns who appreciate the boost that farmers can give to local economies; and organizations working on social welfare in Brazil's cities, who see land occupation as an alternative to shantytowns.

The Mississippi and Hidrovía projects, huge as they are, still constitute only two of the hundreds of agro-industrial developments being challenged around the world. But the coalitions that have formed around them represent the kind of focused response that seems most likely to slow the juggernaut, in part because the solutions these coalitions propose are not vague or quixotic expressions of idealism, but are site-specific and practical. In the case of the alliance forming around the Mississippi River project, the coalition's work has included questioning the assumptions of the Corps of Engineers analysis, lobbying for stronger antitrust examination of agribusiness monopolies, and calling for modification of existing U.S. farm subsidies, which go disproportionately to large farmers. Environmental groups are working to re-establish a balance between use of the Mississippi as a barge mover and as an intact watershed. Sympathetic agricultural extensionists are promoting alternatives to the standard corn-soybean rotation, including certified organic crop production, which can simultaneously bring down

Past and Future: Connecting the Dots

Given the direction and speed of prevailing trends, how far can the decline in farmers go? The lead editorial in the September 13, 1999 issue of *Feedstuffs*, an agribusiness trade journal, notes that "Based on the best estimates of analysts, economists and other sources interviewed for this publication, American agriculture must now quickly consolidate all farmers and livestock producers into about 50 production systems… each with its own brands," in order to maintain competitiveness. Ostensibly, other nations will have to do the same in order to keep up.

To put that in perspective, consider that in traditional agriculture, each farm is an independent production system. In this map of Ireland's farms circa 1930, each dot represents 100 farms, so the country as a whole had many thousands of independent production systems. But if the *Feedstuffs* prognosis were to come to pass, this map would be reduced to a single dot. And even an identically keyed map of the much larger United States would show the country's agriculture reduced to just one dot.

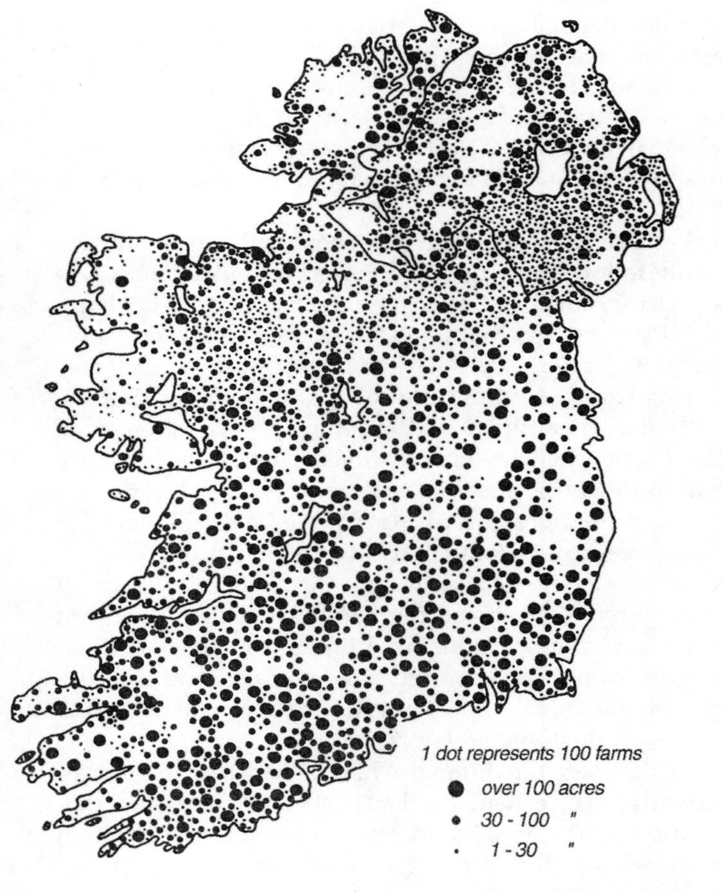

input costs and garner a premium for the final product, and reduce nitrogen pollution.

The United States and Brazil may have made costly mistakes in giving agribusiness such power to reshape the rivers and land to its own use. But the strategy of interlinked coalitions may be mobilizing in time to save much of the world's agricultural health before it is too late. Dave Brubaker, head of the Spira/GRACE Project on Industrial Animal Production at the Johns Hopkins University School of Public Health, sees these diverse coalitions as "the beginning of a revolution in the way we look at the food system, tying in food production with social welfare, human health, and the environment." Brubaker's project brings together public health officials focused on antibiotic overuse and water contamination resulting from hog waste; farmers and local communities who oppose the spread of new factory farms or want to close down existing ones; and a phalanx of natural allies with related campaigns, including animal rights activists, labor unions, religious groups, consumer rights activists, and environmental groups.

"As the circle of interested parties is drawn wider, the alliance ultimately shortens the distance between farmer and consumer," observes Mark Ritchie, president of the Institute for Agriculture and Trade Policy, a research and advocacy group often at the center of these partnerships. This closer proximity may prove critical to the ultimate sustainability of our food supply, since socially and ecologically sound buying habits are not just the passive *result* of changes in the way food is produced, but can actually be the most powerful *drivers of* these changes. The explosion of farmers' markets, community-supported agriculture, and other direct buying arrangements between farmers and consumers points to the growing numbers of nonfarmers who have already shifted their role in the food chain from that of choosing from the tens of thousands of food brands offered by a few dozen companies to bypassing such brands altogether. And, since many of the additives and processing steps that take up the bulk of the food dollar are simply the inevitable consequence of the ever-increasing time commercial food now spends in global transit and storage, this shortening of distance between grower and consumer will not only benefit the culture and ecology of farm communities. It will also give us access to much fresher, more flavorful, and more nutritious food. Luckily, as any food marketer can tell you, these characteristics aren't a hard sell.

Brian Halweil is a staff researcher at the Worldwatch Institute.

Going Cheap

Slave labour plugs neatly into the global economy. **Kevin Bales** argues that it's time to look beyond the cost-benefit analysis.

This past April the world's media zoomed in on the 'slave ship' of Benin. The ship, reported to be carrying 200 enslaved children, was refused entry to Gabon and Cameroon. For two days it disappeared while a search was mounted and fears grew over the fate of the children. When the ship finally reappeared and docked in Benin, it had on board only 43 children and 100 or so adults. After questioning, it was found that most of the children were being trafficked to work in Gabon. In spite of this the ship's captain denied any involvement. The Benin Government then suggested that there was another ship with child slaves, but none was located. Were there other child slaves? Was there another ship? At this point no-one knows.

What we do know is that this confusing incident is just a small part of the regular human traffic between Benin and Gabon. What was news to the world's media is well known in West Africa—on what was once called the Slave Coast, the trade continues. Increasingly, children are bought and sold within and across national borders, forced into domestic work, work in markets or as cheap farm labour. UNICEF estimates there are more than 200,000 children trafficked in West and Central Africa each year.

Child slavery is a significant moneymaker in countries like Benin and Togo. Destitute parents are tricked into giving their children to slave-traders. A local UNICEF worker explains: 'People come and offer the families money and say that their children will work on plantations and send money home. They give the family a little money, from $15 to $30—and then they never see their children again.'

While a slave ship off the African Coast is shocking at the turn of the 21st century, it represents only a tiny part of the world's slavery which has seen a rapid escalation since 1945 and a dramatic change in character.

> If she is ill or injured, she is disposable

Three things have sparked this rapid change. Firstly, the world's population has tripled since 1945 with the bulk of the growth in the Majority World. Secondly, economic change and globalization have driven rural people in poor countries to the cities and into debt. These impoverished and vulnerable people are a bumper crop of potential slaves. Finally, government corruption is essential. When those responsible for law and order can be made to turn a blind eye through bribes, the slave-takers can operate unchecked.

This new slavery is marked by a dramatic shift in the basic economic equation of exploitation—slaves are cheaper today than at any other time in human history. The agricultural slave that cost $1,000 in Alabama in 1850 ($50,000 at today's prices) can be purchased for around $100 today. This fall in price has altered not only the profits to be made from slavery, but the relationship between slave and master as well. The expensive slave of the past was a protected investment; today's slave is cheap and disposable.

A good example is a 14-year-old girl sold into a working-class brothel in Thailand. Her initial purchase price might be less than $1,000. In the brothel she will be told she must repay four times that to gain her freedom—plus rent, food and medicine costs. Even if she has sex with 10-15 men a night, her debt will keep expanding through false accounting and she will never be allowed to leave.

The profit that her 'owners' make from her is very large, as high as 800 per cent. Her annual turnover, the amount men pay for her, is more than $75,000—though she won't see a penny. These profits buy protection from the police, influence with local government, as well as social prestige. Her owners will be lucky to get five years' use from her since HIV is common in the brothels. But because she was so cheap, she is easily replaced. If she is ill or injured or just troublesome, she's disposable.

The brothels of Thailand are just one of the places where new slavery can be found. Slaves tend to be used in simple, non-technological and traditional work. Most work in agriculture. But they are also found in brick-making, mining and quarrying, textiles, leather-working, prostitution, gem-working and jewellery-making, cloth and carpet-making. Or they may work as domestic servants, clear forests, make charcoal or work in shops. Most of this work is aimed at local sale and consumption but slave-made goods filter through the entire global economy and may even end up in western homes.

Studies have documented the slave origins of several international products such as carpets, sugar and jewellery. We may be using slave-made goods or investing in slavery without knowing it. Slave-produced cocoa, for example, goes into the chocolate we buy. Rugs made by slave children in India, Pakistan and Nepal are mainly exported to Europe and the US. The value of global slavery is estimated at $12.3 billion per year, including a significant amount of international trade in slave-produced goods. Despite this outrage few Northern businesses or organizations are taking action. Most trade associations argue that it is impossible to trace the twisted path to a product's origin or, more bluntly, that it's simply not their responsibility. The World Trade Organization has the power to introduce a 'social clause' to block products of forced labour, but it has not done so. And while 'fair trade' programmes are important alternatives to exploitation, they do not directly address the needs of enslaved workers. Obviously, there are many questions yet to be answered both about the economics of slavery and about the most effective strategies for abolition.

Recent studies show that human trafficking is increasing. The US Central Intelligence Agency estimates more than 50,000 persons a year are trafficked into the US. The UN Centre for International Crime Prevention says trafficking is now the third largest money earner for organized crime after drugs and guns. But a lack of reliable information means that governments are scrambling to build databases, develop effective interdiction, work out ways to free and rehabilitate trafficking victims, develop laws and conduct the research needed to address the issue.

Business is also pressed to deal with recent revelations of slavery amongst their suppliers. The filming of slaves on cocoa plantations in Cote d'Ivoire last year led to calls for a boycott of chocolate. Cote d'lvoire produces about half of the world's cocoa. Some local activists claim that up to 90 per cent of the country's plantations use slave labour. Chocolate-producing companies have promised their own investigation.

The situation in Cote d'Ivoire encapsulates much of contemporary slavery. Slaves on the cocoa plantations are mostly from Mali. Desperate for work and tricked by promises of a good job, they can be purchased in village markets for $40 per person. The plantation owners who enslave them are facing a dramatic fall in the world price of cocoa as a result of the World Bank forcing an end to the state marketing monopoly. Meanwhile, Cote d'Ivoire carries $13.5 billion in debt to the Bank and other lenders. With debt payments five times greater than the nation's healthcare budget, there are few resources to protect the enslaved migrants producing its key cash crop.

As well as importing, traffickers in West Africa export slaves to richer countries. Educated young women from Ghana and Cameroon, lured with a chance of further study in the US, have been enslaved as domestics in Washington DC. Large numbers of Nigerian women have been forced into prostitution in Italy. This human traffic into and out of the African coast is mirrored in many countries of the developing and developed world.

In Pakistan and India, across North Africa, in Southeast Asia and in Central and South America, more traditional forms of debt bondage enslave up to 20 million people. These slaves who may be in their third or fourth generation of bondage contribute little to export markets. Laws on bonded labour are either not strict enough, or not enforced. Police are often ignorant of those laws or, as in Brazil and Thailand, they may be profiting from bonded labour themselves.

The result is that underfunded nongovernmental organizations bear the brunt of liberating slaves, sometimes in the face of government resistance. And liberation is just the first step in returning slaves to a life of freedom.

Think for a moment about the 43 children rescued from the Benin slave ship. Questions about their future are every bit as perplexing as questions about their recent past. Many child slaves have suffered physical and psychological abuse and require help. Nearly all have to adjust both to freedom and the challenge of earning a living. With luck, rehabilitation programmes will help them. But few governments are involved in this work.

If there is any good news about modern slavery, it is the dramatic growth in media interest and public awareness. The global coverage of the slave ship was just one example. The UN has several new initiatives on slavery and trafficking, as does the European Union. At the same time, anti-slavery organizations are experiencing an upturn in interest. As one representative of Anti-Slavery International explained recently: 'It is heartening, after years of neglect, to be part of a global movement against slavery. It is still in its infancy, but it is growing everyday.

Kevin Bales is Director of Free the Slaves, the North American sister organization of Anti-Slavery International and the author of *Disposable People: New Slavery in the Global Economy* (University of California Press, 1999), which won the 2000 Viareggio Prize.

From *New Internationalist,* August 2001, pp. 14-15.

UNIT 5
Conflict

Unit Selections

20. **Nasty, Brutish, and Long: America's War on Terrorism**, Ivo H. Daalder and James M. Lindsay
21. **'Why Do They Hate Us?'** Peter Ford
22. **Ten Mistakes in the Middle East**, Bruce Herschensohn
23. **Ethnic Conflict**, Yahya Sadowski
24. **China as Number One**, Soong-Bum Ahn
25. **Battlefield: Space**, Jack Hitt

Key Points to Consider

- Are violent conflicts and warfare increasing or decreasing today? Explain your response.
- What changes have taken place in recent years in the types of conflicts and who participates?
- How is military doctrine changing to reflect new political realities?
- How is the national security policy of the United States likely to change? What about Russia and China?

Links: www.dushkin.com/online/
These sites are annotated in the World Wide Web pages.

DefenseLINK
http://www.defenselink.mil

Federation of American Scientists (FAS)
http://www.fas.org

ISN International Relations and Security Network
http://www.isn.ethz.ch

The NATO Integrated Data Service (NIDS)
http://www.nato.int/structur/nids/nids.htm

Do you lock your doors at night? Do you secure your personal property to avoid theft? These are basic questions that have to do with your sense of personal security. Most individuals take steps to protect what they have, including their lives. The same is true for groups of people, including countries.

In the international arena, governments frequently pursue their national interest by entering into mutually agreeable "deals" with other governments. Social scientists call these types of arrangements "exchanges" (i.e., each side gives up something it values in order to gain something in return that it values even more). On an economic level, it functions like this: "I have the oil that you need. I will sell it to you. In turn I will buy from you the agricultural products that I lack." Whether on the governmental level or the personal level ("If you help me with my homework, then I will drive you home this weekend"), this is the process used by most individuals and groups to "secure" and protect what is of value. The exchange process, however, can break down. When threats and punishments replace mutual exchanges, conflict ensues. Neither side benefits and there are costs to both. Further, each may use threats and hope that the other will capitulate, but if efforts at intimidation and coercion fail, the conflict may escalate into violent confrontation.

With the end of the cold war, issues of national security and the nature of international conflict have changed. In the late 1980s agreements between the former Soviet Union and the United States led to the elimination of superpower support for participants in low-intensity conflicts in Central America, Africa, and Southeast Asia. Fighting the cold war by proxy is now a thing of the past. In addition, cold war military alliances have either collapsed or have been significantly redefined. Despite these historic changes, there is no shortage of conflicts in the world today. The dramatic events of September 11, 2001, have made people around the world fully aware that new threats exist and that the strategy and tactics of warfare have changed.

Many experts initially predicted that the collapse of the Soviet Union would decrease the arms race and diminish the threat of nuclear war. However, some analysts now believe that the threat of nuclear war has in fact increased as control of nuclear weapons has become less centralized and the command structure less reliable. In addition, the proliferation of nuclear weapons into South Asia (India and Pakistan) is a new security issue. Further, there are growing concerns about both dictatorial governments and terrorists obtaining a variety of different types of weapons of mass destruction. What these changing circumstances mean for U.S. policy is a topic of considerable debate.

The unit begins with a timely discussion of three interrelated topics: the war on terrorism, which was precipitated by the attacks on the World Trade Center and the Pentagon on September 11; the conflict in the Middle East; and the general problem of ethnic conflict. In the following articles, the scope of the analysis expands to more strategic issues, including the expanding military role of China. The unit concludes with a broad overview of the rapidly changing technology of warfare with a specific discussion of space-based weapons.

Like all the other global issues described in this anthology, international conflict is a dynamic problem. It is important to understand that conflicts are not random events, but follow patterns and trends. Forty-five years of cold war established discernable patterns of international conflict as the superpowers contained each other with vast expenditures of money and technological know-how. The consequence of this stalemate was often a shift to the developing world for conflict by superpower proxy.

The changing circumstances of the post–cold war era generate a series of important new policy questions: Will there be more nuclear proliferation? Is there an increased danger of so-called "rogue" states destabilizing the international arena? Is the threat of terror a temporary or permanent feature of world affairs? Will there be a growing emphasis on low-intensity conflicts related to the interdiction of drugs, or will some other unforeseen issue determine the world's hot spots? Will the United States and its European allies lose interest in security issues that do not directly involve their economic interests and simply look the other way as age-old ethnic conflicts become brutally violent? Can the international community develop viable institutions to mediate and resolve disputes before they become violent? The answers to these and related questions will determine the patterns of conflict in the twenty-first century.

Article 20

Nasty, Brutish and Long: America's War on Terrorism

"A critical question as the United States enters this new 'cold war' is whether it has learned the lessons of the last—or whether it is destined to repeat its mistakes."

IVO H. DAALDER AND JAMES M. LINDSAY

The post-Cold War era ended abruptly on the morning of September 11, 2001. From the moment terrorists turned jetliners into weapons of mass destruction, the United States was inescapably engaged in a new "war" against global terrorism. The Bush administration now intends to make that war the central organizing principle of America's foreign and defense policies.

This war is not like the one against Iraq a decade ago, when the United States and its allies had a clear territorial objective that could be swiftly achieved. It is also not like the war over Kosovo in 1999, in which the Serbs relented after 78 days of bombing Yugoslavia and NATO suffered no combat deaths. And while the attacks on New York and Washington immediately brought to mind memories of Pearl Harbor, the United States campaign against terrorism will not be like America's effort to force Japan's unconditional surrender.

The campaign against terrorism is instead much more like the cold war of the past century. Like the fight against Soviet communism, today's campaign against terrorism is likely to be nasty, brutish, and long. Because of the diverse nature of the threat, the United States has no clear vision of when or how the war will end. Complete success in the military operations in Afghanistan will not necessarily mean victory. Osama bin Laden's Al Qaeda network of terrorists extends well beyond Afghanistan. It could easily reconstitute itself even if the United States captures or kills bin Laden and his lieutenants. Future attacks might even involve the use of sophisticated germ warfare or radiological weapons, if not nuclear weapons.

As at the start of the cold war, the United States response has begun with the arduous task of assembling a global coalition. President Harry Truman's rousing call in 1947 "to support free peoples who are resisting attempted subjugation by armed minorities or by outside pressures" set the course of United States history for the next four decades. President Bush's invitation to every nation to join the United States in "civilization's fight" was phrased as expansively—and intended to be as enduring. In the new war against terrorism the United States also faces ideologically motivated foes who do not shrink from death. America's fight will end only when, as Defense Secretary Donald Rumsfeld said, Americans can once again get on with their daily lives without fear or thought of a possible terrorist attack. That is a tall order.

A critical question as the United States enters this new "cold war" is whether it has learned the lessons of the last—or whether it is destined to repeat its mistakes. Will Washington again overemphasize military force to achieve its goals and give short shrift to the non-military instruments of statecraft? Will it again focus so narrowly on battle that it forgets other important foreign-policy goals? Will it cut deals today to gain support from other nations that will return to haunt it down the road—in much the same way that supporting the shah led to a deeply hostile Iran and arming Afghan rebels to fight the Soviet Union contributed to the terrorist threat the United States faces today? Will it repudiate its own values at home as it tries to fend off an enemy abroad?

It is crucial that the United States fight its new war against terrorism with the dedication and vigor that President Bush has promised. It is also crucial that it fight that war wisely. Washington must recognize the complexities of its new fight—and the pitfalls that lie before it.

The First Phase

The Bush administration's campaign against terrorism will occur in stages and on multiple fronts. Much of the fight will be conducted through diplomatic pressure; economic, financial, and political sanctions; and intelligence and law enforcement cooperation. But the first phase—capturing or killing bin Laden, destroying his Al Qaeda network in Afghanistan, and deposing the Taliban regime—will be predominantly military.

The administration launched the first phase of its military campaign on October 7, when United States and British forces struck from the air targets in Afghanistan. Administration officials understandably declined to spell out their military strategy in any detail, but early on it appeared to have three components: a Kosovo-style strategic bombing of military targets to weaken the Taliban's hold on power, Somalia-like commando raids to wipe out the terrorists holed up in the unforgiving countryside, and Nicaragua-like support for the Taliban's adversaries (especially the Northern Alliance).

The first weeks of the campaign showed just how difficult things could be. Although United States and British forces quickly destroyed obvious Taliban and Al Qaeda targets, they also hit several civilian sites. These accidents raised tensions within the international coalition the White House had painstakingly assembled in support of the operation, and especially with neighboring countries, such as Pakistan, that fear pro-Taliban sentiments within their own societies. Both bin Laden and Taliban leader Mullah Mohammed Omar escaped capture, perhaps by fleeing to remote caves and valleys. But they may also have taken refuge somewhere in the city of Khandahar, calculating that they would be safe from attack because of the American desire to avoid hitting civilians.

At the same time, United States and British forces initially refrained from attacking front-line Taliban troops around Kabul for fear that doing so would enable Northern Alliance forces to capture Afghanistan's capital before Washington could assemble a new pan-Afghan government. But given the fractious nature of Afghani politics, both within and across ethnic groups, it was far from clear that the political campaign could ever catch up with the military one. When attacks on front-line Taliban forces finally began in the third week of the campaign, they did not produce immediate gains by Northern Alliance forces.

With luck, the military campaign against Afghanistan will end in a matter of weeks or months—with bin Laden and his network inside the country eliminated and the Taliban regime toppled from power. But achieving this set of objectives will require a major and prolonged undertaking with significant costs. And when it succeeds, the campaign against terrorism that Bush promised will only have begun. Just as the Korean War blunted communist expansion but did not end it, the administration will need to turn to a long, grinding, difficult and expensive campaign to disrupt, deter, and defeat terrorist operations elsewhere in the world. And while military force will continue to play some role in this effort, it will be a distinctly secondary role.

Maintaining the International Coalition

Ultimately, for the Bush administration to succeed in its campaign against terrorism it must push ahead on three other fronts. First, it must maintain the anti-terrorism coalition it has assembled in support of military operations in Afghanistan. The coalition is critical because the United States cannot defeat terrorism on its own: it needs other countries to share information about terrorist activities; impose tighter controls over illicit money, weapons and technology flows; isolate and pressure states that sponsor and support terrorists; and strike militarily if targets for action present themselves.

Unfortunately for the Bush administration, the anti-terrorism coalition is not robust. In the Persian Gulf war, more than two dozen countries, including several Arab nations, contributed troops to the fighting. In contrast, American and British forces carried out the initial military operations in Afghanistan alone. Four other countries—Australia, Canada, France, and Germany—have offered to contribute forces at some future point. But significantly, no troops from the Arab or Islamic world participated in the fighting. Only Oman and Pakistan allowed their territory to be used as staging areas for thrusts into Afghan territory. Saudi Arabia, America's main ally in the gulf and host to a large United States Air Force strike force, refused to allow the United States to use its territory as a base for attack (although the air war is coordinated from the United States air control facility at the Prince Sultan airbase located in the middle of the Arabian desert).

The coalition's lack of robustness reflects concerns among the coalition partners over what the campaign against terrorism means for them. Middle Eastern and Islamic governments are crucial to the coalition's success, if only because so many terror groups originate on their soil. These governments fear, however, that joining with Washington will inflame anti-American sentiment in their own societies. Nor are Islamic countries the only ones unsure of how far to follow Washington. Although NATO invoked the organization's Article V provision on mutual defense for the first time 24 hours after the September 11 attacks—ironically, turning an alliance designed to ensure a United States defense of Europe into one in which Europe would help defend the United States—some European countries worry that the United States will go too far in its fight against terrorism.

The issue most likely to fracture the coalition is Iraq. Before September 11, critics speculated that the Bush administration was spoiling for an opportunity to clear up unfinished business from the elder Bush's presidency and would seek to remove Saddam Hussein from power. In the days immediately following the attacks on the World Trade Center and the Pentagon, key administration officials argued for a broad military response that would include Saddam's removal as one of its objectives. President Bush quickly ruled out that option. But in doing so, he embraced an "Afghanistan-first" approach—not the "Afghanistan-only" policy that many in Europe and elsewhere support.

Making Iraq the subject of military attack in a second phase of the campaign against terrorism poses problems for the Bush administration. The United States would almost certainly have to carry out the attack on its own and perhaps even without access to bases in the Persian Gulf area, making it far more difficult to win. Middle Eastern countries argue that attacking Iraq will inflame Arab public opinion and make bin Laden's case that the United States is waging war against Islam. Russia, which has provided Washington with considerable intelligence cooperation since the crisis began, has good relations with Baghdad. Most European governments have long opposed Washington's Iraqi policy. To make matters worse for the administration, these same constraints hold with respect to using military force against Iran or Syria, two countries that have actively sponsored and harbored terrorist groups like Lebanon-based Hezbollah.

Ultimately, the fight against global terrorism is one that the United States cannot win on its own.

Iraq, Iran, and Syria are not the only issues that could fracture the antiterrorism coalition. Should military operations in Afghanistan drag on, or result in large numbers of civilian deaths, the Bush administration could find itself under increasing pressure abroad to end the mission prematurely.

The challenge facing the Bush administration in the near term is to strike the proper balance between its short-term military objectives in Afghanistan and elsewhere and its longer term objective to sustain the international cooperation necessary to conduct a successful fight against global terrorism. In doing so, it will attempt to make the mission define the coalition, rather than letting the coalition define the mission. But it may then find itself confronting what every administration fears: what it wants to do, and perhaps should do, does not mesh with what it can do on its own. There may be times in the campaign against terrorism—as during the cold war itself—when going it alone is both necessary and desirable, but this should be the exception rather than the rule. Ultimately, the fight against global terrorism is one that the United States cannot win on its own.

Securing the Homeland

The second step Washington must take is to improve homeland security. Much of the focus will understandably be on spending more money on the problem, but the immediate challenge will be to ensure that money is spent wisely. And here the core challenge is to organize the government so that it is more effective in providing homeland security. As Dwight D. Eisenhower aptly noted, "although organization cannot make a genius out of an incompetent. . .disorganization can scarcely fail to result in inefficiency and can easily lead to disaster."

President Bush moved swiftly to address the organizational issue. In a September 20 address to Congress, he announced that he would appoint Pennsylvania Governor Tom Ridge head of a new Office of Homeland Security in the White House. The executive order detailing Ridge's duties also created a Homeland Security Council (HSC), modeled after the National Security Council. The HSC's members will consist of the president, vice president, and key cabinet members and agency heads who will advise and assist the president on all aspects of homeland security.

Critics countered that a White House coordinator, even one who was a friend of the president, could not begin to meet the challenge facing the country. They argued that Ridge would have clout only if he were given control of agency budgets or was put in charge of a newly created, cabinet-level department for homeland security that consolidated existing government operations. Proposals along these lines work better in theory than in practice, however. Contrary to the critics, control of budgets or command of an agency is not necessary, or even sufficient, to exercise power in the federal government. National security advisers possess neither, yet no one doubts their authority.

Nor is centralization necessarily the proper prescription. Homeland security to a considerable extent requires decentralization—where the decisions made by people on the "front lines" matter as much if not more than what is decided in Washington. Customs agents need to know what to look for at the border, Coast Guard commanders need to know which ships to interdict, and Immigration and Naturalization Service officers need to know who is to be barred entry. Intelligence officers need to know which pieces of information culled from an overload of data fit together to enable pre-emptive actions. Hospital emergency-room doctors need to know what symptoms indicate possible exposure to a biological attack. Trying to cram these various agencies, and their diverse missions, into a single organization could make the government less effective in battling terrorism, not more.

Another problem with centralization proposals is the sheer number of federal agencies with a stake in counterterrorism—a number that ranges from 46 to 151, depending on who counting. Short of making the entire federal government a counterterrorism agency, that means that any consolidation must be selective. Some agencies and functions critical to the counterterrorism task cannot, by their very nature, be consolidated. The Federal Bureau of Investigation must remain in the Justice Department (where, incidentally, it often resists the attorney general's direction). Further complicating matters is that formal consolidation does not guarantee effective integration. The Department of Energy is the classic cautionary lesson: it was created in 1977 to bring a variety of units under one umbrella, but a quarter of a century later its integration remains far from complete and its effectiveness often questioned. Finally, giving

Ridge command of his own agency would likely destroy his ability to be an "honest broker" who could coordinate conflicting agency demands. Instead, he would, in the eyes of other agencies, simply become another bureaucratic competitor for money and influence.

Thus, the Bush approach of having Ridge coordinate domestic agencies much as the national security adviser coordinates foreign policy agencies makes more sense. His job certainly is more difficult in one key respect: the national security adviser must worry about getting coordinated information to the president in a timely fashion, whereas Ridge must concern himself mainly with how the agencies operate in the field. One factor working in his favor is that September 11 made counterterrorism a priority across all agencies. They not only know that it is a critical mission but also that it is the key to bigger budgets and more authority. The challenge facing Ridge is to forge the channels of formal and informal agency cooperation where they do not exist today—both among domestic agencies and between them and the national security apparatus. Within this coordination framework some agency consolidation may make sense (for example, combining agencies with closely related functions such as the Customs Service, Border Patrol and Coast Guard).

Even if Washington gets organizational matters right, it will not be enough. It must also take major steps to reduce the country's vulnerability to attack. One obvious need is better control over America's borders. Several of the September 11 hijackers were in the United States on expired student visas. Others entered even though they were suspected of ties to Al Qaeda. But to speak of better border enforcement is to acknowledge the difficulty of the task. Millions of people enter the United States each year, legally and illegally, and only a few have any interest in committing terrorist attacks. The United States—Canada border is 4,000 miles long and in most places is uncontrolled-the Border Patrol had only one officer for every 12 miles of border before September 11. America's 2,000-mile-long border with Mexico is also notorious for its porosity.

Another obvious need is to make the country's transportation networks more secure. Congress and the White House took initial steps in this direction immediately after September 11 by tightening aviation security. Much more remains to be done to make rail and vehicular traffic less vulnerable. Reports that Al Qaeda operatives had obtained licenses to drive trucks carrying hazardous materials points only to the beginning of the havoc that terrorists could wreak using ordinary ground transport. And the United States needs to improve the transportation system's equivalent in cyberspace. The Bush administration took an initial organizational step in this direction by appointing a special adviser to the president for cybersecurity, but more must be done to persuade private actors to make their computer networks more secure. That raises the difficult question of who should pay for this "security tax" and whether protection will be best generated by government mandates or incentives.

Washington also needs to improve the ability of federal, state, and local governments to respond once a terrorist attack occurs—especially chemical, biological, and radiological attacks. The anthrax incidents that followed the September 11 attacks broke the taboo against using such weapons and possibly foreshadowed much more devastating future attacks. Congress and the Bush administration have already responded to this need to some extent, especially by deciding to stockpile additional vaccines and antibiotics for biological attacks using communicable diseases such as smallpox. But perhaps just as important, the initial anthrax attacks have made clear the importance of creating a more effective organizational structure for responding. The government's initial response to the release of anthrax in Senate Majority Leader Tom Daschle's office was marked by inconsistent and conflicting statements about the extent of the danger. And federal credibility suffered when two postal workers died of pulmonary anthrax after government officials failed, regrettably though perhaps understandably, to anticipate that Daschle's anthrax-laden letter might have contaminated mailrooms along the way.

Addressing Anti-Americanism Abroad

The campaign against terrorism must also address the sources of the intense anti-Americanism that now roils the Arab and Islamic world and forms the backdrop for Al Qaeda attacks. Hatred of the United States is not peculiar to the Middle East, nor does it translate directly into a desire to launch terrorist attacks. The relationship between the two is more complicated and indirect, akin in many ways to that between oxygen and fire. Oxygen does not cause fires—the spark must come from somewhere else—but fire requires oxygen to rage. In the same fashion, terrorists need anti-American sentiment. It provides them with recruits, and more important, it provides them with people willing to give aid and comfort.

But how can the United States cut off oxygen to the fires of anti-Americanism, especially when the justifiable military operation in Afghanistan and the support it has received from ruling elites in the Arab and Islamic world is likely to feed them? One strategy is to redouble United States efforts to limit and resolve conflicts around the world, especially the one between Israel and the Palestinians. Again, these conflicts did not cause the attacks on the World Trade Center and the Pentagon. They do, however, contribute to the anger that terrorists manipulate to their own, despicable ends.

The payoff from this strategy is questionable; it is easy to call for conflict resolution and hard to deliver it. A Middle East peace deal has been the holy grail of the last six presidential administrations. The escalating violence of the past twelve months has only made it more difficult to persuade Israelis and Palestinians to speak of concession and compromise. The conflict between India and Pakistan over Kashmir—an issue of great concern to Pakistani militants—has dragged on for more than half a century. New Delhi and Islamabad are not about to toss aside their longstanding differences simply because Washington thinks they should. Nor will being seen as actively pursuing peace necessarily do much to deflect Arab and Islamic anger. Former President Bill Clinton's feverish and ultimately unsuccessfully effort in 2000 to broker a Middle East peace deal passed largely unnoticed in the Arab and Islamic world. The frequent complaints about United States policy seldom mention that Washington liberated Kuwait, saved hundreds of thousands of starving Somalis in the early 1990s, fought not one but two wars to protect Muslims in the Balkans, and provided more humanitarian aid than any other country to the people of Afghanistan.

Washington will also need to intensify its support for democracy and economic development—especially in areas like Central Asia and the Arab world, where repression and poverty provide breeding grounds for anti-American sentiments. Prosperous democratic countries are America's best allies against terrorism. But again, this strategy is easier to urge than to carry out. One problem is that while Washington generally knows how to promote economic development, its success in promoting political development is spotty—witness the record in Vietnam, Somalia, and Haiti. The other problem is whether the United States can gracefully extract itself from its current political commitments in the Arab and Islamic world. Calls are likely to mount in the coming months for the United States to distance itself from Cairo and Riyadh unless they enact democratic reforms. Yet that policy could well endanger other important United States foreign policy objectives—not the least securing Egyptian and Saudi cooperation in the fight against terrorism. And it may produce regime change, though not necessarily one that comports with American values. To judge by the slogans of dissidents in Saudi Arabia, greater mass political participation will not deliver a Westminster-style democracy but rather an Iranian-style theocracy steeped in anti-Americanism.

Americans must [recognize] that military force alone is not enough; pretending that it is takes us down a dangerous road.

The focus on big-picture policies like conflict resolution and political development should not obscure small-picture policies that take aim at anti-Americanism. A key here is a concerted public diplomacy campaign, much like the one the United States waged vigorously in the early years of the cold war. Then United States used the media and exchange programs to refute the lies of communist rulers. Today, as President Bush noted in his October 11 press conference, it needs to make a better case for America and to argue that bin Laden represents a perversion of Islam and threatens the stability of all civilizations.

This public diplomacy should use the public relations tools of the cold war, including radio broadcasts, magazines, and cultural centers. But the strategy should also adapt to the times. Bin Laden shrewdly used the Arab-language satellite television channel Al Jazeera to broadcast his hatred to Arabs around the world. Before September 11, however, American officials seldom sought to appear on Al Jazeera and other media outlets in the Arab world to present their case. And the United States needs to press its Middle Eastern allies to do their share in discrediting anti-Americanism. In recent years countries such as Egypt and Saudi Arabia have bought social peace for themselves by ignoring and even encouraging growing hatred toward the United States. Criticizing President Hosni Mubarak on the streets of Cairo will get you arrested; criticizing America will get you applause. Washington must press these governments to confront dangerous distortions of the truth rather than to stoke anti-Americanism.

Hard Lessons

Because the fight against terrorism is a new cold war, some key lessons of the old one are worth remembering. Although the United States ultimately triumphed in that conflict, it made critical mistakes along the way that it must now seek to avoid.

Americans must begin by recognizing that military force alone is not enough; pretending that it is takes us down a dangerous road. The militarization of containment—which elevated military responses over all other tools of policy and culminated in the disastrous United States engagement in Vietnam—undermined the American public's trust in its government. It also weakened the very alliances on which the United States depended to win its confrontation with the Soviet Union.

In calling on the nation to conduct a "war" against terrorism, the Bush administration has helped create the impression that America's victory will be a military one. Again, there is a role for military force in today's fight—to destroy the terrorist infrastructure in Afghanistan, compel an end to continued state-sponsorship of terrorism, and pre-empt any planned terrorist attacks. But the force of arms alone cannot defeat terrorism. The United States also needs better law enforcement, enhanced intelligence, focused diplomacy, and targeted sanctions to succeed.

Second, the United States must avoid creating new threats even as it seeks to defeat the current ones. The most immediate need is to end the cycle of violence in Afghanistan. In the 1980s, the United States armed the mujahideen to help them to defeat the Soviet invaders. When Moscow finally withdrew its troops in 1989, Washington walked away from the scene. We are now living with the consequences.

Washington must not repeat this mistake. The threat of further destabilization in Afghanistan is real. Nearly constant war for more than two decades—first against the Soviet Union and then among Afghans themselves—has created more than 1.5 million refugees and left many hundreds of thousands of others lacking sufficient food or adequate shelter. United States military operations will make matters worse, notwithstanding the efforts to drop relief supplies to those in need. Should Afghanistan's unrest spread, the consequences for neighboring Pakistan—an internally divided and failing state in possession of nuclear weapons—could be severe. The last thing the United States wants or needs is for Islamic fundamentalist sympathizers of bin Laden to take over Pakistan.

United States military operations need to be followed by a concerted effort to stabilize Afghanistan if the United States hopes to discourage its future use as a terrorist haven. Fortunately, the Bush administration, despite a deep-seated hostility to nation-building, has signaled that it understands it must be engaged in Afghanistan. Even if the White House insists that it is not engaged in "nation building" but rather the "stabilization of a future government," these efforts are necessary to increase the prospects for regional stability. The Bush administration wants the United Nations to play a major role in reconstructing Afghanistan, thereby spreading responsibility and perhaps making success more likely, but extensive American involvement is inescapable.

But avoiding policies that inadvertently create new threats also means not carelessly sacrificing other important foreign policy interests and values to serve the cause of defeating global terrorism. During the cold war, Washington made battling the spread of communism an all-consuming fight. Other priorities and interests were jettisoned when they conflicted with the objective of holding Soviet expansion at bay. As a result, the United States embraced unsavory characters (from Spain's Franco to Zaire's Mobutu and Chile's Pinochet), engaged in highly questionable conduct (from assassinations to secret coups), wasted billions of dollars on dead-end interventions and superfluous weapon systems, and ignored a long list of other foreign policy challenges (from human rights to weapons proliferation to the environment).

The same risks exist today. To solicit support for its anti-terror coalition, the Bush administration has lifted sanctions imposed on Pakistan for testing nuclear weapons, begun to side rhetorically with Russia in its brutal fight in Chechnya, and sought assistance from key state sponsors of terrorism such as Iran and Sudan. These and other steps may be needed to address a short-term emergency, but they may come at a hefty price in the long term.

Third, the United States must not needlessly sacrifice its civil liberties as it combats the terrorist threat. The willingness with which Washington and the country as a whole trampled on cherished civil liberties during the McCarthy years of the early cold war is too well known to merit repeating. Perhaps most remarkable about how Americans reacted in the first month after the September 11 attacks was how quickly they acknowledged the importance of not forfeiting America's basic principles as the country met its new challenge. Politicians, the media, and the public emphasized the importance of tolerance. Civil libertarians challenged the merits of some of the administration's proposed changes to law enforcement authority. The question that remains is whether this commitment to fundamental principles of liberty will withstand future terrorist attacks.

In the end, America's campaign to restore the margin of security it enjoyed before September 11 will be neither easy nor quick. The defeat of terrorism will not be achieved or celebrated in one grand moment. There will be no V-E or V-J day, no ticker-tape parade along Fifth Avenue. America's victory will be piecemeal. Every day the United States goes without a terrorist attack will be a triumph. But even that limited achievement requires waging the fight against terrorism with a clear memory that the last war demanded much more than just battlefield bravery. Otherwise, any victory will be tarnished by the new problems the United States will reap.

Article 21

ROBERT HARRISON—STAFF

PROUD FATHER: In a Pakistan pharmacy, pictured above, Amirul Haq (r.), says he is 'satisfied' that his Muslim son was killed in the Kashmir. He's 'against America, because it doesn't care about those who die in Pakistan.'

'Why do they hate us?'

By Peter Ford

Staff writer

asked President Bush in his speech to Congress last Thursday night. It is a question that has ached in America's heart for the past two weeks. Why did those 19 men choose to wreck the icons of US military and economic power?

Most Arabs and Muslims knew the answer, even before they considered who was responsible. Retired Pakistani Air Commodore Sajad Haider—a friend of the US—understood why. Radical Egyptian-born cleric and US enemy Abu Hamza al-Masri understood. And Jimmy Nur Zamzamy, a devout Muslim and advertising executive in Indonesia, understood.

They all understood that this assault was more precisely targeted than an attack on "civilization." First and foremost, it was an attack on America.

In the United States, military planners are deciding how to exact retribution. To many people in the Middle East and beyond, where US policy has bred widespread anti-Americanism, the carnage of Sept. 11 *was* retribution.

And voices across the Muslim world are warning that if America doesn't wage its war on terrorism in a way that the Muslim world considers just, America risks creating even greater animosity.

Mr. Haider is a hero of Pakistan's 1965 war against India, and a sworn friend of America. But he and his neighbors in one of Islamabad's toniest districts are clear about why their warm feelings toward the US are not widely shared in Pakistan.

In his dim office in a north London mosque, Abu Hamza al-Masri sympathizes with the goals of Osama bin Laden, fingered by US officials as the prime suspect behind the Sept. 11 attacks. Abu Hamza has himself directed terrorist operations abroad, according to the British police, although for lack of evidence, they have never brought him to trial.

Mr. Zamzamy, a 30-something advertising executive in Jakarta, knew what was behind the attack, too. Trying to give his ads some zip and still stay within the bounds of his Muslim faith, he is keenly aware of the tensions between Islam and American-style global capitalism.

The 19 men—who US officials say hijacked four American passenger jets and flew them on suicide missions that left more than 7,000 people dead or missing—were all from the Middle East. Most of the hijackers have been identified as Muslims.

The vast majority of Muslims in the Middle East were as shocked and horrified as any American by what they saw happening on their TV screens. And they are frightened of being lumped together in the popular American imagination with the perpetrators of the attack.

But from Jakarta to Cairo, Muslims and Arabs say that on reflection, they are not surprised by it. And they do not share Mr. Bush's view that the perpetrators did what they did because "they hate our freedoms."

Rather, they say, a mood of resentment toward America and its behavior around the world has become so commonplace in their countries that it was bound to breed hostility, and even hatred.

And the buttons that Mr. bin Laden pushes in his statements and interviews—the injustice done to the Palestinians, the cruelty of continued sanctions against Iraq, the presence of US troops in Saudi Arabia, the repressive and corrupt nature of US-backed Gulf governments—win a good deal of popular sympathy.

The resentment of the US has spread through societies demoralized by their recent history. In few of the world's 50 or so Muslim countries have governments offered their citizens either prosperity or democracy. Arab nations have lost three wars against their arch-foe—and America's closest ally—Israel. A sense of failure and injustice is rising in the throats of millions.

Three weeks ago, a leading Arabic newspaper, Al-Hayat, published a poem on its front page. A long lament about the plight of the Arabs, addressed to a dead Syrian poet, it ended:

"Children are dying, but no one makes a move.
Houses are demolished, but no one makes a move.
Holy places are desecrated, but no one makes a move....
I am fed up with life in the world of mortals.
Find me a hole near you. For a life of dignity is in those holes."

It sounds as if it could have been written by a desperate and hopeless man, driven by frustration to seek death, perhaps martyrdom. A young Palestinian refugee planning a suicide bomb attack, maybe. In fact, it was written by the Saudi Arabian ambassador to London, a member of one of the wealthiest and most influential families in the kingdom that is Washington's closest Arab ally.

Against the background of that humiliated mood, America's unchallenged military, economic, and cultural might be seen as an affront even if its policies in the Middle East were neutral. And nobody voices that view.

From one end of the region to the other, the perception is that Israel can get away with murder—literally—and that Washington will turn a blind eye. Clearly, the US and Israel have compelling reasons for their actions. But little that US diplomats have done in recent years to broker a peace deal between Israel and the Palestinians has persuaded Arabs that the US is a fair-minded and equitable judge of Middle Eastern affairs.

Over the past year, Arab TV stations have broadcast countless pictures of Israeli soldiers shooting at Palestinian youths, Israeli tanks plowing into Palestinian homes, Israeli helicopters rocketing Palestinian streets. And they know that the US sends more than $3 billion a year in military and economic aid to Israel.

"You see this every day, and what do you feel?" asks Rafiq Hariri, the portly prime minister of Lebanon, who is not an excitable man. "It hurts me a lot. But for hundreds of thousands of Arabs and Muslims, it drives them crazy. They feel humiliated."

RESENTMENT RISES, AND A RADICAL IS BORN

Ask Sheikh Abdul Majeed Atta why Palestinians may not like the United States, and he does not immediately answer. Instead, he pads barefoot across the red swirls of his living room carpet and reaches for three framed photographs on the floor beside a couch.

The black-and-white prints show dusty, rock-strewn hills dotted with tiny tents and cinderblock houses: the early days of Duheisheh refugee camp, south of Bethlehem in the West Bank. It was where Mr. Atta was born, and where his family has lived for more than half a century. Atta's family village was destroyed in the struggle between Palestinian Arabs and Jews after Britain divided Palestine between them in 1948. For 10 years his family of

13 lived in a tent. The year Atta was born, the United Nations gave them a one-room house.

It doesn't matter to Atta that the United States was not directly involved in "the catastrophe," as Palestinians refer to the events of 1948. Washington averted its eyes when it could have helped, he says, and since then has been firmly on Israel's side.

Heavyset, solid, with a neatly trimmed full beard, Atta is the preacher at a nearby mosque. He looks the part of the community leader, always meticulously turned out in crisp shirts and pressed trousers, gold-rimmed reading glasses tucked into a pocket.

In the past year of the Palestinian-Israeli conflict, Atta has joined Hamas, the radical group responsible for recently sending most of the suicide bombers into Israeli towns. Frustration at watching the rising Palestinian death toll at the hands of the Israeli army played a large part in his decision, he says.

His resentment at Israel, though, dates back to his infancy, and the stories he heard of his village, Ras Abu Amar, which he never knew. That village is still alive for him, just as millions of Palestinians in the West Bank and Gaza Strip, and throughout the Middle East cherish photos, house keys, and deeds to homes that no longer exist or which have housed Israelis for generations.

Today he lives in his own house in Duheisheh, a sprawling tangle of densely packed concrete buildings that crowd snaking, narrow alleys. But he still dreams of the home he never knew, and recalls who took it from him, and remembers who they rely on for their strength.

What happened on Sept. 11 "was an awful thing, a tragedy, and since we live a continuous tragedy, we felt like this touched us," he adds. "But when we see something like this in Israel or the US, we feel a contradiction. We see it's a tragedy, but we remember that these are the people behind our tragedy."

"Even small children know that Israel is nothing without America," says Atta. "And here America means F-16, M-16, Apache helicopters, the tools Israelis use to kill us and destroy our homes."

SUPERPOWER SWAGGER

Such weapons are very much the visible face of American policy in the Middle East, where military might has held the balance of power for 50 years. Thousands of US soldiers stationed in the Gulf, and billions of US dollars each year in military aid to Israel, Egypt, and other allies, have shored up Washington's interests in the strategically crucial, oil-rich region.

That military presence and power looks like swagger to some in the Muslim world, even far from the flashpoints. "Now America is ready with its airplanes to bomb this poor nation [Afghanistan], and most people in Indonesia don't like arrogance," says Imam Budi Prasodjo, an Indonesian sociologist and talk-show host.

"You are a superpower, you are a military superpower, and you can do whatever you want. People don't like that, and this is dangerous," he adds.

"America should spread its culture, rather than weapons or tanks," adds Mohammed el-Sayed Said, deputy director of Cairo's influential Al Ahram think tank. "They need to act like any respectable commander or leader of an army. They can't just project an image of contempt for those they wish to lead."

Ten years ago, at the head of a broad coalition of Western and Arab countries, the United States used its superpower status to kick the Iraqi army out of Kuwait. Since then, however, Washington has found itself alone—save for loyal ally Britain—in its determination to keep bombing Iraq, and to keep imposing strict economic sanctions that the United Nations says are partly responsible for the deaths of half a million Iraqi children.

'We wish the American people could see what their governments are doing in the rest of the world.'

—Saniya Ghussein, whose daughter, Raafat, was killed in the 1986 US bombing raid against Libya

Those deaths, and those bombs (which US and British planes drop regularly, but without fanfare), are felt keenly among fellow Arabs. And Saniya Ghussein knows all about bombs.

A DAUGHTER DIES, AND PARENTS WAIT FOR US APOLOGY

In the middle of the night of April 16, 1986, the deafening sound of anti-aircraft guns woke Saniya Ghussein with a sudden start. "My God," she thought, "there's a war being fought above my house."

She slipped out of bed and ran into the bedroom where her husband Bassem and their 7-year-old daughter Kinda had fallen asleep earlier in the evening. "Bassem, the Americans are here," she said urgently. "It looks like they're going to hit us."

She checked on her other daughter, Raafat. She had been suffering from her annual bout of hay fever, and the 18-year-old art student was in the television room next to the humidifier so she could breathe easier.

Raafat was still sleeping, completely oblivious of all the commotion going on around her, due to the medication she had taken earlier. There was little Saniya felt she could do. She climbed back into bed and pulled the sheets tight around her.

Bassem lay awake on the bed, listening to the appalling noise in the night sky above.

A Palestinian-born Lebanese national, Bassem had worked in Libya as an engineer for Occidental, the American oil giant, for 20 years, helping exploit the country's

ROBERT HARRISON—STAFF

'When Bush talked of a crusade...it was not a slip of the tongue.'
—Sajad Haider, retired Pakistani air force officer

massive oil reserves. He and his family lived in the upmarket Ben Ashour neighborhood of Tripoli, the Libyan capital, on the ground floor of a two-story apartment block.

Bassem never heard the explosion. Instead, he watched in astonishment as the window frame suddenly flew into the room, and the roof collapsed on top of him and his daughter.

Kinda was screaming in the darkness near him. Bassem tried to move, but was pinned by the rubble. He groped in the blackness for Kinda. "Don't worry," he said, squeezing his daughter's hand. "Daddy's here, don't cry, it will be okay."

The blast had knocked Saniya unconscious. She woke to hear Bassem calling from the next room and Kinda screaming. She stumbled in the darkness, barefoot across the rubble and glass shards, choking on the fumes from the missile blast, as she called her daughter's name "Raafat! Raafat!" for several minutes. But there was no response, and Saniya knew with a terrible certainty that her daughter was dead.

"Bassem," she cried. "Raafat has gone."

Pinned beneath the rubble, Bassem heard his wife's words, and he felt a deep sense of anger and resentment well up inside him. His life and that of his family had been shattered, and nothing would ever be the same again.

It took them eight hours to dig Raafat out from under the ruins of the house. "Our pain and agony, which I cannot describe, started at that moment," Saniya says.

Raafat was one of an estimated 55 victims of an air raid mounted by US warplanes against a series of targets in Tripoli and another Libyan city, Benghazi.

The attacks were in retaliation for the bombing of a disco in Berlin, Germany, 10 days earlier in which 200 people were injured, 63 of them US soldiers; one soldier and one civilian were killed. The Reagan administration blamed Libyan leader Muammar Qaddafi.

Bassem and Saniya Ghussein are not natural anti-Americans. Bassem studied in the US before going to work for Esso and then Occidental. He sent Raafat to an American Catholic school, and on family trips to the US, Saniya would take Raafat to Disney World in Florida. "We did all the typical American things," she says.

But since that terrible night 16 years ago, neither Bassem nor Saniya have stepped foot in America. They returned to Beirut in 1994 when Bassem retired.

In 1989, the Libyan government enlisted the help of Ramsey Clark, an attorney general during the Carter administration, to file a lawsuit against President Ronald Reagan and British Prime Minister Margaret Thatcher for the civilian deaths during the air raids. "When Clark came to collect our documents and evidence, I asked him if he thought we had a case," Bassem recalls. "He said 'Oh, definitely. This was murder.' "

But US district court judge Thomas Penfield Jackson disagreed. He dismissed the suit, and fined Clark for presenting a "frivolous" case that "offered no hope whatsoever of success."

Twelve years later, the court's decision still rankles with Bassem. "I will only return to America when I know someone will listen to me and say: 'yes, it was our fault your daughter died, and I am sorry.' So long as they think my daughter's death is 'frivolous,' I won't go back," Bassem says.

The Ghusseins have no sympathy for religious extremism and thoroughly condemn the Sept. 11 suicide bombings in New York and Washington. Yet they both maintain that the devastating attack was a result of America's "arrogant" policies in the Middle East and elsewhere. "We wish the American people could see what their governments are doing in the rest of the world," Saniya says.

A FEELING OF BETRAYAL AMONG FRIENDS

On the other side of Asia, in Pakistan, Air Commodore Haider would sympathize with the Ghusseins' wish. He has always been a friend of the United States, and not just because he enjoyed the 10 years he spent in Washington as his country's military attaché. Like most other members of the ruling elite in Pakistan, in the armed forces, in business, and in the political parties, he sees America as a natural ally.

But not a reliable one. The prevailing mood in Pakistan of anger and suspicion toward the United States springs from a deeply rooted perception that the US has been a fickle friend, Haider says, and not just to Pakistan, but to other nations in the Muslim world.

If there was a moment of betrayal for Haider, it was the 1965 war between India and Pakistan, largely over the future of Kashmir. As Indian tanks advanced on the Pakistani metropolis of Lahore, Haider was head of a squadron of F-86 Sabre jets sent to destroy them. India's Soviet allies helped with money, arms, and diplomatic support. But at a crucial moment, Pakistan's ally, the US, refused to send more weapons. As it turned out, Pakistan was able to defeat the Indian attack on Lahore and elsewhere without US help. Haider's squadron decimated the column of Indian tanks that had reached to within six miles of Lahore. But the lesson lingered: America cannot be trusted.

"There is a feeling of being betrayed, it's a feeling of being let down, and you can only be let down by somebody you care for," says Haider, out for an evening stroll in a tony Islamabad neighborhood.

"They said you will be the bulwark of America and of the free world against Communism. But then they dropped a friend for no good reason."

Today, Haider sees a "convergence of interests" between the United States and Pakistan in the fight against terrorism. But he says that President Bush will need to watch his language when he talks about the Muslim world. "When Bush talked of a Crusade... it was not a slip of the tongue. It was a mindset. When they talk of terrorism, the only thing they have in mind is Islam."

Ultimately, Haider does see a way for America and Muslim nations to become lasting friends, but only if the US begins to give as much weight to the interests of Muslim nations as it does to Israel.

"When you deny justice to people, which you have been doing for several decades in Palestine, and they are intelligent, sensitive people, they are going to find something to do," warns Haider. "They might take shelter in Islam, in fatalism, and some will come to despise you."

How the world views a US military response

In your opinion, once the identity of the terrorists is known, should the American government launch a military attack on the country or countries where the terrorists are based, or should the American government seek to extradite the terrorists to stand trial?

	Launch attack	Try the terrorists	Don't know
Israel	77%	19%	4%
India	72	28	0
United States	54	30	16
Korea	38	54	9
France	29	67	4
Czech Republic	22	64	14
Italy	21	71	8
South Africa	18	75	7
United Kingdom (excluding N. Ireland)	18	75	7
Germany	17	77	6
Bosnia	14	80	6
Colombia	11	85	4
Pakistan	9	69	22
Greece	6	88	6
Mexico	2	94	3

Source: Gallup International surveys Sept. 14 to 17.

AN EGYPTIAN 'INSPIRED' TO JOIN AFGHAN FIGHTERS

Sheikh Abu Hamza al-Masri, the radical Muslim cleric who runs a mosque in a shabby district of north London, has certainly come to despise America.

Abu Hamza says he used to admire the West when he was a young man—so much so that he dropped out of university in his native Alexandria, Egypt, to study in Britain. And he clearly had nothing against the British government when he took a job as a civil engineer at Sandhurst, the British equivalent of West Point, after he graduated.

But as he immersed himself more and more in religious studies, and came into contact with more and more Arab mujahideen, who had travelled from the mountains of Afghanistan to England for medical treatment, he began to change his outlook.

"When you see how happy they are, how anxious to just have a new limb so they can run again and fight again, not thinking of retiring, their main ambition is to get killed in the cause of God... you see another dimension in the verses of the Koran," says Abu Hamza.

Inspired by their example, he took his family to Afghanistan in 1990, to work there as a civil engineer, building roads, tunnels, and "anything I could do." And he also fought with the mujahideen against Afghan President Mohammad Najibullah (seen as a Russian stand-in supported by the Soviets), until he blew both his hands off and lost the sight in his left eye, in a mine explosion.

What transformed him and his comrades-in-arms from anti-Soviet to anti-American militants, he says, was the way Washington abandoned them at the end of the war in Afghanistan, and sought to disarm and disperse them.

"It was when the Americans took the knife out of the Russians and stabbed it in our back, it's as simple as that," says Abu Hamza. "It was a natural turn, not a theoretical one.

"In the meantime, they were bombarding Iraq and occupying the [Arabian] peninsula," he says, referring to the US troops stationed in Saudi Arabia after the Gulf War, "and then with the witch-hunt against the mujahideen, all of it came together, that was a full-scale war, it was very clear."

Abu Hamza would rather see Islamic militants fight corrupt or secular Arab governments before they take on America (indeed, the Yemeni government has sought his extradition from Britain for plotting to overthrow the government in Sana). But he is in no doubt that the American government brought the events of Sept. 11 on its own head.

"The Americans wanted to fight the Russians with Muslim blood, and they could only justify that by triggering the word 'jihad,' " he argues. "Unfortunately for everybody except the Muslims, when that button is pushed, it does not come back that easy. It only keeps going on and on until the Muslim empire swallows every empire existing."

Can he understand the motivation behind the assault on New York and Washington? "The motivation is everywhere," he says, with the current US administration. "When a president stands up before the planet and says an American comes first, he is only preaching hatred. When a president stands up and says we don't honor our missile treaty with the Russians, he is only preaching arrogance. When he refuses to condemn what's happening in Palestine, he is only preaching tyranny.

"American foreign policy has invited everybody, actually, to try to humiliate America, and to give it a bloody nose," he adds.

IN JAKARTA, COUNTERING AMERICAN CULTURE WITHOUT VIOLENCE

You wouldn't catch Rizky "Jimmy" Nur Zamzamy justifying violence that way, though he professes just as deep an attachment to Islam as Abu Hamza.

Mr. Zamzamy, a rangy young Indonesian advertising executive in a pink shirt, is sitting in a Western-style cafe in Jakarta, his cellphone at the ready, and his fried chicken growing cold as he explains how he tries to be a good Muslim by right action, not fighting.

That, he feels, is the best way of countering what he sees as the corrupting influence of American culture and morals on traditional Indonesian ways of life in the largest Muslim country in the world.

Until a few years ago, Zamzamy led a regular secular life, hanging out in bars and dating women. Then he met a Muslim teacher who became his spiritual guide. Now he follows Islamic teachings and donates most of his $1,300 monthly salary to his "guru" to be spent on building mosques and helping the poor.

He says he has made sure that none of the money goes to extremist groups that use violence in the name of Islam, such as the Laskar Jihad group, locked in bloody battle with Christians in the Maluku region of Indonesia.

Two years ago, in line with his growing religious beliefs, he quit the advertising agency he had worked for and set up his own company along Islamic lines: He won't take banks or alcoholic-beverage producers as clients, for example, and he does no business on Friday, the Muslim holy day.

But he is relaxed about those who don't share his beliefs: He does not insist that his wife wear a headscarf, for example, and he is not uncomfortable sitting alongside the rich young Jakartans in the cafe who are flirting and drinking. They must make their own choices, he says.

And though he does not like the sexual overtones of American pop culture, he knows that "you can't hide from American culture." By living his life according to Islamic precepts, he says, "I am fighting America in my own way. But I don't agree with violence."

AMBIVALENCE ABOUT AMERICA

All over the Muslim world, young people like Zamzamy are juggling their sense of Islamic identity with the trappings of a globalized, secular society.

In a classroom of Al Khair University, set in a concrete office park in Islamabad, Nabil Ahmed, a business student, and his classmates are fuming over their president's betrayal of the Pakistani people by pledging to support what they fear will turn into a crusade against Muslims.

Ahmed and his friends are well-dressed, middle-class boys, and represent neither the old-money security of Pakistan's elite nor dirt-poor peasants who make up the bulk of Pakistan's angry conservative masses. They are the silent majority of Pakistan, with their feet firmly planted in both the East and the West. On weekdays, they listen to Whitney Houston and Michael Bolton, wear Dockers and Van Heusen shirts. On weekends, many switch to traditional salwar kameez outfits and go with their fathers to the mosque to pray.

'It is [the] double standard that creates hatred.'

—Nabil Ahmed, a business student at Al Khair University in Islamabad

---

They have much to gain from a Western style of life, and most have plans to move to the United States for a few years to make some money before returning home to Pakistan. Yet despite their attraction to the West, they are wary of it too.

"Most of us here like it both ways, we like American fashion, American music, American movies, but in the end, we are Muslims," says Ahmed. "The Holy Prophet said that all Muslims are like one body, and if one part of the body gets injured, then all parts feel that pain. If one Muslim is injured by non-Muslims in Afghanistan, it is the duty of all Muslims of the world to help him."

Like his friends, Ahmed feels that America has double standards toward its friends and enemies. America attacks Iraq if it invades Kuwait, but allows Israel to bulldoze Palestinian homes in the West Bank and Gaza Strip.

ROBERT HARRISON—STAFF

AFGHAN REFUGEES: These boys are among some 60,000 displaced Afghans at Jalozai refugee camp near Peshawar, Pakistan, along its border with Afghanistan. The camp is crowded, and Pakistan has recently forbidden the UNHCR to register any more refugees.

It ostracizes a Muslim nation like Sudan for oppressing its Christian minority, but allows Russia to bomb its Muslim minority into submission in Chechnya.

And while the US supported many "freedom fighter" movements in the past few decades, including the contra movement in Nicaragua, America labels Pakistan and Afghanistan as terrorist states because they support militant Muslim groups fighting in the Indian state of Kashmir and elsewhere.

'The Americans wanted to fight the Russians with Muslim blood.'

—Sheikh Abu Hamza al-Masri, a radical Muslim cleric who runs a mosque in London

"There is only one way for America to be a friend of Islam," says Ahmed. "And that is if they consider our lives to be as precious as their own. "If Americans are concerned about the 6,500 deaths in the World Trade Center, let them talk also about the deaths in Kashmir, in Palestine, in Chechnya, in Bosnia. It is this double standard that creates hatred."

Ahmed's ambivalence about America—his desire to live and work there, his admiration for its values, but his anger at its behavior around the world—is broadly shared across the Muslim world and Arab world.

"I think they hate us because of what we do, and it seems to contradict who we say we are," says Bruce Lawrence, a professor of religion at Duke University, referring to people in the Middle East. "The major issue is that our policy seems to contradict our own basic values."

That seems clear enough to Muslims who sympathize with the Palestinians, and who say that Washington should force Israel to abide by United Nations resolutions to withdraw from the occupied territories. "The Americans say September 11th was an attack on civilization," says Mr Hariri, the Lebanese prime minister. "But what does civilized society mean if not a society that lives according to the law?"

It also seems clear to citizens of monarchical states in the Gulf, where elections are unknown and women's rights severely restricted. "Since the Cold War ended, America has talked about promoting democracy," says John Esposito, head of the Center for Muslim-Christian Understanding at Georgetown University in Washington. "But we don't do anything about it in repressive regimes in the Middle East, so you can understand widespread anti-Americanism there."

At the same time, the state-run media—which is all the media there is across much of the Middle East—often fan the flames of anti-American and anti-Israel sentiment because that helps focus citizens' minds on something other than their own government's shortcomings.

In Sana, the Yemeni capital, where queues of visa-seekers line up daily outside the US embassy, the ambivalence about America is clear. "When you go there, you really

50 YEARS OF US POLICY IN THE MIDDLE EAST

1947–48
UN votes to partition Palestine into two states—one for Jews, one for Palestinian Arabs. Arab states invade; 300,000 Palestinians flee Jewish-controlled areas. Jewish forces prevail, declaring Israeli independence. US recognizes Israel.

1953
CIA helps Iran's military stage a coup, deposing elected PM Mohammad Mossadeq, whom US sees as communist threat. US oversees installation of Shah Mohammad Reza Pavlavi as ruler of Iran.

1956
Israel attacks Egypt for control of Suez Canal. Britain and France veto US-sponsored UN resolution calling for halt to military action. British forces attack Egypt.

1960
Iran, Iraq, Kuwait, Saudi Arabia, and Venezuela form Organization of Petroleum Exporting Nations (OPEC).

1966
US sells its firs jet bombers to Israel, breaking with a 1956 decision not to sell arms to the Jewish state.

1967
Six-Day War. Israel launches preemptive strike against Arab neighbors, capturing Jerusalem, the Sinai Peninsula, the Gaza Strip, and the Golan Heights. Kuwait and Iraq cut oil supplies to US, UN adopts Resolution 242, calling on Israel to withdraw from captured territory. Israel refuses.

1968
First major hijacking by Arab militants occurs on El Al flight from Rome to Tel Aviv, marking decades of hostage-takings, hijackings, and assassinations as a strategy by Arab militant groups.

1969
Mummar Qaddafi comes to power in Libyan coup and orders US Air Force to evacuate Tripoli.

1972
Eight Arab commandos of Palestinian group Black September kill 11 Israeli athletes at the Munich Olympic Games.

1973
Egypt and Syria attack Israel over its occupation of the Golan Heights and the Sinai Peninsula. US gives $2.2 billion in emergency aid to Israel, turning tide of battle to Israel's favor. Arab states cut US oil shipments.

1974
UN General Assembly recognizes right of Palestinians to independence.

1976
The UN votes on a resolution accusing Israel of war crimes in occupied Arab territories. US casts lone "no" vote. US Ambassador to Lebanon Francis Meloy and an adviser are shot to death in Beirut. US closes Embassy there.

1978
Egypt and Israel sign US-brokered Camp David peace treaty. Eighteen Arab countries impose an economic boycott on Egypt. Egyptian president Anwar Sadat and Israeli Prime Minister Menachem Begin receive Nobel Peace Prize.

1979
Ayatollah Ruhollah Khomeini leads grass-roots Islamic revolution in Iran, deriding the US as "the great Satan." Iranian students storm US Embassy in Tehran, taking 66 Americans hostage for next 15 months. US imposes sanctions. Protesters attack US Embassies in Libya and Pakistan.

1981
Israel bombs Iraqi nuclear reactor. Muslim militants opposed to Egypt's peace treaty with Israel assassinate Egyptian President Sadat.

1982
Israel invades Lebanon to expel the Palestine Liberation Organization, facilitate election of friendly government, and form 25-mile security zone along Israel's border. Defense Minister Ariel Sharon permits Lebanese Christian militiamen to enter the Sabra and Shatila refugee camps outside Beirut. The ensuing three-day massacre kills 600 or more civilian refugees. US and other nations deploy peacekeeping troops in Lebanon.

1983
A truck bomb explodes in US Marines' barracks in Beirut, Lebanon, killing 241 soldiers. US forces withdraw.

1986
Us bombs Libya in retaliation for the bombing of a Berlin nightclub frequented by US servicemen. The airstrike kills 15 people, including the infant daughter of leader Muammar Qaddafi. All Arab nations condemn the attack.

1987
Start of the Palestinian intifada, or uprising, in the West Bank and Gaza Strip.

1990
Iraq invades Kuwait. Saddam Hussein links pullout to Israel's withdrawal from occupied territories. UN imposes sanctions that continue to hobble Iraq's economy in effort to force Iraqi compliance with weapons resolutions.

(continued)

50 YEARS *(continued)*

1991

US and coalition launch attacks against Iraq from Saudi Arabia. Gulf War ends after some three months, but US deployment continues even now, with 17,000 to 24,000 US troops in region at any time.

1993

World Trade Center in New York is bombed, killing six. US Special Forces, deployed as peacekeepers in Somalia, attempt to capture warlord Mohamed Farah Aidid. Eighteen US servicemen are killed. Israeli PM Yitzhak Rabin and Palestinian leader Yasser Arafat sign historic peace declaration in White House ceremony with President Clinton.

1994

Jordan and Israel sign peace treaty. Yasser Arafat, Yitzhak Rabin, and Foreign Minister Shimon Peres receive Nobel Peace Prize for 1993 agreement.

1995

US announces trade ban against Iran, reinforcing sanctions in effect since 1979. Rabin is assassinated, two years after peace deal with Palestinians. In Riyadh, Saudi Arabia, a car bomb explodes outside an office housing US military personnel. Seven are killed, including five Americans. Three Islamist groups claim responsibility.

1996

A truck bomb explodes outside a US military barracks in Khobar, Saudi Arabia, killing 19 US airmen. UN reports that sanctions cause 4,500 Iraqi children under 5 to die each month.

1997

Egyptian Islamic Group massacres 62 people, mostly foreign tourists, in Luxor, Egypt. The group claims it is retaliation for US imprisonment of Sheikh Omar Abdel al-Rahman, who is later convicted in 1993 World Trade Center bombing.

1998

Bombs explode outside US Embassies in Kenya and Tanzania, killing 224 people. US launches cruise-missile attacks on sites in Sudan and Afghanistan allegedly linked to Osama bin Laden. US indicts bin Laden for committing acts of terrorism against Americans abroad.

1999

Islamic militants, traced to bin Laden, are arrested for plot to bomb tourist sites during millennium celebrations.

2000

Camp David negotiations fail. Sharon visits Temple Mount in Jerusalem, sparking current Palestinian uprising. USS Cole bombing in Yemen's Aden harbor kills 17 American sailors. Bin Laden denies responsibility, but applauds the act.

2001

Hijackers crash two planes into World Trade Center in New York, one into Pentagon, and one in Pennsylvania. More than 7,000 people are dead or missing.

Compiled by Julie Finnin Day

SOURCES: "THE MIDDLE EAST" (CONGRESSIONAL QUARTERLY), NEWS REPORTS.

love the United States," says Murad al-Murayri, a US-trained physicist. "You are treated like a human being, much better than in your own country. But when you go back home, you find the US applies justice and fairness to its own people, but not abroad. In this era of globalization, that cannot stand."

Nor has the mood that has gripped Washington over the past two weeks done much to reassure skeptics, says François Burgat, a French social scientist in Yemen.

"When Bush says 'crusade', or that he wants bin Laden 'dead or alive', that is a *fatwa* (religious edict) without any judicial review," he cautions. "It denies all the principles that America is supposed to be."

A *fatwa* is something Amirul Haq, a Pakistani shopkeeper whose son died two years ago in a jihad in Kashmir, understands better than judicial review. "When I heard that my son died, I was satisfied," he says.

It's a sentiment shared by Azad Khan, too. On a hot Sunday afternoon in Mardan, Pakistan, Mr. Khan and his family have laid out a feast in a small guesthouse next to the local mosque. They are celebrating because they have just heard that Mr. Khan's 20-year-old son, Saeed, has been killed in a gun battle with Indian troops in the part of Jammu and Kashmir state that is under Indian control. With his death, Saeed has become another *shahid*, a martyr and heroic defender of the Muslims against the enemies of Islam. According to the Koran, *shahideen* are not actually dead; they are still alive, they just can't be seen. And through acts of bravery, a *shahid* guarantees that his whole family will go to heaven.

"It is not a thing to be mourned. We are happy," says Khan, sitting down to a meal of chicken and mutton, rice and bread, along with leaders of the group with which Saeed had fought. "I told him to take part in jihad [holy war] because he is the son of a Muslim," Khan says. "And just as we fight in Kashmir, if we need to fight against the United States in Afghanistan we are ready, because we are Muslims. It is our duty to fight against any infidels who are threatening our Muslim brothers."

It's not likely that many Pakistanis, or other Muslims, will actually go to Afghanistan to fight the Americans—assuming American soldiers land there. Khan's militant views are not shared by most of his countrymen.

But in a broader sense, and in the longer term, many people in the Middle East fear that the coming war against terrorism—unless it is waged with the utmost caution—could unleash new waves of anti-American sentiment.

Jamal al-Adimi, a US-educated Yemeni lawyer, speaks for many when he warns that "if violence escalates, you bring seeds and water for terrorism. You kill someone's brother or mother, and you will just get more crazy people."

Trying to root out terrorism without re-plowing the soil in which it grows—which means rethinking the policies that breed anti-American sentiment—is unlikely to succeed, say ordinary Middle Easterners and some of their leaders.

On the practical level, Hariri points out, "launching a war is in the hands of the Americans, but winning it needs everybody. And that means everybody should see that he has an interest in joining the coalition" that Washington is building.

On a higher level, argues Bassam Tibi, a professor of international relations at Gottingen University in Germany, and an expert on political Islam, "we need value consensus between the West and Islam on democracy and human rights to combat Islamic fundamentalism. We can't do it with bombs and shooting—that will only exacerbate the problem."

Reported by staff writers Scott Baldauf in Islamabad, Pakistan; Cameron W. Barr in Amman, Jordan; Peter Ford in London; Nicole Gaouette in Jerusalem; Robert Marquand in Beijing; Scott Peterson in Sana, Yemen; Ilene R. Prusher in Tokyo; as well as contributors Nicholas Blanford in Beirut, Lebanon; Sarah Gauch in Cairo; and Simon Montlake in Jakarta, Indonesia.

COMMENTARY

Ten Mistakes in the Middle East

by Bruce Herschensohn

Moses made the first mistake. After going through all the trouble of convincing the pharaoh to let his people go an then leading them on that 40-year walk, he should have told his people to turn right rather than left when they finally reached the eastern edge of the Sinai. Then they could have settled in Saudi Arabia and have had all that oil.

The second mistake was what Israel did after winning the Six Day War of 1967. After gaining the Sinai, Gaza, the Golan Heights, Judea, and Samaria, Israel called them "administered territories," which became internationally known as "occupied territories." It should have called them Israel.

Americans have long since forgotten why that war was fought and why Israel should have claimed those territories. The war was not for the Sinai, nor for Gaza, the Golan Heights, or Judea and Samaria. Egypt already had Sinai and Gaza, Syria had the Golan Heights, and Jordan had Judea and Samaria. (In 1947, with Resolution 181, the United Nations designated an enlarged Gaza, Judea, and Samaria, which became known as the West Bank, as territory to become an independent Arab state, with Jerusalem as an international zone. However, in 1948, Egypt seized Gaza, and Jordan seized Judea and Samaria. Thereafter they prohibited any talk of Palestinian independence in those territories.)

DRIVING ISRAEL INTO THE SEA

The purpose of the coming attack was to take over the entire land of Israel, and, as Nasser put it, to "throw the Zionists into the sea." In 1967, Egyptian President Gamal Nasser blockaded the Gulf of Aqaba to isolate Israel and sent his tanks across the Sinai toward it. UN peacekeepers were in the Sinai to prevent such an invasion, but Nasser told them to leave. The UN secretary-general, U Thant, agreed to their departure.

It was guaranteed that Syria would join Egypt in a joint attack on Israel, and it was probable, but not certain, that Jordan would join the invasion forces as well.

As Egypt prepared its attack from the southwest, with Syria forming a second front from the north, Israel wanted to avoid a third front, which could come from Jordan in the east. Direct dialogue between Israel and Jordan was out of the question because there were no diplomatic relations between the two nations. Therefore, Israel requested that a U.S. emissary go to King Hussein of Jordan to give him a pledge that Israel would leave Jordan alone if Jordan would not join the Egyptians and Syrians in the imminent attacks.

President Lyndon Johnson sent Undersecretary of State Eugene Rostow on the mission to Jordan. The king listened to Rostow but made no commitment. On May 18, 1967, the Voice of the Arabs Radio announced, "The sole method we shall apply against Israel is a total war, which will result in the extermination of Zionist existence."

On May 27, Nasser said, "Our basic objective will be the destruction of Israel. The Arab people want to fight." On June 4, Nasser received Iraq's commitment to join Egypt in the war, with President Aref saying, "Our goal is clear—to wipe Israel off the map."

On June 5, Israel launched a preemptive strike against Egypt's airfields, so the war started with Israel, not Egypt and its allies, in control of the timing. Then King Hussein joined Egypt, making the choice of risking defeat in the war over staying out of the war and facing the wrath of other Arab leaders, who would accuse him of disloyalty.

Many Wrongs Do Not Make It Right

- After gaining the Sinai, Gaza, the Golan Heights, Judea, and Samaria in the Six Day War, Israel called those areas "administered territories." Israel should have called them *Israel*.

- Another mistake was the State Department's refusal to condemn the fate of Arab Palestinians in the territory of Arab nations. Those refugees have become the innocent victims of Arab leaders who profess to be their friends but have held them incarcerated in refugee camps.

- Another misjudgment was made when President Clinton embraced the "Peace Process" negotiated in Oslo. The Peace Process is misnamed since its success rests jointly on Israel and Yasser Arafat, whose lifelong goal has been the subjugation of Israel.

COURTESY OF MELISSA MARENFELD DESIGNS, NEW YORK

Egypt, Syria, and Jordan all lost the war. In six days Egypt lost Sinai and Gaza; Syria lost the Golan Heights; Jordan lost Judea and Samaria, including East Jerusalem. Israel could have gone on to the capital cities of Egypt, Syria, and Jordan, but it now believed it had secure borders.

Decades later, Rostow said of his mission to Jordan, "I myself transmitted the Israeli message to Hussein in 1967, promising him immunity if he did not join the war. If he had stayed out of the war, he would hold the West Bank and Old Jerusalem today."

SUPPORT FOR PALESTINE

After the 1967 war, Egypt, Syria, Jordan, and other Arab states made their first demand for the creation of an independent Palestinian state. Suddenly the 19 years (1948–1967) of Egyptian and Jordanian jurisdiction over the West Bank were lost from the memories of Mideast and U.S. leaders. If the Arabs had wanted an independent Palestinian state, all they needed to have done was to have left the West Bank and Gaza alone in 1948.

After the Six Day War, the United Nations passed Resolution 242, whose most important statement was the affirmation of "withdrawal of Israeli armed forces from territories of recent conflicts." The words *the* and *all* were intentionally absent preceding the phrase "territories of recent conflicts."

The resolution called only for withdrawal "from territories," not stating which ones or how much. It could mean that Israel must give up anywhere from 1 to 100 percent of the territories. (Eleven years later, Israel could have claimed that it was acting in full compliance with UN Resolution 242. By signing the Camp David Accords, returning Sinai to Egypt, Israel gave up 92 percent of the territories gained in the 1967 war).

The third mistake was made by our own State Department in its handling of Israel's victory. When a U.S. enemy conquers territory (as in Southeast Asia, when North Vietnam conquered South Vietnam), the State Department accepts it: It's the past, it's done, the territory belongs to the victor. But when Israel, a friend, won territory in war, the State Department felt differently.

"All right," our State Department reacted, "you've won the war. Now give the territory back." If Israel had as its leader a King Farouk, a Mao Tse-tung, or an Ayatollah Khomeini, the United States would have accepted its 1967 victory and made the best of it.

Although U.S. presidents from Truman onward (with the exception of President Clinton) have sided with Israel in most disputes, many careerists at the State Department try to exert influence favoring Israel's enemies. This is not because the State Department is prejudiced against Israel or Jews. It is because of the reality of human nature in wanting to have a good time.

Even if Israel ceased to exist, Syria would still want to maintain control over Lebanon and would eye a long-held goal of taking over Jordan.

The State Department is largely composed of career foreign service officers who have a succession of two-to-three-year foreign postings. With 22 Arab countries, 20 other Muslim nations, and only one Israel, the odds are high that an officer will serve in numerous Arab or Islamic countries during a career and probably not serve in Israel at all. For a U.S. diplomat, life is easier in a country that endorses U.S. policies, rather than in one that opposes our policies.

And so, through the years, the State Department has leaned toward Arab states, creating the fourth mistake. Diplomats have regarded what they call "the Palestinian question" as the root of the Mideast problems. They know, however, that "the Palestinian question" is not a question but an answer to many Arab rulers, who want to exhibit unity when they, themselves, are the root of the crises through their continual expansionist designs over neighboring lands.

Even if Israel ceased to exist, Syria would still want to maintain control over Lebanon and would eye a long-held goal of taking over Jordan. (And Syria would still plot to take over the Palestinian Authority, while the PA would want to take over Jordan.) Libya would still want to take over Chad, Sudan, and Egypt. Iraq would still hope to take over Kuwait, Saudi Arabia, Iran, and the whole of the Persian Gulf. The Islamic fundamentalist government of Iran would still desire to take over Iraq and Jordan while spreading its Teheran-dictated revolution to every Islamic nation. The only unifying force among so many governments is their opposition to the borders—or even the existence—of Israel.

CAREER REFUGEES

The fifth mistake grew logically from the fourth mistake: the State Department has refused to condemn the fate of Arab Palestinians in Arab territories. Those refugees are the innocent victims of Arab leaders who profess to be their friends but held them incarcerated in refugee camps from 1948 onward.

The world is filled with refugees who were victims of crises such as in Cuba and Vietnam. They have been absorbed into other lands. For most, being a refugee has not been a career but a background. Friendly governments have often taken in the displaced and integrated them after brief stays in refugee camps for examination and relocation arrangements.

But Arab Palestinians are permanent refugees because "friendly" Arab governments have not been friendly. Instead, they have created a career status for Arab-Palestinian refugees, refusing to integrate them.

Three years after the 1967 war, King Hussein fought another war, and this time he was victorious. It was not a war against Israel but a civil war against the PLO, in which Jordan killed 10,000 Arab Palestinians after the PLO tried to take over Jordan. As a result of Jordan's victory, the PLO sought refuge in Lebanon. The PLO's flight created a ministate within Lebanon, with subsequent terror and destruction brought to that nation.

It is purely for public relations reasons that the Jordan-PLO war is no longer talked about by Jordan, the PLO, or other Arab leaders. It is best not to remind the world that Jordan, an Arab state that is in fact 78 percent of Palestine itself, rejected the PLO to the point of warring against it.

When Sadat was a guest on *Meet the Press* in 1979, his honesty trapped him into revealing a closely held secret of the Mideast. Bill Monroe asked him an unexpected question: "Mister President, President Carter says that when he talks privately with Arab leaders, they tell him they do not want an independent Palestinian state. Do you agree with that? Is that your experience as well?" Surprised by the question, Sadat hesitated and then answered, "It is a family business, and I choose better to abstain."

There was no question about the truth of what Sadat was revealing (not that it needed revelation to policymakers). Now the secret would be known throughout the United States and the world if the major media headlined it. They didn't. The State Department breathed a sigh of relief as his statement went by largely unnoticed.

LAND FOR PEACE

President Clinton made the sixth mistake in embracing the falsely named "Peace Process," which called for "Land for Peace." The Peace Process was misnamed because its success rested jointly on Israel and Yasser Arafat. For most of Arafat's adult life, he had (and, we can safely assume, still has) the goal of doing away with Israel.

For decades, Arafat used terrorism to reach that objective. That method didn't work because Israel retaliated against PLO attacks with swiftness and severity. Hamas then took over that role, but it is difficult to believe that Arafat has changed his ultimate objective rather than simply changing his transitory tactics. Hamas wants Israel's demise to come about by terrorism, while Arafat sees a more internationally acceptable way—the slow takeover of sections of Israel one-by-one under the disguise of "Land for Peace."

That phrase should be recognized for what it is: a threat to seize land by war if it isn't given away by peace. Why else would such a phrase have ever become a part of the international vocabulary? The U.S. endorsement of "land for peace," whether it is used to reduce land for Muslims in Bosnia or Jews in Israel, is based on the premise of rewarding the party threatening war.

Let's assume that your residence is in a neighborhood where gangs inhabit most of the houses that surround your home. Would you accept an offer to give up one of your home's rooms for their promise of peace? Of course not.

On an international level, imagine that Mexico becomes a strong military force in the future and its president demands from the United States the return of occupied territory of the "North Bank." Should our president offer "land for peace," returning all land south of San Clemente to Mexico?

Should any amount of land be ceded under threat? At this writing, Israel has given Sinai back to Egypt and most of Gaza to the Palestinian Authority. It has offered 92 percent of Judea and Samaria to the PA and been induced by Clinton to negotiate with Syria regarding the Golan Heights. There is a striking resemblance between the area's pre-June 1967 maps and the scheduled maps of 2007. And all of this is being done in the name of "peace," which in 1967 was a guarantee of war.

Assume, for a naive moment, that Arafat no longer wants all of Israel but merely jurisdiction over Gaza, Samaria, and Judea. Further, assume that with such territory, he plans to live in peace side by side with what is left of Israel. At best, he has control of only the Fatah faction of the old PLO. Apparently he does not have control of Hamas' military wing, Izzadin el-Qassam. He has continually said that he cannot control Hamas or other terrorists among Arab Palestinians. If he cannot control his own people, why should his words and pledges have any validity? If he can't speak for them, why listen to him?

Clinton made the seventh mistake on September 13, 1993, when he invited Arafat to stand with him on the South Lawn of the White House, side by side with Prime Minister Rabin, elevating Arafat to the status of a statesman.

The eighth mistake lasted from that date to the end of Clinton's presidency, as he acted as an "evenhanded" negotiator rather than an ally. For example, he stated on October 17, 2000, that "the United States would develop with the Israelis and Palestinians, as well as in consultation with the UN secretary-general, a committee of fact-finding on the events of the past several weeks and how to prevent their recurrence."

That report, completed after the end of the Clinton presidency in May 2001, was called the Sharm el-Sheikh Fact-Finding Committee Report. It is more popularly known as the Mitchell Report, in recognition of its chairman, former Sen. George Mitchell.

THE TRAP OF MORAL EQUIVALENCE

The conclusions of the Mitchell Report became the ninth mistake. It was written as though there were moral equivalence between Israel and the PA, stating that both sides should implement an "unconditional cessation of violence."

Of course, no sane person wants the violence to continue, but the wording assumes an equality of fault. If Israel had rejected retaliation throughout its history, such a policy would have been tantamount to surrender. How would our nation have reacted during the Persian Gulf War (or any war in which we were engaged) if some representative of a superpower told us that both sides should implement an "unconditional cessation of violence"?

The document further called for "confidence building" so as to "resume negotiations." But negotiated settlements with expansionists have never been successful. U.S. policymakers, above all, should know that. Our only lasting victories were the ones in which we demanded and achieved the unconditional surrenders of those we fought. Israel won such a victory in 1967, but we have insisted that the territory gained in that war should not be kept.

The United States should be an ally of democracies, not a neutral, and surely we should never put nondemocracies on the same plateau as a democracy, or put antagonists on the same plateau as a friend. The Mitchell Report acts as a neutral. Neutrality has always been the friend of totalitarians. As Dante said, "The worst place in hell is reserved for those who are neutral in times of crisis."

In recent years, neutrality has become a kind of Georgetown cocktail-party understanding of world events, with the United States becoming "a super Switzerland." On April 23, 1993, President Clinton said: "The United States should not become involved as a partisan in a war." One year after that, he confirmed the meaning of those words.

On April 15, 1994, in discussing the "ethnic cleansing" of Gorazde in Bosnia, he said, "The United States has no interest in having NATO become involved in this war and trying to gain advantage for one side over the other." He added that the United States had no intention of rolling back Serbian territorial gains and that NATO's role was "to be firm but not provocative and not try to change the military balance." But before his second term ended, he discovered that his dictum did not work. After thousands of deaths, he wisely took a side in Kosovo.

On the night before Sadat's burial, U.S. delegates to the ceremony sat in the lobby of a large Cairo hotel and told stories about the late Egyptian president. One of the most prominent delegates reminded the others that only Sadat welcomed the shah of Iran after he had been forced to leave Iran, United States, Mexico, and Panama. "I said to President Sadat, 'Tell me, Mister President, it must have been a very difficult decision for you to invite the shah, knowing that it might cause some real repercussions.'

Sadat was indignant at my suggestion. He answered me by saying, 'Difficult? Why should it be difficult to decide how to treat a friend? For me there was no difficulty.'" Sadat's clear answer could have been expected because he was not a neutral. His clarity should be the permanent policy of the United States.

President George W. Bush has, so far, wisely acted against the advice of the State Department. He has visited with Prime Minister Ariel Sharon but not Arafat. If President Bush continues to obey his own instincts, he will be a giant in the history of the Mideast.

But if Bush is drawn into the influence of the "expertise" of the State Department, Israel will continue to surrender land for war in the tenth and final mistake.

***Bruce Herschensohn** is a Distinguished Fellow at the Claremont Institute in California. He was formerly director of motion pictures and television for the U.S. Iinformation Agency, deputy special assistant to President Nixon, and Fellow at the John F. Kennedy Insitute of Politics at Harvard.*

ETHNIC CONFLICT

Ethnic conflict seems to have supplanted nuclear war as the most pressing issue on the minds of policymakers. But if yesterday's high priests of mutually assured destruction were guilty of hyper-rationality, today's prophets of anarchy suffer from a collective hysteria triggered by simplistic notions of ethnicity. Debates about intervention in Rwanda or stability in Bosnia demand a more sober perspective.

by Yahya Sadowski

The Number of Ethnic Conflicts Rose Dramatically at the End of the Cold War

Nope. The idea that the number of ethnic conflicts has recently exploded, ushering us into a violent new era of ethnic "pandaemonium," is one of those optical illusions that round-the-clock and round-the-world television coverage has helped to create. Ethnic conflicts have consistently formed the vast majority of wars ever since the epoch of decolonization began to sweep the developing countries after 1945. Although the number of ethnic conflicts has continued to grow since the Cold War ended, it has done so at a slow and steady rate, remaining consistent with the overall trend of the last 50 years.

In 1990 and 1991, however, several new and highly visible ethnic conflicts erupted as a result of the dissolution of the Soviet Union and Yugoslavia. The clashes between the armies of Croatia, Serbia, and Slovenia, and the agonizing battle that pitted Bosnia's Croats, Muslims, and Serbs against each other, occurred on Europe's fringes, within easy reach of television cameras. The wars in Azerbaijan, Chechnya, Georgia, and Tajikistan, while more distant, were still impressive in the way that they humbled the remnants of the former Soviet colossus. Many observers mistook these wars for the start of a new trend. Some were so impressed that they began to reclassify conflicts in Angola, Nicaragua, Peru, and Somalia—once seen as ideological or power struggles—as primarily ethnic conflicts.

The state-formation wars that accompanied the "Leninist extinction" now appear to have been a one-time event—a flash flood rather than a global deluge. Many of these battles have already been brought under control. Indeed, the most striking trend in warfare during the 1990s has been its decline: The Stockholm International Peace Research Institute documented just 27 major armed conflicts (only one of which, India and Pakistan's slow-motion struggle over Kashmir, was an interstate war) in 1996, down from 33 such struggles in 1989. Once the Cold War ended, a long list of seemingly perennial struggles came to a halt: the Lebanese civil war, the Moro insurrection in the Philippines, regional clashes in Chad, the Eritrean secession and related battles in Ethiopia, the Sahrawi independence struggle, fratricide in South Africa, and the guerrilla wars in El Salvador and Nicaragua.

The majority of the wars that survive today are ethnic conflicts—but they are mostly persistent battles that have been simmering for decades. They include the (now possibly defunct) IRA insurgency in the United Kingdom; the struggle for Kurdish autonomy in Iran, Iraq, and Turkey; the Israeli-Palestinian tragedy; the Sri Lankan civil war; and long-standing regional insurrections in Burma, India, and Indonesia.

Most Ethnic Conflicts Are Rooted in Ancient Tribal or Religious Rivalries

No way. The claim that ethnic conflicts have deep roots has long been a standard argument for not getting in-

Ethnic Africa

"Europe's imperial cartographers have been criticized for more than a century for casually drawing up borders that separated ethnic groups or placed long-time rivals in the same colony," observed the *New York Times* in the wake of civil war in Somalia and the breakup of Ethiopia. But as this map of Africa's ethnic groups demonstrates, redrawing borders would be no simple task. This predicament represents the greatest challenge to resolving ethnic conflicts worldwide: There are often no agreed boundaries to retreat behind.

Source: Map reprinted by permission from *Why in the World? Adventures in Geography* by George J. Demko, with Jerome Agel and Eugene Boe, produced by Jerome Agel. © 1992 by Jerome Agel. Published in trade paperback by Anchor Books/Doubleday.

volved. According to political journalist Elizabeth Drew's famous account, President Bill Clinton in 1993 had intended to intervene in Bosnia until he read Robert Kaplan's book *Balkan Ghosts,* which, as Drew said, conveyed the notion that "these people had been killing each other in tribal and religious wars for centuries." But the reality is that most ethnic conflicts are expressions of "modern hate" and largely products of the twentieth century.

The case of Rwanda is typical. When Europeans first stumbled across it, most of the country was already united under a central monarchy whose inhabitants spoke the same language, shared the same cuisine and culture, and practiced the same religion. They were, however, divided into several castes. The largest group, the Hutus, were farmers. The ruling aristocracy, who collected tribute from all other groups, was recruited from the Tutsis, the caste of cattle herders. All groups supplied troops for their common king, and intermarriage was not unusual. Social mobility among castes was quite possible: A rich Hutu who purchased enough cattle could climb into the ranks of

Major Genocides since World War II

COUNTRY	DATES	VICTIMS	NUMBER OF DEATHS (IN THOUSANDS)
USSR	1943–47	Repatriated nationals and ethnic minorities	500–1,100
China	1950–51	Landlords	800–3,000
Sudan	1955–72	Southern nationalists	100–500
Indonesia	1965–66	Communists and ethnic Chinese	80–1,000
China	1966–75	Cultural revolution victims	400–850
Uganda	1971–79	Opponents of Idi Amin	100–500
Pakistan	1971	Bengali nationalists	1,250–3,000
Cambodia	1975–79	Urbanites	800–3,000
Afghanistan	1978–89	Opponents of the regime	1,000
Sudan	1983–98	Southern nationalists	100–1,500
Iraq	1984–91	Kurds	100–282
Bosnia	1991–95	Bosnian Muslims and Croats	25–200
Burundi	1993–98	Hutu, Tutsi	150+
Rwanda	1994	Tutsi	500–1,000

Sources: Barbara Harff, "Victims of the State: Genocides, Politicides and Group Repression since 1945," *International Review of Victimology,* 1 (1989): 23–41; Conflict Resolution Program, *1995–1996 State of World Conflict Report* (Atlanta: Carter Center, 1997); *Los Angeles Times;* and the *Encyclopaedia Britannica.*

the Tutsi; an impoverished Tutsi could fall into the ranks of the Hutu. Anthropologists considered all castes to be members of a single "tribe," the Banyarwanda.

Then came the Belgians. Upon occupying the country after World War I, they transformed the system. Like many colonial powers, the Belgians chose to rule through a local élite—the Tutsis were eager to collaborate in exchange for Belgian guarantees of their local power and for privileged access to modern education. Districts that had been under Hutu leadership were brought under Tutsi rule. Until 1929, about one-third of the chiefs in Rwanda had been Hutu, but then the Belgians decided to "streamline" the provincial administration by eliminating all non-Tutsi chiefs. In 1933, the Belgians issued mandatory identity cards to all Rwandans, eliminating fluid movement between castes and permanently fixing the identity of each individual, and his or her children, as either Hutu or Tutsi. As the colonial administration penetrated and grew more powerful, Belgian backing allowed the Tutsis to increase their exploitation of the Hutus to levels that would have been impossible in earlier times.

In the 1950s, the Belgians came under pressure from the United Nations to grant Rwanda independence. In preparation, Brussels began to accord the majority Hutus—the Tutsis constituted only 14 percent of the population—a share of political power and greater access to education. Although this policy alarmed the Tutsis, it did not come close to satisfying the Hutus: Both groups began to organize to defend their interests, and their confrontations became increasingly militant. Centrist groups that included both Hutus and Tutsis were gradually squeezed out by extremists on both sides. The era of modern communal violence began with the 1959 attack on a Hutu leader by Tutsi extremists; Hutus retaliated, and several hundred people were killed. This set in motion a cycle of violence that culminated in December 1963, when Hutus massacred 10,000 Tutsis and drove another 130,000–150,000 from the country. These tragedies laid the seeds for the genocide of 1994.

The late emergence of ethnic violence, such as in Rwanda, is the norm, not an exception. In Ceylon, riots that pitted Tamils against Sinhalese did not erupt until 1956. In Bosnia, Serbs and Croats coexisted with one another, and both claimed Muslims as members of their communities, until World War II—and peaceful relations resumed even after the bloodshed of that conflict. Turks and Kurds shared a common identity as Ottomans and wore the same uniforms during World War I; in fact, the first Kurdish revolt against Turkish rule was not recorded until 1925. Muslims and Jews in Palestine had no special history of intercommunal hatred (certainly nothing resembling European anti-Semitism) until the riots of 1921, when nascent Arab nationalism began to conflict with the burgeoning Zionist movement. Although Hindu-Muslim clashes had a long history in India, they were highly localized; it was only after 1880 that the contention between these two groups began to gel into large-scale, organized movements. Of course, the agitators in all these conflicts tend to dream up fancy historic pedigrees for their disputes. Bosnian Serbs imagine that they are fighting to

Tribal Wisdom

"For centuries, [Yugoslavia] marked a tense and often violent fault line between empires and religions. The end of the Cold War and the dissolution of that country... surfaced all those ancient tensions again...."

—U.S. president Bill Clinton, addressing the U.S. Naval Academy in 1994

"We are confronted by contradictory phenomena in which both the factors of integration and cooperation and the tendencies of division and dispersal are both apparent. The technological and communications revolution is offset by the eruption of nationalist conflicts and ethnic hatreds."

—Egyptian foreign minister Amr Moussa, before the UN General Assembly in 1996

"In this Europe of ours, where no one would have thought a struggle between ethnic groups possible, tragically this has come about. It may serve to open people's eyes to the unspeakable possibilities in the future, even in unexpected places. Today we are threatened by the danger... of racial, religious, and tribal hatred."

—Italian president Oscar Luigi Scalfaro in 1997

"Yet even as the waves of globalization unfurl so powerfully across our planet, so does a deep and vigorous countertide.... What some have called a 'new tribalism' is shaping the world as profoundly on one level as the 'new globalism' is shaping it on another."

—His Highness the Aga Khan, at the Commonwealth Press Union Conference in Cape Town in 1996

"... all over the world, we see a kind of reversion to tribalism.... We see it in Russia, in Yugoslavia, in Canada, in the United States.... What is it about, all this globalization of communication that is making people return to more—to smaller units of identity?"

—Neil Postman, chair of the department of culture and communication at New York University, in 1995

avenge their defeat by the Ottoman Turks in 1389; Hutus declare that Tutsis have "always" treated them as subhumans; and IRA bombers attack their victims in the name of a nationalist tradition they claim has burned since the Dark Ages. But these mythologies of hatred are themselves largely recent inventions.

Ethnic Conflict Was Powerful Enough to Rip Apart the USSR

Yeah, right. The idea that the Soviet Union was destroyed by an explosion of ethnic atavism has been put forth by a number of influential thinkers, most notably Senator Daniel Patrick Moynihan. But this theory is not only historically inaccurate, it has misleading policy implications. The collapse of states is more often the cause of ethnic conflicts rather than the result.

Prior to 1991, ethnic consciousness within the Soviet Union had only developed into mass nationalism in three regions: the Baltic states, Transcaucasia, and Russia itself. Russian nationalism posed no threat to Soviet rule: It had been so successfully grafted onto communism during World War II that even today Leninists and Russian ultranationalists tend to flock to the same parties. In Transcaucasia, the Armenians and Georgians had developed potent national identities but were much more interested in pursuing local feuds (especially with Muslims) than in dismantling the Soviet Union. Only in the Baltic states, which had remained sovereign and independent until 1940, was powerful nationalist sentiment channeled directly against Moscow.

When the August 1991 coup paralyzed the Communist Party, the last threads holding the Soviet state together dissolved. Only then did rapid efforts to spread nationalism to other regions appear. In Belarus, Ukraine, and across Central Asia, the *nomenklatura*, searching for new instruments to legitimate their rule, began to embrace—and sometimes invent—nationalist mythologies. It was amidst this wave of post-Soviet nationalism that new or rekindled ethnic conflicts broke out in Chechnya, Moldova, Ukraine, and elsewhere. Yet even amid the chaos of state collapse, ethnonationalist movements remained weaker and less violent than many had expected. Despite the predictions of numerous pundits, revivalist Islamic movements only took root in a couple of places (Chechnya and Tajikistan). Relations between indigenous Turkic peoples and Russian immigrants across most of Central Asia remained civil.

Ethnic Conflicts Are More Savage and Genocidal Than Conventional Wars

Wrong. Although this assumption is inaccurate, the truth is not much more comforting. There appears to be no consistent difference between ethnic and nonethnic wars in terms of their lethality. In fact, the percentage of civilians in the share of total casualties is rising for all types of warfare. During World War I, civilian casualties constituted about 15 percent of all deaths. That number skyrocketed to 65 percent during World War II, which, by popularizing the use of strategic bombing, blockade-induced famine, and guerrilla warfare, constituted a real, albeit underappreciated, watershed in the history of human slaughter. Ever since, the number of civilian dead has constituted two-thirds or more of the total fatalities in most wars. Indeed, according to UNICEF, the share of civilian casualties has continued to grow since 1945—rising to almost 90 percent by the end of the 1980s and to more than 90 percent during this decade.

Furthermore, ethnic wars are less likely to be associated with genocide than "conventional" wars. The worst genocides of modern times have not been targeted along primarily ethnic lines. Rather, the genocides within Afghanistan, Cambodia, China, the Soviet Union, and even, to a great extent, Indonesia and Uganda, have focused on liquidating political dissidents: To employ the emerging vocabulary, they were politicides rather than ethnicides. Indeed, the largest genocides of this century were clearly ideologically driven politicides: the mass killings committed by the Maoist regime in China from 1949 to 1976, by the Leninist/Stalinist regime in the Soviet Union between 1917 and 1959, and by the Pol Pot regime in Cambodia between 1975 and 1979.

Finally, some pundits have claimed that ethnic conflicts are more likely to be savage because they are often fought by irregular, or guerrilla, troops. In fact, (a) ethnic wars are usually fought by regular armies, and (b) regular armies are quite capable of vicious massacres. Contrary to the stereotypes played out on television, the worst killing in Bosnia did not occur where combatants were members of irregular militias, reeling drunk on *slivovitz*. The core of the Serb separatist forces consisted of highly disciplined troops that were seconded from the Yugoslav army and led by a spit-and-polish officer corps. It was precisely these units that made the massacres at Srebrenica possible: It required real organizational skill to take between 6,000 and 10,000 Bosnian troops prisoner, disarm and transport them to central locations, and systematically murder them and distribute their bodies among a network of carefully concealed mass graves. Similarly, the wave of ethnic cleansing that followed the seizure of northern and eastern Bosnia by the Serbs in 1991 was not the spontaneous work of crazed irregulars. Transporting the male Bosnian population to concentration camps at Omarska and elsewhere required the talents of men who knew how to coordinate military attacks, read railroad schedules, guard and (under-) supply large prison populations, and organize bus transport for expelling women and children.

Globalization Makes Ethnic Conflict More Likely

Think again. The claim that globalization—the spread of consumer values, democratic institutions, and capitalist enterprise —aggravates ethnic and cultural violence is at the core of Samuel Huntington's "clash of civilizations" hypothesis, Robert Kaplan's vision of "the coming anarchy," and Benjamin Barber's warning that we face a future of "Jihad vs. McWorld." Although these suggestions deserve further study, the early indications are that globalization plays no real role in spreading ethnic conflict and may actually inhibit it.

Despite the fears of cultural critics that the broad appeal of "Baywatch" heralds a collapse of worldwide values, there is not much concrete evidence linking the outbreak of ethnic wars to the global spread of crude materialism via film, television, radio, and boombox. Denmark has just as many television sets as the former Yugoslavia but has not erupted into ethnic carnage or even mass immigrant bashing. Meanwhile, Burundi, sitting on the distant outskirts of the global village with only one television set for every 4,860 people, has witnessed some of the worst violence in this decade.

The spread of democratic values seems a slightly more plausible candidate as a trigger for ethnic violence: The recent progress of democracy in Albania, Armenia, Croatia, Georgia, Moldova, Russia, Serbia, and South Africa has been attended by ethnic feuding in each country. But this is an inconsistent trend. Some of the most savage internal conflicts of the post-Cold War period have occurred in societies that were growing less free, such as Egypt, India (which faced major secessionist challenges by Kashmiris, Sikhs, Tamils, etc.), Iran, and Peru. For that matter, many of the worst recent ethnic conflicts occurred in countries where the regime type was unstable and vacillated back and forth between more and less free forms, as in Azerbaijan, Bosnia, Lebanon, Liberia, Nigeria, and Tajikistan. Conversely, in numerous cases, such as the so-called third wave of democratization that swept Latin America and East Asia during the 1980s, political liberalization seems to have actually reduced most forms of political violence.

Investigating the impact of economic globalization leads to three surprises. First, the countries affected most by globalization—that is, those that have shown the greatest increase in international trade and benefited most significantly from foreign direct investment—are not the newly industrializing economies of East Asia and Latin America but the old industrial societies of Europe and North America. Second, ethnic conflicts are found, in some form or another, in every type of society: They are not concentrated among poor states, nor are they unusually common among countries experiencing economic globalization. Thus, the bad news is that ethnic conflicts do not disappear when societies "modernize."

The good news, however, lies in the third surprise: Ethnic conflicts are likely to be much less lethal in societies that are developed, economically open, and receptive to globalization. Ethnic battles in industrial and industrializing societies tend either to be argued civilly or at least limited to the political violence of marginal groups, such as the provisional IRA in the United Kingdom, Mohawk secessionists in Canada, or the Ku Klux Klan in the United States. The most gruesome ethnic wars are found in poorer societies—Afghanistan and Sudan, for example—where economic frustration reinforces political rage. It seems, therefore, that if economic globalization contributes to a country's prosperity, then it also dampens the level of ethnic violence there.

Fanaticism Makes Ethnic Conflicts Harder to Terminate

Not really. Vojislav Seselj, the commander of one of the most murderous Serb paramilitary groups in Bosnia, once warned that if U.S. forces were used there, "the war [would] be total.... We would have tens of thousands of volunteers, and we would score a glorious victory. The Americans would have to send thousands of body bags. It would be a new Vietnam." Of course, several years later, after Serb forces had been handily defeated by a combination of Croat ground forces and NATO airpower, the president of the Serb separatists, Radovan Karadzic, admitted their leadership had thought all along that "if the West put in 10,000 men to cut off our supply corridors, we Serbs would be finished." Militarily, ethnic conflicts are not intrinsically different from any other type of combat. They can take on the form of guerrilla wars or conventional battles; they can be fought by determined and disciplined cadres or by poorly motivated slobs. How much military force will be required to end the fighting varies widely from one ethnic conflict to the next.

However, achieving a military victory and building a durable peace are two very different matters. Sealing the peace in ethnic conflicts may prove harder for political—not military—reasons. Ethnic conflicts are fought among neighbors, among people who live intermingled with one other, forced to share the same resources and institutions. When two states end a war, they may need only to agree to stop shooting and respect a mutual border. But in ethnic conflicts there are often no established borders to retreat behind. Sometimes, ethnic disputes can be resolved by drawing new borders—creating new states (such as Bangladesh and "rump" Pakistan) that allow the quarreling groups to live apart. Other times, they can be terminated by convincing the combatants that they must share power peaceably and learn to coexist. This is the objective of the Dayton accord on Bosnia.

In either case, ending ethnic warfare often requires the expensive and delicate construction of new political institutions. Not only may this be more difficult than terminating a "normal" interstate war, it may also take much longer. Building truly effective states takes time. For this reason, ethnic wars whose participants are already organized into states or protostates (which was true of the combatants in Croatia and Bosnia) are probably easier to bring to a conclusion than battles in regions—Afghanistan, for example, not to speak of Somalia where real states have yet to congeal.

Want to Know More?

The classic introduction to the study of ethnic conflict is still Donald Horowitz, ***Ethnic Groups in Conflict*** (Berkeley: University of California Press, 1985). The Stockholm International Peace Research Institute (SIPRI) inventories changing patterns of warfare in the ***SIPRI Yearbook*** (Oxford: Oxford University Press, annual). For a specialist's tally of particular ethnic conflicts, see Ted Robert Gurr, ***Minorities at Risk: A Global View of Ethnopolitical Conflicts*** (Washington: U.S. Institute of Peace, 1993). An absorbing overview of the evolving relations between Tutsi and Hutu is Gérard Prunier, ***The Rwanda Crisis: History of a Genocide*** (New York: Columbia University Press, 1995). The Human Rights Watch report, ***Slaughter among Neighbors: The Political Origins of Communal Violence*** (New Haven: Yale University Press, 1995), provides a broader survey of modern hate. An excellent account of the diversity of forms that ethnicity and nationalism have taken in territories of the former Soviet Union is Ronald Grigor Suny's ***The Revenge of the Past: Nationalism, Revolution and the Collapse of the Soviet Union*** (Stanford: Stanford University Press, 1993). Neal Ascherson reflects upon issues of nationality and ethnicity in his book ***Black Sea*** (New York: Hill & Wang, 1995), which chronicles the expansive history of a region that has been a nexus of several Asian and European cultures. David Rohde's chilling ***Endgame: The Betrayal and Fall of Srebrenica*** (New York: Farrar Straus & Giroux, 1997) documents the careful organizational planning underlying the genocide in Bosnia. A recent work that dissects the question of whether, or how, the United States should intervene in ethnic conflicts is David Callahan's ***Unwinnable Wars: American Power and Ethnic Conflict*** (New York: Hill & Wang, 1998).

For links to relevant Web sites, as well as a comprehensive index of related articles, access **www.foreignpolicy.com**.

Article 24

China as Number One

"The inferred assumption in most American scenarios is one in which a dominant China is a threat to its neighbors and the United States. Yet what if China acts as a benevolent hegemon, or at least a benign one?"

SOONG-BUM AHN

Within the next few decades, East Asia will once again become sinocentric. The prospect of an East Asia centered around a more powerful China is not as disastrous as some in the United States have argued. Fears that American interests will be threatened if China dominates the region are largely unfounded and potentially dangerous. Indeed, it is in America's national interest to come to terms with China's historic leadership in the region and foster a positive relationship that will facilitate a constructive role for China. The alternative—a confrontation with China—would set a perilous course for the United States.

Many in the United States who call for global American primacy will attack this argument as counterintuitive—that it advocates a premature American capitulation to the Chinese, and is fundamentally un-American and antithetical to the concept of primacy. Some may even dismiss it as unrealistic naïveté. However, the argument is counterintuitive only to the extent that thinking on these issues is tainted by outmoded cold-war strategies. Political realism would also dictate that we look at China and its future based on how it actually is and not how we would like it to be. To expect that the United States could contain or engage China unilaterally and at whim without serious consequences is unrealistic. Americans must once and for all abandon the concept of a "pro-China" or "anti-China" policy.

The rapid reemergence of China as a global power will return East Asia to a system resembling the region's traditional order. From the American perspective, this will require a reevaluation of roles, interests, and policies in the coming decades. To lay the foundation for a positive United States role in East Asia into the twenty-first century and beyond, the United States needs to review and rethink not only its policy toward China, but also toward Taiwan, the Koreas, and Japan.

THE RETURN TO SINOCENTRISM

The Chinese civil war that established modern China in 1949 was a major challenge to United States foreign policy It represented the "communist threat" on a massive scale and marked the onset of the cold war in Asia, which would cost millions of Asian lives and more than a hundred thousand American lives. America's cold-war record in East Asia is marred by critical policy failures in China and Vietnam—where the United States backed what proved to be the wrong sides—and in Korea, where the United States agreed to the initial division of the peninsula and then failed to protect South Korea by not including it among America's security commitments in Asia. In retrospect, the earlier events and decisions that led to the devastating cold war in East Asia still form the basis for America's current role in the region. The United States is doomed to repeat the tragic aspects of its history in East Asia unless it changes its policies to reflect major events unfolding in the region. In East Asia, China will be preeminent and it is in the United States interest to learn to live with and prosper in that region. The traditional United States foreign policy approach based on bilateral alliances that isolate China will not work. Indeed, this approach may lead to catastrophe.

Significant contrasts mark the Western experience in international relations and the traditional mode of relations among the states of East Asia. Whereas great-power multipolarity characterizes the international structure in Europe, the traditional East Asian system was generally unipolar. China, as the Middle Kingdom, assumed the role of the unipole for lengthy periods of East Asian history. Another point of contrast is the different levels of "anarchy" in the two systems. Modern political realists have based their study of international relations on the dynamics among comparable European states vying for power under an "ordering principle of anarchy." In East Asia, China's mass and gravity brought a hierarchical order to regional dynamics. Along with its power, the Confucian influence on international politics and the tributary system of trade enabled China to manage the regional system in a relatively peaceful manner until the nineteenth century.

The idea that the best way to safeguard United States interests in East Asia is to portray China as a looming threat is short-sighted and dangerous.

The United States is a status quo superpower while China is a revisionist power. Ravaged by modern history, mainly in the form of Western imperialism, modern China under the leadership of the Chinese Communist Party has made national restoration the country's number-one priority. It seeks to undo history and regain its rightful place as a great civilization and power. This has been the major theme and a source of legitimacy for the party. In essence, China must struggle for regional dominance. Its history and size have instilled a need to dominate that is impossible to renounce. At the same time, the Communist Party cannot allow the United States to dominate Asia because the United States government continues to pose the greatest threat to Communist rule in China in the form of its military alliances with the surrounding states and because of its regular condemnation of Beijing's policies. Amid the gap in perception and divergence in goals, the best way for the United States to make an enemy out of China is to portray it as such—a potentially devastating case of a self-fulfilling prophecy.

In international relations, the perception of intent is more important than the intent itself. A large gap in perception divides the United States and China. Although current United States policy toward China may very well be generally defensive and benign, the Chinese see it in more malignant terms. United States attempts to prod and cajole the Chinese into playing by America's rules and, in particular, America's duplicitous relationship with Taiwan, are seen in Beijing as meddling and an attempt to set up roadblocks to Chinese progress. The more the United States tries to persuade China of the legitimacy of these policies, the more the Chinese are convinced to the contrary. This gap in perception widened considerably as a result of the United States bombing of the Chinese embassy in Belgrade during NATO's Kosovo air war in 1999, the recent spy-plane incident off Hainan Island, and the diplomatic fallout that ensued after each incident.

Obviously, a return to the traditional sinocentric tributary system is impossible to envision under modern international conditions. However, the emergence of an East Asia that is centered on a modernized, powerful China is not difficult to imagine. China would be the center of gravity for the region in terms of population, landmass, economy, and military strength. In terms of economic activity, China, with its large and growing middle class of consumers, is already an attractive market for the exporting economies of East Asia as well as a good source of low-cost products and raw materials. Additionally, the cultural aspect of China's role in the region cannot be ignored. To varying degrees, Chinese culture has had an enduring impact on most of the societies of East Asia. This element in the relationships adds to China's influence.

Admittedly, the region's future security environment will depend largely on Chinese behavior and the perception its neighbors form of its intent.[1] America's evolving relationship with China will largely determine the course and nature of China's emerging role. If the Chinese achieve domination after a long hegemonic struggle with the United States, that supremacy is likely to be harsh, destructive, and based on military power. If, however, Chinese primacy comes about under a positive Sino-American relationship, then China is likely to be a benign or even a benevolent regional power. The regional states will once again learn to live within a China-dominated East Asia, and a United States role in the region will be affirmed. In that case, we are likely to witness a China-dominated regional system not susceptible to American influence and coercion, but open to American engagement and trade.

The coming Chinese challenge is in the realm of national wealth, not ideology. Very few in Beijing would place ideology before profits.

AGAINST AMERICAN PESSIMISM

The inferred assumption in most American scenarios is one in which a dominant China is a threat to its neighbors and the United States. Yet what if China acts as a benevolent hegemon, or at least a benign one? Many, including prominent scholars such as the late Gerald Segal in his book *Defending China*, have argued that historically, Chinese military action has been defensive or punitive in nature and seldom imperialistic. And the People's Republic's "Five Principles of Peaceful Coexistence," as laid out by the late Prime Minister Zhou Enlai, are based on the concepts of noninterference and no stationing of troops outside one's own territory. Thus, from the Chinese perspective, military force is used only for domestic stability (as in the case of Tibet and Taiwan) or national defense (as in the case of Korea, India, and Vietnam).

As East Asia continues to emerge as a regional system, a form of "soft balance" may be achieved whereby China's power is checked by other states in the region and by the United States. This would not constitute an unstable balance of military power in the traditional sense. Rather, in response to pressures placed on it by its economic interdependence with the other states, China would seek to form consensus on regional issues with the other players rather than risk conflict and enmity through bullying. In the larger context of Asia, India and Russia will be factors in an overall structure for balance. The United States can play the crucial role of offshore balancer.

The core of future United States engagement in East Asia is economics. This does not mean that the United States must maintain dominance in East Asia to secure its economic interests there. If this were the case, every global economic power would seek to gain dominance and monopoly over regions key to its economic health. Even after its dominance is secured, China would gain little from disrupting the stability that enables economic exchange and prosperity in the region: a breakdown of the relationships across the Pacific would be disastrous for the Chinese. Roughly 35 percent of China's exports go to the United States. Moreover, two of its most important trading partners, Japan and South Korea, also depend on their ability to export to the American market. With China's forthcoming membership in the World Trade Organization, mutual reliance on this trans-Pacific trading network will continue to expand. Admittedly, East Asia and the Pacific are far behind Europe in terms of regional cooperation and integration. However, it is erroneous to think that a rising China will inevitably set off arms races and instability. The shared desire for peace and prosperity that undergird the European Union are at work in East Asia as well. The coming Chinese challenge is in the realm of national wealth, not ideology. Very few in Beijing would place ideology before profits and even fewer would risk stability and wealth to spread a defunct ideology. To argue otherwise is hyperbole and primordialist.

The Unacceptable Alternative

A change in the global distribution of power has usually been a traumatic event in world politics, with the emergence of a new dominant power often accompanied by war. Historically, war has caused the downfall of a superpower, enabling the emergence of a new power, or two rival states have fought each other for supremacy. In the latter case, war resulted because the reigning hegemon resisted the challenge of the emerging global power. The United States must avoid this trap.

The idea that the best way to safeguard United States interests in East Asia is to portray China as a looming threat is short-sighted and dangerous. Playing this new China card may arouse American concerns, and gather some domestic support for an aggressive United States security policy to deal with the "threat." The East Asian reaction, however, will be counter to United States interests. China will respond by reallocating resources. Japan and South Korea may decide that United States policy is flawed and pursue independent policies to accommodate China.

Historically China has been a continental power and will continue to maintain its strategic focus on the Asian landmass. Given this continental outlook, any potential adversary must be prepared to engage in protracted land campaigns that would require troop-intensive formations and the expectation of large numbers of casualties. Fighting China in a protracted land war in Asia would be a disaster for the United States because American forces would not be able to threaten China's traditional centers of gravity—its vast landmass and population—without great loss of American life. In the absence of a direct threat to United States national security, it is difficult to imagine a scenario where the American public would support a conflict with China over dominance in East Asia, especially in light of the American aversion to casualties and mishaps, even minor ones.

For example, on Taiwan the United States opposes the use of military force and implies that it would risk a confrontation with China for the "security" of the island (President George W. Bush has made this more explicit by stating in a rather unstatesmanlike manner that the United States would indeed come to the aid of Taiwan). Yet a great asymmetry can be seen in the importance that China and the United States place on this issue. Rhetoric aside, the People's Republic is fully committed to preventing Taiwanese secession, even at the cost of a large-scale military conflict with the United States. Conversely, it is hard to imagine the United States sacrificing large numbers of Americans in a war with China for the sake of Taiwanese "security" (an assessment the Chinese also share).

Any future conflict scenario for East Asia must assume that China will fight for survival as a coherent state, whereas America will fight for a precarious dominance over a region that sees it as a distant foreign power. For the United States, a hegemonic war with China in East Asia would prove too costly, and in the end, unwinnable.

Korea: Balancing or Bandwagoning?

The Chinese strategic view of Korea was historically that of a reliable client state and buffer on China's eastern flank. Today the Chinese consider a divided Korea a way to maintain the regional balance of power and a check against the United States. Barring the continuation of the status quo on the peninsula, China's desired outcome is a peaceful reunification process resulting in a pro-Chinese Korean state without an alliance with the United States and without foreign troops. One could even envision a Finlandization process whereby Korea assumes a neutral status within the Chinese sphere. Some lesser-desired scenarios for China are Korean reunification resulting in the strengthening of the current South Korea–United States alliance, or worse yet, a truly independent Korean state with strategic capability.

According to the literature on international relations, states facing a threat generally have two options: balance against the threat, or "bandwagon" or align with the threat. In the case of Korea with regard to China, it appears that, if forced to make a choice, a reunified Korea will bandwagon with China. Besides the historical precedent for its close relations with China, compelling geopolitical reasons can be made for Korean bandwagoning, such as lack of a reliable long-term ally, geographic proximity to China, and the overwhelming nature of the potential threat. The preferred strategic option for Korea is to align with a distant power to balance against the local threat. The United States has been the ideal distant ally. However, as China continues to grow in importance and the rationale for a United States presence fades, Korea will lean toward China.

China also looms large for Korea in the context of south-north reconciliation and reunification. During a transition period on the peninsula, China will exert its considerable influence to shape the resulting political-military landscape. Considering China's potential impact on reunification for good or ill, it is clearly in Korea's interest to consider how to gain China's support for a reunified Korea. And China will leverage the Korean yearning for reunification to win political concessions.

Korea's strategic calculations are unique in that its disadvantageous geopolitical position requires it to be constantly mindful of the plans of the greater powers around it. For this reason, China is a major factor in Korean strategic calculations. When China does come to dominate East Asia, Korea will thus likely lean toward it to safeguard its national interests.

JAPAN'S DILEMMA

From the Chinese perspective, Japan has historically posed a threat. The failed Hideyoshi invasions of Korea in the sixteenth century were intended to provide a staging area for the conquest of China. At the end of the nineteenth century, after remaking itself in the image of the Western imperialist powers, Japan began to assert itself on the Asian continent, defeating a weakened China and Russia, annexing Korea, and establishing a puppet state in northeast China.

Since the end of World War II, Japan has served as the center of the United States presence in the region and host to numerous United States military bases. The end of the cold war and the diminished North Korean threat put into question the rationale for these bases and the United States–Japan alliance itself. The danger that the alliance will be perceived as an anti-China front is real and should concern all in the region. From the Chinese perspective, the purpose of such an alliance is to thwart the rise of China and maintain the status quo in East Asia. The Bush administration's abandonment of former President Bill Clinton's "strategic partnership" rhetoric, the identification of China as a potential future adversary by defense officials, and Deputy Secretary of State Richard Armitage's call for an increase in Japan's military capabilities add weight to China's perception.

Like Korea, Japan will probably choose to lean toward China, especially if it begins to question United States resolve and commitment. As in the Korean case, the perception of United States commitment to the region will be crucial to Japan's decision to continue to link its national security to the United States. Also as with Korea, the United States will not be able to offer a security commitment to Japan sufficient to convince Japan to maintain the alliance, at least in its current form. United States defense-treaty commitments would ring hollow without a military presence. However, that presence is already questioned in both countries, with organized calls for reduction or withdrawal. In the near future, absent a clear Chinese threat, the United States will find itself in the difficult position of advocating a forward presence to show resolve while opposition in the host countries gains increasing support.

Japan will be the most likely battleground in a China–United States rivalry in East Asia. It cannot afford to bear the brunt of the negative fallout from a Sino-American confrontation. If Japan concludes that China's hegemony is inevitable, that it will not be malevolent, and that the United States commitment is less than assured, it may disengage itself from the United States, seeking an equidistant relationship between the United States and China or even an accommodation with China. China and Japan share many common, long-term interests that can lead to compromise and cooperation.

Absent an alliance with the United States, Japan does have more options than Korea but they will be difficult and dangerous to bring to fruition. For Japan, balancing against China through an independent defense buildup will not be easy. Any sizable Japanese remilitarization is likely to make the region more unstable. And it would be dangerous if Japan were to pursue such a policy, since it would likely force China (and Korea) to adopt an aggressive posture toward Japan, thus making Japan more vulnerable.

For China, Japan will continue to be a crucial source of technology and capital as it modernizes its economy. Likewise, as its economy and its middle class continue to grow, China will become an important market for Japan's consumer goods. It is already a large market for low-cost goods and an important source of raw materials. Even in the age of rapid globalization, the attractiveness of such a huge regional market has the potential to overshadow the economic linkages across the Pacific Ocean. China's regional dominance will afford both China and Japan easier and more reliable access to the assets crucial to their long-term development.

Finally, China's fear of a resurgent Japan (and hence its implicit support of continued United States military presence) is much exaggerated. This "cork-in-the-bottle" argument is useful as a rhetorical tool but lacks power to be considered seriously. All factors, including Japan and the Japanese, are fundamentally different today than they were before World War II. As discussed earlier, without a clear and direct Chinese threat to Japan, any attempts at Japanese remilitarization would prove counterproductive, and hence be a poor policy option. Also, China's desire to supplant the United States as the dominant power in East Asia overshadows any benefit China currently derives from the United States presence in the region.

AMERICAN IMPERATIVES

Since the end of the cold war, the American foreign policy community has been searching for a new paradigm and a new focus. As America looks at China, its perceptions are distorted by the lingering effects of obsolete cold-war strategies. The concept of a threatening China, as reflected in a number of Chinese "threat" articles, is an example of this. American policymakers cannot adopt a single ideology or theory as a guide for the future. The United States must abandon zero-sum calculations that dictate an either/or dichotomy that ultimately leads to a China–United States conflict. Likewise, it should be wary of overly sanguine perspectives that predict peace and prosperity for all. The actual consequences of China's rise in East Asia will be more a function of the nature of the China–United States relationship and the environment in which the transition takes place rather than a predetermined chain of inescapable events based on theory. America should reject policies based on short-term interests and view its East Asia role through a long-term perspective based on enlightened self-interest.

Looking to the midterm future in East Asia, the United States should assess its interests within the context of a regional order centered on China. America's main source of influence will come from its regional economic linkages. Therefore, it should intensify economic cooperation with the states of East Asia, especially China and its key trading partners, Japan and Korea. In the near term, the United States should help restructure the Sino-American relationship into an equal partnership in East Asia to aid in the transition of power from the United States to China over the next several decades. This will enable the United States to play a guiding role as China continues to reform and ascend, allowing for a smooth transition to Chinese dominance and minimizing the possibility for conflict during this unstable period. The United States should abandon its policy of engaging China only if it fits into its own design for the region. No real progress in the Sino-American relationship can occur if the United States insists that everyone must play only by its rules. Historical precedent shows that the Chinese will not engage the United States under those conditions.

Based on their partnership, China and the United States should promote multilateralism. This would facilitate the development of a formalized regional framework of military, economic, and political ties. Building on existing relationships and influence, China and the United States could facilitate confidence building, gradually producing frameworks for stability and cooperation in East Asia. In addition, Americans must recognize that values are in fact relative across different levels of political and economic development and across different cultures, and that the gap in values between most of East Asia and the United States is still quite large. The United States should thus stop promoting American values regarding human rights and democracy to the societies of East Asia, which resent this intrusion. Although this will be difficult, the United States government must not overreact to the insecure belligerence of the Chinese Communist Party and the Chinese military. American policymakers must see beyond Communist rule and seek to establish a relationship with the Chinese people that is based on mutual respect and cooperation; the system in Beijing is bound to change eventually. Finally, the United States should be consistent in its dealing with the states in the region.

For Taiwan, the current United States policy is ill conceived and dangerous and must be brought in line with its commitment to the one-China policy. American allies in the region have already expressed their concern over what they see as a dangerous United States tendency to entangle them in a conflict with China. A war over Taiwan will rupture the United States-centered bilateral alliance structure in Asia. An American abandonment of or setback in Taiwan, at a time of crisis, also would be a major blow to United States prestige and credibility since it would confirm suspicions regarding the "hollowness" of United States might.

The continued United States support of Taiwan also militates against its interest in promoting democratization in China. Although the Chinese are split on many issues, they are uniformly supportive of the Communist Party's stance that Taiwan is an integral part of China and that the issue is strictly an internal matter. Taiwan is a good way for the party to muster popular support and firm up national solidarity, especially in times of domestic turmoil. And the United States in effect helps the Communists maintain a monopoly on power in Beijing by continuing to raise Taiwan as a banner for the party to wave. The best way to secure Taiwanese security and encourage peaceful Beijing–Taipei interaction is to reaffirm America's commitment to Chinese sovereignty by cutting all military ties to Taiwan and insisting that the island abide by the one-China policy.

For Korea, the United States must recognize the unique geostrategic position that Korea occupies. The United States must also recognize that a reunified Korea will once again lean toward China as it seeks to secure its interests. A key factor is that the Sino-American relationship will greatly determine the nature of the United States–Korea relationship. For now, China and the United States should foster close relations with both South and North Korea so as to play constructive roles during the reunification process.

For Japan, the United States must help it normalize relations with its neighbors. East Asian security and prosperity and Japan's place in the region cannot be fully secured as long as Japan's relations with its neighbors are constrained by history. Japan's failure to fully reconcile with its past is a lasting obstacle to better relations with its two most immediate neighbors, China and Korea. Correspondingly, the focus of the United States–Japan alliance should shift from security concerns to economic and global issues. This will demilitarize United States–Japan ties and enhance the ability of both countries to deal with global issues. It will also minimize Chinese anxiety and mistrust.

The best outcome for the entire region would be a network of densely interconnected relationships regionally and across the Pacific that would balance all actors, moderate their behavior, and promote cooperation. This would be a long-term stable arrangement that accommodates China's overall regional primacy while safeguarding American economic interests and establishing a regional balance of power by nonmilitary means.

This vision of East Asia's future bears out the dangers of current United States policy and its probable negative outcome. It also acknowledges China as the long-term regional dominant power and maintains that peace and prosperity can be achieved only through mutual compromise by the two powers. It seeks to prevent the emergence of a new bipolar confrontation in the region and recognizes that the realist-based tendencies of China will require the United States to come to terms with it sooner rather than later. And it recognizes that the United States can work with China now to ensure that East Asia develops into a peaceful and prosperous region from which the United States will benefit.

A NEW OUTLOOK

United States interests in East Asia have changed since the cold war, and the United States needs to build a new foundation for its role and policies in the region. China's rise to displace the United States regionally in the coming decades will test America's capacity to respond to a change of this magnitude. United States interests lie in a stable and open region in which it continues to play a significant role while China assumes the mantle of dominant regional power and police officer. Taking on the number-two role in East Asia would allow the United States to continue to benefit from a dynamic region and at the same time contribute to the maintenance of peace and prosperity. A reduced United States role would mean a significant trimming of its massive array of military assets in the region; the current costs incurred by United States primacy would be greatly reduced across the Pacific. Another important outcome is that the United States and China will be better able to form a durable relationship. As a committed revisionist power, China will most likely not reconcile with a United States that is dominant in a region that China sees as its own sphere. The United States as number two will no longer represent the Western imperialism that the Chinese consider a major cause of their historic downfall and current second-rate status. A China that is number one is less likely to behave aggressively or threaten its neighbors to secure its position and interests. Rather, it will find it in its interest to promote regional cooperation and global stability. The United States can assure a smooth transition to this new structure in East Asia by engaging China in a constructive partnership today.

According to Samuel Huntington, in a multipolar world "there is no reason why Americans should take responsibility for maintaining order if it can be done locally." For years, the United States has provided the common good of stability in East Asia, and all have benefited. It is time to let the Chinese provide this common good so the United States can benefit.

Note

1. Currently, China's interests are served by a United States military presence in East Asia because it promotes stability. However, once the North Korean threat is substantially reduced or removed, an American military presence will no longer be in China's interest. A precondition for continued United States military presence in East Asia is American leadership in the region, a role in direct opposition to the Chinese view of China's rightful place in the region. A comprehensive regional framework for security cooperation is one scenario where a limited United States military presence may coexist with a regionally dominant China. This would require a formal multilateral structure where a United States military presence would clearly be for regional collective security and not part of an anti-China alliance.

LIEUTENANT COLONEL SOONG-BUM AHN *wrote this essay while serving as a United States Army Research Fellow at RAND. He is currently the United States Army Senior Service College Fellow at the Korean Institute for Defense Analysis in Seoul. The views expressed here are solely those of the author.*

Battlefield: Space

Space-based warfare used to seem pure fantasy. Now, to the delight of war planners, and to the dismay of many civilians, it's closer to reality than you'd think.

By Jack Hitt

The Defense Department's newest satellite technology, Warfighter I, sits inside a protected clean room in Germantown, Md. To enter, you must run your shoes through a cleaning device and then don a "bunny suit," a layered hooded outfit that covers every part of your body except your eyes.

"Human skin sloughs off as many 30,000 particles a second," says the program manager, Michael Lembeck, as we step onto a tacky mat, essentially an enormous piece of flypaper. "If one speck of skin got on the Warfighter's lens," he adds with friendly hyperbole, "it would set us back 20 years."

The satellite, which is not much bigger than a college sophomore's dorm refrigerator, is undergoing final tests. Several different machines—producing an artificial magnetic field, digitally created blinking stars, phony sunshine and computer-generated Global Positioning System signals—are fooling the satellite into acting as if it were in real orbit. Several lights click on and motors grind. "It must think it just cleared the North Pole," Lembeck says, "and is reorienting itself toward the sun."

After a few more tests confirm the on-board systems are working, Lembeck says, "We'll get all the graybeards in the room, tell them what we've done here and they will bless us and say, 'Go fly.'"

The Next Generation

The U.S. military has plans for a diverse arsenal in space. Microsatellites could sabotage enemy satellites with high-power microwave beams. Flechettes are rods that could theoretically be dropped from space to smash into targets on earth. And laser cannons could, the Pentagon hopes, zap targets anywhere on the planet.

In fact, Warfighter I is an extremely powerful camera, one that will give the Pentagon revolutionary new powers of surveillance. But its importance goes beyond its technological wizardry. The launch of Warfighter—scheduled for early September—will mark the latest effort by the Pentagon to end a new threat to American security. According to the nation's war planners, America has had a free ride in space during the last 40 years, when the only country capable of even getting there was Russia. Now there is a satellite rush in the final frontier, with both countries and companies entering space. Commercial space launches started to outnumber military ones in 1998. Of the 1,000 active satellites currently in orbit, about an eighth belong to the U.S. military, and that percentage will diminish by the end of the decade, when experts estimate that operating satellites in space will reach 2,000. (Warfighter is being launched by a private company called Orbital Imaging, itself a sign of the times.)

America's war planners fear that we could soon lose our advantage in space. As a result, the military has commissioned numerous studies and long-range plans, all of them coming to the same conclusion. Space, the Pentagon believes, is the ultimate military "high ground"—the tower from which to pour boiling oil. Therefore, America's goal there should be, in the felicitous phrase used in an early study, "Global Battlespace Dominance."

Perhaps that term sounded a little too Strangelove, for the Pentagon's preferred phrase has since become "Full Spectrum Dominance." Last year, the Air Force developed its Strategic Master Plan for space, which states our goal bluntly: "To maintain space superiority, we must have the ability to control the 'high ground' of space. To do so, we must be able to operate freely in space, deny the use of space to our adversaries, protect ourselves from attack in and through space and develop and deploy a N.M.D. capability."

N.M.D. stands for national missile defense, the controversial $8.3 billion missile shield that President Bush and his secretary of Defense, Donald Rumsfeld, have championed. (Last month, the Pentagon announced that it was ready to pour concrete on the first missile-defense test site, in Alaska.) And yet the political attention devoted to national missile defense, which is an updated version of President Reagan's Strategic Defensive Initiative, has obscured its larger purpose. According to the Strategic Master Plan, N.M.D. is but one part of a triad of technologies—along with improved space surveillance and antisatellite offensive weaponry—that, the Air Force hopes, will lead to total "space control." George Friedman, an intelligence consultant and the author of "The Future of War," calls the national missile defense plan a "Trojan horse" for the real issue: the coming weaponization of space.

The cost of expanding our space assets is only now beginning to show itself. Many of the specific systems for space have had their budgets increased in President Bush's first defense-spending proposal, which has been otherwise criticized for being stingy. A new system of space sensors went from $239 million to $420 million. (By comparison, the Air Force's new F-22 Raptor fighter plane has a price tag of $180 million.) A previously unfunded space-based radar program is budgeted at $50 million. And a line for "space control technology"—a euphemism for antisatellite weaponry—was expanded from $8 million to $33 million. Carefully budgeted space technologies like the Warfighter will cost only $42 million, but the more exotic ideas face a long climb up the technological curve and will cost billions.

Warfighter's camera features a new form of imaging called hyperspectral. Space is already home to multispectral cameras, which can take a picture of an ecosystem and discern conifer from deciduous trees. But hyperspectral goes much further, distinguishing the subtle "light signatures" that separate a field of oats from barley and telling you the precise *species* of oats. And then whether the field contains natural or genetically altered oats. And then whether the field is infested with insects or damaged by nitrogen depletion.

The eventual commercial potential of such a technology is obvious. But if you talk to enough colonels and experience what old Pentagon hands call "death by briefing,"—and I have—you will hear mentions of hyperspectral quickly followed by the new mantra of contemporary war planners: *tanks under trees*. To put it briefly: as with oats, so with tanks. Warfighter I will be able to discern the unique light signatures of extremely specific things—like tanks hiding under trees or tanks covered in camouflage or tanks painted with a paint meant to make them not look like tanks.

Consider what such space-assisted technology would have meant to a commander in, say, Kosovo two years ago. He could have swept the contested area with Warfighter I and zeroed in on every enemy tank, missile, ammo dump or plane, almost no matter how hard the Serbs tried to conceal them. Then the commander could have called in a cruise missile to blast each one. In theory, the entire conflict could have been finished off in time for lunch. It's a nice, sweet, hammock-tempting image if you're a war planner.

In preparation, space planners have already engaged in some feverish brainstorming. They envision a high-tech arsenal that will take full advantage of the military potential of space, ranging from the near-term possible to long-term notional: kinetic energy rods, microwave guns, space-based lasers, pyrotechnic electromagnetic pulses, holographic decoys, robo-bugs, suppression clouds, 360-degree helmet-mounted displays, cluster satellites, oxygen suckers, microsatellites, destructo swarmbots, to name a few.

Some civilians find these plans deeply troubling. "If you start talking about putting actual weapons in space, you can take the unhappiness that our allies, Russia and China already have with the missile shield and multiply it by 10," warns Lisbeth Gronlund, a physicist with the Union of Concerned Scientists. Such critics see the Pentagon's effort to weaponize space as profoundly dangerous for national security—not to mention expensive and potentially unfeasible.

"Once you start spinning this baby out," says Dan Smith, an analyst with the Center for Defense Information, "it becomes more complex, more expensive and more impossible to protect ourselves. After the next country introduces space weaponry, *then* what do we do? Live with a new, unpredictable threat orbiting right above us? Or commit an act of war by pre-emptively removing their weapons from space? The basis of security is that it never works for just one. You have to have security for everyone or it fails."

Not surprisingly, the *Realpolitik* leadership at the Pentagon disagrees. Just before taking over Defense, Rumsfeld led a space commission that was established not long after Congressional Republicans grew enraged that Clinton had line-item-vetoed funds for a space plane, antisatellite weapons and a missile-defense technology. The commission issued its report nine days before Bush was sworn in as president, and it concluded: "Every medium—air, land and sea—has seen conflict. Reality indicates that space will be no different." And Warfighter I, it turns out, is the beginning of a many-splendored arsenal to ensure we're ready for battle when it does.

MUCH OF THE MILITARY'S RESEARCH INTO SPACE TECHNOLOGY takes place at the Space Research Lab. It is divided into 10 missions scattered across the country, ranging from the Propulsion Directorate to the Munitions Directorate. On a blazing hot afternoon in June, I arrive at Kirtland Air Force Base in Albuquerque to get cleared into the Space Vehicles Directorate, which specializes in satellite technology. Many outposts of the emerging bureaucracy of space distill their enthusiasms into a shoulder patch. The First Space Operations's patch shows stars and a plane above the words "Always in Control." The 50th Space Wing's logo is an image of Pegasus above the claim "Master of Space." Some divisions have more informal slogans. The motto of the Space Warfare Center is "In Your Face From Outer Space."

I first meet with Alok Das, the head of the Space Vehicle Directorate's innovative concepts group. His latest work has been perfecting the microsatellite. Unlike traditional satellites, which can weigh tons, microsatellites are the size of a suitcase and weigh about 200 pounds. Since it costs "a bar of gold to launch a can of Coke," as Das put it, lightweight microsatellites will be much cheaper to launch than their obese precursors. The idea is to send microsatellites into space in flocks. In this cluster, they would be reprogrammable, able to switch to new tasks when the

Pentagon required it. They might be set in linear formation to conduct ground reconnaissance or grouped in a circle to serve as a communications satellite. "It's like going from a mainframe computer to a network of PC's," Das says brightly. "Together, they'd form a larger virtual satellite."

Yet a flock could also be launched with separate missions. One microsatellite might refuel a larger satellite or upgrade its software. Others might scoot about with small on-board cameras to provide live video feeds from space—a capability no nation currently has.

A microsatellite could do both surveillance and sabotage. As one official explains, 'It could go right up to an enemy satellite and look at it real close—maybe even bump it.'

As I am escorted into a clean room to the see the first microsatellite under construction, one officer offhandedly confides, "It could also go right up to an enemy satellite and look at it real close—maybe even *bump* it."

That's how easy it is to go from peaceful mission to offensive weapon. A suitcase-size microsatellite would just have to put a little shoulder and some thrust into an S.U.V.-size satellite to push it off its proper orbit and render it temporarily unable to communicate with the ground. Another idea is to mount a microwave gun on board so that once the microsatellite maneuvered right beside an enemy satellite, it could emit a pulse of microwaves and fry the electronics permanently. Space planners call this application a high-power microwave pill. Better yet, this microsatellite's sabotage operations would be covert, undetectable from earth. It would give a nation complete deniability: that Chinese satellite that Saddam Hussein has been using doesn't work? Must have been a solar storm.

The first microsatellite launch is planned for this fall.

Later, I talk with the lab's experts in hyperspectral imaging. How, I ask them, will the Warfighter learn the precise "light signature" of, say, a tank hiding beneath a pine-forest canopy?

"Think of them as fingerprints," says Tom Cooley, one of the lab's top researchers. "The wavelength of any kind of camouflage, regardless of composition, can be distinguished—by the dyes, cotton, different lignants from plants. If you look at black-and-white images of camouflage next to scrub brush, they look the same. But a leaf from the scrub brush does not look at all like camouflage to hyperspectral. It would be sharply different."

Before hyperspectral can work, it will require some novel research and testing, says Col. Jack Anthony, chief of space experiments. "Take a tank under a tree," he says, explaining some coming tests. "We'll take some panels made of wood and paint them with different paints, government paint, some paint you might buy at a store. Then we'll take some images with the Warfighter I, and that will give us what's called 'truth.'"

To build what Anthony calls "a library of light signatures," a lot of truth will have to be collected. All possible contingencies—tank under trees, tank under branches, tank under government paint—must be cataloged, one by one. "So if the bad guys are hiding tanks under trees," Anthony explains, "and you have a good idea what the bad guy's tank is made out of and you know what the local trees look like, then you can screen out the trees' wavelength and just see the tank's signature. Then you're going to know there's something bad under that tree. And we can arm our soldiers accordingly."

Cooley adds that "anything from Somalia to Bosnia to Haiti would have dramatically different backgrounds," making it necessary to bank in a library the differences among, say, Honduran swamps and Libyan deserts. "And by the way, water vapor is terribly opaque and will cause the special signature to be completely invisible." However, Cooley continues, another project will be to gather data in order to "correct for water vapor that may blur some of those special features."

To a civilian, hyperspectral surveillance can sound amazing and then—once you hear about light-signature libraries and water-vapor snafus—it can seem a bit iffy, about as dependable as launching a Xerox machine into the stress of low-earth orbit and then counting on it to work during a war.

That's how the Pentagon's critics see it. "There are *already* countermeasures for this kind of technology," Lisbeth Gronlund says. She describes a new kind of camouflage that entails bundling, say, two dozen Mylar balloons beside a nuclear warhead. After launch and the boost phase, the balloons and the warhead are scattered into space. Each has a slightly different light signature. So which target do you shoot down? "The military is *very* sensitive about this problem," Gronlund says.

Yet Anthony is doggedly optimistic. He believes that hyperspectral could be working successfully in the battlefield before the end of the decade. And he thinks the technology will help save lives: "It makes me feel good if I can help a soldier, sailor, airman, marine to know there is something bad hiding on the other side of that hill. We're just putting another arrow in our quiver."

Anthony's robust enthusiasm for space is shared among the research scientists. This enthusiasm is extraordinary. The Nasdaq bubble that burst around election time last year has not affected the military. Space-wise, war planners are prebubble techno-enthusiasts. (And their visions of space warfare are as cinematic as a summer blockbuster. Just look at the language: "Full Spectrum Dominance," "destructo swarmbots," "robobugs." It's hard to imagine the Pentagon's idea of space without Hollywood's.)

Inside the military, all technological setbacks—like the fact that two out of the four major missile-defense simulations conducted so far have failed—are set aside as part of the natural arc of any technological testing. Failure is just proof that there needs to be more research. But the real reason the military is so excited by space is that so much that is already up there, both civilian and military, works splendidly. Nearly all the emblems of our technologically quotidian life—the A.T.M., credit-card transactions, cell phones, the Internet—rely upon satellites.

When space technology has catastrophically failed, the public's reaction has not been greater skepticism but mere annoyance. In May 1998, the Galaxy IV satellite malfunctioned, causing 45 million pagers to shut down and credit-card transactions to cease. The public did not decide to return to making house calls, paying cash and reading by candlelight: it simply expected it to be fixed because it has so internalized the presumption that such technology works, and works wonders. And so has the military.

If the A.T.M. is the shorthand symbol of how easy modern space-based technology has made our lives, then the precision-guided munition is that symbol for the average grunt. The invention of a missile that can be aimed after it has been fired has fundamentally changed modern warfare. It is why arguments about the possible failure of new technologies bounce off space researchers as if off a force field.

Back in World War II, it took, on average, 5,000 bombs to take out one target like a bridge. By the time of the Vietnam War, the ratio had dropped to 500. But in all those wars, bombs were dumb, meaning once you let go of them, they fell in the general direction in which they were pitched.

Then came the gulf war. During this conflict, the U.S. military used space to conduct nearly all of its secret communications, reconnaissance missions and bombing raids. And space-based technology guided new "smart bombs" with such accuracy that the hit ratio plummeted to 1 in 10. "The 500-year history of ballistic warfare has come to an end," George Friedman says. "The gulf war was the first space war."

Although not of the same scale, one notable fact of the Kosovo conflict of 1999 is that no Americans died in combat. Military planners credit that result in part to munitions directed by the Global Positioning System, a constellation of 24 satellites orbiting the earth that is capable of precisely geo-locating any object equipped with the proper receiver. Couple such technological progress with the ultimate lesson of Vietnam—no body bags on TV—and you begin to understand the military's profound enthusiasm about space and why there has been so much blue-sky planning to maintain "Full Spectrum Dominance."

INSIDE THE LAB OF THE DIRECTED ENERGY DIRECTORATE, where research on everything from microwave beams to lasers begins, the machines thrum to a start. A long pipe of fuzzy purple light in a large tube seems to vibrate like a plucked string. In an adjacent chamber that has had most of the air removed to mimic the high altitude of a missile trajectory, a piece of carbonized steel like that which might clad a rocket fuel tank is set in a grip. It begins to spin rapidly to simulate a missile in its ascent. Visual access to the vacuum room is supplied by a closed-circuit television. Technicians call out from one system to another that they are ready. The machines screech into action. On the TV screen, the piece of spinning metal is suddenly blasted with bursts of columnated light that scorch it, back-splashing in a dramatic laser fan.

"We're testing the laser's effect on what would be the body of a rocket spinning in flight," says Capt. Eric Moomey, the chief of this facility. (His insignia reads "Peace Through Light.") In effect, what I am seeing is a small part of what might one day become the national missile-defense shield.

At one point, Moomey clamps a four-inch-square piece of thick plexiglass in a C-clamp and orders the crew to fire up the laser. We all put on safety goggles as the laser shouts for a portion of a second. Burned neatly in the center is an indentation, just big enough, the captain tells me as he hands me the square, to hold a coffee cup. It is holding mine right now. I suspect that my souvenir coaster is not the first of its kind.

Such laser parlor tricks suggest just how far we've come since President Reagan first suggested this idea. Back then, the technology was far off and impossible. The Strategic Defense Initiative amounted to a bluff against the Soviets, and in the end it collapsed amid political ridicule. Back in the early 80's, the idea of shooting down a missile with another missile was widely scoffed at as trying to "shoot a bullet with a bullet." The Star Wars program specifically designed to do this was called Brilliant Pebbles. Besides being technologically complex, it frightened many people with its inherent idea: ringing the planet with thousands of space-borne projectiles, each of which could drop down into the atmosphere to collide with an enemy's missile.

Brilliant Pebbles is now being revived by President Bush, but given the instantaneous speed of lasers, it may soon be joined by a companion technology. With the ability to lock onto the trajectory of a missile, Moomey explains, you might be able to aim an air-based laser at an enemy missile's fuel tank and rapidly heat up the cladding so that "the liquid propulsion vents out and it rips open like a tin can." Moomey says that this kind of laser defense weapon, budgeted at $11 billion, should be operational sometime around 2010.

I next speak with Doug Beason, another expert on laser weaponry. Colonel Beason is a thin, amiable man and a widely read scientist. His magazine rack has well-thumbed editions of Sky and Telescope, Science and Wired. He is the author (sometimes co-author) of 10 novels, including "Virtual Destruction," "Assemblers of Infinity" and "Assault on Alpha Base." A few of his works have just been issued in paperback. When I casually use the word "sci-fi" in a sentence, Beason stops me politely to say that "techno-thriller" is the genre in which he labors. Sci-fi is a "50's expression," he says, trying to be cordial, even though it's clear that I've committed a faux pas on the order of asking Jane Campion about her next chick flick. There are bright lines in Beason's world—between techno-thriller and science fiction, but also between research that looks great on paper and technology he can help put in the hands of an American space warrior.

"The time between invention and mass use of the fluorescent lamp was 79 years," he says. "For the jet engine, 14 years; for the wireless, 8 years."

> The Warfighter I camera, riding on [a] satellite, uses "hyperspectral" technology to identify enemy targets on earth—even those hidden beneath camouflage. The results of such surveillance could be beamed to an Air Force bomber pilot.

This lag time is shrinking rapidly, he says. "We have the tools to exploit the technology, and that's why I'm so excited. Lasers, for example, are no longer used just for CD's and light pointers."

As a result, the Pentagon has its hopes set on a space-based laser. President Bush doubled the research budget this year to $165 million. The estimated cost for a working space laser test is about $5 billion. Actual testing in space is expected to take place as early as 2008.

"This is the technology that can provide the next revolution in military affairs," Beason says, "the Buck Rogers kind of thing."

He adds that lasers have many warfare applications besides outright weaponry. "We've also been working on a flexible-membrane mirror," Beason says, one that would be deployed in space. Then, from earth, a commander could fire a certain frequency of laser, bounce it off the mirror and "onto the battlefield to light up the night only to people with certain types of goggles."

Whenever I express any sense that these technologies sound a bit too, um, sci-fi, Beason responds the same way all his colleagues do. "These are all *concepts*," he explains, "and like any weaponry in a mature technological arsenal, it all depends on how much money you want to spend." Men like Beason are supremely confident in the technology; it's the political will to have space-based weapons that's the problem.

The peculiar thing about space warfare is that many of the innovations that sound the most far-fetched—like illuminating a battlefield at night with light that only one side can see or the deployment of high-power microwave pills—are actually much closer to existence, technologically, than some items that might seem more logically in line for development. Consider the spaceplane. It would be a tremendous tool for the military, since it could get to any point on the globe in a few hours. But building a manned craft that can quickly glide in and out of low orbits has proved incredibly daunting. Earlier this year, the X-33, NASA's big experiment in flying into space, ended in failure. The image that most people have of "Star Wars"-style combat—manned spaceplanes engaging in dogfights near the moon—is very far off. But the use of space for weaponry directed back at earth or guided from space is pretty much at hand.

"I'm particularly excited about high-power microwaves," Beason tells me. Lacking the thousand-mile reach of lasers, H.P.M.'s, as they are called, can be projected only about a half-mile. But were an unmanned plane guided from space able to transport a high-powered microwave device close to a battlefield, the possibilities could push the Pentagon's bomb-to-target ratio even closer to perfection. To an invading army of modern soldiers, a massive hit by high-powered microwave could ground their high-tech weapons, leaving them to wage modern warfare with their fists.

The time lag between the current R.&D. on microwaves and its application in the battlefield may be a while. Beason himself estimates 15 years, although one use is on the verge of showing up in battlefields soon. On the ground, a microwave weapon could be used to drive back an invading squadron. "It'll feel like opening the door of an oven," Beason says. "We're testing it on humans now." He pauses and worries that he is bumping up against classified information. "If you want to know more," he adds, "you'll have to contact the Human Effectiveness Directorate."

THE PENTAGON'S PASSION FOR SPACE ALSO DERIVES FROM the thrill of discovering the medium's own peculiar disadvantages and advantages. True, you have to worry about new problems—space debris traveling at 16,000 miles per hour, solar flares, the Van Allen radiation belt. But it is never overcast in space, the field of vision is planetary and the speed of light is really, really fast. For the far term, war planners have conceived scores of new and exciting weapons. Talking about them is not a conversation the military wants to have in public, given the gnarly debate over the missile shield, but it is one they have been having in private for some time.

Among the internal reports generated by the war colleges and service branches are a half-dozen that imagine how space will be integrated into the U.S. military: The Strategic Master Plan, New World Vistas, Long Range Plan, Guardians of the High Frontier, Almanac 2000, Joint Vision 2010, Spacecast 2020 and Air Force 2025. Taken together, they form an encyclopedia of our war planners' dreams.

Any military response in the future would rely heavily on technologies aloft in space or directed from there. As a result, the U.S. Air Force will little resemble the service as we now romantically conceive it. According to a study entitled Counterair: The Cutting Edge, "uninhabited aerial vehicles will be widespread in 2025." Our new fleet of pilot-free planes would be directed from space and would range from small devices permitting a squadron leader to see over a hill to much larger craft that could deliver powerful weapons to a distant battlefield with tremendous speed. For example, one notion for an unmanned space-directed vehicle—called Strike Star—could "loiter over an area of operations for 24 hours" to deliver "'stun bombs' producing overbearing noise and light effects to disrupt and disorient groups of individuals."

Weapons like the Strike Star would exist on earth but be orchestrated from space. If we can get used to the idea of weapons actually in space, though, then a new arsenal would emerge. For example, if a laser cannon were to be inserted in space, its potential as an offensive weapon would make a cruise missile look like a firecracker. Why? Because, according to one study on directed energy, "a full-power beam can successfully attack ground or airborne targets by melting or cracking cockpit canopies, burning through control cables, exploding fuel tanks, melting or burning sensor assemblies and antenna arrays, exploding or melting munitions pods, destroying ground communications and power grids and melting or burning a large variety of strategic targets (e.g., dams, industrial and defense facilities and munitions factories)—all in a fraction of a second."

Just as the sea and the air presented different advantages in maneuverability, so will space. Having a weapon up there means being at the top of the "gravity well" so that the force that frustrates rocketeering is suddenly your friend. "Kinetic energy weapons" are the subject of a study included in Air Force 2025, with one application being rods, or "flechettes," designed to be tossed down to earth from space. Like the legendary penny tossed off the Empire State Building boring 10 feet into the sidewalk, flechettes could travel at supersonic speed (by aiming a laser just in front of them to create an "air spike," eliminating most of the effects of shock and heat). At such a speed, they could pierce the earth's surface to a depth of one-half mile and obliterate a hidden underground bunker.

Another idea is to set into orbit a number of "giant mirrors" that would take a boy's notion of burning ants with a magnifying lens and loft it into space. "This concept constructs a 10-kilometer magnifying glass or focusing element in space to illuminate targets on the ground or in space," reads one report touting it. "This illumination can turn night to day on the ground, scorch facilities or overheat satellite components." There is a database of such ideas at the Air War College in Alabama. This "solar energy weapon" is colloquially known as "concept No. 900163."

What precisely some of these concepts do is not known, but their names can be tantalizingly glimpsed in footnotes throughout the reports that reference the space database. For example: No. 901178, "space debris repulsion field"; No. 900168, "meteors as a weapon"; No. 900231, "gnat robot threat detectors"; No. 900288, "swarms of micromachines"; No. 900390, "holographic battlefield deception"; No. 900522, "space-based AI-driven intelligence master mind."

In these internal documents, real-world constraints like political will are postponed and the enormous issue of cost is finessed. The one roadblock that is seriously addressed is the bureaucratic resistance from pilots upset at the very concept of unmanned warcraft. In such moments, the tone of the language is melancholic—the problem referred to sorrowfully as "pro-pilot bias"—and suggests that listening to such woes is akin to hearing out the complaints of old sergeants a century ago harrumphing about all that crazy talk of a horseless cavalry.

On a clear blue Colorado afternoon, a bus with high-security officers, civilian engineers and computer techies rumbles into the entrance tunnel to Cheyenne Mountain, the underground cold-war city built on giant springs to withstand a Soviet ICBM attack. I have come here to try to see the emerging space bureaucracy, the elements that may one day make up a new branch of the military, the United States Space Force. At the first checkpoint, we set out on foot. A cool persistent wind practically pushes us through the 30-ton blast doors. For most of the last 40 years, Cheyenne was famous for being the home of Norad, the North American Aerospace Defense Command—the U.S.-Canadian early-warning system that scanned the globe looking for the telltale launch plume of an intercontinental ballistic missile. In fact, it is a Canadian officer from Norad who escorts me into the command room and to the chair where a commanding general would make the decision to launch a nuclear weapon.

"Don't mash the distress button under the desk there," the Canadian warns me, "or armed guards will storm the room." Before me are a wall of television screens reporting global data. (On account of my presence, several are draped with blankets marked Top Secret.) And right away, the shift toward space is obvious. The main screen reads "Combined Command Center for NORAD/USSPACECOM."

The U.S. Space Command is the proto-bureaucracy of our emerging space force. Its current commander, a four-star general named Ralph E. Eberhardt, was given more prominence last May when Rumsfeld reorganized the space command structure. Eberhardt is being touted as the possible next chairman of the Joint Chiefs. Should he be appointed, it will be the most powerful signal yet that President Bush's campaign promise to "leapfrog" to the next generation of weaponry will mean the militarization of space.

The clearest evidence is across town from Cheyenne at Schriever Air Force Base. The Space Warfare Center was established there in 1993. It has three branches, the Space Battle Lab (patch: "Above All Others"); the Space Warfare School (patch: image of missile shooting off lightning bolts); and, as of last October, the 527th Space Aggressor Squadron (patch: image of cartoon bird standing on a cloud tossing a missile to earth). A good deal of the theory about how space can assist our troops during wartime on earth—today—is being developed here. It is the Space Battle Lab that will soon be figuring out how to take a reading from the hyperspectral camera aboard Warfighter I and make that information meaningful to a pilot flying an Air Force bomber.

"We are trying to bring the utility of space *directly* to the fighter," says the battle lab commander, Col. Ron Oholendt, "by either increasing lethality or mission effectiveness." Another project under way is to make better use of space for "bomb-impact assessment."

"As a cruise missile is heading for its target," Oholendt says, "it would transmit a data burst into space just before impact. It might tell us, 'I'm armed; here's where I am; the scene I see matches the target I was given.' So we'd have a confidence it was successful. Or it might say, 'I'm here; I don't see anything familiar so I'm going to blow up some dirt.' After we downloaded the information from the satellite, we'd be fairly confident that site would have to be retargeted."

Rumsfeld has said that the military must prepare itself to avoid a "space Pearl Harbor." This is where such preparations are being made. The commander of the space aggressor squadron, Col. Conrad Widman, spends his days envisioning how an enemy might exploit space—in order to train our forces how to react.

"The one thing you don't want to do is go to war and encounter the enemy's capability for the first time," Widman says. In one simulation exercise, he and the 527th posed as an Iranian terrorist cell set against some real U.S. troops stationed in South Asia. During the exercise, Widman hired a French satellite to take a picture, which can be paid for with a credit card.

"The guys on the Iranian team were able to count airplanes and see entry control points," Widman explains. "They could even see the tent-city area and figure out how many people they had deployed. They could also tell there was some kind of air-defense batteries. They knew that Patriot missiles often played that role, so they went to the Raytheon home page and learned that Patriot batteries are normally laid out in a format with the radar in the center." By the time the 527th had finished the simulation, they had learned the surrounding landscape, the best approach path and the entry points into the concertina-wire-protected camp.

"Is this how the terrorists in Yemen figured where the U.S.S. Cole was?" Widman says chillingly. Widman's work repeatedly reveals that technologies once carefully held as national-security secrets are now commonplace because of satellite proliferation and the Internet. "More and more," Widman's colleague Col. James Rogers says, "the problem is not another superpower, but a guy with a credit card."

As a sign of space's growing importance to the military, the first large-scale war game devoted to space issues was held for five days in January. The hypothetical conflict was set in the year 2017 and involved fighting a space battle with a "near-peer competitor" country named Red that resembled China. During the simulation exercise, which involved 250 people, the two main weapons used to duke it out were laser cannons and microsatellites. Even though select journalists were invited to "watch," the Pentagon did not provide many details of the fighting, except to say that the conflict hinged on attempts to blind each other's satellites as a first step toward waging war. The message of the demonstration, however, was clear: whoever doesn't control space in the next conflict will lose.

The future of space depends a great deal on how we describe it, a struggle that is largely metaphorical. Is space merely an extension of the air or an entirely separate arena?

THE FUTURE OF SPACE DEPENDS A GREAT DEAL ON HOW WE describe it, a struggle that is largely metaphorical. Is space merely an extension of the air and therefore the province of the Air Force? Or is it an entirely separate medium for power, like the land or sea, in need of a new doctrine? The first comparison more easily allows a militarization of space as just more of what we already have, while the second challenges us to debate space as the frontier it still is.

Rumsfeld leans toward the first comparison. His reorganization of the space command structure two months ago put Eberhardt and the Air Force in charge. The changes are even linguistic; the Air Force has revived the antique word "aerospace" to remarry the two domains. The Strategic Master Plan, for example, describes the current Air Force as being engaged in a "transition from a cold-war garrison force to an expeditionary aerospace force" in order to train "21st-century aerospace warriors."

At every stop, I was reminded of the incremental militarization of air after World War I. The Air Force began as a wing of the Army, flying over enemy territory and providing surveillance. Then the pilots began shooting one another down; later they started to drop bombs. Space can be seen as undergoing the same process, progressing out of its current stage as an arena of surveillance to microsatellites attacking other satellites to, finally, space-based lasers aiming down at fighter jets to blast them from the sky.

Yet at some point the future of space will emerge as a great American debate. Over and over, as I interviewed military scientists and generals assigned to space, I was reminded that the decision to move into space will, at the end of the day, be made in Washington. Already, a few politicians have foreseen this conversation and staked out positions.

"Space is our next manifest destiny," explains Senator Bob Smith, Republican of New Hampshire, "because it's a dangerous world out there." Smith says that we have to weaponize space before somebody else does or face the consequences: "I don't want to see a president in the position where he has to step up to the microphones and say that the next Iraq has threatened us with a full-scale attack tomorrow, and we've either got to surrender or nuke them."

On the other side is Representative Dennis Kucinich, Democrat of Ohio. This fall, he intends to introduce a bill to ban completely the weaponization of space. "It's bad enough that we've turned space into a junkyard, but they want to turn space into a place of death," he says. "Think about the metaphysics. For all of human history, space was a place of wonder, of dreams, of aspirations—an almost visual portrayal of Browning's poem: 'Ah, but a man's reach should exceed his grasp,/Or what's a heaven for?' "

Ugh. Maybe this is how the debate must begin—duck-and-cover fear-mongering versus mawkish piety. Yet both positions are really built around the same fear: *weaponizing space is terrifying*. Smith resolves his fear by weaponizing first; Kucinich by appealing to a pristine notion of space that hasn't existed for 40 years. But this fear is real precisely because space weapons, unlike those at sea or on land, would orbit invisibly above us all. That fear would be irresolvable, like the nuclear nightmares of the last century, with their bomb shelters, gas masks and decades of mass-destruction anxiety. It is bad enough that space-surveillance technology has conspiracy theorists convinced the government can see them stepping out of the shower. Can you imagine the global neuroses if deadly lasers could be fired from space?

There is, however, a middle ground between hang-nukes-from-every-star and leave-space-the-inky-domain-of-magi, one that is occupied by some civilian theorists and military war planners.

"If we aggressively move weaponry into space," warns Michael Krepon of the Stimson Center, a Washington think tank, "then we will start an arms race." By inspiring nations to compete directly and immediately with our space-based assets, we will almost certainly guarantee the loss of the very advantages we seek to protect. Krepon supports a doctrine called "space sanctuary," a woolly phrase that sounds more feel-good than it is. His position is really that of a space pragmatist.

Pragmatists like Krepon want the military to continue research into space technologies; it would be foolish not to do so. But instead of testing or deploying a space-based arsenal, pragmatists would hold up a threat: if any rival country goes into space to test armaments, then America will go up with its own devices immediately. In the meantime, pragmatists believe, the United States should be promoting efforts to create rules of the road for space. As a model, Krepon suggests the bilateral agreements that currently regulate behavior among blue-water ships on the oceans. They are informally negotiated navy to navy, rather than through the more potentially hostile venues of governments and treaty arrangements.

Space pragmatists also believe there is great danger in abandoning the treaties that so far have guided behavior in space: the 1967 Outer Space Treaty, which forbids putting weapons of mass destruction in space, and the 1972 Antiballistic Missile Treaty, which created the surveillance system to prevent nuclear conflict (and forbids most antimissile testing). President Bush has roundly condemned the ABM treaty as a "relic" and has said that he will test antimissile technology no matter what—prompting precisely the kind of reaction Krepon fears. Even our allies have expressed "concern."

"If the ABM treaty is trashed, its protections of satellites also go by the boards," Krepon cautions. "The ABM treaty contains the most explicit protections of satellites on the books. They pertain only to those satellites that monitor treaty provisions, but when you kill the treaty, you also remove the protections." Indeed, if the U.S. abandons the treaty, a rogue nation might well respond by tossing into orbit what experts call a "keg of nails"—that is, putting thousands of metal shards into a 16,000-mile-per-hour counterorbit against our low-orbit satellites.

Kaboom.

The Pentagon's certainty that "Full Spectrum Dominance" is the only answer is curious because its own actions undercut the theory. Throughout all the conversations I had, I was perplexed by one glaring paradox. The linchpin of our precision-guided munitions is the Global Positioning System. After making the system public in the 90's, we opened it up further two years ago so that anyone on the earth can use its efficacy down to one meter of accuracy. This is an amazing gift to the world. Why did we make it? I kept asking the officers this question and heard an answer that didn't quite satisfy: "American businessmen could make some money off it."

But there is one other theory that is not stated so publicly: if we permitted everyone to use it, then no one would feel driven to build a competing system. Rather, everyone would become dependent on it. And, in fact, everyone has. The world has incorporated our G.P.S. into its daily life as rapidly as Americans took up the A.T.M. banking network, and the rules of the G.P.S. road are getting written. The entire military forces of Australia now rely upon our G.P.S., and the new generation of cell phones will automatically locate a 911 caller.

By sharing G.P.S., no one feels so threatened to compete with it. And its use is so ubiquitous internationally that any country that damaged it would provoke a global fury. There is a sense of transparency on our part by giving away access to the G.P.S., even a feeling of generosity. Naturally, there are encryption devices on our satellites. In a crisis, we could block a bellicose nation's access to G.P.S. What was done with G.P.S. is a kind of space pragmatism.

A similar protocol could be done for introducing direct video access to space. Once it is developed, the U.S. military could make technology that allows us to see and confirm exactly what is happening up in space publicly available. This would, once again, be viewed as American generosity. It would ease competitive tensions since there would be mutually assured awareness in space. A nation with a defunct satellite would be able to confirm that it was not sabotage but the usual wear and tear of, say, subatomic bombardment (another new space hazard) that caused a breakdown. The benefit for us would be that when the crunch time of a crisis came, the visual infrastructure to see precisely what's going on in space, like G.P.S., could be made unavailable to a hostile force.

The strength of the pragmatic position is that it seeks neither to march into space while locking and loading nor does it naïvely strive for a purity that no longer exists. Space pragmatism doesn't pretend to keep space unsullied, because it can't. Without a doubt, more and more satellites will go up. More businesses will operate there, new uses will be discovered and quarrels will occur. And gradually, a military presence that is already there will get expanded. But the pragmatist intent is to hold the line at surveillance.

Can we? Can we hold the line without necessarily filling space with weaponry? The pragmatist position holds out the hope that by writing rules now—and by sharing technology—the United States could make it much harder for anyone to ever breach that line. On the other hand, if we plan, test and deploy aggressively as the lone superpower, we make certain that after a brief respite from the cold war's nuclear competition, we will once again embark on a fresh and costly arms race. And with it, assume the dark burden of policing a rapid evolution in battlespace.

Jack Hitt is a contributing writer for the magazine.

UNIT 6

Cooperation

Unit Selections

26. **Reforming the United Nations**, Maurice Strong
27. **Justice Goes Global**, *Time*
28. **Enforcing Human Rights**, Karl E. Meyer
29. **Meet the World's Top Cop**, *Foreign Policy*
30. **Tribes Under the Microscope**, Vida Foubister

Key Points to Consider

- Itemize the products you own that were manufactured in another country.
- What recent contacts have you had with people from other countries? How was it possible for you to have these contacts?
- Do you use the Internet to access people or Web sites in other countries?
- Identify nongovernmental organizations in your community that are involved in international cooperation (e.g., Rotary International).
- What are the prospects for international governance? How would a trend in this direction enhance or threaten American values and constitutional rights?
- How can the conflict and rivalry be transformed into meaningful cooperation?

Links: www.dushkin.com/online/
These sites are annotated in the World Wide Web pages.

American Foreign Service Association
http://www.afsa.org/related.html

Carnegie Endowment for International Peace
http://www.ceip.org

Commission on Global Governance
http://www.cgg.ch

OECD/FDI Statistics
http://www.oecd.org/statistics/

U.S. Institute of Peace
http://www.usip.org

An individual can write a letter to another person who is located just about anywhere in the world and, assuming it is properly addressed, the sender can be relatively certain that the letter will be delivered. This is true even though the sender pays for postage only in the country of origin and not in the country where it is delivered. A similar pattern of international cooperation is true when an individual boards an airplane in one country and never gives a second thought to the issues of potential language and technical barriers, even though the flight's destination is halfway around the world.

Many of the most basic activities of our lives are the direct result of multinational cooperation. International organizational structures, for example, have been created to monitor threats to public health and to scientifically evaluate changing weather conditions. The flow of mail, the safety of airlines, and the mo.nitoring of changing international conditions are just some of the examples of individual governments recognizing that their self-interest directly benefits from cooperation (in some cases by giving up some of their sovereignty through the creation of international governmental organizations, or IGOs).

Transnational activities are not limited to the governmental level. There are now tens of thousands of international nongovernmental organizations (INGOs). The activities of INGOs range from staging the Olympic Games to organizing scientific meetings to actively discouraging the hunting of seals. The number of INGOs along with their influence has grown tremendously in the past 50 years.

During the same period in which the growth in importance of IGOs and INGOs has taken place, there also has been a parallel expansion of corporate activity across international borders. Most U.S. consumers are as familiar with Japanese or German brand-name products as they are with items made in their own country. The multinational corporation (MNC) is an important nonstate actor. The value of goods and services produced by the biggest MNCs is far greater than the gross domestic product (GDP) of many countries. The international structures that make it possible to buy a Swedish automobile in Sacramento or a Swiss watch in Singapore have been developed over many years. They are the result of governments negotiating treaties that create IGOs to implement the agreements (e.g., the World Trade Organization). As a result, corporations engaged in international trade and manufacturing have created complex transnational networks of sales, distribution, and service that employ millions of people.

To some observers these trends indicate that the era of the nation-state as the dominant player in international politics is passing. Other experts have observed these same trends and have concluded that the state system has a monopoly of power and that the diverse variety of transnational organizations depends on the state system and, in significant ways, perpetuates it.

In many of the articles that appear elsewhere in this book, the authors have concluded their analysis by calling for greater international cooperation to solve the world's most pressing problems. The articles in this section provide examples of successful cooperation. In the midst of a lot of bad news, it is easy to overlook the fact that we are surrounded by international cooperation and that basic day-to-day activities in our lives often directly benefit from it.

REFORMING THE UNITED NATIONS

A Canadian with long experience as a UN official gives a frank assessment of the global institution's prospects and possibilities.

By Maurice Strong

UN/DPI PHOTO #187456C BY L. BIANCO

Reformers meet in Geneva in 1997: UN Secretary-General Kofi Annan (center) chairs the organization's Administrative Committee on Coordination. The author, Maurice Strong, sits under the UN flag. The ACC attempts to coordinate the activities of the independent agencies that make up the UN family—the World Bank, the International Monetary Fund, the Food and Agricultural Organization, the World Health Organization, UNESCO, and others. Miles Stoby (far left) is deputy executive coordinator for UN Reform. Patricio Civili, the ACC secretary, and Vladimir Petrovsky, director-general of the UN's Geneva office, sit right.

What kind of United Nations does the world need for the twenty-first century? Will it—should it—evolve into a world government?

Let me make my own position clear: World government is just not on; it is not necessary, not feasible, and not desirable.

This is not to say that we can aspire to a world without systems of rules. Far from it. A chaotic world would pose equal or even greater danger than world government. The challenge is to strike a balance so that the management of global affairs is responsive to the interests of all people in a secure and sustainable future.

Today a sense of internationalism has become a necessary ingredient of sound national policies. No nation can make progress heedless of insecurity and deprivation elsewhere. We have to share a global neighborhood and strengthen it so that it may offer the promise of a good and secure life to all our neighbors.

The fear that international organizations represent a creeping movement toward world government may be understandable, but it is simply not valid. Indeed, the idea is both dangerous and counterproductive.

Mistrust of Government

As the need for more of what I call "co-operative governance" increases, paradoxically, there is an increasing mistrust of government in all its forms and a growing reluctance to entrust governments with more power, authority, and control over resources. There has been strong support for right-wing calls to "get governments off the backs of the people" and to reverse the trend toward ever-bigger government that has characterized the post-Second World War period. This has been especially evident in the United States, but there is a similar trend in other Western countries and more recently in some developing countries.

A parallel push is for reduced support for international organizations, also nourished by strongly voiced fears that they're likely to subvert national sovereignty and, indeed, represent a movement toward world government. This fear—not to say paranoia—has been greatly exaggerated by extreme right-wing elements in the United States, which in turn have had a disproportionate influence on the U.S. Congress. Such fear has undoubtedly contributed to the American retreat from financial commitments to the United Nations, as well as from support of other international organizations.

The fear that international organizations represent a creeping movement toward world government may be understandable, but it is simply not valid. Indeed, the idea is both dangerous and counterproductive, to the extent that it undermines the principal instruments that governments must use to cooperate for the protection and benefit of their own citizens.

At a time when even the strongest national governments are experiencing difficulties and constraints on their capacity to perform the duties already entrusted to them, establishing a central world government would compound the problem, not solve it. What is needed instead is an improved system of international agreements and international law and more streamlined international organizations to service and support the cooperation among governments and other key actors that will be required.

The United Nations, the Bretton Woods institutions (the World Bank and International Monetary Fund), and the many other regional and specialized international organizations that now exist provide the basic elements for such a system. Of course, they need continuing reform, restructuring, rationalization, and reorientation to make them more effective and more efficient and to prepare them for the enlarged functions they will be called on to undertake in the period ahead. But even more than this, they need revitalized mandates and a renewal of the political and financial support that is essential for their effective functioning. This will not be possible without a much broader understanding and more positive appreciation of the role of the United Nations and other multilateral organizations and their relevance to the issues that affect the lives and prospects of individuals.

These basic considerations provided the philosophical underpinnings of the UN reforms undertaken by Secretary-General Kofi Annan, in which I was involved. But, as the secretary-general has frequently made clear, reform is not a single event but a continuing process. And it is a process that must be embraced by all international organizations.

There is very limited understanding, and much misunderstanding, about the nature of international organizations. They are not governments but the servants of governments, and they lack the basic attributes of governments.

In democratic societies, local, state, and national governments are elected directly by the people and are accountable to them. They have taxing and borrowing power to raise the revenues and capital required to act as mandated by their people. National governments have their own military establishments.

The United Nations has none of these features. It was created by national governments, which are its members; they provide and control its finances and determine its functions and activities. It cannot tax or borrow and has no source of revenue independent of governments. The United Nations has no military forces or capacity of its own to carry out missions mandated by the Security Council or to enforce its decisions. It has no direct relationship with the people of its member countries, despite the fact that the preamble to the UN charter begins with "We the Peoples...."

The United Nations is therefore totally dependent on its member governments; it can only undertake activities that its members agree to and only to the extent that the same governments provide the wherewithal. Because member governments frequently fail to supply the funding and military support to carry out the decisions, the United Nations becomes a scapegoat for delinquent governments.

There is another important difference between the United Nations and governments. In nation-states, the various departments (finance, foreign affairs, and so on) are an integral part of government, subject to its overall control and direction. Not so in the United Nations. The specialized agencies of the UN, such as the World Bank, the International Monetary Fund, the World Health Organization, the Food and Agriculture Organization, and UNESCO, are the international counterparts of the related departments of national governments, but they are not integrated into the central body of the United Nations. Each has been established through a separate international agreement among the governments that become members of the organization, and these generally, but not entirely, parallel the membership of the United Nations. They are therefore autonomous organizations within the extended UN family, or "system," but each reports separately to its own governing body, consisting of the governments of its member countries, and is financed separately by them.

Two Principles to Guide Reform

1. Apply the principle of subsidiarity.

I am a great believer in the principle of subsidiarity—that government is most effective when it is carried out at the level closest to the people its decisions affect. Many of the powers and functions that national governments have taken on in recent years could be more logically and effectively performed at the state, local, or in some cases regional levels. In most Western countries there has already been a significant movement in this direction. By the same token, more and more of the responsibilities and functions of national governments require international cooperation for treaties, conventions, and agreements.

There are a number of activities performed by UN organizations and agencies

UN/DPI PHOTO BY MILTON GRANT

The Security Council, one of the main bodies of the United Nations, meets at the Millennium Summit, 2000. The UN offers nations the opportunity to seek common ground on issues of global importance; but it is not and should not be a world government, says author Maurice Strong.

The United Nations: A Few Salient Points

The UN General Assembly, the central political forum, is composed of 188 members, including virtually all the world's nation-states. Two-thirds of members are developing countries, which account for about three-quarters of the world's population.

Reaching decisions is difficult, especially since all agreements by custom must be reached by consensus. As a result, important agreements are often held hostage by narrow special interests, and most agreements are reached only by reducing them to their lowest common denominators. But the real question, Maurice Strong believes, is whether the major countries of the world will allow democracy to function at the highest level.

The Security Council, which is responsible for peace and security, deals with issues of the greatest political importance. The Council has only 15 members so it can meet frequently and deal with crises. Once impotent due to Cold War rivalries, it has regained much of the authority accorded by the UN charter.

The Council is effectively controlled by its five permanent members—the United States, Great Britain, France, Russia, and China. The other 10 members are chosen through an intensive election process in the General Assembly.

Strong believes the Council needs to be enlarged to reflect today's geopolitical realities—the political and economic power of Japan and Germany, the tripling of the UN membership, and the growing power of its developing-country majority.

The Economic and Social Council is the principal forum for dealing with globalization in its various manifestations—development, humanitarian, environment and gender issues, the spread of crime, terrorism, and drug trafficking.

The Council, known as ECOSOC, is the sole body with a broad enough mandate to provide the political forum for issues that cut across institutional boundaries, Strong says. Only when governments recognize the need for such a forum at the global level will they provide the support that will enable ECOSOC to perform its tasks effectively.

A new Trusteeship Council might provide the principal forum through which the nations of the world would come together to exercise their collective trusteeship for the global environment and the global commons—the oceans, the atmosphere, the Antarctic, and outer space. The commons transcend national boundaries and can only be managed effectively through cooperation.

—Edward Cornish

that in today's context could be better or more appropriately handled by other regional and special-purpose organizations, including those of a nongovernmental nature. In other cases it makes more sense for the United Nations, as the only world organization with a global membership and mandate, to provide the framework for actions by national governments and others.

It's not easy, though, to devolve issues away from the agenda of the UN General Assembly, since each agenda item is the special interest of one or more member governments.

2. Define the "boundary conditions" that should prescribe global priorities.

What should remain on the UN agenda? I believe the issues that should be accorded highest priority at the international level are those that can have a major effect on the security, survival, and well-being of the entire human community or major portions of it. These center on what I call the "boundary conditions," by which I mean the outer limits that humankind as a whole must respect to protect us all from major risks to our common future—and, of course, to realize major opportunities that cannot otherwise be achieved. It is these "boundaries" that the world community needs to accept and to find ways of managing cooperatively.

Security will remain a major preoccupation of nations and of the international community, but in today's complex, interdependent technological civilization, traditional concepts of security of one nation vis-à-vis other nations need to be expanded to include human and environmental security.

Initially, agreement on such boundary conditions should be limited to a small number of areas—those with the highest degree of potential risk, which call for early action. This would be my "starter list":

1. Strictly controlling the manufacture and use of nuclear, biological, and chemical weapons of mass destruction.
2. Limiting the amount of carbon dioxide and other greenhouse gases from human sources that can be allowed to build up in the atmosphere.
3. Limiting the destruction or compromise of the earth's biological resources.
4. Limiting the discharge or transport by any country of hazardous and noxious substances that can inflict damage beyond its borders.
5. Limiting a country's intrusion into or undermining of the security or economy of other countries.
6. Defining the extent to which a government can suppress human rights or commit violence against its own people without justifying redressive action on the part of the international community.
7. Protecting the global commons—the oceans, the atmosphere, the Antarctic, and outer space.

Need to Focus on Security

The central bodies of the United Nations—the General Assembly, the Security Council, the Economic and Social Council, and a refurbished Trusteeship Council—need to function as the principal political forums of the world community at the global level. They should therefore concentrate on those issues that are global in nature or importance, or require a global context for national, regional, or sectoral action. The United Nations should be prepared to divest other issues to the regional or special-purpose organization best suited to deal with them.

Security will remain a major preoccupation of nations and of the international community, but in today's complex, interdependent technological civilization, traditional concepts of security of one nation vis-à-vis other nations need to be expanded to include human and environmental security. Even in respect of military security it is not realistic to expect the security of all nations to be achieved through a single global security pact. More plausibly, we should build on the existing patchwork of multilateral and bilateral security arrangements. That way, we could realistically achieve a global system based on a series of regional security agreements guaranteed by the international community through the United Nations.

Growing threats to the earth's life-support systems present more danger to the future of life than the threats we face from conflicts with each other. I contend, therefore, that the basic concept of security must be enlarged to accommodate this new reality.

In the armed conflicts that are proliferating within states, particularly in the developing world, the magnitude of civilian casualties in recent times has been on the order of 75%. Human security—the security of individuals—and civic security—the security of communities—have now moved onto the international agenda. These are the main priorities of the University for Peace, established by international agreement and approved by the UN General Assembly in 1980 to serve and support the peace and security goals of the United Nations through education, training, and research. The University for Peace is allied with the Earth Council, headquartered in Costa Rica, which was established as a result of the Earth Summit to support community and grassroots action for sustainable development. The two organizations cooperate in programs designed to foster environmental security, particularly through anticipation, prevention, and resolution of conflicts arising from competition and disputes over water, natural resources, and cross-boundary environmental impacts.

The Future of the Nation-State

Will the nation-state just fade away? Will the idea of "national sovereignty" be tossed at last into the dustbin of history?

Well, no... and yes.

The way we govern our own societies and the world community as a whole will, I am sure, be the central issue of the twenty-first century. Only by an effective system of governance will we be able to manage successfully the host of other issues that human survival and well-being depend on. I have already affirmed my own belief in the principle of subsidiarity—the idea that every function of government should be carried out at the closest possible level to the people affected. Rigorous application of this principle would undoubtedly affect national governments most of all. They will need to yield jurisdiction over many issues to regional, state, and local governments that are better able to deal with them, and they will also need to delegate more authority to international organizations, as cooperation with other governments becomes more and more necessary.

It is entirely possible that we will see a reemergence of a modern version of the classical city-state of medieval and Renaissance Europe. We will also see ad hoc alliances—groupings of states into blocs (whether for trade, defense, or simply mutual self-interest). None of this means that the nation-state will just disappear. It will almost certainly continue to be the single strongest and most important level of governance and the indispensable link between various levels and sectors of national society with the institutions and activities of the international community.

So nation-states will, and should, survive. But they will likely become smaller and almost certainly more numerous.

Key Actions to Secure the World's Future

Maurice Strong believes that the next 30 years are critical. During this period, decisions must be made and actions taken in order to secure the human future. "The doomsday clock is ticking toward a day of reckoning if we fail to change our ways," he says in *Where on Earth Are We Going?*

Besides implementing and building on the Earth Summit's Agenda 21 and accompanying agreements, Strong urges 12 "key actions":

1. Promote the greening of the market system, such as through "emissions trading." It is essential to institute incentives and financial mechanisms to ensure that private capital will support development that is sustainable.

2. Revamp subsidies. Governments are spending vast amounts of money on unnecessary and counter-productive subsidies to various sectors of their economies. A recent Earth Council study estimated that these subsidies amount to at least $700 billion a year in the water, transport, energy, and agriculture sectors alone.

3. Manage "Earth Incorporated" using sound business principles, including full accounting for environmental costs and taxing products and activities that are environmentally harmful.

4. Accelerate the transition to environmentally sound energy. Strong incentives are needed to produce new alternative sources of energy. Hydrogen, fuel cells, solar, and other renewable sources offer significant promise, and they all have a place in the energy mix of the future, though none at this point seems a likely candidate for the primary fuel. Strong has proposed that the OECD countries make a fivefold increase in their expenditures on research and development to improve the performance of existing fuels and find alternatives. "I can think of no better investment in long-term environmental security," he writes.

5. Close the knowledge gap between rich and poor countries and between science and policy making. It's important to support the developing countries in their efforts to extend their own scientific and technological capabilities so that they, too, can be generators of knowledge, especially in areas where they have a potential advantage. Developing countries also need to allocate a much larger proportion of their domestic resources to strengthening their scientific and technological capacities.

6. Move away from foreign aid. The era of foreign aid as we know it is coming to an end, and more complex and sophisticated relationships are needed. To be successful, development must be homegrown, rooted in the political and economic management of each country, its policies and priorities, and driven by the shared aspirations of the people and their willingness to accept the attendant responsibilities.

7. Move to more flexible, incentive-based regulation. As globalization has new dimensions of interdependence, there has been a need for a much greater degree of international cooperation and agreement to harmonize international regulations and standards. There is a need to ensure that the people of one country are not disadvantaged vis-à-vis others and to provide for the effective functioning of the many activities and services that are by their nature international, such as trade, investment, air transport, shipping, telecommunications, disease control, and the environment.

8. Provide more effective trusteeship over the global commons. The oceans beyond national jurisdictions constitute some 70% of the earth's surface; the Antarctic is in reality a global commons area; the high atmosphere and outer space are the newest frontiers of the commons. Management of these areas can only be carried out cooperatively, and we must devise a much better means of doing so. We need a global forum where commons issues can be overseen, where arrangements for managing the commons can be discussed, and where the various organizations undertaking activities are accountable. A ready-made vehicle for providing this forum exists in the UN Trusteeship Council.

9. Prepare for natural disasters and extraterrestrial threats. There is much we can do to anticipate disasters, prepare to deal with them when they occur, and mitigate their effects. The UN's humanitarian efforts, and those of private humanitarian agencies, are being focused more and more on anticipatory measures. Environmental neglect and mismanagement contribute significantly to the likelihood and costs of mudslides, avalanches, and floods. Recent examples include the devastating consequences of Hurricane Mitch in Central America and the Yangtze flood in China. Another factor is the growing concentration of population in some areas where disasters occur.

10. Rejoice in diversity and encourage it. A human society that sustains and enhances diversity will not only optimize freedom and quality of life but will also be stronger and more sustainable.

11. Encourage lifestyles of "sophisticated modesty." Reducing one's impact on the environment is a continuing process of trying to break bad habits and to obtain the kind of services and products that will help accomplish one's goals.

12. Learn from those in enclave communities. People seeking refuge from a turbulent and materialistic world have for many centuries formed monastic communities, many of them self-reliant. Recently there has been a resurgence in the movement toward establishing such communities by secular as well as spiritual groups. These communities represent not so much an escape from the "real world" as an opportunity to experience it under conditions more congenial and sustainable than those outside. Such communities can set an example of ways of life that can be pursued anywhere, any time.

Source: *Where on Earth Are We Going?*

One of the apparent paradoxes of our time is that, while nations are coalescing in trade, economics, and, in the case of the European Union, political blocs, there is a countertrend toward the fragmentation of existing nations. Important and distinctive (even if only in their own eyes) ethnic groups or regions are asserting their demands for autonomy or independence. But this is no paradox, really. In fact, these trends represent opposite sides of the same coin. It is becoming more and more feasible for smaller units to achieve the same level of security and economic advantages that they currently obtain from being part of a larger nation, through membership in regional and global organizations.

The European Union is an innovative governance structure that seems likely to provide a model that will influence others in the period ahead. It is neither a multilateral organization nor national government. But it *is* a government—in the sense that its members, all of them national governments, have vested in it responsibilities formally and normally exercised by the governments of its member countries, together with the constitutional powers to carry out these responsibilities.

The United Nations now has 188 members, some of them micro-states like Andorra, Monaco, and Liechtenstein. The fact that they have full status in the community of nations is not lost on other groups, which can see that, if they were separate nations, they would be much more visible and possibly more viable. Quebec, for example, would be the 32nd-largest nation in terms of its economy if it were to separate—a useful reminder to Canadians that both Quebec and the rest of Canada could be viable separately by the standards of today's international community.

The running of our planet, as the Commission on Global Governance has said, "now involves not only governments and intergovernmental institutions but also nongovernmental organizations (NGOs), citizens' movements, transnational corporations, academia, and the mass media. The emergence of a global civil society, with many movements reinforcing a sense of human solidarity, reflects a large increase in the capacity and will of people to take control of their own lives."

The rise of civil society in the twentieth century can be compared to the rise of the nation-state in the nineteenth, according to Johns Hopkins political scientist Lester Salamon. This exaggerates the realities somewhat but it does underscore the importance of civil society movements. I attach special importance to the need to "support and empower people in building a more secure, equitable, and sustainable future," which is the stated goal of the Earth Council.

Of course, not all the organizations and activities of nongovernmental sectors of society are "civil." While crime has always been with us, technology and the processes of globalization have vastly multiplied the capacities of criminal elements to undermine and exploit our societies. I am convinced that international crime is emerging as one of the principal challenges of the twenty-first century, confronting nations and the international community with the need to mobilize their resources for an entirely new kind of war, in which the enemy is powerful, versatile, and largely invisible. It is a war that no nation can wage alone, as organized crime is clearly highly adept at using the instruments of globalization to move people and resources across national boundaries.

The future is in our hands. We have the ability to control our own destiny—and the responsibility to manage it. The time frame in which we must act is very short. It is not that the demise of our civilization could occur rapidly, but that the decisions and actions that would determine its ultimate fate are likely to emerge within the first part of the new century and particularly within the next two decades. Disaster is not inevitable. It is still avoidable if we effect the kind of "change of course" called for at the Earth Summit in Rio in 1992. (See "Key Actions to Secure the World's Future.")

The future is ours to make and our children's to inherit. And the Earth is our future.

About the Author

Maurice Strong is currently chairman and chief executive officer of the Earth Council, United Nations, New York, as well as president of the Council, the University for Peace, San Juan, Costa Rica. E-mail lois@un.org.

This article draws on material in his book *Where on Earth Are We Going?*

Originally published in the September/October 2001, issue of *The Futurist,* pp. 19-25. Used with permission from the World Future Society, 7910 Woodmont Avenue, Suite 450, Bethesda, Maryland 20814. Telephone: 310/656-8274; Fax: 301/951-0394; http://www.wfs.org).

Justice Goes Global

(International Criminal Court Is Created)

More than 160 nations voted to establish the International Criminal Court, which will be located in The Hague, Netherlands. The U.S. refused to sign the treaty to create the global tribunal to judge war crimes because of reservations about sovereignty and jurisdiction.

Despite U.S. dissent the world community finally creates a new court to judge the crimes of war.

The spectre of the century's slaughtered millions haunted Rome as the world's nations struggled for five weeks to create the first permanent international body dedicated to punishing the crimes of war. "Victims of past crimes and potential victims are watching us," said U.N. Secretary-General Kofi Annan. "They will not forgive us if we fail."

They did not fail. Cheers and applause echoed as representatives of some 160 nations, assisted by more than 200 non-governmental organizations, gathered last week in the plush maze of the U.N. Food and Agriculture Organization's building, voted overwhelmingly to create the International Criminal Court (I.C.C.). But success came only after frantic last-minute negotiations to bridge philosophical divides that left the U.S. in opposition to the treaty and at odds with most of its major allies. Just how viable the court will be if the world's superpower carries out its threat to "actively oppose" the new institution remains to be seen, but 18 judges will gather in The Hague within the next few years, ready to try cases of genocide, war crimes and crimes against humanity.

The duality of mankind's urges to both wage war and curb its own bellicosity is virtually as old as warfare itself. But it was only in the 19th century that refinements in the technology of battle concentrated minds on serious attempts to find judicial ways to combat their brutality. The laws and customs of war were codified at Conventions in The Hague in 1899 and 1907, and efforts continued between the two World Wars. But those laudable agreements were impotent in face of the unprecedented carnage of the 20th century's first half, when an estimated 58 million died in Europe alone. After World War II, international tribunals at Nuremburg and Tokyo tried and convicted the conflict's instigators for war crimes, crimes against peace and against humanity itself. But these judgments were carried out within a temporary judicial framework imposed by the victors.

The Geneva Conventions of 1949 continued to build a body of international law governing the conduct of war, but the problem of applying the provisions remained. The newly formed U.N. had commissioned a study in 1948 to look into establishing a permanent tribunal, but the cold war prevented any real progress. The topic surfaced again only in 1989, when the International Law Commission began preparing a draft statute for an International Criminal Court. But what really galvanized the international community was the chaotic disintegration of Yugoslavia and the atrocities that accompanied it.

The U.N. eventually moved to create an ad hoc criminal tribunal on the crimes committed during the Bosnian war in 1993, followed a year later by another one-off body for Rwanda. The distinguished South African jurist Richard Goldstone, the original chief prosecutor for both tribunals, says that those courts represented "the first real international attempt to enforce international humanitarian law." But establishing those bodies took up to two years of preparatory work and negotiation. "The thing is to avoid having to spend six months looking for a prosecutor," notes Theodor Meron, professor of international law at New York University Law School, "and a year looking for a building."

Even though Bosnia's most notorious accused war criminals have not yet been brought before The Hague tribunal, it has indicted some 60 people, holds 27 men in custody and has handed down two judgments. This month the court launched the first genocide prosecution in Europe. Deputy Prosecutor Graham Blewitt says that "We have been a model for the creation of the new court."

International law has always involved an inherent tension between national sovereignty and accountability. But the continuing carnage since 1945—another 18 million dead and the likes of Idi Amin, Pol Pot and Saddam Hussein reigning in terror—reinforced the U.N.'s determination to act. As it did so, Washington began to fret. Michael Scharf, currently professor of law at New England Law School, was the State Department's point man on the court under President George Bush. "One of my jobs, which I did not enjoy," recalls Scharf, "was to find ways to stall it forever." President Clinton has been far more supportive, but his administration, too, developed serious qualms. Recalling the invasions of Grenada and Panama, and the bombing of Libya, the U.S. worried that similar actions in the future could involve officials all the way up the chain of command being hauled before the I.C.C.

As the conference convened in Rome on June 15, it was beset by disagreement. The most divisive questions revolved around the precise definition of the crimes to be within the court's jurisdiction, the breadth of that jurisdiction and just who would determine which cases should be brought. The U.S. went in with goals that allied it uncomfortably with China, Russia and India, as well as Libya and Algeria, but put it at odds with most of its usual friends who gathered among the so-called Like-Minded Nations seeking a strong and independent Court. "We are not here," said Washington's U.N. ambassador, Bill Richardson, "to create a court that sits in judgment on national systems." The U.S. is concerned that its many soldiers serving overseas could become involved in confrontations that would make them vulnerable to what an Administration official called "frivolous claims by politically motivated governments."

The Washington negotiators—who rejected universal jurisdiction, subjecting any state, signatory or not, to the court's remit—agreed that the court should have automatic jurisdiction in the case of genocide, giving it the ability to prosecute individuals of any country that had signed the treaty. But they sought a clause allowing countries to opt out of the court's jurisdiction on war crimes and crimes against humanity for 10 years. The agreed statute allows states to opt out of the court's jurisdictions only on war crimes and only for seven years. It also includes the crime of "aggression" within the court's jurisdiction, subject to a precise definition of aggression. Washington had also wanted to give only the Security Council and states party to the agreement the right to bring cases to the court. The statute, however, also empowers the prosecutor to initiate cases. The U.S. did manage to get a compromise, promoted by Singapore, allowing the Security Council to call a 12-month renewable halt to investigations and prosecutions included in the text. "If states can simply opt in or out when they want, the court will be unworkable," said a senior official in the German delegation. Without an independent prosecutor, he added, "crimes will be passed over for political reasons."

Although conference chairman Philippe Kirsch of Canada had already successfully chaired at least eight international conferences—brokering agreements on issues such as terrorism and the protection of war victims—all his undoubted mediation skills failed to resolve the disputes. As Washington became increasingly isolated, a copy of U.S. "talking points" circulated among the delegations, suggesting that if the court did not meet U.S. requirements Washington might retaliate by withdrawing its troops overseas, including those in Europe. Although few believed in that possibility and the Administration downplayed it, State Department spokesman Jamie Rubin explained that "The U.S. has a special responsibility that other governments do not have."

After all the wrangling, what emerged was a court to be located in The Hague—where the International Court of Justice already deals with cases brought on a civil basis by states against other states. It is to contain four elements: a Presidency with three judges; a section encompassing an appeals division, trial and pre-trial divisions; a Prosecutor's office; and a Registry to handle administration. The court, which will act only when national courts are "unwilling or unable genuinely" to proceed, will confine its maximum penalty to life imprisonment.

How the court will fare without the support of the U.S. is unclear. Washington has provided vital political backing for the Yugoslav and Rwanda tribunals and continues to be their leading financier. "We have shown that the only way to get war criminals to trial is for the U.S. to take a prominent role," said one Administration official last week. "If the U.S. is not a lead player in the creation of this court, it doesn't happen."

Nevertheless, the fact that a court with teeth has actually been created was an unprecedented move by the world community to make the rule of law finally prevail over brute force—a step towards fulfilling Secretary-General Annan's pledge that "At long last we aim to prove we mean it when we say 'Never Again.'"

Enforcing Human Rights

Karl E. Meyer

In the century's surprising finale, human rights in its many guises has become a pervasive global cause, culminating in the most unusual of modern wars, the NATO intervention in Kosovo. As never before, the foreign news is seemingly dominated by demands for basic political rights and protests against internal repression. Stories involving human rights, or their absence, flow from lands of every description, ranging from the Vale of Kashmir to tiny East Timor in Asia, from every region of Africa, and from almost every ex-Soviet republic from the Baltic to the Caspian Sea. So strong is the tide that human rights offenses long past are being tried anew, either in British courts in the case of Chile's General Augusto Pinochet, or in American films and academic treatises in the case of African slavery.

Politics and technology help explain this development. Public diplomacy abhors a void, and with the end of the Cold War, there has been a palpable hunger for a unifying doctrine. Thus, the long ignored and most blatantly flouted of international covenants, the Universal Declaration of Human Rights, adopted by the United Nations in 1948, has assumed a robust second life. Its principles are advanced by an aggressive phalanx of nongovernmental organizations, notably Amnesty International, Doctors Without Borders, and Human Rights Watch. With an assist from pop stars and British royals, most Westerners are now conversant with the current vocabulary of human rights: boat people, "ethnic cleansing," Free Tibet, land mines, Live Aid, female mutilation, and that most misleading media mantra, the "international community." For Westerners, what happened in Kosovo was a good deal more than "a quarrel in a far away country between people of whom we know nothing," as Neville Chamberlain said of Czechoslovakia in 1938 (a phrase echoed by Secretary of State Warren Christopher, speaking about Bosnia in 1993).

For non-Westerners stifled by authoritarian regimes, human rights have acquired a different resonance. They provide a weapon of opposition that can generate foreign attention and even in some cases (Kosovo, for example) trigger intervention. On its face, prospects for moving forward appear promising. Earlier debates on the alleged conflict between "Asian values" and the U.N. declaration have abated, and the consensus on universal norms seems broad and hopeful. The failure of communism has given widespread and practical luster to such democratic values as free speech, civil society, the rule of law, and electoral accountability. Propitiously, new technologies have bored holes in closed frontiers. Fax machines, cellular telephones, and the Internet now feed the agitation against the hard-line ayatollahs of Iran and the Burmese jailers of Aung San Suu Kyi.

Yet however welcome to human rights activists, these favorable developments have raised expectations that cannot plausibly be realized. The American role is critical. No forward movement is possible without Washington's support and leadership, but the very exercise of such leadership stirs an outcry against U.S. hegemony abroad and a backlash from left and right at home. In truth, American policy has neither direction nor strategy but is a melange of bromidic phrases. At a recent panel discussion in New York, a Peruvian human rights worker confessed he could not understand why the Clinton administration, having uttered the right sentiments about repression in his country, went on to help finance a draconian narcotics sweep by the hated security police, bent U.S. laws to sell advanced warplanes to the all-too powerful military, and gave its blessing to fiscal measures that punish the poor and undermine Peruvian democracy. Asked what he most sought from Washington, he offered a one-word answer: "Coherence."

Wilsonian Trappings in the Real World

The rebuke is valid, but in the circumstances, inescapable. There is no "international community" in any meaningful sense, only its simulacrum in the form of an enfeebled (and insolvent) United Nations and a toothless World Court. Despite all the Wilsonian trappings, the world today substantially resembles that of 1900: one global superpower (America, in place of Britain), a dozen or so pivotal powers (Britain, Germany, France, Russia, China, Japan, India, Brazil, Indonesia, Israel, Turkey, Pakistan, and South Africa), and upward of 150 lesser entities, most of them poor and dependent. Granted, the old colonial empires have melted away, but from the human rights vantage, this is not always a plus. For reasons of crass self-interest, colonial powers maintained a monopoly on the use of force, put down regional and ethnic separatists, and imposed a rough Hobbesian peace. As we have seen in Rwanda, Bosnia, and Somalia, the "international community" has failed to devise a more acceptable, and effective, substitute.

In the nineteenth century, it is worth recalling, a "power" was defined as a country strong enough to resist foreign intervention. The distinction still holds. It is highly unlikely, putting it mildly, that the "international community" would ever intervene forcibly on human rights grounds against any of the pivotal powers. To be sure, sanctions of various degrees of severity are feasible, and can have teeth, as in the case of South Africa during the apartheid era. But this was an exception. In the post—Cold War era, pivotal powers generally get a human rights pass: consider Turkey and the Kurds, China and the Tibetans, Russia and the Chechens. Thus, harsher measures invariably apply to the weak, the poor, and the pariah (Serbia and Iraq). There is no equal justice under world law.

All this is known to policymakers. As the writer David Rieff usefully reminds us, officials reserve their lofty phrases for the public pulpit, and in private employ terms that Bismark would have no trouble understanding.[1] In that realistic spirit, one should attempt to sort out the policy choices for the United States in the coming decades. In my view, they boil down to three. Washington could dispense with cant and unilaterally proclaim a Pax Americana, dispatching Marines or cruise missiles, when necessary, to rush in humanitarian aid, prevent massacres, and punish tyrants. A second option would be to heed George Kennan's advice: abjure interventionist meddling, address our own neglected ills, and lead by moral example. Or Washington could, for the first time, make a serious commitment to collective action, building on structures that already exist, and thereby give some meaning to the hollow phrase "international community."

The perils of the first course were apparent in the Clinton administration's punitive air strikes in 1998 against presumed terrorists in Afghanistan and Sudan. The suspicion that President Clinton was trying to change the subject during the impeachment proceedings against him sharpened when the Pentagon could not confirm that a factory it destroyed in Khartoum actually produced chemical weapons. To the peril of seeming cynical and incompetent when operations misfire is added the peril of seeming a hegemonic bully when missions succeed. In any case, unilateral military adventures are easier to initiate than to end. Previous American "police actions" in Haiti, the Dominican Republic, and Nicaragua turned into occupations that endured through six American administrations, from William Howard Taft to Franklin D. Roosevelt (who is still remembered in Latin America as the good neighbor who pulled out the Marines).

The problem with George Kennan's prescription is its unfeasibility in a multiethnic democracy in which legislators play so important a role in foreign policy. One may sympathize with Kennan's distaste for moralizing bombast from members of Congress, but that is the price of popular democracy. Indeed, examined more closely, our melting-pot diplomacy, whatever its periodic excesses, has also had its triumphs. While serving as secretary of state, Henry Kissinger deplored the Jackson-Vanik Act that attached human rights conditions to most-favored-nation trade benefits, and he was at best lukewarm about the human rights provisions in the 1975 Helsinki Accords that gave all signatories the right to inquire into and judge compliance—yet both helped to legitimize internal opposition to Soviet repression. We tend as well to forget that in enacting economic sanctions against South Africa, Congress overrode President Reagan's veto—an instance in which a legislative measure palpably fostered peaceful change in another country. All these measures were attributable to human rights agitation and melting-pot politics, and all involved the kind of moralizing intervention that George Kennan too indiscriminately deplores.

If popular involvement in foreign policy is integral to our system, why not turn this to advantage? Why not tap the undoubted reserves of American goodwill and generosity, as evidenced in the continuing vitality of the Peace Corps? For starters, the next president could reverse course and support the 1998 Rome Statute creating an International Criminal Court, ending the need for ad hoc tribunals to try accused war criminals. Why not take the braver course—sign the statute and address its shortcomings while moving forward to full ratification? It is hard to believe that Americans lack the legal wit to safeguard U.S. troops from frivolous prosecutions—cited by the Clinton administration as a major reason for refusing to sign. Had Harry Truman heeded similar warnings from lawyers, to whom every precedent is a slippery slope, the Nuremberg Tribunal would never have been established. (Indeed, a British initiative to give the tribunal permanent status was among the sadder political casualties of the Cold War.)

Additionally, the next president could call upon the country to join with willing foreign partners, notably Canada and the Netherlands, finally to establish a voluntary standby force under the United Nations capable of responding swiftly when genocidal disasters threaten. Of the regrettable features of the NATO intervention in Kosovo, two stand out: the reliance on massive air power to avoid NATO casualties, thus all but destroying the country that was to be saved, and the use of a regional military alliance to bypass authorization by the U.N. Security Council. These were precedents far graver than any of the claimed pitfalls in the Rome Statute, and it would require courage for a presidential contender to say as much. But absent that kind of courage, it is hard to see how anything like a real "international community" will ever emerge.

Washington's Frosty Response

In George Kennan's telling phrase, American support for human rights has been declaratory in nature, not contractual. This was so from the outset. The Truman administration was delighted when Eleanor Roosevelt gained unanimous General Assembly approval in 1948 for the Universal Declaration of Human Rights (48 in favor, none opposed, two absent, and eight abstentions, mostly Soviet bloc delegates). As the first chairman of the U.N. Human Rights Commission, Mrs. Roosevelt adroitly coaxed support for language that emphasized individual rights, while it also recognized social and economic rights. Article One paraphrases Jefferson's Declaration, *sans* Creator: "All human beings are born free and equal in dignity and rights. They are endowed with reason and conscience and should act toward one another in the spirit of brotherhood."

Yet when Mrs. Roosevelt, "the First Lady of the World," pressed for ratification of implementing covenants, she met with a frosty response in Washington. As the writer Michael Ignatieff has remarked, American human rights policy is distinctive and paradoxical, "a nation with a great rights tradition that leads the world in denouncing human rights violations but which behaves like a rogue state in relation to international legal conventions."[2] The Senate has refused to approve, or has imposed demeaning reservations on, nearly every important U.N. covenant with respect to human rights. The U.S. Senate, typically enough, deliberated for nearly four decades before ratifying, with qualifying conditions, the 1948 Genocide Convention. (It needs adding that Sen. William Proxmire for three years took the floor daily to express his dismay at this shaming lassitude.)

To be sure, the constitutional requirement of a two-thirds vote for ratifying treaties gives inordinate leverage to a Senate minority. Granted as well, during the Cold War's glacial phase, the United Nations fell so far in American esteem that a Reagan administration delegate invited the organization to sail into the sunset (a geographic impossibility from New York harbor), a sentiment seconded by Mayor Ed Koch, a Democrat. Many Americans, not all of them conservatives, found it unconscionable to be lectured on human rights by members of the Soviet bloc and the Third World majority in the General Assembly. This is now history. The Soviet Union no longer exists, the General Assembly has rescinded its resolution equating Zionism with racism, most of the basic fiscal and management reforms demanded by Washington have been undertaken—yet the Clinton administration and the U.S. Congress still regard the United Nations as something like an unfriendly foreign power, unworthy of real trust, or even indeed of its $1.6 billion in treaty-mandated back dues and assessments.

The result, in the words of Brian Urquhart, is a weak, divided and underfinanced international system, on which the world must prayerfully count to prevent wars (internal and regional), genocide, nuclear proliferation, and environmental calamities. Urquhart, a former under-secretary general of the United Nations, offers a gloomy but accurate summary of what this means: "More than ever it is clear that there is a large hole in this ramshackle international structure—the absence of consistent and effective international authority in vital international matters. The very notion of international authority is anathema to many governments, great and small, until they are looking disaster in the face, by which time it is usually too late for useful international action.[3]

The next president has a history-given opportunity to treat Americans as grownups, by stating plainly that this country has neither the wit nor the resources to be the world's sheriff, that sharing global obligations makes political and fiscal sense, that a new administration wishes to work with others to clear out land mines everywhere, that it welcomes proposals for training international police, and indeed would even consider (as David Rieff suggests) some form of long-term authority in places like Kosovo, where creating stable political arrangements may take a generation.

A specific and useful proposal is already on the table: the creation of a multinational standby force that could be rapidly deployed to check genocidal massacres. No matter that such crises are infrequent: when they occur, the aftershocks endure for decades. Interestingly, when such a force was first proposed in 1992, it was endorsed by candidate Bill Clinton: "We should explore the possibility of creating a standby, voluntary U.N. rapid deployment force to deter aggression against small states and to protect humanitarian relief shipments."

The standby proposal originated in "An Agenda for Peace," a report to the Security Council by Egypt's Boutros Boutros-Ghali, a smart, abrasive, and unpopular U.N. secretary general. As he was at pains to emphasize, he was not suggesting the formation of a U.N. army but instead asking as many nations as possible to make available troops on a standby basis, so operations could get underway in days, not months. Such a force was envisioned in Article 43 of the U.N. Charter, under which all members "undertake to make available to the Security Council, on its call and in accordance with a special agreement… armed forces, assistance, and facilities, including rights of passage, necessary for the purpose of maintaining international peace and security."

Fatal Timing

Boutros-Ghali's proposal had merit, but his timing was fatal. In 1993, the untested Clinton team inherited from the Bush administration a muddled humanitarian mission in Somalia meant to feed a stricken people without taking sides in a civil war. Although nominally under U.N. auspices, Operation Restore Hope was directly controlled by the United States, which provided most of the troops. On October 3, 1993, eighteen U.S. Rangers were killed in a skirmish, a shaken President Clinton pulled back and out, and hopes for a multinational standby force died in the mean streets of Mogadishu.

The need for such a force was underscored with horrific finality in April 1994, with the outbreak of ethnic massacres in Rwanda. A small U.N. force of 2,500 troops was instantly withdrawn from the Rwandan capital, Kigali, and Washington blocked Security Council authorization for a stronger force, among the gravest foreign affairs mistakes by the Clinton White House. Around 800,000 Rwandans were slain; the slaughter was followed by the exodus of 2.5 million refugees and a cycle of violence in Central Africa whose end is not in sight. In his memoirs, Boutros-Ghali recalls a White House meeting in May 1994 at which, to his surprise, the president all but shrugged off Rwanda to discuss the appointment of an inspector general at the United Nations and the naming of his candidate as the director of the United Nations International Children's Emergency Fund (UNICEF). (Years later, it should be noted, President Clinton more creditably acknowledged American culpability in failing to respond to the Rwanda genocide.)

The Canadian commander of the U.N. force in Kigali, Gen. Romeo Dallaire, asserts that even with two or three thousand troops he could have substantially limited the killings—a judgment supported by Scott R. Fell in a report to the Carnegie Commission on Preventing Deadly Conflict. Fell estimates that a trained force of 5,000 soldiers, deployed in April 1994 could have significantly reduced the toll.[4]

In its indifference to the United Nations, the Clinton administration expressed Washington's abiding bipartisan distaste for multilateral operations in any form, unless there is clear demonstration of American national interest (for example, the Desert Storm operation against Iraq) or an American is in charge (as at the World Bank and UNICEF). Even so, the case for a standby force has gained converts in Washington. In 1998, the Department of Defense quietly won approval for providing $200,000 as seed money for a fund to finance a rapid deployment mission headquarters under Bernard Miyet, the undersecretary general for peacekeeping.

The fund grows out of a Canadian proposal in 1995 for the establishment of such a force, a suggestion strongly seconded by the Dutch. Interestingly, as of July 1999, 85 countries, ranging from Argentina to Zambia, have officially expressed willingness to participate in standby arrangements. The French and the British have offered to make available 5,000 and 10,000 troops respectively. Participants would be obliged to train and pay costs while the forces remained on standby, with the U.N. providing reimbursements after the deployed troops left their country. Of the 85 volunteers, 24 states have already signed a memorandum of understanding with the United Nations, 14 have provided planning data, 23 (including the United States) have listed their capabilities, and 24 have expressed a willingness to take part. Adding the first three groups together, the United Nations on paper could mobilize 84,000 reserves, 56,700 support troops, 1,600 military observers, and 2,050 civilian police.

This is not a standing U.N. army. Its American equivalent is a trained volunteer fire department, able to respond quickly in emergencies. Deployment would be subject to approval of the Security Council, whose five permanent members—the United States, Russia, China, Britain, and France—each wield a veto. Even so, given America's resistance to multilateral operations, winning approval for such a volunteer standby army would require a fair measure of presidential imagination, persuasiveness, and courage.

How refreshing it would be if the next chief executive reported to Americans on the world as it really is, warned human rights activists that frustration and disappointments were unavoidable, acknowledged that double standards exist and that the "international community" has yet to be created, added that the most likely threats to peace and human rights will arise from civil strife within sovereign frontiers, that to deal with this threat the world needed both regional and international standby reserves, that Washington would do what it could to help, and that as a first step he or she would seek to persuade Americans that it was in their interest to pay the dues owed an organization inspired by American ideals and located in the world's most ethnically diverse city. How refreshing, and how necessary.

Notes

1. See David Rieff, "A New Age of Liberal Imperialism?" *World Policy Journal*, vol. 16 (summer 1999).
2. Michael Ignatieff, "Human Rights: The Midlife Crisis," *New York Review of Books*, May 20, 1999.
3. Brian Urquhart, "Looking for the Sheriff," *New York Review of Books*, July 16, 1998.
4. See *Preventing Genocide: How the Early Use of Force Might Have Succeeded in Rwanda*, which is available, along with the Carnegie Commission's final report on Rwanda, at http://www.ccpdc.org. For Boutros Boutros-Ghali's version of the U.S. response to Rwanda, see his memoir, *Unvanquished: A United States-United Nations Saga* (New York: Random House, 1999). For the pros and cons of the Rome Statute, see the monograph, *Toward an International Court* (New York: Council on Foreign Relations, 1999).

Karl E. Meyer has written extensively on human rights as a member of the New York Times *Editorial Board, 1979–98. He is the author, with Shareen Brysac, of* Tournament of Shadows: The Great Game and Race for Empire in Central Asia, *published in November by Counterpoint.*

From *World Policy Journal,* Fall 1999, pp. 45-50. © 1999 by Karl E. Meyer. Reprinted by permission.

Meet the World's Top Cop

Interpol's Raymond Kendall explains why today's world has him worried.

What is a city cop to do? In the same way that businesses have relocated to profit from a shrinking world, crime networks have stretched thousands of miles to penetrate new markets, find new sources of revenue and influence, or get an edge on the compensation at home. Governments have been less adroit, especially at building effective multilateral mechanisms to meet this more sophisticated threat to their citizens. For the last 15 years, Raymond Kendall has been secretary general of Interpol, a kind of United Nations for the world's police forces. As he prepared to step down in November of last year, Kendall met for several hours with *FP* Editor Moisés Naím in New York City for an exclusive interview on the state of global crime. The world needs to change the way it fights back, he argues. Legalize drug use? Privatize police intelligence? Globalize the courts? Everything is on the table.

FOREIGN POLICY: In your 15 years at the helm of Interpol, what have you learned about global crime that the world doesn't seem to understand?

Raymond Kendall: Well, I'm not sure whether the world is conscious of how rapidly the magnitude of crime has grown. Take the film *The French Connection,* which was a hit almost 30 years ago when I was starting at Interpol. The criminals in *The French Connection* are trying to move 100 kilos of heroin from Marseilles to New York City. Now in those days, there were a few registered heroin addicts in the United Kingdom, but there was no real drug problem in Europe. By today's standards, 100 kilos of heroin is nothing.

Take Operation Icicle, which involved Interpol offices in Athens, London, Ljubljana, Rome, and Vienna, plus Interpol's General Secretariat Analytical Criminal Intelligence Unit, or ACIU. In July 1999, British police found out that a suspect container was due to arrive in Italy. When the container arrived, Italian police searched it and discovered 1,400 kilograms of cocaine. The police decided to leave 500 kilograms of cocaine in the container and follow it to its final destination. It went from Greece, to Macedonia, back to Italy, and then to Vienna, where the cocaine was seized, and its recipients arrested. People read about it in the newspapers and are concerned. But what the world does not quite understand is how much networks have penetrated all countries, how entrenched and dangerous they are.

FP: So complacency reigns?

RK: It really frightens me to see how, in this period of 25 years, we have gone from a situation where there were virtually no drugs to a situation where, quite frankly, today the European continent is pretty well flooded in drugs. And everything else that goes with them. Public outrage has not grown in the same proportion.

FP: The scale of crime, then, has increased globally. Have the kinds of crimes you encounter changed as much? What new crimes have emerged since you've been involved in law enforcement?

RK: I don't think there have been what we might call new, really new, types of crime. There have been changes in intensity, changes in methodology, changes in the way criminals use technology—really, a more businesslike approach to what they do. Local organized crime still exists. But at the same time, criminal groups on the European continent, and extending around the world, instead of specializing in particular types of criminal activity—whether it's drug trafficking, trafficking weapons, trafficking stolen art objects, and more recently trafficking people as a commodity—they have diversified, created networks through which, at any given time, they can adapt themselves to evade capture and profit from many types of criminal activity.

FP: Your job is huge. The world needs to fight a U.S. $400-billion drug trade. The United Nations estimates that criminal syndicates worldwide are making U.S. $1.5 trillion a year. The International Monetary Fund (IMF) estimates that U.S. $600 billion is laundered every year. More than 60,000 works of art are missing. The trade in people is soaring. Terrorism is on the rise. Then you have the stolen cars, the pirated software, and the cybercrime. Recently, you had to deal with more political matters—the extradition of Gen. Augusto Pinochet of Chile and the arrest warrant against Slobodan Milosevic of Yugoslavia. And for all of that, Interpol has a budget of U.S. $23 million?

RK: Yes.

Once Upon a Crime

The idea for Interpol was born in 1914 when Monaco's Prince Albert convened more than 20 countries to discuss international crime. The outbreak of World War I killed their plans for a new international police organization. But in 1923, Vienna's chief of police, Johann Schober, resuscitated the idea, joining up with 138 delegates from 20 countries to form the International Criminal Police Commission (ICPC). Based in Vienna, the ICPC aimed to facilitate international police cooperation.

During World War II, the Nazis took over the ICPC and moved the headquarters to a town near Berlin. Under the command of Reinhold Heydrich, the Nazis used ICPC files, which recorded a suspect's religion and sexual orientation, to track down European Jews and homosexuals.

After the war, Belgian Inspector-General Florent Louwage formed a committee that rebuilt the ICPC as it was intended. In 1946, the organization, then with delegates from 17 countries, chose ICPC's telegraphic address, "Interpol," as its new name and relocated to Paris—then to Saint-Cloud, France, in 1966, and finally, in 1989, to Lyon. Today, Interpol boasts 178 member states.

Interpol has never had policing powers of its own. Rather, it acts as a global clearinghouse for information on crime and maintains vast databases of fingerprints, mug shots, reproductions of missing art, license plate numbers of stolen cars, and more. A system of notices, ranging from red notices for criminals wanted for extradition to green notices for informational purposes, keeps its National Central Bureaus up-to-date. Interpol also helps police bureaus counter a wide range of crimes, from trafficking in human beings and drugs to terrorism. At the request of Interpol Moscow, for instance, U.S. immigration officials located, arrested, and in June 1999 deported a Russian murder fugitive. In October 1999, Interpol assisted the South African Endangered Species Protection Unit and the Portuguese police in arresting four suspects who were smuggling 150 African elephant tusks and 1,000 kilograms of cannabis.

Interpol's 373-person bureaucracy of about 120 police experts and 200-plus support staffers runs on a budget financed by the annual contributions of member states. When a new state joins Interpol, it agrees to pay fixed annual dues ranging from 2 to 100 "units," according to its resources, G7 (Group of Seven) countries pay the maximum contribution. The General Assembly, Interpol's supreme governing body—made up of approximately 400 delegates appointed by the member states—determines the budget at annual meetings by deciding how much money each unit will be worth. In 2000, those units added up to 177 million French francs (U.S. $23 million). The General Assembly also elects officials, such as the secretary general, and decides how to allocate money to Interpol's various programs and initiatives.

In addition to helping countries connect, Interpol now cooperates with agencies within states, as well as non-governmental and international organizations. In October 2000, Interpol agreed to help the Tequila Regulating Council in Mexico combat the export of adulterated tequila by affixing the Interpol hologram on export permits. The United Nations is a frequent partner as well. In 1996, the United Nations granted Interpol "Permanent Observer" status to the United Nations General Assembly, which entitles Interpol to participate in U.N.-sponsored international conferences. And last year, the United Nations Educational, Scientific, and Cultural Organization collaborated with Interpol to create a CD-ROM that reproduces and profiles more than 14,000 stolen works of art.

—*FP*

FP: Didn't you feel at times that perhaps it was pointless? That there is no point in trying to fight so much and so many different kinds of crimes with $23 million a year?

RK: We are a small-budget organization if you compare us with the challenges we face. One of my biggest frustrations, and maybe I have a certain responsibility for this, I don't know, has been how to get the people and politicians to recognize this. In the last few years, for example, at the G8 [Group of Eight] meetings, they say their number-one priority is to deal with organized crime, drug trafficking, and terrorism—and then some of the people at those meetings go back home and immediately reduce their local law-enforcement budgets by 10 percent or something like that. I have seen that happen many times.

FP: Which countries?

RK: It's not a matter of one particular country. It is a general trend—spending lots of time talking about international crime, but acting only when something happens. For instance, in June of last year, 58 Chinese people suffocated in a truck that was going from Belgium to England. And suddenly French politicians decided that the illegal movement of people is a problem, that they must do something. But in fact, trafficking in people is something we've been concerned about, and asking governments to do something about, for at least 10 years.

FP: Sure. But isn't there a long tradition of the police bashing politicians, accusing politicians of getting interested in their problems only when a high-visibility crime generates a public reaction?

RK: You're absolutely right. Politicians make decisions on the basis of good information. It seems that effective communication between police and governments is not there.

FP: Could it be that communication is breaking down because of Interpol? That governments do not trust Interpol, and therefore they would rather bypass you and develop relationships with specific foreign police departments? For instance, when the case of money laundering at the Bank of New York broke, you said you were reluctant to share information with your Russian counterparts because you had a sense that the information could end up in the wrong hands.

RK: I think that is a fact of international political life. We have to manage as best we can. We cooperate with nations that have so many different types of regimes, so many different types of police systems, so many possibilities for corruption. The misconception on the part of the people who have this mistrust is that they think that any information that comes into an organization like ours will be automatically distributed to all the member countries simply because they are members. This is absolutely untrue. We don't own any information, we are entrusted with it. The country that gives us information sets the conditions under which we can share it.

FP: Is Interpol really that secure? A former senior U.S. intelligence official told me with certainty that Interpol had been compromised.

RK: Interpol is secure. We may have, from time to time, like in any organization, some corruption. But I can remember only one such incident at the General Secretariat in almost 30 years.

FP: Tell me, what can Interpol do well and what can it not do well?

RK: There are some basic things that only Interpol can do. For example, being able to circulate throughout the world, throughout 178 countries, information about a wanted person, a stolen work of art, or a missing child. What it cannot do is undertake street action. Interpol cannot do that, and I don't believe it will ever be able to do that in the foreseeable future.

FP: Our sources tell us that recently, Interpol has launched a new project, a new kind of information database. That you have moved from sharing basic criminal information tied to specific events to sharing criminal intelligence and analysis. We are told that a core of 50 or so Interpol member states, including the United States, is collaborating on a project designed to track the activities of Eurasian organized crime in and outside of the former Soviet sphere. Is this true?

RK: It is true.

FP: How is this project an innovation for Interpol?

RK: Before, a lot of information was passed to us that then went into a database that was never exploited. Now, all that data is being examined globally from the intelligence point of view. The key role of strategic intelligence is not to identify specific operational targets, but rather to focus attention on new threats, identifying changing situations and providing the basis for forecasting future trends. We look at such things as the movement of people or goods to find if there is any way we can predict where the next organized activity is going, where we should be looking next.

FP: What is Interpol's Millennium Project?

RK: A majority of European countries are participating in the Millennium Project, providing intelligence information on the newest and most dynamic of the major international organized criminal groups—gangs from the former Soviet Union. The latest estimates are that about 1,000 Russian organized-crime groups are operating internationally, plus 8,000 to 10,000 operating in the area of the former Soviet Union. Each group ranges in size from 50 to 1,000 members. They are best understood as loose networks; they may work together in specific cases and cooperate against common threats, but there is little top-down control and coordination. Their activities include cigarette and other contraband smuggling, drug smuggling, illegal immigration, extortion, prostitution, vehicle theft, and arms dealing. The Millennium Project has demonstrated the difficulties in investigating these organizations in one country or even bilaterally. They operate from several countries and are diversified enough to make it extremely difficult to investigate using traditional methods. Unless approached in a truly multilateral way, with countries really collaborating efficiently, these criminal groups will always have the upper hand.

FP: The millennium Project has been quite effective in tracking property that Russian crime bosses are buying in Columbia.

RK: Yes, that's correct.

CRIME'S NEW POLITICS

FP: What was the most controversial decision you made in your 15-year tenure?

RK: Perhaps the Rainbow Warrior case. As you may recall, in 1985 a ship belonging to Greenpeace was sunk in the harbor in northern New Zealand. The people who claimed to be responsible for the attack were carrying, of course, Swiss passports. To cut a long story short, it turned out that they were members of the French Secret Service. The New Zealand president's position was that the crime has been committed, people should be punished, this is a criminal matter. The French authorities said, "You should not be dealing with this case. This is a political case." Well, I said, "No, this is a criminal case."

FP: What other controversial decision or what other decision looms large in your memory?

RK: Several cases led to controversy when Interpol cooperation was requested. When Interpol refused to help in an investigation of the Chinese religious group Faun Gong, for instance, or an investigation of the instigators of a coup in Qatar. And of course, there was Interpol's involvement in the Pinochet case.

FP: How did the decision to go after General Pinochet come about?

RK: It was initiated by a Spanish judge. If the British had said they didn't agree, that this action shouldn't involve Interpol, then I would have never made the decision to say, "Well, I think it should." But I didn't have to make the decision. Nobody objected.

FP: What was your role, Interpol's role?

RK: Interpol supplied the official channel to enable the Spanish magistrate to contact the British police and provided the legal cover to Spain's extradition request.

FP: And now you're charged with the capture of Slobodan Milosevic.

RK: When I heard there were plans to create this international tribunal for dealing with war crimes in the former Yugoslavia, I said, well, that's fine to have a tribunal, but how are they going to bring people before it? So I wrote to [then United Nations Secretary-General] Boutros Boutros-Ghali and said we will place at the U.N.'s disposal Interpol's system for circulating warrants on these people. At the moment I think there are something like 40 or 50 of these warrants in existence, including one for Milosevic.

FP: And of those that were issued, how many have been captured?

RK: I think about half a dozen. It's kind of interesting that, in fact, there can be real international legal action. And the plan now to create an international criminal tribunal, which unfortunately is being opposed by a certain number of countries, including the United Kingdom and the United States, is a good sign that we will see more of this.

FP: We are increasingly witnessing how countries cede some specific aspects of their sovereignty to an international body such as the World Trade Organization or the IMF. We are also beginning to see more frequent instances in the area of international law enforcement. Do you think that the world is heading toward more and more global tribunals and, perhaps one day, a global justice systems?

RK: The movement started with the war-crimes tribunal that was created for Yugoslavia and was then extended to Rwanda. I think you will find that inevitably it will become a global thing and not restricted to certain countries. The more crime becomes global, the more justice and law enforcement in general will have to become global.

THE CASE FOR DECRIMINALIZATION

FP: You've repeatedly made governments furious by deciding early on and publicly stating that the criminalization of drug use is wrong.

RK: Part of the confusion in attitudes comes from terminology. Words like "depenalization," "liberalization," "decriminalization," and so on can be interpreted a bit freely. I have always strongly believed that a drug abuser is not the same as a criminal. He is not victimizing somebody else, he's not stealing anything. He has a problem, a personal problem that leads him to take drugs. Over the years, I have advocated not reducing the amount we spend on law enforcement, but balancing whatever we spend on repression with at least an equal sum dealing with treatment, education, and so on. That way, we reduce the demand, so producing countries can't say it's not their problem. Because they have a point. It's not really fair to accuse them all the time of being responsible for our problems.

FP: The Clinton administration's drug czar, Gen. Barry McCaffrey, has said that your way of thinking would result in "significantly higher rates of drug abuse particularly among young people and exponential increase in human and social costs to society." How would you respond?

RK: I met General McCaffrey in Brussels a couple of years ago, and he was sympathetic, shall I say, maybe not agreeing of course, but he was sympathetic to the way I view things—making clear what we mean by "decriminalization," as I just did.

FP: Bottom line, your position is that if somebody is captured with cocaine, and there's no evidence that this person has been trafficking or reselling cocaine, this person should not go to jail.

RK: There should be an alternative that enables him to go for treatment. And the only reason, I repeat, the only reason I think there has to be some administrative way of sending people for treatment is because it has been shown that the drug addict, unless you force him, will not voluntarily seek treatment.

FP: A generation or so from now, do you think your successors will look back at the way we fought the drug war these last two or three decades as a big mistake?

RK: Yes.

FP: A big misallocation of resources and—

RK: Now let's be clear about this. I'm not saying that you should take resources away from what the law-enforcement people are doing and put them elsewhere. I say that the mistake is in not giving equal resources to deal with treatment.

FP: How does the balance fall now, globally?

RK: At the global level something like 80 percent is spent on law enforcement and only 20 percent on treatment.

FP: What are the most powerful tools to deal, not with drug consumers, but with the people who are actively engaged in drug production, funding, trafficking, and distribution?

RK: In terms of producers, a good, if limited example, is what the U.N. has tried to do with crop substitution for Bolivia's coca fields. There are a number of approaches like this. If our job in law enforcement is to interrupt the supply of drugs, then our most powerful tool for attack would be international cooperation, good international intelligence, and so on. We produce at the moment a weekly drug-intelligence bulletin. Even our U.S. critics would have to recognize that quite a number of the big recent seizures they've made were based on information coming from our bulletin.

THE CHALLENGE OF CYBERCRIME

FP: You have said that governments were caught unaware by Internet crime and were unprepared to deal with it. But even if they had been aware, what could they have done? What can they do?

RK: I don't think that governments can deal with this issue unless they do it with the private sector. Governments may say they are concerned about cybercrime, that they have created a special group to deal with it, and what does that mean? They just take somebody from the drug squad, somebody from the money-laundering squad, and pull them into a group and call it a cybercrime squad. The kind of expertise we need in this area, the kind of research and development we need, are all in the private sector. And even if you want to recruit the appropriate, qualified people, you can't, because you can't compete with the private sector in terms of salaries and incentives.

FP: Do you have a cybercrime unit at Interpol?

RK: I have a unit, which I would not claim to be better than those government units I spoke about. My people don't have the expertise of those in the private sector. I'm willing to listen to anybody in the private sector who can come up with something we can do.

FP: Have you sought the help of the private sector?

RK: We are exploring a collaboration with a firm called Atomic Tangerine, an independent consulting firm based in Menlo Park, California. We are exploring plans to provide relevant Interpol information to private firms, and, in return, to have those private firms, through Interpol, advise member nations of Internet threats. In the future, more private companies will have access to global intelligence, without cost, to assist them in defending their Internet activities from cyberterrorism and "hactivism." At the same time, law enforcement agencies will be able to benefit from sophisticated technology intelligence gathered by leading Internet firms.

TERRORISM'S CHANGING FACE

FP: What percentage of Interpol's time and resources is spent combating terrorism?

RK: The General Secretariat dedicates 8 percent of its police staff resources—mainly police experts seconded by countries that were, or are, victims of terrorism, such as Italy, Germany, and Spain—to fighting terrorism.

FP: How are the terrorists you encounter today different from the ones you encountered when you took your position at Interpol 15 years ago? And before that, when you were a British police officer?

RK: From exclusively politically motivated or funded terrorism in the 1970s and 1980s, we see a new era of terrorism motivated by pseudo-religious purposes. In fact, these "religious" terrorists are simply criminals. Osama bin Laden comes to mind. Extortion of funds is among the most usual motivations of terrorists, but hidden by ideological cover—the Irish Republican Army, Basque ETA, or Corsican FNLC.

FP: Do you think your successor will have to deal with terrorist organizations that have nuclear weapons at their disposal?

RK: I personally don't think this is a serious threat. Making a nuclear bomb is not an easy thing to do. We have worked with atomic-energy authorities in a group of countries to try and assess the nature of the threat. The general conclusion up until now has always been that for a terrorist organization to do something like that, it would need a great deal of—There are other ways they can do things without going that far.

FP: Are you thinking about terrorism with biological or chemical weapons of mass destruction?

RK: Yes, that is a possibility, though still unlikely. It would be more likely in that area than in the atomic area, in my view.

FP: Would you say the world is doing a better job fighting terrorism than fighting drug trafficking?

RK: Yes, I think so.

FP: Why:

RK: Well, the nature of the problem is such that people other than police become involved to a much greater extent, even at the highest political level. Politicians seem more interested in combating terrorism that drug cartels.

FP: Is there anything that can be learned from the fight against terrorism and applied to the fight against drugs?

RK: Intelligence. A greater application of the methods used to deal with terrorist organizations.

FP: For instance?

RK: Intelligence collection and intelligence analysis again and again, undercover operations, satellite observation, phone and mobile-phone tapping, e-mail interception, and use of information technology.

FP: Which countries have the most effective approach to counterterrorism?

RK: I think the British have always had an approach to subversion that puts them in a good position, in the same ways the United States is in a good position. Also maybe the French. Any country that has a history of battling subversion is better able to handle terrorism than others.

FP: And the failures? Which countries frustrate you in their inability to fight terrorism effectively?

RK: Those countries where politics have prevented them from eradicating terrorism within their borders, and those countries that have used or are still using terrorism as a political tool. I won't give you any names, but open your newspaper on any given day and you will recognize them.

ENDGAME

FP: You said that you are relieved to be leaving your job. Was it a mistake for you to run last time, five years ago?

RK: I don't think it was a mistake. I thought the last time I hadn't really gotten far enough into completing all there was to be done. For instance, I hadn't had time to adapt Interpol's finances to future missions. Member countries request more and more from Interpol, but they refuse to increase our budget. Another term didn't help, though. A solution will have to be found by my successor. Interpol needs more money.

FP: So now it's time to retire?

RK: I think that it's time for somebody else to take over. I don't know why, but there are clear indications that the moment has come to turn the page. One of them, purely coincidental, was the death of Jean Nepote, my predecessor, a man who recreated and built up this organization immediately after World War II. He was a Frenchman, a farsighted person and, in a way, a little bit my mentor.

FP: What kind of advice did he give you?

RK: Mr. Nepote gave me a lot of advice, even after his retirement. The advice that has been most important to the organization was that Interpol needed to adapt to the information technology era.

FP: What have you done in the last 15 years at Interpol that makes you very proud?

RK: Well, I think the fact that the organization has reached the status that it has, in the United Nations General Assembly for instance. That puts you in a stronger position to deal with things than before. I mean, I personally have a kind of status that I did not have 10 years ago. When I started, if I visited a country, I never got to see the interior minister or somebody at that upper level. Recognition for Interpol is something I've struggled for, to get some recognition at the political level.

FP: But I'm interested in specifics. What were Interpol's greatest moments during your tenure? The ones where it showed what it can do, or hinted at its true potential?

RK: The G7 (Group of Seven] summer meetings held in Lyon, France, in 1996, when we gained official recognition of Interpol's prominent role in the fight against transnational terrorism; a day in June 1998 when I delivered my first speech to the United Nations General Assembly in New York; my numerous meetings with U.S. presidents in Washington, D.C., and Davos, Switzerland—these were among the greatest moments in my career.

FP: I am surprised by that answer. I would have thought that you would have singled out specific achievements in your fight against criminals.

RK: There were many of those, but without the political support for Interpol I was fighting for, our efforts to fight criminals would have been doomed.

FP: Is your successor, the U.S. lawyer Ronald Noble, the best person available? Was that a good pick?

RK: Time will tell. But I don't think I should comment on that.

FP: How does one get elected to head Interpol?

RK: You need a two-thirds majority, two thirds of the country representatives present to vote. That's usually about 140 to 150 members. Of course, it's not as if people are being asked to vote from a selection of candidates, there's a preelection procedure.

FP: And how does that work?

RK: There are 13 countries on our executive board. They choose one person out of a number of candidates presented by their member countries for the job. Then that one has to go before Interpol's General Assembly.

FP: So 13 people meet in a small room and decide who the next head of Interpol will be, and then they take it to the General Assembly for rubber stamping. Would that be an unfair characterization?

RK: I think it would be unfair. Those men sitting around in a small group are all individually elected by groups of countries. There are three members from each continent. So it's a bit like countries that have a system where their president is elected by their parliament as opposed to being elected directly by all the citizens of the country.

FP: Throughout the multilateral world, every time there is a need to pick a leader of a multilateral organization, be it the leader of the IMF, the World Trade Organization, or the U.N., there is always a highly political process. Many critics say that the process is so political that very often, the merits of the candidates are not as central to the selection as they should be. Is Interpol different?

RK: When I was appointed, I came from within the organization. I was head of the criminal division, I was seen as the natural successor. The organization had to invent the process for my successor. What is tricky is that now, Interpol has reached the point where political considerations have become very important.

FP: Among Interpol's staff, as well as in the secretary general's office, no? One of the criticisms that has been leveled against Interpol is that the organization gets stuck with either second-rate police officers who countries can afford to do without and send off to your headquarters in Lyon, or officers who are good at milking the system and have their eyes on the easy life of an Interpol functionary.

RK: I can agree with that as a general criticism. Once, perhaps it was true. I think it's no longer valid in the same way. There are ways of fighting that sort of thing, but it remains an issue. Still, so long as the organization doesn't pay its staff directly, totally finance its staff, there will be a problem. The situation has changed in the last decade, and now countries are recognizing the fact that sending highly qualified staff to Lyon contributes to their profile in global police cooperation. But if we want to have a good staff, we need to pay them accordingly.

FP: So, you have drug trafficking that cannot be contained. You have cybercrime that cannot be fought without recruiting the help of the private sector. You have international trafficking in individuals, including children. You have frail democratic regimes that are prone to corruption and capture by criminal organizations. You have international networks that are capable of matching governments technology for technology. And facing all of that, you have a multilateral organization, Interpol, that is neither staffed with the best people nor funded sufficiently to keep up with fast-moving crime. Are you pessimistic?

RK: If I were totally pessimistic, then I would not have remained in office. The feeling I have is that we have been doing a lot of experimentation, without a true strategy to deal with crime globally. Part of it has to do with the major disparity between developed and underdeveloped countries. But then again, there are sufficient indications of successes to go with the failures. For instance, although the world production of counterfeit currency has probably increased by something like 30 percent in the last few years, if we look at the counterfeiting of U.S. dollars, that seems to have gone down. We do have bits and pieces of good news here and there. But the global picture is certainly not cause for celebration.

FP: The European Union has established Europol, and the countries of the Associations of Southeast Asian Nations have launched Aseanpol. These groups of countries all seem to be setting up their own shop. What does that say about the performance of Interpol?

RK: All it says to me is that people have decided, all for different reasons, to reinforce their crime-fighting capabilities. Let's take the European Union. Here we have 15 like-minded countries that came together for political or economic reasons. Inevitably, they will become interested in their internal security, which is very laudable. And if they are willing to put resources into it, that's fine. But they have to understand that there are no drugs, other than synthetic drugs, produced in the EU. So to confront even a basic problem like drug trafficking, they are going to have to look outside the union. And then there is a need for cooperation with European countries outside the EU.

FP: And that's where Interpol comes in?

RK: No group of countries can act in isolation, period. The value and the power of an organization like ours is to be able to create a global frame within which these other people can work together. Unless the world learns how to do that quickly and effectively, international crime will continue to grow.

Want to Know More?

For broad surveys of global crime, see ***Law Enforcement in a New Century and a Changing World: Improving the Administration of Federal Law Enforcement*** (Commission on the Advancement of Federal Law Enforcement, January 2000); Claire Sterling's ***Crime without Frontiers: The Worldwide Expansion of Organized Crime and the Pax Mafiosa*** (London: Little, Brown & Co., 1994) and ***Thieves' World: The Threat of the New Global Network of Organized Crime*** (New York: Simon & Schuster, 1994); and H. Richard Friman and Peter Andreas, eds. ***The Illicit Global Economy and State Power*** (Lanham: Rowman & Littlefield Publishers, 1999).

On the decriminalization of drug use, read Ethan A. Nadelmann's ***"Commonsense Drug Policy"*** (*Foreign Affairs,* January/February 1998). For studies of regional crime, see Raimondo Catanzaro's ***Men of Respect; A Social History of the Sicilian Mafia*** (New York: Free Press, 1992); Gerard P. Burke and Frank J. Cilluffo, eds. ***Russian Organized Crime*** (Washington: Center for Strategic and International Studies, 1997); Martin Booth's ***The Dragon Syndicates: The Global Phenomenon of the Triads*** (Chicago: Carroll & Graf Publishers, 2000); Paul Klebnikov's ***Godfather of the Kremlin*** (New York: Harcourt, 2000); and a special double issue of ***Transnational Organized Crime*** (nos. 2.2 and 2.3, 1997), edited by Phil Williams. On terrorist organizations operating around the world, read the U.S. State Department's ***Patterns of Global Terrorism Index.*** On nuclear terrorism, see Brian Jenkins's valuable article **"Will Terrorists Go Nuclear?"** (*Orbis,* Fall 1985). FOREIGN POLICY has provided regular analysis of terrorist threats, including: **"The Great Superterrorism Scare"** (Fall 1998) and **"Rational Fanatics"** (September/October 2000), both by Ehud Sprinzak; **"Think Again: Terrorism"** (Fall 1997) by John Deutch; and **"Is Europe Soft on Terrorism?"** (Summer 1999) by Bruce Hoffman.

For links to relevant Web sites, as well as a comprehensive index of related FOREIGN POLICY articles, access **www.foreignpolicy.com.**

Article 30

TRIBES UNDER THE MICROSCOPE

Genetic researchers view the world's indigenous cultures as "living laboratories"—but what happens when new science clashes with ancient beliefs?

by Vida Foubister

Patauaki is my sacred mountain

Rangitaiki is my sacred river. Ngati Awa is my tribe, Ngati Pahipoto my sub-tribe, and Kokohinau my meeting place. Mataatua is the canoe whose genealogy binds me to my tribe, the nine tribes of my region and the other tribes of the North whose genealogy stems from the same ancestors as mine."

This traditional Maori introduction, translated by Aroha Te Pareake Mead, manager of Cultural Heritage and Indigenous Issues for the Ministry of Maori Development in Wellington, New Zealand, reveals his identity and standing in the world as it is interpreted by his people.

The Maori, the indigenous people of New Zealand, have a detailed genealogy that traces back to their account of creation, in which Ranginui, the Sky Father, and Papatuanuku, the Earth Mother, sacrifice their deep love for each other and separate because their earthly embrace is suffocating their children, the Maori.

The Maori's belief in this epic love story is strong, and Western notions of evolution and genetic inheritance, despite being presented as scientific fact, do not compete as credible alternatives. Likewise, other indigenous peoples throughout the world hold just as strongly to their own traditional cosmologies.

It is against this backdrop that science, especially gene-based medical research, finds itself increasingly viewed with suspicion by the very populations that would make perfect "living laboratories"—indigenous tribes and other isolated groups whose members share common ancestors and, thus, many distinct genetic traits.

For example, as the Human Genome Project, the publicly funded international effort to sequence or "map" the human genetic code known as DNA (deoxyribonucleic acid), nears its completion, researchers are becoming increasingly interested in the genetic variations between populations. They theorize that analyzing these small differences will help them to identify which genes or genetic mutations put some people at risk for specific diseases, which could lead to medical breakthroughs. Such differences are easier to isolate if the study groups have their genetic homogeneity largely intact.

But here is where science clashes with traditional beliefs. To begin with, such analysis requires genetic sampling, usually by obtaining small amounts of blood, hair or saliva from the subjects. These procedures are simple, but loaded with cultural implications in the case of subjects who identify themselves not just as individuals, but—often more strongly—as members of a tribe or other distinct group.

"There's a basic ideological conflict when it comes to DNA and genes and parts of the body in general," says Debra Harry, executive director of the Indigenous Peoples Council on Biocolonialism in Nixon, Nevada, USA, and a member of the Northern Paiute tribe of American Indians.

"From an indigenous perspective, we are not the owners of our DNA," she says. "We don't have a right to change it and fix it and manipulate it or sell it because it belongs to our future generations. We also have spiritual beliefs about the body, that you don't take a piece of somebody's body from them because it also has a part of their spirit."

Says Barbara Burns McGrath, RN, PhD, a medical anthropologist at the University of Washington in Seattle: "Genetic research is based on Western ideas of improvement and progress and the benefits of science. We're going headstrong into this new biology without really recognizing the fact that not all people, not all cultures, share these values to the same extent."

Mead adds that the whole empirical concept of "true or false" carries little weight where deep-seated cultural beliefs are concerned. "Those who dispel the Maori view, or any indigenous cosmological view, don't seem to realize that the main message of any knowledge system is not whether it is true or false," he says. "It's not about ideas being proven or unproved. The purpose of any people's evolutionary framework is, and always will be, the social, cultural and ethical values that it promotes among its members."

Another problem is that current ethics protocols for obtaining informed consent from study subjects may not address the implications that genetic research can have on family members or the extended cultural group.

"As soon as you say 'Navajo' [an American Indian tribe], then you're talking about not just that person, but a nation," explains Brett Lee Shelton, an attorney in Boulder, Colorado, USA, and a member of the Oglala Lakota tribe. "That person can't speak for the nation, so their sample can't stand for the nation unless the nation agrees."

Such concerns led to opposition that essentially derailed the Human Genome Diversity Project (HGDP), an international effort launched in 1993 to determine the origins and migration patterns of the world's populations. Currently, the HGDP is collecting genetic samples only in China and Southwest Asia and lacks the funding to do so in North America.

But private companies, eager to develop gene-based medicines, are picking up where the HGDP left off.

"Now that the commercial importance of this information is becoming much bigger, that's where all the research is going on," says Julie Delahanty, researcher and program manager for the Rural Advancement Foundation International (RAFI) in Winnipeg, Manitoba, Canada.

Several genomics companies that have sprung up in the past decade are pioneering this research, often in partnership with major pharmaceutical companies.

"Most of the genetic research that's done in isolated communities is driven by companies," agrees Bernard Zinman MD, a senior scientist at Mount Sinai Hospital's Samuel Lunenfeld Research Institute in Toronto. "Sometimes they have agreements [with the study groups], and sometimes they just take the DNA and they do what they want."

This push to study genetic variation is bringing some scientists into contact with indigenous groups for the first time, driving the issue of cultural sensitivity to the forefront.

"There are researchers who work with Native American populations their whole lives and who are very sensitive to their needs," says George J. Annas, a health law professor at Boston University School of Public Health. "There are others who really haven't thought about Native Americans at all and they have no understanding of Native American history or culture or values."

These scientists not only need to overcome indigenous people's concerns about genetic research, but to meet their cultural expectations as well.

William L. Freeman, MD, MPH, director of the U.S. Indian Health Service research program in Rockville, Maryland, USA, says many Native Americans automatically place a visiting medical researcher in the same category as their own traditional healers, often highly esteemed and respected members of the group, which can lead to misunderstandings if expectations aren't met. "They expect a caring relationship, and if the researcher falls into that role without even knowing it and doesn't meet the demands of that role, then people can get very upset about it," he says.

Researchers often are unaware of any cultural blunders they might have made during a project. Often equally unaware is the office or committee set up to monitor ethics protocols.

One relatively simple solution to the problem is to proactively involve the communities in the research projects. One approach, called "community consultation," strives to educate the target community about the nature and significance of the project and invites local input, increasing the likelihood that the project will fulfill cultural expectations and garner willing participation.

"We can be more than people landing in the village square announcing the research project and, when it's over, leaving without a trace," says Timothy F. Murphy, PhD, head of Medical Humanities at the University of Illinois at Chicago.

"As tribal members, we have an obligation to our people. It's our people first and ourselves second."

Other models go further by requiring official community consent for members to participate. Though there's considerable debate about whether or not community leaders should have the right to decide who takes part in certain research projects, tribal governments in the United States already have this jurisdiction on reservation land. Federally recognized tribes are considered sovereign nations within a sovereign nation, and people who choose to live there respect the power of their elected leaders.

"As a native woman, what my elders have said is what I'm doing, and that's protecting the DNA of my people," says Judy Gobert, who serves as the spokeswoman on genetic research for the Confederated Salish and Kootenai Tribes of the Flathead Reservation in Montana. "As tribal members, we have an obligation to our people. It's our people first and ourselves second."

While genetic research holds tremendous promise, and many experts expect the anticipated high-tech breakthroughs will soon change the way medicine is practiced, some question its relevance to the indigenous groups—very often low-income people who even now lack access to basic health care and nutrition.

"The concern that I have is that the cures they're looking for are not going to benefit all of humankind," Gobert said, referring to the fact that much of the research is to combat diseases prevalent in the Western world, not among the populations being studied.

For example, Rural Advancement Foundation International recently cited a Columbia University study conducted in a remote Pakistani village with a high incidence of a genetic disease that leaves men and women completely hairless. The researchers were seeking a genetic cure for baldness, a condition for which consumers in the United States alone spend an estimate $7 billion annually in hair replacement therapies, drugs and other treatments.

"What they're really looking at are diseases of affluent Americans willing to pay for therapies that have nothing to do with health," Delahanty says.

Another widely cited case occurred a few years ago, when the U.S. National Institutes of Health took out a patent on the "cell line" of a study subject who was a member of the Hagahai tribe of Papua New Guinea. A cell line is a family of cells derived from a single parent cell that will replicate indefinitely under the right laboratory conditions, a trait that makes it a valuable commodity in the research world. Some laboratory animals, such as rodents, yield cell lines easily, but establishing cell lines from human tissue is considered difficult.

International pressure from human rights groups and foreign governments, which charged that informed consent had not been sought or given by the Hagahai subject, led the NIH to drop the patent in 1996. The Hagahai cell line, however, remains commercially available through the American Type Culture Collection, a nonprofit organization that authenticates and distributes biological resources worldwide.

In general, however, the odds of finding a lucrative commercial use for any genetic finding are "in the nature of a lottery ticket," says attorney Hank Greely, co-director of the Stanford University program in genomics, ethics and society.

But there's increasing recognition that communities still should have the right to share in the commercial potential, however remote. At the very least, some ethicists contend, scientists should ensure that the communities receive some benefit from participating in research projects.

"Some of us do that by hiring members from the community to be part of the research team," Dr. McGrath says. "This has the dual benefit of sharing some research funds with the community, as well as recognizing their expertise."

Other options include the funding of special health clinics or developing health promotion and disease prevention programs tailored to the community.

An example of a successful collaboration between researchers and their study group is a diabetes project involving the Sandy Lake First Nation, a community of Oji-Cree people in remote, northwestern Ontario, Canada. The partnership began nearly a decade ago when the tribe's chief and council, concerned about the community's unusually high rate of diabetes—five times the national average—invited medical researchers from Toronto to investigate. The project led to the discovery of a genetic mutation—a specific change in the DNA related to diabetes—that places the people at greater risk for the disease.

Originally, the mutation likely was a survival mechanism that evolved hundreds of years ago, when the tribe was a hunting-and-gathering society, explains Dr. Zinman of Toronto's Mount Sinai Hospital. It allowed them to store calories to survive seasonal feast-and-famine cycles. But the mutation became a liability in recent generations as the tribe developed a more settled lifestyle with regular access to commercial food.

The agreement between the researchers and the tribe guaranteed Sandy Lake a 20 percent share of any commercial value that resulted from the study. That hasn't happened yet, but the discovery itself has prompted an aggressive public health and awareness campaign that has convinced many in the community to adopt more healthful lifestyles. The local grocery store now uses Oji-Cree icons to identify low-fat products. Walking trails have been built to encourage exercise, and elementary school children now receive culturally appropriate lessons in healthful living.

> "Researchers have a moral obligation to respect the values and interests of communities..."

"We started with very little understanding about the problem," says Sandy Lake Deputy Chief Harry Meekis. "Consultation and participation have opened our eyes and the minds of those who for years have accepted diabetes as a problem without hope."

The Sandy Lake agreement appears to have succeeded in helping both science and the community, but if it had gone awry, the Oji-Cree would have had little recourse beyond filing a lawsuit, a situation which puts many money-strapped tribal governments at a distinct disadvantage.

"That places all of the burden of policing it on the tribes," says Gobert, of the Flathead Reservation in Montana. "No responsibility is laid on the researchers."

That's why Charles Weijer, MD, PhD, a bioethicist at Dalhousie University in Halifax, Nova Scotia, Canada, wants to see the Belmont Report, the U.S. government's ethics blueprint for medical research involving human subjects, amended to include a "respect for communities" clause.

Meanwhile, groups such as RAFI are pushing several international bodies, including the United Nations Human Rights Commission, the World Health Organization and the United Nations Educational, Scientific and Cultural Organization's International Bioethics Committee, to regulate genetic diversity research as it applies to indigenous populations.

Until such protections are in place, indigenous peoples likely will continue to be wary of gene-based research and its effects on their traditions, beliefs and status as culturally distinct populations.

Says Dr. Weijer: "Researchers have a moral obligation to respect the values and interests of communities and, wherever possible, protect communities in research from harm."

A Canadian citizen, Vida Foubister is a healthcare journalist and freelance writer based in Chicago. She holds a bachelor's degree in cell biotechnology and a master's degree in biochemistry.

UNIT 7

Values and Visions

Unit Selections

31. **Are Human Rights Universal?** Shashi Tharoor
32. **The Grameen Bank**, Muhammad Yunus
33. **Why Environmental Ethics Matters to International Relations**, John Barkdull
34. **Women Waging Peace**, Swanee Hunt and Cristina Posa
35. **Modernization's Challenge to Traditional Values: Who's Afraid of Ronald McDonald?** Ronald Inglehart and Wayne E. Baker
36. **Will the Corporation Survive? Yes, But Not as We Know It**, *The Economist*

Key Points to Consider

- Comment on the idea that it is naive to speak of international politics and economics in terms of ethics. What role can governments, international organizations, and the individual play in making the world a more ethical place?
- The consumption of resources is the foundation of the modern economic system. What are the values underlying this economic system, and how resistant to change are they?
- How easily are the values of democracy transferred to new settings?
- What are the characteristics of leadership?
- In addition to the ideas presented here, what other new ideas are being expressed, and how likely are they to be widely accepted?

Links: www.dushkin.com/online/
These sites are annotated in the World Wide Web pages.

Human Rights Web
http://www.hrweb.org

InterAction
http://www.interaction.org

The final unit of this book considers how humanity's view of itself is changing. Values, like all other elements discussed in this anthology, are dynamic. Visionary people with new ideas can have a profound impact on how a society deals with problems and adapts to changing circumstances. Therefore, to understand the forces at work in the world today, values, visions, and new ideas in many ways are every bit as important as new technology or changing demographics.

Novelist Herman Wouk, in his book *War and Remembrance,* observed that many institutions have been so embedded in the social fabric of their time that people assumed that they were part of human nature. Slavery and human sacrifice are two examples. However, forward-thinking people opposed these institutions. Many knew that they would never see the abolition of these social systems within their own lifetimes, but they pressed on in the hope that someday these institutions would be eliminated.

Wouk believes the same is true for warfare. He states, "Either we are finished with war or war will finish us." Aspects of society such as warfare, slavery, racism, and the secondary status of women are creations of the human mind; history suggests that they can be changed by the human spirit.

The articles of this unit have been selected with the previous six units in mind. Each explores some aspect of world affairs from the perspective of values and alternative visions of the future.

New ideas are critical to meeting these challenges. The examination of well-known issues from new perspectives can yield new insights into old problems. It was feminist Susan B. Anthony who once remarked that "social change is never made by the masses, only by educated minorities." The redefinition of human values (which, by necessity, will accompany the successful confrontation of important global issues) is a task that few people take on willingly. Nevertheless, in order to deal with the dangers of nuclear war, overpopulation, and environmental degradation, educated people must take a broad view of history. This is going to require considerable effort and much personal sacrifice.

When people first begin to consider the magnitude of contemporary global problems, many often become disheartened and depressed. Some ask: What can I do? What does it matter? Who cares? There are no easy answers to these questions, but people need only look around to see good news as well as bad. How individuals react to the world is not solely a function of so-called objective reality but a reflection of themselves. Different people react differently to the same world.

As stated at the beginning of the first unit, the study of global issues is the study of people. The study of people, furthermore, is the study of both values and the level of commitment supporting these values and beliefs.

It is one of the goals of this book to stimulate you, the reader, to react intellectually and emotionally to the discussion and description of various global challenges. In the process of studying these issues, hopefully you have had some new insights into your own values and commitments. In the presentation of the allegory of the balloon, the third color added represented the "meta" component, all of those qualities that make human beings unique. It is these qualities that have brought us to this "special moment in time," and it will be these same qualities that will determine the outcome of our historically unique challenges.

Article 31

Are Human Rights Universal?

Shashi Tharoor

The growing consensus in the West that human rights are universal has been fiercely opposed by critics in other parts of the world. At the very least, the idea may well pose as many questions as it answers. Beyond the more general, philosophical question of whether anything in our pluri-cultural multipolar world is truly universal, the issue of whether human rights is an essentially Western concept—ignoring the very different cultural, economic, and political realities of the other parts of the world—cannot simply be dismissed. Can the values of the consumer society be applied to societies that have nothing to consume? Isn't talking about universal rights rather like saying that the rich and the poor both have the same right to fly first class and to sleep under bridges? Don't human rights as laid out in the international convenants ignore the traditions, the religions, and the socio-cultural patterns of what used to be called the Third World? And at the risk of sounding frivolous, when you stop a man in traditional dress from beating his wife, are you upholding her human rights or violating his?

This is anything but an abstract debate. To the contrary, our is an era in which wars have been waged in the name of human rights, and in which many of the major developments in international law have presupposed the universality of the concept. By the same token, the perception that human rights as a universal discourse is increasingly serving as a flag of convenience for other, far more questionable political agendas, accounts for the degree to which the very ideas of human rights is being questioned and resisted by both intellectuals and states. These objections need to be taken very seriously.

The philosophical objection asserts essentially that nothing can be universal; that all rights and values are defined and limited by cultural perceptions. If there is no universal culture, there can be no universal human rights. In fact, some philosophers have objected that the concept of human rights is founded on an anthropocentric, that is, a human-centered, view of the world, predicated upon an individualistic view of man as an autonomous being whose greatest need is to be free from interference by the state—free to enjoy what one Western writer summed up as the "right to private property, the right to freedom of contract, and the right to be left alone." But this view would seem to clash with the communitarian one propounded by other ideologies and cultures where society is conceived of as far more than the sum of its individual members.

Who Defines Human Rights?

Implicit in this is a series of broad, culturally grounded objections. Historically, in a number of non-Western cultures, individuals are not accorded rights in the same way as they are in the West. Critics of the universal idea of human rights contend that in the Confucian or Vedic traditions, duties are considered more important than rights, while in Africa it is the community that protects and nurtures the individual. One African writer summed up the African philosophy of existence as: "I am because we are, and because we are therefore I am." Some Africans have argued that they have a complex structure of communal entitlements and obligations grouped around what one might call four "r's": not "rights," but respect, restraint, responsibility, and reciprocity. They argue that in most African societies group rights have always taken precedence over individual rights, and political decisions have been made through group consensus, not through individual assertions of rights.

These cultural differences, to the extent that they are real, have practical implications. Many in developing countries argue that some human rights are simply not relevant to their societies—the right, for instance, to political pluralism, the right to paid vacations (always good for a laugh in the sweatshops of the Third World), and, inevitably, the rights of women. It is not just that some societies claim they are simply unable to provide certain rights to all their citizens, but rather that they see the "universal" conception of human rights as little more than an attempt to impose alien Western values on them.

Rights promoting the equality of the sexes are a contentious case in point. How, critics demand, can women's rights be universal in the face of widespread divergences of cultural practice, when in many societies, for example, marriage is not seen as a contract between two individuals but as an alliance between lineages, and when the permissible behavior of womenfolk is central to the society's perception of its honor?

And, inseparable from the issues of tradition, is the issue of religion. For religious critics of the universalist definition of human rights, nothing can be universal that is not founded on transcendent values, symbolized by God, and sanctioned by the guardians of the various faiths. They point out that the cardinal document of the contemporary human rights movement, the Universal Declaration of Human Rights, can claim no such heritage.

Recently, the fiftieth anniversary of the Universal Declaration was celebrated with much fanfare. But critics from countries that were still colonies in 1948 suggest that its provisions reflect the ethnocentric bias of the time. They go on to argue that the concept of human rights is really a cover for Western interventionism in the affairs of the developing world, and that "human rights" are merely an instrument of Western political neocolonialism. One critic in the 1970s wrote of his fear that "Human Rights might turn out to be a Trojan horse, surreptitiously introduced into other civilizations, which will then be obliged to accept those ways of living, thinking and feeling for which Human Rights is the proper solution in cases of conflict."

In practice, this argument tends to be as much about development as about civilizational integrity. Critics argue that the developing countries often cannot afford human rights, since the tasks of nation building, economic development, and the consolidation of the state structure to these ends are still unfinished. Authoritarianism, they argue, is more efficient in promoting development and economic growth. This is the premise behind the so-called Asian values case, which attributes the economic growth of Southeast Asia to the Confucian virtues of obedience, order, and respect for authority. The argument is even a little more subtle than that, because the suspension or limiting of human rights is also portrayed as the sacrifice of the few for the benefit of the many. The human rights concept is understood, applied, and argued over only, critics say, by a small Westernized minority in developing countries. Universality in these circumstances would be the universality of the privileged. Human rights is for the few who have the concerns of Westerners; it does not extend to the lowest rungs of the ladder.

The Case for the Defense

That is the case for the prosecution—the indictment of the assumption of the universality of human rights. There is, of course, a case for the defense. The philosophical objection is, perhaps surprisingly, the easiest to counter. After all, concepts of justice and law, the legitimacy of government, the dignity of the individual, protection from oppressive or arbitrary rule, and participation in the affairs of the community are found in every society on the face of this earth. Far from being difficult to identify, the number of philosophical common denominators between different cultures and political traditions makes universalism anything but a distortion of reality.

Historically, a number of developing countries—notably India, China, Chile, Cuba, Lebanon, and Panama—played an active and highly influential part in the drafting of the Universal Declaration of Human Rights. In the case of the human rights covenants, in the 1 1960s the developing world actually made the decisive contribution; it was the "new majority" of the Third World states emerging from colonialism—particularly Ghana and Nigeria—that broke the logjam, ending the East–West stalemate that had held up adoption of the covenants for nearly two decades. The principles of human rights have been widely adopted, imitated, and ratified by developing countries; the fact that therefore they were devised by less than a third of the states now in existence is really irrelevant.

In reality, many of the current objections to the universality of human rights reflect a false opposition between the primacy of the individual and the paramountcy of society. Many of the civil and political rights protect groups, while many of the social and economic rights protect individuals. Thus, crucially, the two sets of rights, and the two covenants that codify them, are like Siamese twins—inseparable and interdependent, sustaining and nourishing each other.

Still, while the conflict between group rights and individual rights may not be inevitable, it would be native to pretend that conflict would never occur. But while groups may collectively exercise rights, the individuals within them should also be permitted the exercise of their rights within the group, rights that the group may not infringe upon.

A Hidden Agenda?

Those who champion the view that human rights are not universal frequently insist that their adversaries have hidden agendas. In fairness, the same accusation can be leveled against at least some of those who cite culture as a defense against human rights. Authoritarian regimes who appeal to their own cultural traditions are cheerfully willing to crush culture domestically when it suits them to do so. Also, the "traditional culture" that is sometimes advanced to justify the nonobservance of human rights, including in Africa, in practice no longer exists in a pure form at the national level anywhere. The societies of developing countries have not remained in a pristine, pre-Western state; all have been subject to change and distortion by external influence, both as a result of colonialism in many cases and through participation in modern interstate relations.

You cannot impose the model of a "modern" nation-state cutting across tribal boundaries and conventions on your country, appoint a president and an ambassador to the United Nations, and then argue that tribal traditions should be applied to judge the human rights conduct of the resulting modern state.

In any case, there should be nothing sacrosanct about culture. Culture is constantly evolving in any living society, responding to both internal and external stimuli, and there is much in every culture that societies quite naturally outgrow and reject. Am I, as an Indian, obliged to defend, in the name of my culture, the practice of suttee, which was banned 160 years ago, of obliging widows to immolate themselves on their husbands' funeral pyres? The fact that slavery was acceptable across the world for at least 2,000 years does not make it acceptable to us now; the deep historical roots of anti-Semitism in European culture cannot justify discrimination against Jews today.

The problem with the culture argument is that it subsumes all members of a society under a cultural framework that may in fact be inimical to them. It is one thing to advocate the cultural argument with an escape clause—that is, one that does not seek to coerce the dissenters but permits individuals to opt out and to assert their individual rights. Those who freely choose to live by and to be treated according to their traditional cultures are welcome to do so, provided others who wish to be free are not oppressed in the name of a culture they prefer to disavow.

A controversial but pertinent example of an approach that seeks to strengthen both cultural integrity and individual freedom is India's Muslim Women (Protection of Rights upon Divorce) Act. This piece of legislation was enacted following the famous Shah Banu case, in which the Supreme Court upheld the right of a divorced Muslim woman to alimony, prompting howls of outrage from Muslim traditionalists who claimed this violated their religious beliefs that divorced women were only entitled to the return of the bride price paid upon marriage. The Indian parliament then passed a law to override the court's judgment, under which Muslim women married under Muslim law would be obliged to accept the return of the bride price as the only payment of alimony, but that the official Muslim charity, the Waqf Board, would assist them.

Many Muslim women and feminists were outraged by this. But the interesting point is that if a Muslim woman does not want to be subject to the provisions of the act, she can marry under the civil code; if she marries under Muslim personal law, she will be subject to its provisions. That may be the kind of balance that can be struck between the rights of Muslims as a group to protect their traditional practices and the right of a particular Muslim woman, who may not choose to be subject to that particular law, to exempt herself from it.

It needs to be emphasized that the objections that are voiced to specific (allegedly Western) rights very frequently involve the rights of women, and are usually vociferously argued by men. Even conceding, for argument's sake, that child marriage, widow inheritance, female circumcision, and the like are not found reprehensible by many societies, how do the victims of these practices feel about them? How many teenage girls who have had their genitalia mutilated would have agreed to undergo circumcision if they had the human right to refuse to permit it? For me, the standard is simple: where coercion exists, rights are violated, and these violations must be condemned whatever the traditional justification. So it is not culture that is the test, it is coercion.

Not with Faith, But with the Faithful

Nor can religion be deployed to sanction the status quo. Every religion seeks to embody certain verities that are applicable to all mankind—justice, truth, mercy, compassion—though the details of their interpretation vary according to the historical and geographical context in which the religion originated. As U.N. secretary general Kofi Annan has often said, the problem is usually not with the faith, but with the faithful. In any case, freedom is not a value found only in Western faiths: it is highly prized in Buddhism and in different aspects of Hinduism and Islam.

If religion cannot be fairly used to sanction oppression, it should be equally obvious that authoritarianism promotes repression, not development. Development is about change, but repression prevents change. The Nobel Prize–winning economist Amartya Sen has pointed out in a number of interesting pieces that there is now a generally agreed-upon list of policies that are helpful to economic development— "openness to competition, the use of international markets, a high level of literacy and school education, successful land reforms, and public provision of incentives for investment, export and industrialization"—none of which requires authoritarianism; none is incompatible with human rights. Indeed, it is the availability of political and civil rights that gives people the opportunity to draw attention to their needs and to demand action from the government. Sen's work has established, for example, that no substantial famine has ever occurred in any independent and democratic country with a relatively free press. That is striking; though there may be cases where authoritarian societies have had success in achieving economic growth, a country like Botswana, an exemplar of democracy in Africa, has grown faster than most authoritarian states.

In any case, when one hears of the unsuitability or inapplicability or ethnocentrism of human rights, it is important to ask what the unstated assumptions of this view really are. What exactly are these human rights that it is so unreasonable to promote? If one picks up the more contentious covenant—the one on civil and political rights— and looks through the list, what can one find that someone in a developing country can easily do without? Not the right to life, one trusts. Freedom from torture? The right not to be enslaved, not to be physically assaulted, not to be arbitrarily arrested, imprisoned, executed? No one actually advocates in so many words the abridgement of any of these rights. As Kofi Annan asked at a speech in Tehran University in 1997: "When have you heard a free voice demand an end to freedom? Where have you heard a slave argue for slavery? When have you heard a victim of torture endorse the ways of the torturer? Where have you heard the tolerant cry out for intolerance?"

Tolerance and mercy have always, and in all cultures, been ideals of government rule and human behavior. If we do not unequivocally assert the universality of the rights that oppressive governments abuse, and if we admit that these rights can be diluted and changed, ultimately we risk giving oppressive governments an intellectual justification for the morally indefensible. Objections to the applicability of international human rights standards have all too frequently been voiced by authoritarian rulers and power elites to rationalize their violations of human rights—violations that serve primarily, if not solely, to sustain them in power. Just as the Devil can quote scripture for his purpose, Third World communitarianism can be the slogan of a deracinated tyrant trained, as in the case of Pol Pot, at the Sorbonne. The authentic voices of the Third World know how to cry out in pain. It is time to heed them.

The "Right to Development"

At the same time, particularly in a world in which market capitalism is triumphant, it is important to stress that the right to development is also a universal human right. The very concept of development evolved in tune with the concept of human rights; decolonization and self-determination advanced side by side with a consciousness of the need to improve the standards of living of subject peoples. The idea that human rights could be ensured merely by the state not interfering with individual freedom cannot survive confrontation with a billion hungry, deprived, illiterate, and jobless human beings around the globe. Human rights, in one memorable phrase, start with breakfast.

For the sake of the deprived, the notion of human rights has to be a positive, active one: not just protection from the state but also the protection of the state, to permit these human beings to fulfill the basic aspirations of growth and development that are frustrated by poverty and scarce resources. We have to accept that social deprivation and economic exploitation are just as evil as political oppression or racial persecution. This calls for a more profound approach to both human rights and to development. Without development, human rights could not be truly universal, since universality must be predicated upon the most underprivileged in developing countries achieving empowerment. We can not exclude the poorest of the poor from the universality of the rich.

After all, do some societies have the right to deny human beings the opportunity to fulfill their aspirations for growth and fulfillment legally and in freedom, while other societies organize themselves in such a way as to permit and encourage human beings freely to fulfill the same needs? On what basis can we accept a double standard that says that an Australian's need to develop his own potential is a right, while an Angolan's or an Albanian's is a luxury?

Universality, Not Uniformity

But it is essential to recognize that universality does not presuppose uniformity. To assert the universality of human rights is not to suggest that our views of human rights transcend all possible philosophical, cultural, or religious differences or represent a magical aggregation of the world's ethical and philosophical systems. Rather, it is enough that they do not fundamentally contradict the ideals and aspirations of any society, and that they reflect our common universal humanity, from which no human being must be excluded.

Most basically, human rights derive from the mere fact of being human; they are not the gift of a particular government or legal code. But the standards being proclaimed internationally can become reality only when applied by countries within their own legal systems. The challenge is to work towards the "indigenization" of human rights, and their assertion within each country's traditions and history. If different approaches are welcomed within the established framework—if, in other words, eclecticism can be encouraged as part of the consensus and not be seen as a threat to it—this flexibility can guarantee universality, enrich the intellectual and philosophical debate, and so complement, rather than undermine, the concept of worldwide human rights. Paradoxical as it may seem, it is a universal idea of human rights that can in fact help make the world safe for diversity.

Note

This article was adapted from the first Mahbub-ul-Haq Memorial Lecture, South Asia Forum, October 1998.

Shashi Tharoor is Director of Communications and Special Projects in the Office of the Secretary General of the United Nations. The views expressed here are the author's own and do not necessarily reflect the positions of the United Nations.

The Grameen Bank

A small experiment begun in Bangladesh has turned into a major new concept in eradicating poverty

by Muhammad Yunus

Over many years, Amena Begum had become resigned to a life of grinding poverty and physical abuse. Her family was among the poorest in Bangladesh—one of thousands that own virtually nothing, surviving as squatters on desolate tracts of land and earning a living as day laborers.

In early 1993 Amena convinced her husband to move to the village of Kholshi, 112 kilometers (70 miles) west of Dhaka. She hoped the presence of a nearby relative would reduce the number and severity of the beatings that her husband inflicted on her. The abuse continued, however—until she joined the Grameen Bank. Oloka Ghosh, a neighbor, told Amena that Grameen was forming a new group in Kholshi and encouraged her to join. Amena doubted that anyone would want her in their group. But Oloka persisted with words of encouragement. "We're all poor—or at least we all were when we joined. I'll stick up for you because I know you'll succeed in business.

Amena's group joined a Grameen Bank Center in April 1993. When she received her first loan of $60, she used it to start her own business raising chickens and ducks. When she repaid her initial loan and began preparing a proposal for a second loan of $110, her friend Oloka gave her some sage advice: "Tell your husband that Grameen does not allow borrowers who are beaten by their spouses to remain members and take loans." From that day on, Amena suffered significantly less physical abuse at the hands of her husband. Today her business continues to grow and provide for the basic needs of her family.

Unlike Amena, the majority of people in Asia, Africa and Latin America have few opportunities to escape from poverty. According to the World Bank, more than 1.3 billion people live on less than a dollar a day. Poverty has not been eradicated in the 50 years since the Universal Declaration on Human Rights asserted that each individual has a right to:

> A standard of living adequate for the health and well-being of himself and of his family, including food, clothing, housing and medical care and necessary social services, and the right to security in the event of unemployment, sickness, disability, widowhood, old age or other lack of livelihood in circumstances beyond his control.

Will poverty still be with us 50 years from now? My own experience suggests that it need not.

After completing my Ph.D. at Vanderbilt University, I returned to Bangladesh in 1972 to teach economics at Chittagong University. I was excited about the possibilities for my newly independent country. But in 1974 we were hit with a terrible famine. Faced with death and starvation outside my classroom, I began to question the very economic theories I was teaching. I started feeling there was a great distance between the actual life of poor and hungry people and the abstract world of economic theory.

I wanted to learn the real economics of the poor. Because Chittagong University is located in a rural area, it was easy for me to visit impoverished households in the neighboring village of Jobra. Over the course of many visits, I learned all about the lives of my struggling neighbors and much about economics that is never taught in the classroom. I was dismayed to see how the indigent in Jobra suffered because they could not come up with small amounts of working capital. Frequently they needed less than a dollar a person but could get that money only on extremely unfair terms. In most cases, people were required to sell their goods to moneylenders at prices fixed by the latter.

This daily tragedy moved me to action. With the help of my graduate students, I made a list of those who needed small amounts of money. We came up with 42 people. The total amount they needed was $27.

I was shocked. It was nothing for us to talk about millions of dollars in the classroom, but we were ignoring the minuscule capital needs of 42 hardworking, skilled people next door. From my own pocket, I lent $27 to those on my list.

Still, there were many others who could benefit from access to credit. I decided to approach the university's bank and try to persuade it to lend to the local poor. The branch manager said, however, that the bank could not give loans to the needy: the villagers, he argued, were not creditworthy.

I could not convince him otherwise. I met with higher officials in the banking hierarchy with similar results. Finally, I offered myself as a guarantor to get the loans.

In 1976 I took a loan from the local bank and distributed the money to poverty-stricken individuals in Jobra. Without exception, the villagers paid back their loans. Confronted with this evidence, the bank still refused to grant them loans directly. And so I tried my experiment in another village, and again it was successful. I kept expanding my work, from two to five, to 20, to 50, to 100 villages, all to convince the bankers that they should be lending to the poor. Although each time we expanded to a new village the loans were repaid, the bankers still would not change their view of those who had no collateral.

Because I could not change the banks, I decided to create a separate bank for the impoverished. After a great deal of work and negotiation with the government, the Grameen Bank ("village bank" in Bengali) was established in 1983.

From the outset, Grameen was built on principles that ran counter to the conventional wisdom of banking. We sought out the very poorest borrowers, and we required no collateral. The bank rests on the strength of its borrowers. They are required to join the bank in self-formed groups of five. The group members provide one another with peer support in the form of mutual assistance and advice. In addition, they allow for peer discipline by evaluating business viability and ensuring repayment. If one member fails to repay a loan, all members risk having their line of credit suspended or reduced.

The Power of Peers

Typically a new group submits loan proposals from two members, each requiring between $25 and $100. After these two borrowers successfully repay their first five weekly installments, the next two group members become eligible to apply for their own loans. Once they make five repayments, the final member of the group may apply. After 50 installments have been repaid, a borrower pays her interest, which is slightly above the commercial rate. The borrower is now eligible to apply for a larger loan.

The bank does not wait for borrowers to come to the bank; it brings the bank to the people. Loan payments are made in weekly meetings consisting of six to eight groups, held in the villages where the members live. Grameen staff attend these meetings and often visit individual borrowers' homes to see how the business—whether it be raising goats or growing vegetables or hawking utensils—is faring.

Today Grameen is established in nearly 39,000 villages in Bangladesh. It lends to approximately 2.4 million borrowers, 94 percent of whom are women. Grameen reached its first $1 billion in cumulative loans in March 1995, 18 years after it began in Jobra. It took only two more years to reach the $2-billion mark. After 20 years of work, Grameen's average loan size now stands at $180. The repayment rate hovers between 96 and 100 percent.

A year after joining the bank, a borrower becomes eligible to buy shares in Grameen. At present, 94 percent of the bank is owned by its borrowers. Of the 13 members of the board of directors, nine are elected from among the borrowers; the rest are government representatives, academics, myself and others.

A study carried out by Sydney R. Schuler of John Snow, Inc., a private research group, and her colleagues concluded that a Grameen loan empowers a woman by increasing her economic security and status within the family. In 1998 a study by Shahidur R. Khandker an economist with the World Bank, and others noted that participation in Grameen also has a significant positive effect on the schooling and nutrition of children—as long as women rather than men receive the loans. (Such a tendency was clear from the early days of the bank and is one reason Grameen lends primarily to women: all too often men spend the money on themselves.) In particular, a 10 percent increase in borrowing by women resulted in the arm circumference of girls—a common measure of nutritional status—expanding by 6 percent. And for every 10 percent increase in borrowing by a member the likelihood of her daughter being enrolled in school increased by almost 20 percent.

Not all the benefits derive directly from credit. When joining the bank, each member is required to memorize a list of 16 resolutions. These include commonsense items about hygiene and health—drinking clean water, growing and eating vegetables, digging and using a pit latrine, and so on—as well as social dictums such as refusing dowry and managing family size. The women usually recite the entire list at the weekly branch meetings, but the resolutions are not otherwise enforced.

Even so, Schuler's study revealed that women use contraception more consistently after joining the bank. Curiously, it appears that women who live in villages where Grameen operates, but who are not themselves members, are also more likely to adopt contraception. The population growth rate in Bangladesh has fallen dramatically in the past two decades, and it is possible that Grameen's influence has accelerated the trend.

In a typical year 5 percent of Grameen borrowers—representing 125,000 families—rise above the poverty level. Khandker concluded that among these borrowers extreme poverty (defined by consumption of less than 80 percent of the minimum requirement stipulated by the Food and Agriculture Organization of the United Nations) declined by more than 70 percent within five years of their joining the bank.

To be sure, making a microcredit program work well—so that it meets its social goals and also stays economi-

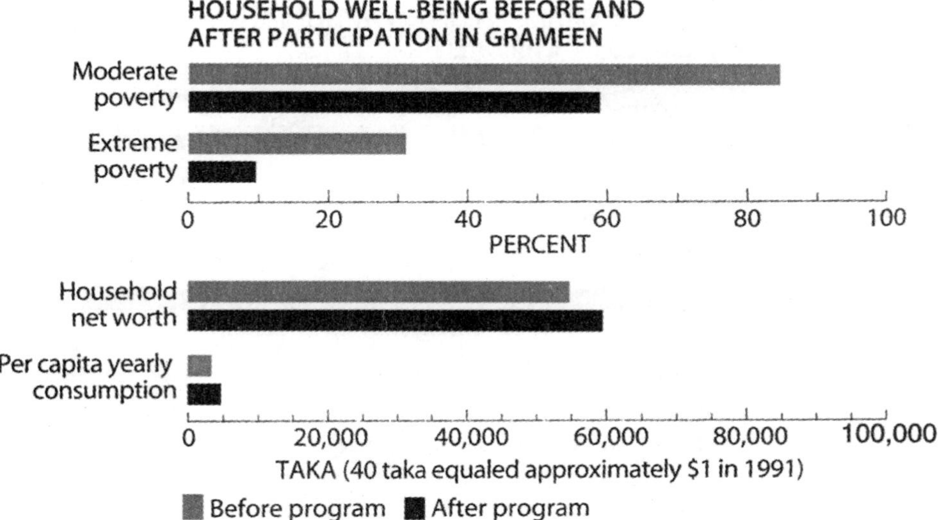

cally sound—is not easy. We try to ensure that the bank serves the poorest: only those living at less than half the poverty line are eligible for loans. Mixing poor participants with those who are better off would lead to the latter dominating the groups. In practice, however, it can be hard to include the most abjectly poor, who might be excluded by their peers when the borrowing groups are being formed. And despite our best efforts, it does sometimes happen that the money lent to a woman is appropriated by her husband.

Given its size and spread, the Grameen Bank has had to evolve ways to monitor the performance of its branch managers and to guarantee honesty and transparency. A manager is not allowed to remain in the same village for long, for fear that he may develop local connections that impede his performance. Moreover, a manager is never posted near his home. Because of such constraints—and because managers are required to have university degrees—very few of them are women. As a result, Grameen has been accused of adhering to a paternalistic pattern. We are sensitive to this argument and are trying to change the situation by finding new ways to recruit women.

Grameen has also often been criticized for being not a charity but a profit-making institution. Yet that status, I am convinced, is essential to its viability. Last year a disastrous flood washed away the homes, cattle and most other belongings of hundreds of thousands of Grameen borrowers. We did not forgive the loans, although we did issue new ones, and give borrowers more time to repay. Writing off loans would banish accountability, a key factor in the bank's success.

Liberating Their Potential

The Grameen model has now been applied in 40 countries. The first replication, begun in Malaysia in 1986, currently serves 40,000 poor families; their repayment rate has consistently stayed near 100 percent. In Bolivia, microcredit has allowed women to make the transition from "food for work" programs to managing their own businesses. Within two years the majority of women in the program acquire enough credit history and financial skills to qualify for loans from mainstream banks. Similar success stories are coming in from programs in poor countries everywhere. These banks all target the most impoverished, lend to groups and usually lend primarily to women.

The Grameen Bank in Bangladesh has been economically self-sufficient since 1995. Similar institutions in other countries are slowly making their way toward self-reliance. A few small programs are also running in the U.S., such as in innercity Chicago. Unfortunately, because labor costs are much higher in the U.S. than in developing countries—which often have a large pool of educated unemployed who can serve as managers or accountants—the operations are more expensive there. As a result, the U.S. programs have had to be heavily subsidized.

In all, about 22 million poor people around the world now have access to small loans. Microcredit Summit, an institution based in Washington, D.C., serves as a resource center for the various regional microcredit institutions and organizes yearly conferences. Last year the attendees pledged to provide 100 million of the world's poorest families, especially their women, with credit by the year 2005. The campaign has grown to include more than 2,000 organizations, ranging from banks to religious institutions to nongovernmental organizations to United Nations agencies.

The standard scenario for economic development in a poor country calls for industrialization via investment. In this "topdown" view, creating opportunities for employment is the only way to end poverty. But for much of the developing world, increased employment exacerbates migration from the countryside to the cities and creates low-paying jobs in miserable conditions. I firmly believe that, instead, the eradication of poverty starts with people

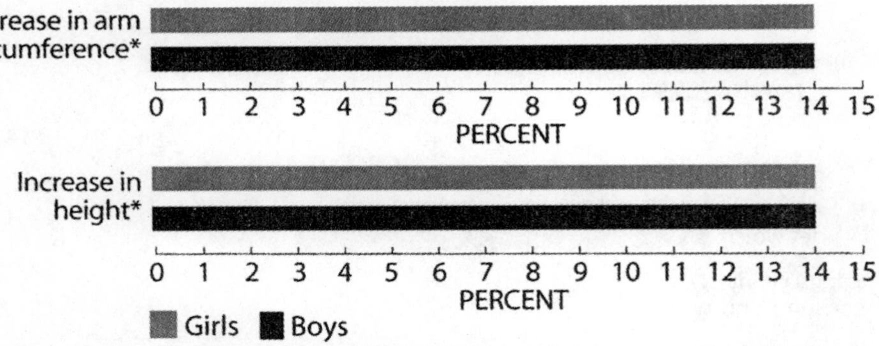

*Bars reflect changes accompanying a 10 percent increase in credit to women.

being able to control their own fates. It is not by creating jobs that we will save the poor but rather by providing them with the opportunity to realize their potential. Time and time again I have seen that the poor are poor not because they are lazy or untrained or illiterate but because they cannot keep the genuine returns on their labor.

Self-employment may be the only solution for such people, whom our economies refuse to hire and our taxpayers will not support. Microcredit views each person as a potential entrepreneur and turns on the tiny economic engines of a rejected portion of society. Once a large number of these engines start working, the stage can be set for enormous socioeconomic change.

Applying this philosophy, Grameen has established more than a dozen enterprises, often in partnership with other entrepreneurs. By assisting microborrowers and microsavers to take ownership of large enterprises and even infrastructure companies, we are trying to speed the process of overcoming poverty. Grameen Phone, for instance, is a cellular telephone company that aims to serve urban and rural Bangladesh. After a pilot study in 65 villages, Grameen Phone has taken a loan to extend its activities to all villages in which the bank is active. Some 50,000 women, many of whom have never seen a telephone or even an electric light, will become the providers of telephone service in their villages. Ultimately, they will become the owners of the company itself by buying its shares. Our latest innovation, Grameen Investments, allows U.S. individuals to support companies such as Grameen Phone while receiving interest on their investment. This is a significant step toward putting commercial funds to work to end poverty.

I believe it is the responsibility of any civilized society to ensure human dignity to all members and to offer each individual the best opportunity to reveal his or her creativity. Let us remember that poverty is not created by the poor but by the institutions and policies that we, the better off, have established. We can solve the problem not by means of the old concepts but by adopting radically new ones.

The Author

MUHAMMAD YUNUS, the founder and managing director of the Grameen Bank, was born in Bangladesh. He obtained a Ph.D. in economics from Vanderbilt University in 1970 and soon after returned to his home country to teach at Chittagong University. In 1976 he started the Grameen project, to which he has devoted all his time for the past decade. He has served on many advisory committees: for the government of Bangladesh, the United Nations, and other bodies concerned with poverty, women and health. He has received the World Food Prize, the Ramon Magsaysay Award, the Humanitarian Award, the Man for Peace Award and numerous other distinctions as well as six honorary degrees.

Further Reading

GRAMEEN BANK: PERFORMANCE AND SUSTAINABILITY. Shahidur R. Khandker, Baqui Khalily and Zahed Khan. World Bank Discussion Papers, No. 306. ISBN 0-8213-3463-8. World Bank, 1995.

GIVE US CREDIT. Alex Counts. Times Books (Random House), 1996.

FIGHTING POVERTY WITH MICROCREDIT: EXPERIENCE IN BANGLADESH. Shahidur R. Khandker. Oxford University Press, 1998.

Grameen Bank site is available at www.grameenfoundation.org on the World Wide Web.

Article 33

Why Environmental Ethics Matters to International Relations

"Environmental ethics [should] not be seen as an add-on to be approached after the important issues of security and economics have been settled. Instead, we [should] recognize that all our important social choices are inherently about the 'natural' world we create."

JOHN BARKDULL

What challenge does environmental ethics pose for international relations? International relations is usually understood as the realm of power politics, a world in which military might and the quest to survive dominate. In this world, moral concern for other human beings, much less nature, is limited or entirely lacking. Environmental ethics—a set of principles to guide human interaction with the earth—calls on us to extend moral consideration beyond humans to other living things and to natural "wholes" such as bioregions and ecosystems. Is it possible to introduce environmental ethics' far-reaching moral claims into the competitive, militarized, economically unequal world political system?

Although explorations in environmental ethics now have a long resumé, the dialogue over the human debt to the natural environment has proceeded largely without reference to international politics, to international relations theory, or even to the literature on international ethics. Practical politics is thus often removed from consideration. And scholars of international relations have barely considered the relationship between their studies and environmental ethics.

Bringing the two fields into the same conversation is possible. International political theory has profound implications for understanding how humans ought to relate to the environment. Realism and liberal institutionalism (the mainstream of international relations theory), by suggesting what political, economic, and social goals are desirable, also imply what environmental values should prevail. They indicate what kind of world humans should or can create and thus tell us how we should relate to the environment. The question then is not whether environmental ethics should matter in world politics, but in which way: which environmental ethic does in fact matter, which should, and what obstacles prevent needed changes in political practices from being made?

WHICH ENVIRONMENTAL ETHICS?

Environmental ethics can be anthropocentric, biocentric, or ecocentric. Anthropocentric ethics is about what humans owe each other. It evaluates environmental policies with regard to how they affect human well-being. For example, exploitation of natural resources such as minerals can destroy forests on which indigenous peoples depend. Moral evaluation of the environmental destruction proceeds in terms of the rights, happiness, or just treatment of all human parties, including the displaced tribes and the consumers who benefit from the minerals. Anthropocentric environmental ethics generally calls for more environmental protection than we now undertake; current unsustainable resource-use patterns and conversion of land to agricultural or urban uses mean that existing practices do more harm to humans than good, especially when future generations are considered. Still, many observers find anthropocentric environmental ethics unsatisfactory because it appears not to recognize other creatures' inherent right to share the planet and considers only their value to human beings.

Biocentric environmental ethics seeks to correct this deficiency by according moral standing to non-human creatures. Humans have moral worth but only as one species among many living things that also have moral standing. The grizzly bear's right to sufficient domain for sustaining life and reproduction has as much moral weight (if not more) as a logging company's desire to make a profit in that domain. Even if maintaining the grizzly bear's habitat means some humans must live in somewhat less spacious homes, the loss of human utility by no means cancels the animal's moral claim to the forest. In short, animals have rights. Which animals have moral standing and whether plants do as well remain matters of dispute among biocentric theorists. Nonetheless, biocentric theory expands the moral realm beyond humans and hence implies greater moral obligations than anthropocentric ethics.[1]

Ecocentric theory tackles a problem at the heart of biocentric theory. In reality, ecosystems work on the principle of eat and be eaten. We may accord the grizzly "rights" but the bear survives by consuming salmon, rodents, and so forth, thus violating other living creatures' right to life. Humans are simply part of a complex food chain or web of life. Given this, ecocentric theory asserts that moral status should attach to ecological wholes, from bioregions to the planetary ecosystem (sometimes called Gaia). Ecocentric theorists are not concerned about particular animals or even species, but with the entire evolutionary process. Evolution involves the "land" broadly understood to include all its organic and nonorganic components. To disrupt or destroy the evolutionary process, reducing the diversity of life and the stability and beauty of the natural system, is unethical. As Aldo Leopold, the environmental philosopher who first developed the land ethic, put it in his 1949 book, *A Sand County Almanac and Sketches Here and There*, "A thing is right when it tends to preserve the integrity, stability, and beauty of the biotic community. It is wrong when it tends otherwise." The emphasis here is on the word "community."

Each of these approaches suggests the need for change in the practice of international politics. Anthropocentric environmental ethics implies the least extensive reform, although these still could be far-reaching, especially with regard to current economic arrangements. Developed industrial economies rely heavily on the global commons for "free" natural services, such as areas to dispose of pollutants. For example, reliance on fossil fuels leads to increases in CO_2 in the atmosphere, and in turn to global warming. Developing countries undergoing industrialization will draw on the atmosphere's capacity to absorb greenhouse gases. The added load, along with already high levels of emissions from developed countries, could push the environment beyond a critical threshold, setting off catastrophic climate changes because of global warming. These climatic upheavals could lead to crop failures and destructive storms battering coastal cities. What is fair under these circumstances? Should developed countries make radical changes—such as decentralizing and deindustrializing—in their economic arrangements? Should they refrain from adding the potentially disastrous increment of greenhouse gases that will push the climate over the threshold of climatic catastrophe? If yes, then anthropocentric environmental ethics calls for far-reaching social and economic reform.

Biocentric environmental ethics also implies considerable economic reform. If animals have moral standing, then killing them or destroying their habitat for human benefit is unacceptable. In particular, the massive species loss resulting from deforestation is a moral failure even if humans profit. Likewise, agricultural practices that rely on pesticides and fertilizers that harm nonhuman species should be curtailed. Warfare's effects on nonhuman living things would also need to be evaluated. Just-war theory generally evaluates collateral damage's significance in the context of civilians killed or injured due to military operations. Yet collateral damage also kills and injures animals that have even less stake and less say in the conflict than civilians. Should their right to life be considered? Biocentric ethics would say yes. If so, virtually the entire practice of modern war might be held as inherently immoral.

Ecocentric ethics implies the strongest critique of current practices. Disrupting the ecological cycle or the evolutionary process is morally unacceptable. Most current economic or military practices would not pass muster. Indeed, in its strong form, ecocentric ethics would require a major reduction in the human population, since the 6 billion people now on earth are already disrupting the evolutionary process and will continue to do so as world population grows to 10 billion or more. Political institutions must be replaced, either with one-world government capable of implementing ecocentric environmental policy, or with ecologically based bioregional political units (ecocentric theorists hold differing views on whether authoritarian government or more democracy is needed to make ecocentrism effective in practice). If bioregionalism were adopted, world trade would come to a halt since each bioregion would be self-sustaining. Wasteful resource use would be curtailed. Long-term sustainability in harmony with the needs of other living things would be the desired end. For some ecocentric thinkers, the model is a hunter-gatherer society or a peasant agriculture society.

The gap between what environmental ethics calls for and what international political theory postulates may find its bridge in the land ethic.

Environmental ethics in each form carries important implications for the practice of international politics. Yet the environmental ethics literature usually pays little attention to obvious features of the international system. This is not to say that environmental ethics bears no relationship to political realities. If realism (the theory of power politics) and liberal institutionalism (the theory emphasizing interdependence and the possibilities for cooperation) both contain implicit environmental ethics, then environmental ethics contains implicit political theory. Yet without explicit attention to international political theory, environmental ethics lacks the basis to determine which of its recommendations is feasible, and which utopian.

Bridging the Gap

The gap between what environmental ethics calls for and what international political theory postulates may find its bridge in the land ethic. The land ethic, as formulated by J. Baird Callicott, recognizes that environmental obligations are only part of our moral world.[2] Although the land ethic implies significant change in existing practices, it does not necessarily call for abandoning the sovereign state, relinquishing national identity or authority to a world government, or even abolishing capitalism. Rather, it asks for balance between human needs and the requisites of preserving the diversity of life flowing from the evolutionary process. The land ethic simply states that which enhances the integrity, stability, and beauty of the land is good, and that which does not is bad. Human intervention can serve good purposes by this standard. (Indeed, Aldo Leopold was himself a hunter, and found no contradiction between that pursuit and his commitment to the land ethic.) Presumably, human-induced changes to the landscape must be evaluated in context, assessing positive and negative effects.

Yet if the land ethic is to provide guidance for international politics, it needs to identify the other values that must be balanced with its requirements. In international politics, these can be determined in terms of mainstream international political theory, realism and liberal institutionalism. Realism and liberal insitutionalism capture much about how the international system works and what values shape international political practices. Thus we can observe the world for clues as to what international theory entails for the kind of world we should create. Although the verdict is not positive for existing practices, this does not foreclose the possibility of change within either paradigm. But how specifically does realism and liberal institutionalism see the relationship of humans to nature?

Realism and the Environment

Realism is generally understood to be amoral. States do as they must to survive. Survival can justify breaking agreements, lying, deception, violence, and theft. Those who fail to play the game disappear. Those who are best at the game dominate the others. Morality, when invoked, is usually a cover for state interests. Certainly, some prominent realists have said otherwise. Hans Morgenthau recognized the moral content of foreign policy, as did E. H. Carr and Reinhold Niebuhr. Nonetheless, realists usually observe the human capacity for "evil" when the stakes are high.

But this negative perspective on morality obscures realism's highly moral claims. Realism asserts that humans naturally form groups, which experience conflicts of interest because resources are scarce. Maintaining the group's autonomy and freedom is the highest good. On it depends the ability of a people to work out their destiny within the borders of the state. Implicitly, this moral project justifies the extreme measures states undertake. Environmental ethics must recognize this as an extremely powerful moral claim. At the same time, international relations theory must recognize that staking this claim, which superficially appears to be a social question, implies a view of how humans should relate to the natural world.

Realism assumes that the state system, or at least some form of power politics involving contending groups, will characterize human relations as long as humans inhabit the planet. The possibilities for environmental (or any other) ethics are limited by this evidently permanent institutional arrangement. Virtually every state action must be evaluated in terms of the relative gains it offers with other states. The struggle for survival and dominance is an endless game in which any minor advantage today could have profound consequences tomorrow. Moreover, as Machiavelli observed, chance plays such a large role in human affairs that immediate advantage is all the prudent policymaker can consider. Thus, to think about long-term environmental trends, for example, is impractical, because an actor that sacrifices present advantage for future gains may not be around to enjoy the fruits.

Perhaps the most significant implication of realism lies in its emphasis on military security. Military imperatives dictate that states develop and deploy the most effective military technology available. The effects on the land of the particular choices made are little considered. No military technology could be more environmentally damaging than nuclear weapons, but these weapons confer maximum national power. Thus the environmental effects of producing, storing, deploying, and dismantling them (not to mention the effects they would have on the environment if ever used) are considered secondary. Here we see how realism as an international political theory is at the same time an implicit environmental ethic: land has little or no moral worth. This is a choice about how humans are to relate to the natural world, not only a choice about how states (or humans) are to relate to one another. A similar argument could be made about the entire range of military technologies, from cluster bombs to napalm to defoliants to biological weapons.

According to realism, the economic institutions of a society must support the most effective military establishment. Societies that attempt to structure economic relations along other lines, such as long-term sustainability, will soon find themselves overwhelmed by other states that make choices geared toward military dominance. States that wish to survive will emulate the most successful economic systems of other states and constantly seek economic innovations that will give them the edge. Capitalism as practiced in the United States and other major Western nations seems to be most compatible with military preponderance.

Realism thus implicitly endorses capitalism, albeit only because it is the most successful economic system at present for enhancing national power (as the former Soviet Union discovered). Capitalism has put the United States at the top of the international order. Others fail to emulate the United States at their peril. Moreover, realism would suggest that because economic growth facilitates military preparedness, autonomous economic growth should override other goals, including environmental protection. Saving a wetland will not contribute as much to national security as producing goods for export. Consequently, realism's emphasis on security leads to embracing the market in its most environmentally heedless form.

Realism's attitude toward the land is that it is territory, an asset of the state, a form of property. The land's status is as a mere resource with no moral standing apart from human uses. It has no life of its own. Prudent management is the most that is morally required. Hence realism shares the modern notion of nature as a spiritless "other" that humans can rightfully manipulate to serve their own ends.

We see that realism's strong moral claim—that a people's right to determine their own destiny, to define and develop their own idea of freedom and the good society, without interference from others—contradicts the institutional arrangements that realism produces. In practice, few alternatives are available. A people who decide that their destiny is to live in harmony with the land, to follow the land ethic's central precept, would quickly lose the freedom to do so through conquest and domination by other states. Aside from the evident fact that many environmental problems require cooperation across political jurisdictions, the competitiveness of the state system ensures that environmental consciousness will not long guide state policy.[3] Realism thus implies an environmental ethic; unfortunately, it is a most pernicious one. Equally unfortunate for environmental ethics is that realism is an undoubtedly incomplete, but not inaccurate, description of how the international system works.

Yet realism's historical and social argument rests on the moral claim that the group is the highest value: that it is within the group that some conception of the good society can be pursued. But surely a good society is one that fosters environmental values, a goal that suffers when nations pursue national security at all costs. As environmental crises mount, the contradiction at the heart of realist ethics becomes more obvious. Perhaps this can lead to changed conceptions of morality.

Ethical standards change. Nationalism, which underpins today's state system, has not driven human behavior for all history (nationalism, for example, had little influence in feudal Europe). Humans can change their view of how best to pursue a vision of the good society. To the extent that the land ethic becomes part of the moral dialogue, institutional change to bring about a healthier human-environment relationship is possible. Nonetheless, realism reminds us that the road to ethical change toward a land ethic likely will be long and hard.

Liberal Institutionalism and the Environment

Liberal institutionalism is far more ready to accept that universal values such as respect for the land exist. Unlike realism, the liberal perspective considers human rights standards to apply across boundaries and cultures. Individuals are the moral agents and moral objects of liberal thought. Individuals have rights that exist regardless of their cultural heritage.

Furthermore, liberalism asserts that these individuals have a particular character. Partly self-interested and partly altruistic, individuals are aware of their dependence on collective action to obtain the good life. The liberal individual also acts, or should, through enlightened self-interest, which is the best way to secure the means of life and protection against bodily harm. Liberal individuals are predisposed to make certain choices. But would they choose a different way of life, namely, one more in harmony with the land?

The question becomes pertinent because it is not at all clear that liberal society is sustainable. Liberalism as manifested in practice is strongly committed to the market system. Indeed, the entire point of liberal institutional international political economy is to find the means to open the world economy to free trade and investment. From this perspective, environmental problems become unintended side-effects of otherwise desirable industrialization and economic growth. The problem for liberalism is simply managing these unfortunate consequences in ways that maintain the open economy. But as the modern market system encompasses more of the globe and penetrates deeper into social life, profound social choices occur, the result of the incremental effects of countless discrete, uncoordinated individual actions. Liberals are comfortable with this way of making social choices due to their faith in progress; the mounting ecological catastrophe might speak against this optimistic view.

Liberal institutionalism cannot escape its entanglement with and commitment to the capitalist market system. In effect, this means that liberal institutionalism can only with difficulty critique that system as it has developed in history. Hence liberal institutionalism will continue to see normal diplomacy and statecraft, the operations of multinational corporations, the growth of free trade and investment, and rising interdependence as progress toward a better world. This in turn exhibits liberal institutionalism's environmental ethic: managerial, limited to mitigation of the market's worst effects, and committed to economic growth and development. The world we should build is on display. It is embodied in the more enlightened liberal states, those that combine commitment to individual liberty, representative democracy, and free enterprise with some degree of environmental awareness. It is industrialized, or postindustrial. It is technologically advanced. It provides a wide range of goods and services to consumers. Environmental concerns enter by way of interest groups devoted to the "issue" rather than as fundamental values that determine which practices to retain and which to abandon.

Like realism, liberal institutionalism captures a large part of the truth about how contemporary international politics operates. It suggests emphasizing certain trends in the hope of dampening others; strengthening the forces for globalization to reduce the impact of military competition. But its commitment to the predominant global economic institutions leaves little room for a land ethic. Liberal institutionalism's anthropocentrism and consequent emphasis on economic growth leads to a relative lack of concern for the stability, integrity, and beauty of the land. Nonetheless, liberal institutionalism is far more open to the possibility of value change and political transformation than is realism. Liberal theory's faith in progress can imply that liberalism itself eventually will be transcended in favor of more earth-centered ethics. Yet current liberal international theory does not recognize or embrace this possibility. To the extent that theory is practice, liberal international theory contributes to the worsening environmental crisis rather than offering a way out.

A NEW DIALOGUE

Both realism and liberal institutionalism are implicitly environmental ethics. They tell us the relationship humans should have with nature, even if they largely base their claims not on ethical choice but on what we must do under existing circumstances. But humans can make conscious choices about what kind of international order to create and maintain. The realist imperative to play the game of power politics or be eliminated from the system depends on a prior choice about ethics and practice. It precludes the possibility of collaboratively engaging the "other" in democratic dialogue aimed at discovering different social practices that do not, for example, lead to environmentally heedless arms races. The "other" must always remain other in realist thought, an assumption that is far from proven. Likewise, liberalism's imperative to rely on the market if we are to achieve individual liberty and social progress is open to question. If the individual is constituted in community—that is, by social practices—then the self-definition of the community can change. Acquisitive individualism and consumerism need not define the individuals.

How is change to come about? More authentic democracy, based on unforced, open discourse, affords the opportunity to choose consciously the kind of world we are to build. The choice need not come about indirectly, as the result of more immediate decisions on how to achieve national security, nor need it occur unintentionally as individuals make the best of circumstances not of their choosing. Engaging in this dialogue will require abandoning the notion that nature and the social are distinct. The social and the natural are inextricable. We constitute nature through our practices at the same time that we constitute the social world. Thus an ecologically informed political discourse will be one that recognizes the environmental ethics embedded in all political worldviews.

Environmental ethics will not be seen as an add-on to be approached after the important issues of security and economics have been settled. Instead, we will recognize that all our important social choices are inherently about the "natural" world we create. We will consciously raise the question of what this particular action means for that world, and we will recognize that it is our responsibility, not something external to us.

NOTES

1. For more on anthropocentric and biocentric ethics, see J. Baird Callicott, *In Defense of the Land Ethic: Essays for Environmental Philosophy* (Albany: State University of New York Press, 1989).
2. See Callicott, *In Defense of the Land Ethic*.
3. This competition also influences the abilities of states to cooperate to deal with transnational environmental problems. States are expected to attempt to free ride or otherwise exploit the global "commons." If environmental cooperation occurs, it is likely due to a hegemonic power or small group of large powers imposing an international regime. Of course, the Hobbesian use of power to make and enforce law is the antithesis of democratic decision making (which could well be a major element of the society's vision of the good life). But because states are and must be short-sighted and self-interested, no alternative to coercive imposition of regimes exists. Whether such regimes would conform to the requisites of long-term environmental sustainability—much less to the integrity, beauty, and stability of the land—is doubtful.

JOHN BARKDULL *is an associate professor of political science at Texas Tech University. His research interests include international political theory, international ethics, and environmental policy.*

Article 34

Women Waging Peace

You can't end wars simply by declaring peace. "Inclusive security" rests on the principle that fundamental social changes are necessary to prevent renewed hostilities. Women have proven time and again their unique ability to bridge seemingly insurmountable divides. So why aren't they at the negotiating table?

By Swanee Hunt and Cristina Posa

Allowing men who plan wars to plan peace is a bad habit. But international negotiators and policymakers can break that habit by including peace promoters, not just warriors, at the negotiating table. More often than not, those peace promoters are women. Certainly, some extraordinary men have changed the course of history with their peacemaking; likewise, a few belligerent women have made it to the top of the political ladder or, at the grass-roots level, have taken the roles of suicide bombers or soldiers. Exceptions aside, however, women are often the most powerful voices for moderation in times of conflict. While most men come to the negotiating table directly from the war room and battlefield, women usually arrive straight out of civil activism and—take a deep breath—family care.

Yet, traditional thinking about war and peace either ignores women or regards them as victims. This oversight costs the world dearly. The wars of the last decade have gripped the public conscience largely because civilians were not merely caught in the crossfire; they were targeted, deliberately and brutally, by military strategists. Just as warfare has become "inclusive"—with civilian deaths more common than soldiers'—so too must our approach toward ending conflict. Today, the goal is not simply the absence of war, but the creation of sustainable peace by fostering fundamental societal changes. In this respect, the United States and other countries could take a lesson from Canada, whose innovative "human security" initiative—by making human beings and their communities, rather than states, its point of reference—focuses on safety and protection, particularly of the most vulnerable segments of a population.

The concept of "inclusive security," a diverse, citizen-driven approach to global stability, emphasizes women's agency, not their vulnerability. Rather than motivated by gender fairness, this concept is driven by efficiency: Women are crucial to inclusive security since they are often at the center of nongovernmental organizations (NGOs), popular protests, electoral referendums, and other citizen-empowering movements whose influence has grown with the global spread of democracy. An inclusive security approach expands the array of tools available to police, military, and diplomatic structures by adding collaboration with local efforts to achieve peace. Every effort to bridge divides, even if unsuccessful, has value, both in lessons learned and links to be built on later. Local actors with crucial experience resolving conflicts, organizing political movements, managing relief efforts, or working with military forces bring that experience into ongoing peace processes.

International organizations are slowly recognizing the indispensable role that women play in preventing war and sustaining peace. On October 31, 2000, the United Nations Security Council issued Resolution 1325 urging the secretary-general to expand the role of women in U.N. field-based operations, especially among military observers, civilian police, human rights workers, and humanitarian personnel. The Organization for Security and Co-operation in Europe (OSCE) is working to move women off the gender sidelines and into the everyday activities of the organization—particularly in the Office for Democratic Institutions and Human Rights, which has been useful in monitoring elections and human rights throughout Europe and the former Soviet Union. Last November, the European Parliament passed a hard-hitting resolution calling on European Union members (and the European Commission and Council) to promote the equal participation of women in diplomatic conflict resolution; to ensure that women fill at least 40 percent of all reconciliation, peacekeeping, peace-enforcement, peace-building, and conflict-prevention posts; and to support the creation and strengthening of NGOs (including women's organizations) that focus on conflict prevention, peace building, and post-conflict reconstruction.

Ironically, women's status as second-class citizens is a source of empowerment, since it has made women adept at finding innovative ways to cope with problems.

But such strides by international organizations have done little to correct the deplorable extent to which local women have been relegated to the margins of police, military, and diplomatic efforts. Consider that Bosnian women were not invited to participate in the Dayton talks, which ended the war in Bosnia, even though during the conflict 40 women's associations remained organized and active across ethnic lines. Not surprisingly, this exclusion has subsequently characterized—and undermined—the implementation of the Dayton accord. During a 1997 trip to Bosnia, U.S. President Bill Clinton, Secretary of State Madeleine Albright, and National Security Advisor Samuel Berger had a miserable meeting with intransigent politicians elected under the ethnic-based requirements of Dayton. During the same period, First Lady Hillary Rodham Clinton engaged a dozen women from across the country who shared story after story of their courageous and remarkably effective work to restore their communities. At the end of the day, a grim Berger faced the press, offering no encouraging word from the meetings with the political dinosaurs. The first lady's meeting with the energetic women activists was never mentioned.

We can ignore women's work as peacemakers, or we can harness its full force across a wide range of activities relevant to the security sphere: bridging the divide between groups in conflict, influencing local security forces, collaborating with international organizations, and seeking political office.

BRIDGING THE DIVIDE

The idea of women as peacemakers is not political correctness run amok. Social science research supports the stereotype of women as generally more collaborative than men and thus more inclined toward consensus and compromise. Ironically, women's status as second-class citizens is a source of empowerment, since it has made women adept at finding innovative ways to cope with problems. Because women are not ensconced within the mainstream, those in power consider them less threatening, allowing women to work unimpeded and "below the radar screen." Since they usually have not been behind a rifle, women, in contrast to men, have less psychological distance to reach across a conflict line. (They are also more accepted on the "other side," because it is assumed that they did not do any of the actual killing.) Women often choose an identity, notably that of mothers, that cuts across international borders and ethnic enclaves. Given their roles as family nurturers, women have a huge investment in the stability of their communities. And since women know their communities, they can predict the acceptance of peace initiatives, as well as broker agreements in their own neighborhoods.

As U.N. Secretary-General Kofi Annan remarked in October 2000 to the Security Council, "For generations, women have served as peace educators, both in their families and in their societies. They have proved instrumental in building bridges rather than walls." Women have been able to bridge the divide even in situations where leaders have deemed conflict resolution futile in the face of so-called intractable ethnic hatreds. Striking examples of women making the impossible possible come from Sudan, a country splintered by decades of civil war. In the south, women working together in the New Sudan Council of Churches conducted their own version of shuttle diplomacy—perhaps without the panache of jetting between capitals—and organized the Wunlit tribal summit in February 1999 to bring an end to bloody hostilities between the Dinka and Nuer peoples. As a result, the Wunlit Covenant guaranteed peace between the Dinka and the Nuer, who agreed to share rights to water, fishing, and grazing land, which had been key points of disagreement. The covenant also returned prisoners and guaranteed freedom of movement for members of both tribes.

On another continent, women have bridged the seemingly insurmountable differences between India and Pakistan by organizing huge rallies to unite citizens from both countries. Since 1994, the Pakistan-India People's Forum for Peace and Democracy has worked to overcome the hysterics of the nationalist media and jingoistic governing elites by holding annual conventions where Indians and Pakistanis can affirm their shared histories, forge networks, and act together on specific initiatives. In 1995, for instance, activists joined forces on behalf of fishers and their children who were languishing in each side's jails because they had strayed across maritime boundaries. As a result, the adversarial governments released the prisoners and their boats.

In addition to laying the foundation for broader accords by tackling the smaller, everyday problems that keep people apart, women have also taken the initiative in drafting principles for comprehensive settlements. The platform of Jerusalem Link, a federation of Palestinian and Israeli women's groups, served as a blueprint for negotiations over the final status of Jerusalem during the Oslo process. Former President Clinton, the week of the failed Camp David talks in July 2000, remarked simply, "If we'd had women at Camp David, we'd have an agreement."

Sometimes conflict resolution requires unshackling the media. Journalists can nourish a fair and tolerant vision of society or feed the public poisonous, one-sided, and untruthful accounts of the "news" that stimulate violent conflict. Supreme Allied Commander of Europe Wesley Clark understood as much when he ordered NATO to bomb transmitters in Kosovo to prevent the Milosevic media machine from spewing ever more inflammatory rhetoric. One of the founders of the independent Kosovo radio station RTV-21 realized that there were "many instances of male colleagues reporting with anger, which served to raise the tensions rather than lower them." As a result, RTV-

21 now runs workshops in radio, print, and TV journalism to cultivate a core of female journalists with a noninflammatory style. The OSCE and the BBC, which train promising local journalists in Kosovo and Bosnia, would do well to seek out women, who generally bring with them a reputation for moderation in unstable situations.

Nelson Mandela suggested at last summer's Arusha peace talks that if Burundian men began fighting again, their women should withhold "conjugal rights" (like cooking, he added).

INFLUENCING SECURITY FORCES

The influence of women on warriors dates back to the ancient Greek play *Lysistrata*. Borrowing from that play's story, former South African President Nelson Mandela suggested at last summer's Arusha peace talks on the conflict in Burundi that if Burundian men began fighting again, their women should withhold "conjugal rights" (like cooking, he added).

Women can also act as a valuable interface between their countries' security forces (police and military) and the public, especially in cases when rapid response is necessary to head off violence. Women in Northern Ireland, for example, have helped calm the often deadly "marching season" by facilitating mediations between Protestant unionists and Catholic nationalists. The women bring together key members of each community, many of whom are released prisoners, as mediators to calm tensions. This circle of mediators works with local police throughout the marching season, meeting quietly and maintaining contacts on a 24-hour basis. This intervention provides a powerful extension of the limited tools of the local police and security forces.

Likewise, an early goal of the Sudanese Women's Voice for Peace was to meet and talk with the military leaders of the various rebel armies. These contacts secured women's access to areas controlled by the revolutionary movements, a critical variable in the success or failure of humanitarian efforts in war zones. Women have also worked with the military to search for missing people, a common element in the cycle of violence. In Colombia, for example, women were so persistent in their demands for information regarding 150 people abducted from a church in 1999 that the army eventually gave them space on a military base for an information and strategy center. The military worked alongside the women and their families trying to track down the missing people. In short, through moral suasion, local women often have influence where outsiders, such as international human rights agencies, do not.

That influence may have allowed a female investigative reporter like Maria Cristina Caballero to go where a man could not go, venturing on horseback alone, eight hours into the jungle to tape a four-hour interview with the head of the paramilitary forces in Colombia. She also interviewed another guerilla leader and published an award-winning comparison of the transcripts, showing where the two mortal enemies shared the same vision. "This [was] bigger than a story," she later said, "this [was] hope for peace." Risking their lives to move back and forth across the divide, women like Caballero perform work that is just as important for regional stabilization as the grandest Plan Colombia.

INTERNATIONAL COLLABORATION

Given the nature of "inclusive" war, security forces are increasingly called upon to ensure the safe passage of humanitarian relief across conflict zones. Women serve as indispensable contacts between civilians, warring parties, and relief organizations. Without women's knowledge of the local scene, the mandate of the military to support NGOs would often be severely hindered, if not impossible.

In rebel-controlled areas of Sudan, women have worked closely with humanitarian organizations to prevent food from being diverted from those who need it most. According to Catherine Loria Duku Jeremano of Oxfam: "The normal pattern was to hand out relief to the men, who were then expected to take it home to be distributed to their family. However, many of the men did what they pleased with the food they received: either selling it directly, often in exchange for alcohol, or giving food to the wives they favored." Sudanese women worked closely with tribal chiefs and relief organizations to establish a system allowing women to pick up the food for their families, despite contrary cultural norms.

In Pristina, Kosovo, Vjosa Dobruna, a pediatric neurologist and human rights leader, is now the joint administrator for civil society for the U.N. Interim Administration Mission in Kosovo (UNMIK). In September 2000, at the request of NATO, she organized a multiethnic strategic planning session to integrate women throughout UNMIK. Before that gathering, women who had played very significant roles in their communities felt shunned by the international organizations that descended on Kosovo following the bombing campaign. Vjosa's conference pulled them back into the mainstream, bringing international players into the conference to hear from local women what stabilizing measures they were planning, rather than the other way around. There, as in Bosnia, the OSCE has created a quota system for elected office, mandating that women comprise one third of each party's candidate list; leaders like Vjosa helped turn that policy into reality.

In addition to helping aid organizations find better ways to distribute relief or helping the U.N. and OSCE implement their ambitious mandates, women also work closely with them to locate and exchange prisoners of war. As the peace processes in Northern Ireland, Bosnia, and the Middle East illustrate, a deadlock on the exchange and release of prisoners can be a major obstacle to achieving a final settlement. Women activists in Armenia and Azerbaijan have worked closely with the International Helsinki Citizens Assembly and the OSCE for the release

The Black and the Green

Grass-roots women's organizations in Israel come in two colors: black and green. The Women in Black, founded in 1988, and the Women in Green, founded in 1993, could not be further apart on the political spectrum, but both claim the mantle of "womanhood" and "motherhood" in the ongoing struggle to end the Israeli-Palestinian conflict.

One month after the Palestinian intifada broke out in December 1988, a small group of women decided to meet every Friday afternoon at a busy Jerusalem intersection wearing all black and holding hand-shaped signs that read: "Stop the Occupation." The weekly gatherings continued and soon spread across Israel to Europe, the United States, and then to Asia.

While the movement was originally dedicated to achieving peace in the Middle East, other groups soon protested against repression in the Balkans and India. For these activists, their status as women lends them a special authority when it comes to demanding peace. In the words of the Asian Women's Human Rights Council: "We are the Women in Black... women, unmasking the many horrific faces of more public 'legitimate' forms of violence—state repression, communalism, ethnic cleansing, nationalism, and wars...."

Today, the Women in Black in Israel continue their nonviolent opposition to the occupation in cooperation with the umbrella group Coalition of Women for a Just Peace. They have been demonstrating against the closures of various Palestinian cities, arguing that the blockades prevent pregnant women from accessing healthcare services and keep students from attending school. The group also calls for the full participation of women in peace negotiations.

While the Women in Black stood in silent protest worldwide, a group of "grandmothers, mothers, wives, and daughters; housewives and professionals; secular and religious" formed the far-right Women in Green in 1993 out of "a shared love, devotion and concern for Israel." Known for the signature green hats they wear at rallies, the Women in Green emerged as a protest to the Oslo accords on the grounds that Israel made too many concessions to Yasir Arafat's Palestinian Liberation Organization. The group opposes returning the Golan Heights to Syria, sharing sovereignty over Jerusalem with the Palestinians, and insists that "Israel remain a Jewish state."

The Women in Green boast some 15,000 members in Israel, and while they have not garnered the global support of the Women in Black, 15,000 Americans have joined their cause. An ardent supporter of Israeli Prime Minister Ariel Sharon, the group seeks to educate the Israeli electorate through weekly street theater and public demonstrations, as well as articles, posters, and newspaper advertisements.

White the groups' messages and methods diverge, their existence and influence demonstrate that women can mobilize support for political change—no matter what color they wear.

—FP

of hostages in the disputed region of Nagorno-Karabakh, where tens of thousands of people have been killed. In fact, these women's knowledge of the local players and the situation on the ground would make them indispensable in peace negotiations to end this 13-year-old conflict.

> The grass-roots, get-out-the-vote work of Vox Femina convinced hesitant Yugoslav women to vote for change; those votes contributed to the margin that ousted President Slobodan Milosevic.

REACHING FOR POLITICAL OFFICE

In 1977, women organizers in Northern Ireland won the Nobel Peace Prize for their nonsectarian public demonstrations. Two decades later, Northern Irish women are showing how diligently women must still work not only to ensure a place at the negotiating table but also to sustain peace by reaching critical mass in political office. In 1996, peace activists Monica McWilliams (now a member of the Northern Ireland Assembly) and May Blood (now a member of the House of Lords) were told that only leaders of the top 10 political parties—all men—would be included in the peace talks. With only six weeks to organize, McWilliams and Blood gathered 10,000 signatures to create a new political party (the Northern Ireland Women's Coalition, or NIWC) and got themselves on the ballot. They were voted into the top 10 and earned a place at the table.

The NIWC's efforts paid off. The women drafted key clauses of the Good Friday Agreement regarding the importance of mixed housing, the particular difficulties of young people, and the need for resources to address these problems. The NIWC also lobbied for the early release and reintegration of political prisoners in order to combat social exclusion and pushed for a comprehensive review of the police service so that all members of society would accept it. Clearly, the women's prior work with individuals and families affected by "the Troubles" enabled them to formulate such salient contributions to the agreement. In the subsequent public referendum on the Good Friday Agreement, Mo Mowlam, then British secretary of state for Northern Ireland, attributed the overwhelming success of the YES Campaign to the NIWC's persistent canvassing and lobbying.

Women in the former Yugoslavia are also stepping forward to wrest the reins of political control from extremists (including women, such as ultranationalist Bosnian Serb President Biljana Plavsic) who destroyed their country. Last December, Zorica Trifunovic, founding member of the local Women in Black (an antiwar group formed in Belgrade in October 1991), led a meeting that united 90 women leaders of pro-democracy political campaigns across the former Yugoslavia. According to polling by the National Democratic Institute, the grass-roots, get-out-the-vote work of groups such as Vox Femina (a local NGO that participated in the December meeting) convinced hesitant women to vote for change; those votes contributed to the margin that ousted President Slobodan Milosevic.

International security forces and diplomats will find no better allies than these mobilized mothers, who are tackling the toughest, most hardened hostilities.

Argentina provides another example of women making the transition from protesters to politicians: Several leaders of the Madres de la Plaza de Mayo movement, formed in the 1970s to protest the "disappearances" of their children at the hands of the military regime, have now been elected to political office. And in Russia, the Committee of Soldiers' Mothers—a protest group founded in 1989 demanding their sons' rights amidst cruel conditions in the Russian military—has grown into a powerful organization with 300 chapters and official political status. In January, U.S. Ambassador to Moscow Jim Collins described the committee as a significant factor in countering the most aggressive voices promoting military force in Chechnya. Similar mothers' groups have sprung up across the former Soviet Union and beyond—including the Mothers of Tiananmen Square. International security forces and diplomats will find no better allies than these mobilized mothers, who are tackling the toughest, most hardened hostilities.

YOU'VE COME A LONG WAY, MAYBE

Common sense dictates that women should be central to peacemaking, where they can bring their experience in conflict resolution to bear. Yet, despite all of the instances where women have been able to play a role in peace negotiations, women remain relegated to the sidelines. Part of the problem is structural: Even though more and more women are legislators and soldiers, underrepresentation persists in the highest levels of political and military hierarchies. The presidents, prime ministers, party leaders, cabinet secretaries, and generals who typically negotiate peace settlements are overwhelmingly men. There is also a psychological barrier that precludes women from sitting in on negotiations: Waging war is still thought of as a "man's job," and as such, the task of stopping war often is delegated to men (although if we could begin to think about the process not in terms of stopping war but promoting peace, women would emerge as the more logical choice). But the key reason behind women's marginalization may be that everyone recognizes just how good women are at forging peace. A U.N. official once stated that, in Africa, women are often excluded from negotiating teams because the war leaders "are afraid the women will compromise" and give away too much.

Some encouraging signs of change, however, are emerging. Rwandan President Paul Kagame, dismayed at his difficulty in attracting international aid to his genocide-ravaged country, recently distinguished Rwanda from the prevailing image of brutality in central Africa by appointing three women to his negotiating team for the conflict in the Democratic Republic of the Congo. In an unusually healthy tit for tat, the Ugandans responded by immediately appointing a woman to their team.

Will those women make a difference? Negotiators sometimes worry that having women participate in the discussion may change the tone of the meeting. They're right: A British participant in the Northern Ireland peace talks insightfully noted that when the parties became bogged down by abstract issues and past offenses, "the women would come and talk about their loved ones, their bereavement, their children and their hopes for the future." These deeply personal comments, rather than being a diversion, helped keep the talks focused. The women's experiences reminded the parties that security for all citizens was what really mattered.

The role of women as peacemakers can be expanded in many ways. Mediators can and should insist on gender balance among negotiators to ensure a peace plan that is workable at the community level. Cultural barriers can be overcome if high-level visitors require that a critical mass (usually one third) of the local interlocutors be women (and not simply present as wives). When drafting principles for negotiation, diplomats should determine whether women's groups have already agreed upon key conflict-bridging principles, and whether their approach can serve as a basis for general negotiations.

Moreover, to foster a larger pool of potential peacemakers, embassies in conflict areas should broaden their regular contact with local women leaders and sponsor women in training programs, both at home and abroad. Governments can also do their part by providing information technology and training to women activists through private and public partnerships. Internet communication allows women peace builders to network among themselves, as well as exchange tactics and strategies with their global counterparts.

"Women understood the cost of the war and were genuinely interested in peace," recalls retired Admiral Jonathan Howe, reflecting on his experience leading the U.N. mission in Somalia in the early 1990s. "They'd had it with their warrior husbands. They were a force willing to say enough is enough. The men were sitting around talking and chewing qat, while the women were working away. They were such a positive force.... You have to look at all elements in society and be ready to tap into those that will be constructive."

Want to Know More?

The Internet is invaluable in enabling the inclusive security approach advocated in this article. The Web offers not only a wealth of information but, just as important, relatively cheap and easy access for citizens worldwide. Most of the women's peace-building activities and strategies explored in this article can be found on the Web site of **Women Waging Peace**—a collaborative venture of Harvard University's John F. Kennedy School of Government and the nonprofit organization Hunt Alternatives, which recognize the essential role and contribution of women in preventing violent conflict, stopping war, reconstructing ravaged societies, and sustaining peace in fragile areas around the world. On the site, women active in conflict areas can communicate with each other without fear of retribution via a secure server. The women submit narratives detailing their strategies, which can then be read on the public Web site. The site also features a video archive of interviews with each of these women. You need a password to view these interviews, so contact Women Waging Peace online or call (617) 868-3910.

The Organization for Security and Co-operation in Europe (OSCE) is an outstanding resource for qualitative and quantitative studies of women's involvement in conflict prevention. Start with the final report of the ***OSCE Supplementary Implementation Meeting: Gender Issues*** (Vienna: UNIFEM, 1999), posted on the group's Web site. **The United Nations Development Fund for Women** (UNIFEM) also publishes reports on its colorful and easy-to-navigate site. The fund's informative book, ***Women at the Peace Table: Making a Difference*** (New York: UNIFEM, 2000), available online, features interviews with some of today's most prominent women peacemakers, including Hanan Ashrawi and Mo Mowlam.

For a look at how globalization is changing women's roles in governments, companies, and militaries, read Cynthia Enloe's ***Bananas, Beaches and Bases: Making Feminist Sense of International Politics*** (Berkeley: University of California Press, 2001). In ***Maneuvers: The International Politics of Militarizing Women's Lives*** (Berkeley: University of California Press, 2000), Enloe examines the military's effects on women, whether they are soldiers or soldiers' spouses. For a more general discussion of where feminism fits into academia and policymaking, see **"Searching for the Princess? Feminist Perspectives in International Relations"** (*The Harvard International Review*, Fall 1999) by J. Ann Tickner, associate professor of international relations at the University of Southern California.

The Fall 1997 issue of FOREIGN POLICY magazine features two articles that highlight how women worldwide are simultaneously gaining political clout but also bearing the brunt of poverty: **"Women in Power: From Tokenism to Critical Mass"** by Jane S. Jaquette and **"Women in Poverty: A New Global Underclass"** by Mayra Buvinic.

• For links to relevant Web sites, as well as a comprehensive index of related FOREIGN POLICY articles, access **www.foreignpolicy.com**.

Lasting peace must be homegrown. Inclusive security helps police forces, military leaders, and diplomats do their jobs more effectively by creating coalitions with the people most invested in stability and most adept at building peace. Women working on the ground are eager to join forces. Just let them in.

Swanee Hunt is director of the Women in Public Policy Program at Harvard University's John F. Kennedy School of Government. As the United States' ambassador to Austria (1993–97), she founded the "Vital Voices: Women in Democracy" initiative. Cristina Posa, a former judicial clerk at the United Nations International Criminal Tribunal for the former Yugoslavia, is an attorney at Cleary, Gottlieb, Steen & Hamilton in New York.

Modernization's Challenge to Traditional Values: Who's Afraid of Ronald McDonald?

"Modernization" means "Americanization" to many who fear a coming McWorld. But a study by two social researchers indicates that traditional values will keep most countries from becoming clones of the United States.

By Ronald Inglehart and Wayne E. Baker

The World Values Survey—a two-decade-long examination of the values of 65 societies coordinated by the University of Michigan's Institute for Social Research—is the largest investigation ever conducted of attitudes, values, and beliefs around the world. This study has carried out three waves of representative national surveys: the first in 1981–1982, the second in 1990–1991, and the third in 1995–1998. The fourth wave is being completed in 1999–2001. The study now represents some 80% of the world's population. These societies have per capita GNPs ranging from $300 to more than $30,000. Their political systems range from long-established stable democracies to authoritarian states.

The World Values Survey data have been used by researchers around the world for hundreds of publications in more than a dozen languages. Studies that have been based on the data cover a wide range of topics, including volunteerism in Europe, political partisanship and social class in Ireland, democratization in Korea, liberalization in Mexico, future values in Japan, and the religious vote in Western Europe.

This article examines the relationship between cultural values and economic globalization and modernization: What impact does economic development have on the values of a culture, and vice versa? Is a future "McWorld" inevitable?

Rich Values, Poor Values

The World Values Survey data show us that the world views of the people of rich societies differ systematically from those of low-income societies across a wide range of political, social, and religious norms and beliefs. The two most significant dimensions that emerged reflected, first, a polarization between *traditional* and *secular-rational* orientations toward authority and, second, a polarization between *survival* and *self-expression* values. By *traditional* we mean those societies that are relatively authoritarian, place strong emphasis on religion, and exhibit a mainstream version of preindustrial values such as an emphasis on male dominance in economic and political life, respect for authority, and relatively low levels of tolerance for abortion and divorce. Advanced societies, or *secular-rational*, tend to have the opposite characteristics.

A central component of the survival vs. self-expression dimension involves the polarization between materialist and postmaterialist values. Massive evidence indicates that a cultural shift throughout advanced industrial society is emerging among generations who have grown up taking survival for granted. Values among this group emphasize environmental protection, the women's movement, and rising demand for participation in decision making in economic and political life. During the past 25 years, these values have become increasingly widespread in almost all advanced industrial societies for which extensive time-series evidence is available.

Economic development brings with it sweeping cultural change, some modernization theorists tell us. Others argue that cultural values are enduring and exert more influence on society than does economic change. Who's right?

One goal of the World Values Survey is to study links between economic development and changes in values. A key question that we ask is whether the globalization of the economy will necessarily produce a homogenization (or, more specifically, an Americanization) of culture—a so-called "McWorld."

In the nineteenth century, modernization theorists such as Karl Marx and Friedrich Nietzsche made bold predictions about the future of industrial society, such as the rise of labor and the decline of religion. In the twentieth century, non-Western societies were expected to abandon their traditional cultures and assimilate the technologically and morally "superior" ways of the West.

Clearly now, at the start of the twenty-first century, we need to rethink "modernization." Few people today anticipate a proletarian revolution, and non-western societies such as East Asia have surpassed their Western role models in key aspects of modernization, such as rates of economic growth. And few observers today attribute moral superiority to the West.

Two Dimensions of Cross-Cultural Variation

1. Traditional vs. Secular-Rational Values
   Traditional values emphasize the following:
   - God is very important in respondent's life.
   - Respondent believes it is more important for a child to learn obedience and religious faith than independence and determination.
   - Respondent believes abortion is never justifiable.
   - Respondent has strong sense of national pride.
   - Respondent favors more respect for authority.

   Secular-Rational values emphasize the opposite.
2. Survival vs. Self-Expression Values
   Survival values emphasize the following:
   - Respondent gives priority to economic and physical security over self-expression and quality of life.
   - Respondent describes self as not very happy.
   - Respondent has not signed and would not sign a petition.
   - Respondent believes homosexuality is never justifiable.
   - Respondent believes you have to be very careful about trusting people.

   Self-Expression values emphasize the opposite.

Source: World Values Survey (http://wvs.isr.umich.edu)

On the other hand, one core concept of modernization theory still seems valid: Industrialization produces pervasive social and cultural consequences, such as rising educational levels, shifting attitudes toward authority, broader political participation, declining fertility rates, and changing gender roles. On the basis of the World Values Surveys, we believe that economic development has systematic and, to some extent, predictable cultural and political consequences. Once a society has embarked on industrialization—the central element of the modernization process—certain changes are highly likely to occur. But economic development is not the *only* force at work.

In the past few decades, modernization has become associated with *post*-industrialization: the rise of the knowledge and service-oriented economy. These changes in the nature of work had major political and cultural consequences, too. Rather than growing more materialistic with increased prosperity, postindustrial societies are experiencing an increasing emphasis on quality-of-life issues, environmental protection, and self-expression.

While industrialization increased human dominance over the environment—and consequently created a dwindling role for religious belief—the emergence of postindustrial society is stimulating further evolution of prevailing world views in a different direction. Life in postindustrial societies centers on services rather than material objects, and more effort is focused on communicating and processing information. Most people spend their productive hours dealing with other people and symbols.

Thus, the rise of postindustrial society leads to a growing emphasis on self-expression. Today's unprecedented wealth in advanced societies means an increasing share of the population grows up taking survival for granted. Their value priorities shift from an overwhelming emphasis on economic and physical security toward an increasing emphasis on subjective well-being and quality of life. "Modernization," thus, is not linear—it moves in new directions.

How Values Shape Culture

Different societies follow different trajectories even when they are subjected to the same forces of economic development, in part because situation-specific factors, such as a society's cultural heritage, also shape how a particular society develops. Recently, Samuel Huntington, author of *The Clash of Civilizations* (Simon & Schuster, 1996), has focused on the role of religion in shaping the world's eight major civilizations or "cultural zones": Western Christianity, Orthodox, Islam, Confucian, Japanese, Hindu, African, and Latin American. These zones were shaped by religious traditions that are still powerful today, despite the forces of modernization.

Distinctive cultural zones persist two centuries after the industrial revolution began.

Other scholars observe other distinctive cultural traits that endure over long periods of time and continue to shape a society's political and economic performance. For example, the regions of Italy in which democratic institutions function most successfully today are those in which civil society was relatively well developed in the nineteenth century and even earlier, as Robert Putnam notes in *Making Democracy Work* (Princeton University Press, 1993). And a cultural heritage of "low trust" puts a society at a competitive disadvantage in global markets because it is less able to develop large and complex social institutions, Francis Fukuyama argues in *Trust: The Social Virtues and the Creation of Prosperity* (Free Press, 1995).

The impression that we are moving toward a uniform "McWorld" is partly an illusion. The seemingly identical McDonald's restaurants that have spread throughout the world actually have different social meanings and fulfill dif-

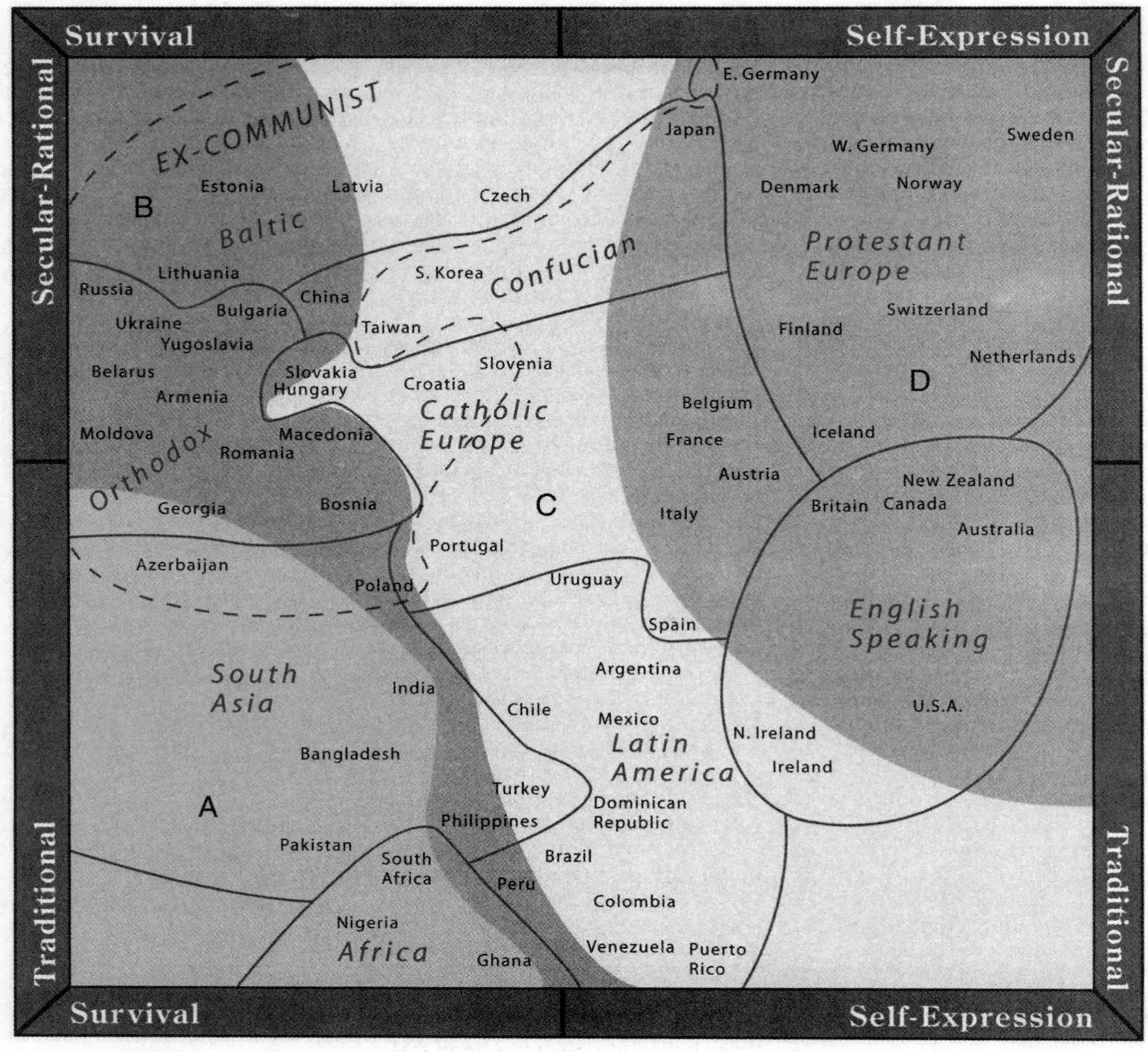

Less than $2,000 GNP per capita A C $5,000 to $15,000 GNP per capita

$2,000 to $5,000 GNP per capita B D More than $15,000 GNP per capita

ferent social functions in different cultural zones. Eating in a McDonald's restaurant in Japan is a different social experience from eating in one in the United States, Europe, or China.

Likewise, the globalization of communication is unmistakable, but its effects may be overestimated. It is certainly apparent that young people around the world are wearing jeans and listening to U.S. pop music; what is less apparent is the persistence of underlying value differences.

Mapping and Predicting Values

Using the 1995–1998 wave of the World Values Survey, we produced a map of the world's values, showing the locations of 65 societies on the two cross-cultural dimensions—traditional vs. secular-rational values and survival vs. self-expression values.

What the map shows us is that cross-cultural variation is highly constrained. That is, if the people of a given society place a strong emphasis on religion, that society's relative position on many other variables can be predicted—such as attitudes toward abortion, national pride, respect for authority, and childrearing. Similarly, survival vs. self-expression values reflect wide-ranging but tightly correlated clusters of values: Materialistic (survival-oriented) societies can be predicted to value maintaining order and fighting inflation, while postmaterialistic (self-expression-oriented) societies can be predicted to value freedom, interpersonal trust, and tolerance of outgroups.

Economic development seems to have a powerful impact on cultural values: The value systems of rich countries differ systematically from those of poor countries. If we superimpose an income "map" over the values map, we see that all 19 societies with an annual per capita GNP of over $15,000 rank relatively high on both dimensions, placing them in the upper right-hand corner. This economic zone cuts across the boundaries of the Protestant, ex-Communist, Confucian, Catholic, and English-speaking cultural zones.

On the other hand, all societies with per capita GNPs below $2,000 fall into a cluster at the lower left of the map, in an economic zone that cuts across the African, South Asian, ex-Communist, and Orthodox cultural zones. The remaining societies fall into two intermediate cultural-economic zones. Economic development seems to move societies in a common direction, regardless of their cultural heritage. Nevertheless, distinctive cultural zones persist two centuries after the industrial revolution began.

Of course, per capita GNP is only one indicator of a society's level of economic development. Another might be the percentage of the labor force engaged in the agricultural sector, the industrial sector, or the service sector. The shift from an agrarian mode of production to industrial production seems to bring with it a shift from traditional values toward increasing rationalization and secularization.

But a society's cultural heritage also plays a role: All four of the Confucian-influenced societies (China, Taiwan, South Korea, and Japan) have relatively secular values, regardless of the proportion of their labor forces in the industrial sector. Conversely, the historically Roman Catholic societies (e.g., Italy, Portugal, and Spain) display relatively traditional values when compared with Confucian or ex-Communist societies with the same proportion of industrial workers. And virtually all of the historically Protestant societies (e.g., West Germany, Denmark, Norway, and Sweden) rank higher on the survival/self-expression dimension than do all of the historically Roman Catholic societies, regardless of the extent to which their labor forces are engaged in the service sector.

We can conclude from this that changes in GNP and occupational structure have important influences on prevailing world views, but traditional cultural influences persist.

Religious traditions appear to have had an enduring impact on the contemporary value systems of the 65 societies. But a society's culture reflects its entire historical heritage. A central historical event of the twentieth century was the rise and fall of a Communist empire that once ruled one-third of the world's population. Communism left a clear imprint on the value systems of those who lived under it. East Germany remains culturally close to West Germany despite four decades of Communist rule, but its value system has been drawn toward the Communist zone. And although China is a member of the Confucian zone, it also falls within a broad Communist-influenced zone. Similarly, Azerbaijan, though part of the Islamic cluster, also falls within the Communist superzone that dominated it for decades.

The Deviant U.S.

The World Value Map clearly shows that the United States is a deviant case. We do not believe it is a prototype of cultural modernization for other societies to follow, as some postwar modernization theorists have naively assumed. The United States has a much more traditional value system than any other advanced industrial society.

On the traditional/secular-rational dimension, the United States ranks far below other rich societies, with levels of religiosity and national pride comparable to those found in developing societies. The United States does rank among the most advanced societies along the survival/self-expression dimension, but even here it does not lead the world. The Swedes and the Dutch seem closer to the cutting edge of cultural change than do the Americans.

Modernization theory implies that as societies develop economically their cultures tend to shift in a predictable direction. Our data supports this prediction. Economic differences are linked with large and pervasive cultural differences. But we find clear evidence of the influence of long-established cultural zones.

Do these cultural clusters simply reflect economic differences? For example, do the societies of Protestant Europe have similar values simply because they are rich? No. The impact of a society's historical-cultural heritage persists when we control for GDP per capita and the structure of the labor force. On a value such as *interpersonal trust* (a variable on the surival / self-expression dimension), even rich Catholic societies rank lower than rich Protestant ones.

Within a given society, however, Catholics rank about as high on *interpersonal trust* as do Protestants. The shared historical experience of given nations, not individual personality, is crucial. Once established, the cross-cultural differences linked with religion have become part of a national culture that is transmitted by the educational institutions and mass media of given societies to the people of that nation. Despite globalization, the nation remains a key unit of shared experience, and its educational and cultural institutions shape the values of almost everyone in that society.

The Persistence of Religious and Spiritual Beliefs

As a society shifts from an agrarian to an industrial economy and survival comes to be taken for granted, traditional religious beliefs tend to decline. Nevertheless, as the twenty-first century opens, cleavages along religious lines remain strong. Why has religion been so slow to disappear?

History has taken an ironic turn: Communist-style industrialization was especially favorable to secularization, but the collapse of Communism has given rise to pervasive insecurity—

and a return to religious beliefs. Five of the seven ex-Communist societies for which we have time-series data show rising church attendance.

Throughout advanced industrial societies we see two contrasting trends: the decline of attendance at religious services on the one hand, and on the other the persistence of religious beliefs and the rise of spirituality. The need for answers to spiritual questions such as why we are here and where we are going does not die out in postindustrial society. Spiritual concerns will probably always be part of the human outlook. In fact, in the three successive waves of the World Values Survey, concern for the meaning and purpose of life became *stronger* in most advanced industrial societies.

Conclusion: Whither Modernization?

Economic development is associated with pervasive, and to an extent predictable, cultural changes. Industrialization promotes a shift from traditional to secular-rational values; postindustrialization promotes a shift toward more trust, tolerance, and emphasis on well-being. Economic collapse propels societies in the opposite direction.

Economic development tends to push societies in a common direction, but rather than converging they seem to move along paths shaped by their cultural heritages. Therefore, we doubt that the forces of modernization will produce a homogenized world culture in the foreseeable future.

Certainly it is misleading to view cultural change as "Americanization." Industrializing societies in general are not becoming like the United States. In fact, the United States seems to be a deviant case: Its people hold much more traditional values and beliefs than do those in any other equally prosperous society. If any societies exemplify the cutting edge of cultural change, it would be the Nordic countries.

Finally, modernization is probabilistic, not deterministic. Economic development tends to transform a given society in a predictable direction, but the process and path are not inevitable. Many factors are involved, so any prediction must be contingent on the historical and cultural context of the society in question.

Nevertheless, the central prediction of modernization theory finds broad support: Economic development is associated with major changes in prevailing values and beliefs. The world views of rich societies differ markedly from those of poor societies. This does not necessarily imply cultural convergence, but it does predict the general direction of cultural change and (insofar as the process is based on intergenerational population replacement) even gives some idea of the rate at which such change is likely to occur.

In short, economic development will cause shifts in the values of people in developing nations, but it will not produce a uniform global culture. The future may *look* like McWorld, but it won't feel like one.

Modernization and McDonald's

McDonald's restaurants have become a dominant symbol of the globalization of the economy and target of the wrath of globalization's many opponents. But local values still wield great influence on culture, so don't look for McWorld to emerge anytime soon, say social researchers Ronald Inglehart and Wayne E. Baker.

About the Authors

Ronald Inglehart is professor of political science and program director at the Institute for Social Research, University of Michigan, Ann Arbor, Michigan 48106. E-mail RFI@umich.edu. The World Values Survey Web site is http://wvs.isr.umich.edu/.

Wayne E. Baker is professor of organizational behavior and director of the Center for Society and Economy, University of Michigan Business School, and faculty associate at the Institute for Social Research. He may be reached by e-mail at wayneb@umich.edu; his Web site is www.bus.umich.edu/cse.

This article draws on their paper "Modernization, Cultural Change, and the Persistence of Traditional Values" in the American Sociological Review (February 2000).

Originally published in the March/April 2001 issue of *The Futurist,* pp. 16-21. Used with permission from the World Future Society, 7910 Woodmont Avenue, Suite 450, Bethesda, Maryland 20814. Telephone: 310/656-8274; Fax: 301/951-0394; (http://www.wfs.org).

Will the corporation survive?

Yes, but not as we know it

FOR most of the time since the corporation was invented around 1870, the following five basic points have been assumed to apply:

- The corporation is the "master", the employee is the "servant". Because the corporation owns the means of production without which the employee could not make a living, the employee needs the corporation more than vice versa.
- The great majority of employees work full-time for the corporation. The pay they get for the job is their only income and provides their livelihood.
- The most efficient way to produce anything is to bring together under one management as many as possible of the activities needed to turn out the product.

The theory underlying this was not developed until after the second world war, by Ronald Coase, an Anglo-American economist, who argued that bringing together activities into one company lowers "transactional costs", and especially the cost of communications (for which theory he received the 1991 Nobel prize in economics). But the concept itself was discovered and put into practice 70 or 80 years earlier by John D. Rockefeller. He saw that to put exploration, production, transport, refining and selling into one corporate structure resulted in the most efficient and lowest-cost petroleum operation. On this insight he built the Standard Oil Trust, probably the most profitable large enterprise in business history. The concept was carried to an extreme by Henry Ford in the early 1920s. The Ford Motor Company not only produced all parts of the automobile and assembled it, but it also made its own steel, its own glass and its own tyres. It owned the plantations in the Amazon that grew the rubber trees, owned and ran the railroad that carried supplies to the plant and carried the finished cars from it, and planned eventually to sell and service Ford cars too (though it never did).

- Suppliers and especially manufacturers have market power because they have information about a product or a service that the customer does not and cannot have, and does not need if he can trust the brand. This explains the profitability of brands.
- To any one particular technology pertains one and only one industry, and conversely, to any one particular industry pertains one and only one technology. This means that all technology needed to make steel is peculiar to the steel industry; and conversely, that whatever technology is being used to make steel comes out of the steel industry itself. The same applies to the paper industry, to agriculture or to banking and commerce.

On this assumption were founded the industrial research labs, beginning with Siemens's, started in Germany in 1869, and ending with IBM's, the last of the great traditional labs, founded in America in 1952. Each of them concentrated on the technology needed for a single industry, and each assumed that its discoveries would be applied only in that industry.

Everything in its place

Similarly, everybody took it for granted that every product or service had a specific application, and that for every application there was a specific product or material. So beer and milk were sold only in glass bottles; car bodies were made only from steel; working capital for a business was supplied by a commercial bank through a commercial loan; and so on. Competition therefore took place mainly within an industry. By and large, it was obvious what the business of a given company was and what its markets were.

Every one of these assumptions remained valid for a whole century, but from 1970 onwards every one of them has been turned upside down. The list now reads as follows:

- The means of production is knowledge, which is owned by knowledge workers and is highly portable. This applies equally to high-knowledge workers such as research scientists and to knowledge technologists such as physiotherapists, computer technicians and paralegals. Knowledge workers provide "capital" just as much as does the provider of money. The two are dependent on each other. This makes the knowledge worker an equal—an associate or a partner.
- Many employees, perhaps a majority, will still have full-time jobs with a salary that provides their only or main income. But a growing number of people who work for an organisation will not be full-time employees but part-timers, temporaries, consultants or contractors. Even of those who do have a full-time job, a large and growing number may not be employees of the organisation for

which they work, but employees of, eg, an outsourcing contractor.

• There always were limits to the importance of transactional costs. Henry Ford's all-inclusive Ford Motor Company proved unmanageable and became a disaster. But now the traditional axiom that an enterprise should aim for maximum integration has become almost entirely invalidated. One reason is that the knowledge needed for any activity has become highly specialised. It is therefore increasingly expensive, and also increasingly difficult, to maintain enough critical mass for every major task within an enterprise. And because knowledge rapidly deteriorates unless it is used constantly, maintaining within an organisation an activity that is used only intermittently guarantees incompetence.

The second reason why maximum integration is no longer needed is that communications costs have come down so fast as to become insignificant. This decline began well before the information revolution. Perhaps its biggest cause has been the growth and spread of business literacy. When Rockefeller built his Standard Oil Trust, he had great difficulty finding people who knew even the most elementary book-keeping or had heard of the most common business terms. At the time there were no business textbooks or business courses, so the transactional costs of making oneself understood were extremely high. Sixty years later, by 1950 or 1960, the large oil companies that succeeded the Standard Oil Trust could confidently assume that their more senior employees were business literate.

By now the new information technology—Internet and e-mail—have practically eliminated the physical costs of communications. This has meant that the most productive and most profitable way to organise is to disintegrate. This is being extended to more and more activities. Outsourcing the management of an institution's information technology, data processing and computer system has become routine. In the early 1990s most American computer firms, eg, Apple, even outsourced the production of their hardware to manufacturers in Japan or Singapore. In the late 1990s practically every Japanese consumer-electronics company repaid the compliment by outsourcing the manufacturing of its products for the American market to American contract manufacturers.

In the past few years the entire human-resources management of more than 2m American workers—hiring, firing, training, benefits and so on—has been outsourced to professional employee organisations. This sector, which ten years ago barely existed, is now growing at a rate of 30% a year. It originally concentrated on small and medium-sized companies, but the biggest of the firms, Exult, founded only in 1998, now manages employment issues for a number of *Fortune* 500 companies, including BP, a British-American oil giant, and Unisys, a computer maker. According to a study by McKinsey, a consultancy, outsourcing human-relations management in this way can save up to 30% of the cost, and increase employee satisfaction as well.

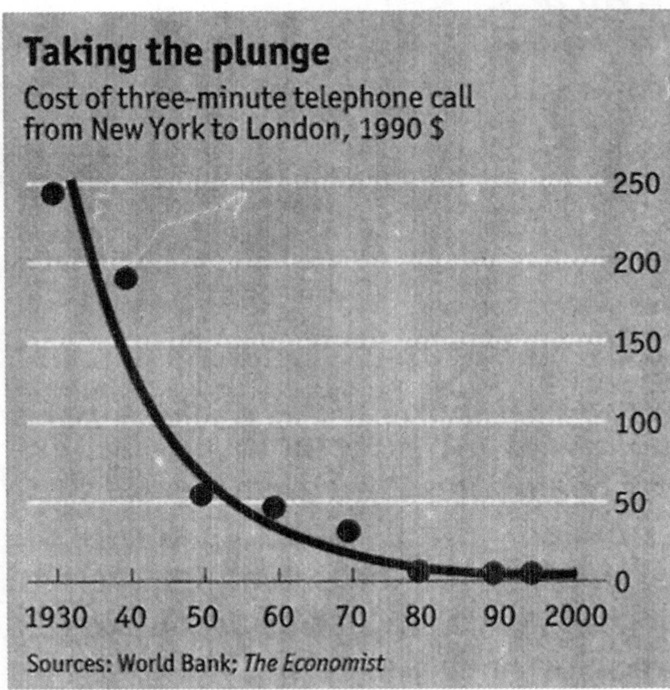

• The customer now has the information. As yet, the Internet lacks the equivalent of a telephone book that would make it easy for users to find what they are looking for. It still requires pecking and hunting. But the information is somewhere on a website, and search firms to find it for a fee are rapidly developing. Whoever has the information has the power. Power is thus shifting to the customer, be it another business or the ultimate consumer. Specifically, that means the supplier, eg, the manufacturer, will cease to be a seller and instead become a buyer for the customer. This is already happening.

General Motors (GM), still the world's largest manufacturer and for many years its most successful selling organisation, last year announced the creation of a major business that will buy for the ultimate car consumer. Although wholly owned by GM, the business will be autonomous, and will buy not only General Motors cars, but whatever car and model most closely fits the individual customer's preferences, values and wallet.

• Lastly, there are few unique technologies any more. Increasingly, the knowledge needed in a given industry comes out of some totally different technology with which, very often, the people in the industry are unfamiliar. No one in the telephone industry knew anything about fibreglass cables. They were developed by a glass company, Corning. Conversely, more than half the important inventions developed since the second world war by the most productive of the great research labs, the Bell Laboratory, have been applied mainly outside the telephone industry.

The Bell Lab's most significant invention of the past 50 years was the transistor, which created the modern electronics industry. But the telephone company saw so little use for this revolutionary new device that it practically gave it away to anybody who asked for it—which is what put Sony, and with it the Japanese, into the consumer-electronics business.

Who needs a research lab?

Research directors, as well as high-tech industrialists, now tend to believe that the company-owned research lab, that proud 19th-century invention, has become obsolete. This explains why, increasingly, development and growth of a business is taking place not inside the corporation itself but through partnerships, joint ventures, alliances, minority participation and know-how agreements with institutions in different industries and with a different technology. Something that only 50 years ago would have been unthinkable is becoming common: alliances between institutions of a totally different character, say a profit-making company and a university department, or a city or state government and a business that contracts for a specific service such as cleaning the streets or running prisons.

Practically no product or service any longer has either a single specific end-use or application, or its own market. Commercial paper competes with the banks' commercial loans. Cardboard, plastic and aluminium compete with glass for the bottle market. Glass is replacing copper in cables. Steel is competing with wood and plastic in providing the studs around which the American one-family home is constructed. The deferred annuity is pushing aside traditional life insurance—but, in turn, insurance companies rather than financial-service institutions are becoming the managers of commercial risks.

A "glass company" may therefore have to redefine itself by what it is good at doing rather than by the material in which it has specialised in the past. One of the world's largest glass makers, Corning, sold its profitable business making traditional glass products to become the number one producer and supplier of high-tech materials. Merck, America's largest pharmaceutical company, diversified from making drugs into wholesaling every kind of pharmacy product, most of them not even made by Merck, and a good many by competitors.

The same sort of thing is happening in the non-business sectors of the economy. One example is the free-standing "birthing centre" run by a group of obstetricians that competes with the American hospital's maternity ward. And Britain, long before the Internet, created the "Open University", which allowed people to get a university education and obtain a degree without ever setting foot in a classroom or attending a lecture.

The next company

One thing is almost certain: in future there will be not one kind of corporation but several different ones. The modern company was invented simultaneously but independently in three countries: America, Germany and Japan. It was a complete novelty and bore no resemblance to the economic organisation that had been the "economic enterprise" for millennia: the small, privately owned and personally run firm. As late as 1832, England's McLane Report—the first statistical survey of business—found that nearly all firms were privately owned and had fewer than ten employees. The only exceptions were quasi-governmental organisations such as the Bank of England or the East India Company. Forty years later a new kind of organisation with thousands of employees had appeared on the scene, eg, the American railroads, built with federal and state support, and Germany's Deutsche Bank.

Wherever the corporation went, it acquired some national characteristics and adapted to different legal rules in each country. Moreover, very large corporations everywhere are being run quite differently from the small owner-managed kind. And there are substantial internal differences in culture, values and rhetoric between corporations in different industries. Banks everywhere are very much alike, and so are retailers or manufacturers. But banks everywhere are different from retailers or manufacturers. Otherwise, however, the differences between corporations everywhere are more of style than of substance. The same is true of all other organisations in modern society: government agencies, armed forces, hospitals, universities and so on.

The tide turned around 1970, first with the emergence of new institutional investors such as pension funds and mutual trusts as the new owners, then—more decisively—with the emergence of knowledge workers as the economy's big new resource and the society's representative class. The result has been a fundamental change in the corporation.

A bank in the next society will still not look like a hospital, nor be run like one. But different banks may be quite different from one another, depending on how each of them responds to the changes in its workforce, technology and markets. A number of different models is likely to emerge, especially of organisation and structure, but perhaps also of recognitions and rewards.

The same legal entity—eg, a business, a government agency or a large not-for-profit organisation—may well contain several different human organisations that interlock, but are managed separately and differently. One of these is likely to be a traditional organisation of full-time employees. Yet there may also be a closely linked but separately managed human organisation made up mainly of older people who are not employees but associates or affiliates. And there are likely to be "perimeter" groups such as the people who work for the organisation, even full-time, but as employees of an outsourcing contractor or of a contract manufacturer. These people have no contractual relationship with the business they work for, which in turn has no control over them. They may not have to be "managed", but they have to be made productive. They will therefore have to be deployed where their specialised knowledge can make the greatest contribution. Despite all the present talk of "knowledge management", no one yet really knows how to do it.

Just as important, the people in every one of these organisational categories will have to be satisfied. Attracting them and holding them will become the central task of people management. We already know what does not work: bribery. In the past ten or 15 years many businesses in America have used bonuses or stock options to attract and keep knowledge workers. It always fails.

According to an old saying, you cannot hire a hand: the whole man always comes with it. But you cannot hire a man either; the spouse almost always comes with it. And the spouse has already spent the money when falling profits eliminate the bonus or falling stock prices make the option worthless. Then both the employee and the spouse feel bitter and betrayed.

Of course knowledge workers need to be satisfied with their pay, because dissatisfaction with income and benefits is a powerful disincentive. The incentives, however, are different. The management of knowledge workers should be based on the assumption that the corporation needs them more than they need the corporation. They know they can leave. They have both mobility and self-confidence. This means they have to be treated and managed as volunteers, in the same way as volunteers who work for not-for-profit organisations. The first thing such people want to know is what the company is trying to do and where it is going. Next, they are interested in personal achievement and personal responsibility—which means they have to be put in the right job. Knowledge workers expect continuous learning and continuous training. Above all, they want respect, not so much for themselves but for their area of knowledge. In that regard, they have moved several steps beyond traditional workers, who used to expect to be told what to do, although later they were increasingly expected to "participate". Knowledge workers, by contrast, expect to make the decisions in their own area.

From corporation to confederation

Eighty years ago, GM first developed both the organisational concepts and the organisational structure on which today's large corporations everywhere are based. It also invented the idea of a distinct top management. Now it is experimenting with a range of new organisational models. It has been changing itself from a unitary corporation held together by control through ownership into a group held together by management control, with GM often holding only a minority stake. GM now controls but does not own Fiat, itself one of the oldest and largest car makers. It also controls Saab in Sweden and two smaller Japanese car makers, Suzuki and Isuzu.

At the same time GM has divested itself of much of its manufacturing by spinning off into a separate company, called Delphi, the making of parts and accessories that together account for 60–70% of the cost of producing a car. Instead of owning—or at least controlling—the suppliers of parts and accessories, GM will in future buy them at auction and on the Internet. It has joined up with its American competitors, Ford and DaimlerChrysler, to create an independent purchasing co-operative that will buy for its members from whatever source offers the best deal. All the other car makers have been invited to join.

GM will still design its cars, it will still make engines, and it will still assemble. It will also still sell its cars through its dealer network. But in addition to selling its own cars, GM intends to become a car merchant and a buyer for the ultimate consumer, finding the right car for the buyer no matter who makes it.

The Toyota way

GM is still the world's largest car manufacturer, but for the past 20 years Toyota has been the most successful one. Like GM, Toyota is building a worldwide group, but unlike GM, Toyota has organised its group round its core competence in manufacturing. The company is moving away from having multiple suppliers of parts and accessories, ultimately aiming for no more than two suppliers for any one part. These suppliers will be separate and independent companies, owned locally, but Toyota will in effect run their manufacturing operation for them. They will get the Toyota business only if they agree to being inspected and "advised" by a special Toyota manufacturing consulting organisation. And Toyota will also do most of the design work for the suppliers.

This is not a new idea. Sears Roebuck did the same for its suppliers in the 1920s and 1930s. Britain's Marks & Spencer, although in deep trouble now, was the world's most successful retailer for 50 years, maintaining its pre-eminence largely by keeping an iron grip on its suppliers. It is rumoured in Japan that Toyota intends ultimately to market its manufacturing consultancy to non-car companies, turning its manufacturing core competence into a separate big business.

Yet another approach is being explored by a large manufacturer of branded and packaged consumer goods. Some 60% of the company's products are sold in the developed countries through some 150 retail chains. The company plans to create a worldwide website that will take orders direct from customers in all countries, either to be picked up in the retail store nearest to them or to be delivered by that store to their home. But—and this is the true innovation—the website will also take orders for non-competing packaged and branded consumer products made by other, and especially smaller, firms. Such firms have great difficulty in getting their wares on to increasingly crowded supermarket shelves. The multina-

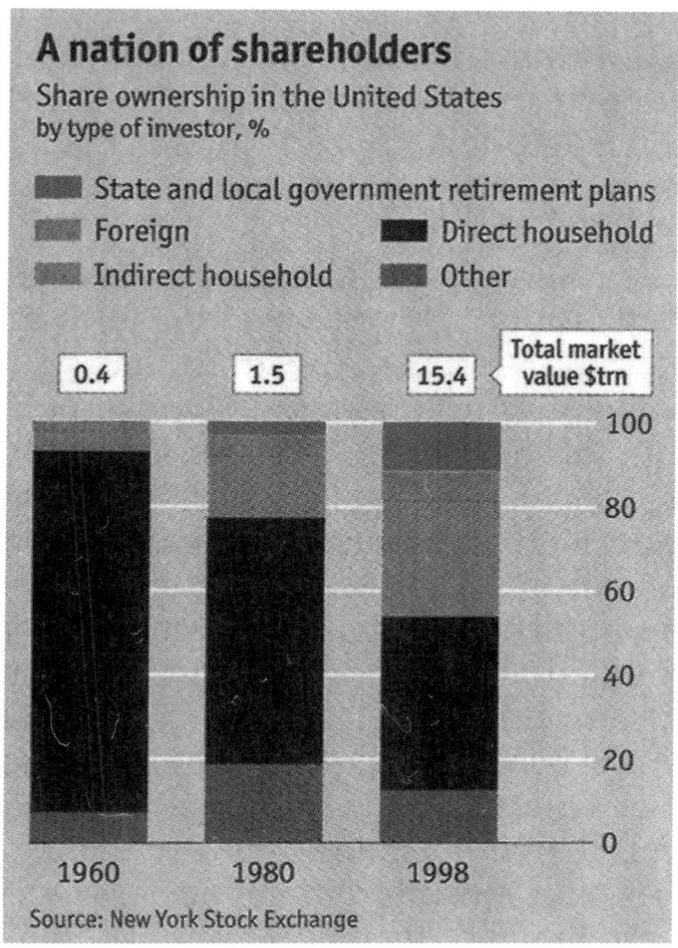

tional's website could offer them direct access to customers and delivery through an established large retailer. The pay-off for the multinational and the retailer would be that both get a decent commission without having to invest any money of their own, without risk and without sacrificing shelf space to slow-moving items.

There are already a good many variations on this theme: the American contract manufacturers, already mentioned, who now make the products for half a dozen competing Japanese consumer-electronics firms; a few independent specialists who design software for competing information-hardware makers; the independent specialists who design credit cards for competing American banks and also often market and clear the cards for the bank. All the bank does is the financing.

These approaches, however different, still all take the traditional corporation as their point of departure. But there are also some new ideas that do away with the corporate model altogether. One example is a "syndicate" being tested by several non-competing manufacturers in the European Union. Each of the constituent companies is medium-sized, family-owned and owner-managed. Each is a leader in a narrow, highly engineered product line. Each is heavily export-dependent. The individual companies intend to remain independent, and to continue to design their products separately. They will also continue to make them in their own plants for their main markets, and to sell them in these markets. But for other markets, and especially for emerging or less developed countries, the syndicate will arrange for the making of the products, either in syndicate-owned plants producing for several of the members or by local contract manufacturers. The syndicate will handle the delivery of all members' products and service them in all markets. Each member will own a share of the syndicate, and the syndicate, in turn, will own a small share of each member's capital. If this sounds familiar, it is because the model is the 19th century farmers' co-operative.

As the corporation moves towards a confederation or a syndicate, it will increasingly need a top management that is separate, powerful and accountable. This top management's responsibilities will cover the entire organisation's direction, planning, strategy, values and principles; its structure and its relationship between its various members; its alliances, partnerships and joint ventures; and its research, design and innovation. It will have to take charge of the management of the two resources common to all units of the organisation: key people and money. It will represent the corporation to the outside world and maintain relationships with governments, the public, the media and organised labour.

Life at the top

An equally important task for top management in the next society's corporation will be to balance the three dimensions of the corporation: as an economic organisation, as a human organisation and as an increasingly important social organisation. Each of the three models of the corporation developed in the past half-century stressed one of these dimensions and subordinated the other two. The German model of the "social market economy" put the emphasis on the social dimension, the Japanese one on the human dimension and the American one ("shareholder sovereignty") on the economic dimension.

None of the three is adequate on its own. The German model achieved both economic success and social stability, but at the price of high unemployment and dangerous labour-market rigidity. The Japanese model was strikingly successful for 20 years, but faltered at the first serious challenge; indeed it has become a major obstacle to recovery from Japan's present recession. Shareholder sovereignty is also bound to flounder. It is a fair-weather model that works well only in times of prosperity. Obviously the enterprise can fulfill its human and social functions only if it prospers as a business. But now that knowledge workers are becoming the key employees, a company also needs to be a desirable employer to be successful.

Crucially, the claim to the absolute primacy of business gains that made shareholder sovereignty possible has also highlighted the importance of the corporation's social function. The new shareholders whose emergence since 1960 or 1970 produced shareholder sovereignty are not "capitalists". They are employees who own a stake in the business through their retirement and pension funds. By 2000, pension funds and mutual funds had come to own the majority of the share capital of America's large companies. This has given shareholders the power to demand short-term rewards. But the need for a secure retirement income will increasingly focus people's minds on the future value of the investment. Corporations, therefore, will have to pay attention both to their short-term business results and to their long-term performance as providers of retirement benefits. The two are not irreconcilable, but they are different, and they will have to be balanced.

Over the past decade or two, managing a large corporation has changed out of all recognition. That explains the emergence of the "CEO superman", such as Jack Welch of GE, Andy Grove of Intel or Sanford Weill of Citigroup. But organisations cannot rely on finding supermen to run them; the supply is both unpredictable and far too limited. Organisations survive only if they can be run by competent people who take their job seriously. That it takes genius today to be the boss of a big organisation clearly indicates that top management is in crisis.

Impossible jobs

The recent failure rate of chief executives in big American companies points in the same direction. A large proportion of CEOs of such companies appointed in the past ten years were fired as failures within a year or two. But each of these people had been picked for his proven competence, and each had been highly successful in his previous jobs. This suggests that the jobs they took on had become undoable. The American record suggests not human failure but systems failure. Top management in big organisations needs a new concept.

Some elements of such a concept are beginning to emerge. For instance, Jack Welch at GE has built a top-management team in which the company's chief financial officer and its chief human-resources officer are near-equals to the chief executive, and are both excluded from the succession to the top job. He has also given himself and his team a clear and publicly announced priority task on which to concentrate. During his 20 years in the top job, Mr Welch has had three such priorities, each occupying him for five years or more. Each time he has delegated everything else to the top managements of the operating businesses within the GE confederation.

A different approach has been taken by Asea Brown Boveri (ABB), a huge Swedish-Swiss engineering multinational. Goran Lindahl, who retired as chief executive earlier this year, went even further than GE in making the individual units within the company into separate worldwide businesses and building up a strong top management team of a few non-operating people. But he also defined for himself a new role as a one-man information system for the company, travelling incessantly to get to know all the senior managers personally, listening to them and telling them what went on within the organisation.

A largish financial-services company tried another idea: appointing not one CEO but six. The head of each of the five operating businesses is also CEO for the whole company in one top management area, such as corporate planning and strategy or human resources. The company's chairman represents the company to the outside world and is also directly concerned with obtaining, allocating and managing capital. All six people meet twice a week as the top management committee. This seems to work well, but only because none of the five operating CEOs wants the chairman's job; each prefers to stay in operations. Even the man who designed the system, and then himself took the chairman's job, doubts that the system will survive once he is gone.

In their different ways, the top people at all of these companies were trying to do the same thing: to establish their organisation's unique personality. And that may well be the most important task for top management in the next society's big organisations. In the half-century after the second world war, the business corporation has brilliantly proved itself as an economic organisation, ie, a creator of wealth and jobs. In the next society, the biggest challenge for the large company—especially for the multinational—may be its social legitimacy: its values, its mission, its vision. Increasingly, in the next society's corporation, top management will, in fact, be the company. Everything else can be outsourced.

Will the corporation survive? Yes, after a fashion. Something akin to a corporation will have to co-ordinate the next society's economic resources. Legally and perhaps financially, it may even look much the same as today's corporation. But instead of there being a single model adopted by everyone, there will be a range of models to choose from.

Index

Index

O

P

R

S

T

U

V

W

Y

Z

Test Your Knowledge Form

We encourage you to photocopy and use this page as a tool to assess how the articles in *Annual Editions* expand on the information in your textbook. By reflecting on the articles you will gain enhanced text information. You can also access this useful form on a product's book support Web site at *http://www.dushkin.com/online/*.

NAME: DATE:

TITLE AND NUMBER OF ARTICLE:

BRIEFLY STATE THE MAIN IDEA OF THIS ARTICLE:

LIST THREE IMPORTANT FACTS THAT THE AUTHOR USES TO SUPPORT THE MAIN IDEA:

WHAT INFORMATION OR IDEAS DISCUSSED IN THIS ARTICLE ARE ALSO DISCUSSED IN YOUR TEXTBOOK OR OTHER READINGS THAT YOU HAVE DONE? LIST THE TEXTBOOK CHAPTERS AND PAGE NUMBERS:

LIST ANY EXAMPLES OF BIAS OR FAULTY REASONING THAT YOU FOUND IN THE ARTICLE:

LIST ANY NEW TERMS/CONCEPTS THAT WERE DISCUSSED IN THE ARTICLE, AND WRITE A SHORT DEFINITION:

We Want Your Advice

ANNUAL EDITIONS revisions depend on two major opinion sources: one is our Advisory Board, listed in the front of this volume, which works with us in scanning the thousands of articles published in the public press each year; the other is you—the person a ctu- ally using the book. Please help us and the users of the next edition by completing the prepaid article rating form on this page and returning it to us. Thank you for your help!

ANNUAL EDITIONS: Global Issues 02/03

ARTICLE RATING FORM

Here is an opportunity for you to have direct input into the next revision of this volume. We would like you to rate each of the articles listed below, using the following scale:

1. **Excellent: should definitely be retained**
2. **Above average: should probably be retained**
3. **Below average: should probably be deleted**
4. **Poor: should definitely be deleted**

Your ratings will play a vital part in the next revision. Please mail this prepaid form to us as soon as possible. Thanks for your help!

RATING	ARTICLE
________	1. A Special Moment in History
________	2. The Many Faces of the Future
________	3. The Clash of Ignorance
________	4. Mr. Order Meets Mr. Chaos
________	5. The Big Crunch
________	6. Breaking *Out* or Breaking *Down*
________	7. Grains of Hope
________	8. The Global Challenge
________	9. The Energy Question, Again
________	10. Invasive Species: Pathogens of Globalization
________	11. We *Can* Build a Sustainable Economy
________	12. The Complexities and Contradictions of Globalization
________	13. The Great Divide in the Global Village
________	14. Dueling Globalizations: A Debate Between Thomas L. Friedman and Ignacio Ramonet
________	15. Will Globalization Go Bankrupt?
________	16. America's Two-Front Economic Conflict
________	17. What's Wrong With This Picture?
________	18. Where Have All the Farmers Gone?
________	19. Going Cheap
________	20. Nasty, Brutish, and Long: America's War on Terrorism
________	21. 'Why Do They Hate Us?'
________	22. Ten Mistakes in the Middle East
________	23. Ethnic Conflict
________	24. China as Number One
________	25. Battlefield: Space
________	26. Reforming the United Nations
________	27. Justice Goes Global
________	28. Enforcing Human Rights
________	29. Meet the World's Top Cop
________	30. Tribes Under the Microscope
________	31. Are Human Rights Universal?
________	32. The Grameen Bank
________	33. Why Environmental Ethics Matters to International Relations
________	34. Women Waging Peace
________	35. Modernization's Challenge to Traditional Values: Who's Afraid of Ronald McDonald?
________	36. Will the Corporation Survive? Yes, But Not as We Know It

(Continued on next page)

NO POSTAGE NECESSARY IF MAILED IN THE UNITED STATES

BUSINESS REPLY MAIL
FIRST-CLASS MAIL PERMIT NO. 84 GUILFORD CT
POSTAGE WILL BE PAID BY ADDRESSEE

McGraw-Hill/Dushkin
530 Old Whitfield Street
Guilford, Ct 06437-9989

ABOUT YOU

Name _______________ Date _______________

Are you a teacher? ❒ A student? ❒
Your school's name _______________

Department _______________

Address _______________ City _______________ State _______________ Zip _______________

School telephone # _______________

YOUR COMMENTS ARE IMPORTANT TO US!

Please fill in the following information:
For which course did you use this book? _______________

Did you use a text with this ANNUAL EDITION? ❒ yes ❒ no
What was the title of the text? _______________

What are your general reactions to the *Annual Editions* concept? _______________

Have you read any pertinent articles recently that you think should be included in the next edition? Explain. _______________

Are there any articles that you feel should be replaced in the next edition? Why? _______________

Are there any World Wide Web sites that you feel should be included in the next edition? Please annotate. _______________

May we contact you for editorial input? ❒ yes ❒ no
May we quote your comments? ❒ yes ❒ no